SHARING IV
A Manual for Volunteer Teachers

After graduation from Marquette University in 1969, Tom Zanzig began to use his training in theology and sociology as a director of religious education for Holy Name Parish in Kimberly, Wisconsin. Two years later he accepted the position of executive director of the Appleton Catholic Education Council in Appleton, Wisconsin. In that position Tom was responsible for creating and directing a high school religious education program for five parishes, a program that eventually attracted some seven hundred students a year. Tom continued to refine the curriculum during his seven years of work in Appleton. The entire program was then published by Saint Mary's Press between 1976 and 1979 under the title *Sharing the Christian Message*, or, more popularly, "the SHARING Program."

In 1978 Tom joined Saint Mary's Press as a consultant and author. In 1980 his first textbook intended for use in Catholic high schools was published—*Understanding Your Faith: An Introduction to Catholic Christianity for Freshmen*. It became immediately popular in Catholic high schools all over the United States. A textbook on Christology followed in 1982—*Jesus of History, Christ of Faith: A Gospel Portrait for Young People*. An adult version of that textbook was then published under the title *Jesus Is Lord! A Basic Christology for Adults*.

In 1988, Tom revised his first textbook, *Understanding Your Faith*, under the title *Understanding Catholic Christianity*.

Tom has written a number of articles for the respected religious education journal *PACE*. He has recorded two videotapes: a four-session workshop for directors and teachers of religious education, *Effective Adolescent Religious Education*, and an hour-long discussion on the Gospel and how it touches each of us, *Jesus: The Good News Proclaimed to Youth*.

During 1983–84, Tom worked nearly full-time on thoroughly revising the first three manuals of the original SHARING Program. Utilizing information and ideas from users of SHARING gained through his frequent travel, workshops, convention speaking, and correspondence, Tom was able to build creatively and effectively on the solid foundation of the original SHARING Program. In 1987, he completed writing SHARING IV, and the result is a remarkably comprehensive, integrated, and successful religious education program for high school students—the revised SHARING Program.

Tom resides in Winona, Minnesota, with his wife, Kate, and their two children, Adam and Barbara.

Sharing the Christian Message:
A comprehensive four-year religious education program
for high school students

SHARING IV

A Manual for Volunteer Teachers

Revised Edition

by Thomas Zanzig

**Saint Mary's Press
Christian Brothers Publications
Winona, Minnesota**

Nihil Obstat: Rev. Donald P. Schmitz
                Censor Deputatus
                1 May 1988
Imprimatur: †John G. Vlazny
              Bishop of Winona
              1 May 1988

The publishing team included Robert P. Stamschror, editor; Lynn Dahdal, manuscript editor; Holly Schmidt, production editor; and Carolyn St. George, designer and illustrator. The cover photograph is by Michael Goldberg.

The acknowledgments continue on page 237.

Copyright © 1988 by Saint Mary's Press, Terrace Heights, Winona, MN 55987. All rights reserved. Permission is granted to reproduce only those materials intended for distribution to the students. No other part of this manual may be reproduced by any means without the written permission of the publisher.

Printed in the United States of America

Printing: 6 5 4 3 2 1

Year: 1995 94 93 92 91 90 89 88

ISBN 0-88489-166-6

Contents

Introduction   7

Part 1
New Perspectives on Some Old Questions

"Forming Faith" or "Teaching Religion"   19

Faith Formation: Putting Theory into Practice   23

Faith Development and Adolescence: At the Crossroads   29

Effective Teaching: Making Molehills out of Mountains   38

The Teacher as a Witness of Faith   45

Part 2
Seven 2-Hour Sessions

Session 1
The Next Challenge: Moving into Adulthood   51

Session 2
The Future Is in My Hands: Turning Dreams into Realities   66

Session 3
Choices: Deciding How to Decide   80

Session 4
Connections: Building Healthful Relationships   91

Session 5
Communication: The Tie That Binds All Relationships   102

Session 6
The Search for Intimacy: A Risk Worth Taking   114

Session 7
Faith and the Young Adult: Seeking Intimacy with God   133

Part 3
SHARING IV Weekend Retreat Program

SHARING IV Designed Retreat   147

Retreat Planning Guide for SHARING IV   170

Part 4
Learning to Meditate: A Way to God

The Meditation Program: An Introduction   179

Directing the Meditation Program   185

A Guide for Meditation: Instructions and Photocopy Masters   204

Photocopy Masters for Student Handouts   237

Introduction

The Revised SHARING Program: What and Why?

The original SHARING Program was published between 1976, beginning with the publication of SHARING 9 for freshmen, and 1979, when the introduction of the SHARING 11/12 manual for the junior and senior years "completed" the SHARING Program. The SHARING Program called for a rather dramatic shift in our approach to high school religious education. But many who were willing to give it a try found it highly successful, and so the word spread. Since joining Saint Mary's Press in 1978 as an author and consultant, I have had the opportunity to travel a great deal—giving workshops, speaking at conventions, and meeting many professionals and volunteers working in youth ministry and adolescent catechesis. In my travels I am continually gratified—and, admittedly, a bit proud—to find that SHARING has been generally accepted as the most effective parish religious education program for adolescents available today.

Nevertheless, talk of doing a revision of SHARING began as early as 1981, usually in response to questions or comments about the dating of some of the session materials, films, and so on. Initially I viewed any revision as relatively minor and rather easily accomplished. The process of actually revising the program turned out to be neither. It required a full year of evaluation by people in the field, extensive planning, another year and a half of full-time writing on my part, and then six months in design and production. If the original SHARING was so well received and apparently effective, why all the changes?

Making a Good Program Better

In a nutshell, my intention as I began the revision process was to make a good program better. SHARING appeared to be meeting too many needs to be allowed to simply fade away, but it clearly needed some work if it was going to respond to a rapidly changing scene in Catholic youth ministry. The question I faced was this: How do I maintain all the strengths and positive characteristics of the original program while making changes or additions to improve those areas of SHARING that need work? Ultimately there is only one way to make such judgments—listen to the people. And so I did.

I just mentioned my extensive traveling. Over the last several years I have conducted workshops or spoken at conventions in thirty-five states. Everywhere I went I met people who were using SHARING, and I listened to their suggestions, criticisms, insights, and ideas. In 1982 Saint Mary's Press began to publish a free newsletter, the **SHARING News,** to encourage those using SHARING to write or call with their observations on how SHARING might be improved. That newsletter reached an audience of over three thousand. Those **SHARING News** subscribers then became the focal point of the most extensive level of the evaluation and revision of the original SHARING Program.

I wrote to all **SHARING News** subscribers and asked that parishes interested in working with me on the evaluation process do so by recruiting a "revision coordinator" in their parish who would serve as a liaison between me and all parish staff and volunteers involved with SHARING. An initial—and quite incredible—two hundred parishes responded. Of those, ninety-five maintained contact with me throughout the entire revision process—evaluating the original SHARING, responding to all my proposals for the revision, reading and reacting to ideas as I developed them. It required a lot of time and effort for all of us, but it paid off in a program that is far richer and more solid than ever. Those revision coordinators are recognized in the director's manual, and I am indebted to them for all they have done for me and, ultimately, for the young people who will benefit from their generosity.

Where Did It All Lead?

What did all this evaluation, planning, and writing eventually lead to? First, the revised SHARING does, I feel, maintain all those proven qualities and characteristics that I first discovered when developing the program over the course of my ten years of work as a parish director of high school religious education programs. Among the most significant of these foundational characteristics are the following:

1. The revised SHARING maintains a commitment to respond to the felt needs and developmental characteristics of adolescents. In fact, one of the major reasons SHARING has been substantially revised is that young people today are significantly different than when SHARING was originally developed. More on that later.

2. The revised SHARING remains committed to the effective formation of a faith relationship between young people and God rather than simply to the teaching of religious doctrines, beliefs, and practices. One of the most exciting and far-reaching developments in the Church since SHARING was originally conceived has been the growth of a vision of total ministry to and with young people. The original SHARING was developed with a tacit commitment on my part to total youth ministry, but with very little understanding of what that vision meant concretely. In the past several years I have learned a great deal, and my expanded understanding and richer experience have influenced the revised SHARING dramatically.

3. As was true with the original SHARING Program, I remain committed in the revised SHARING to creative teaching methods, unique scheduling, a comfortable learning environment, and a warm and affirming teacher-student relationship. All these will be explained more fully in the introductory chapters of this manual.

4. I remain convinced of the need for very detailed session plans, a fact perhaps of greatest interest to the volunteer. I would rather risk insulting experienced teachers by explaining too much than fail to meet the needs of novices by offering too little. I have been told repeatedly that one of the best characteristics of SHARING is that it leads the volunteer teacher step by step through every phase of a session, relieving a lot of tension and assuring far greater success. The revised SHARING, I trust, will maintain and even enhance that reputation.

So, What's New?

Along with a consistent commitment to the basic philosophy and pedagogy that made the original SHARING effective, I have recognized a need for significant change. Some changes were required because the SHARING Program was incomplete in the first place, missing or inadequately dealing with important topics such as sexuality, the Scriptures, and Christian lifestyles. These are now included in the revised SHARING. Other alterations were required because young people and their relationship to Christian faith and the Church have changed since SHARING began to evolve in the early- to mid-seventies. The major revisions reflecting this shift in student readiness and youth ministry in the Church are the following:

1. More—more fully integrated and more challenging content at all levels. The original SHARING 9, for example, was developed with the conviction that freshmen were often antagonistic toward or at best indifferent about religious education programs. It offered far fewer sessions than were normally expected of ninth graders at that time, and the content of those sessions was much more person-centered than content-centered. Its chief goal was to win the students' confidence and develop a level of openness that would allow deeper discussions in later stages of the program. For many people, SHARING 9 achieved those goals.

But many things have changed among young people in the last decade—some things for the worse, perhaps, but many things undoubtedly for the better. Specifically in the area of faith development and religious education, there have been many signs of hope—signs that our earlier decisions and shifts in ministry are bearing fruit. Among the most encouraging indicators has been the consistent comment from people over the last few years that students were ready for more than what SHARING was offering them. They wanted to meet more often, and they wanted more depth. In the revised SHARING, we have responded very creatively and concretely to these changing attitudes and needs.

The original SHARING 9 and 10 programs offered five 2-½-hour "Core Sessions," optional "Follow-Up Sessions" of 1-½ hours each, and an overnight retreat experience. A person participating in all of the program would receive some thirty-three hours of formal religious education—certainly not inadequate—but often presented in the context of ten or fewer meetings during the year. By comparison, the new SHARING III Program provides detailed session plans for sixteen 2-hour sessions, plus an overnight retreat option, for a total of some fifty or more solid hours of program material.

But the content of a program cannot be judged simply by the *quantity* of sessions offered. The *quality* of the total curriculum design and of individual session plans is of far greater significance. The original SHARING evolved slowly over the course of nearly ten years. After it was all published, I could recognize many gaps in content, inconsistencies in style, and so on—if for no other reason than that I had learned a lot myself between the time SHARING 9 was developed and the time SHARING 11/12 was finished. In the process of revising, all of that experience has been utilized. Not only is each session improved in the revised SHARING, but the arrangement of each phase of the entire program is far more integrated, cohesive, and complete than was possible in the original. Consequently, themes flow more naturally, content is richer, methodologies are more balanced, and the progression from one manual to the next is more logical and theologically sound. I know of no other parish religious education program for high school students that even attempts, much less achieves, this kind of integrated, progressive, and complete four-year curriculum.

2. A shift from "the school model" to a needs-based, developmental program design. Most religious education programs designed for use with adolescents in parish programs either (*a*) offer so little direction that the teacher is not sure with which students to use what materials or (*b*) direct the material too precisely to certain age-groups, denying the possibility of a wide divergence of student readiness from one parish to another. The original SHARING erred, perhaps, in the latter manner. By identifying the SHARING manuals as specifically 9, 10, and 11/12, it seemed clear that teachers should use the first with ninth graders, the second with sophomores, and so on. Quite candidly, that is what I had in mind when I designed the program. Each manual, for example, gave psychological sketches of each grade level. The problem is that the real world simply is not that rigid, at least not in terms of readiness for religious education. As a result, sometimes when people used SHARING 11/12 with their juniors, the material was simply too advanced, irrelevant, and often ineffective.

You will note that the revised SHARING no longer identifies its component manuals in terms of grades 9 through 12. Rather, I now offer SHARING I through IV. This is intended to make very clear that the director and teachers must evaluate their particular groups in terms of their *real needs* based on the students' prior experience with religious education programs.

The SHARING I manual, for example, is a very enjoyable, highly relational program aimed at the evangelization of students *regardless of their age*. It will be very effective with most, if not all, ninth graders. But it will also work very well for juniors who have had no previous effective religious education. Therefore, if your parish is just introducing SHARING in its high school religious education programming, you might do well to use SHARING I with *all* high school students the first year, introducing SHARING II for sophomores through seniors the second year, SHARING III for juniors and seniors the third year, and so on. In this way it may take four years before each grade is using a separate manual, SHARING I through IV, sequentially. This seems far more reasonable, realistic, and ultimately successful than those programs—the original SHARING included—that are too strictly designed in terms of grades in school.

A workable and reasonable alternative to the above approach might be to introduce SHARING into the parish by using SHARING I for the ninth and tenth graders and SHARING II for eleventh and twelfth graders during the first year. In the second year, ninth graders would use SHARING I, tenth graders SHARING II, and eleventh and twelfth graders SHARING III. It would then be in the third year of use of the SHARING Program that you would finally be ready for SHARING IV with seniors.

The point here is to emphasize two extremely important factors in your use of the SHARING Program generally or the SHARING IV manual specifically: (1) You have a great deal of flexibility in the SHARING Program, so take time to plan thoughtfully and imaginatively. (2) Always base your decisions on a clear understanding of the starting point of the group with which you will work, rather than on anyone's preconceived notions of what is needed for a particular grade level. Your students have specific needs, and the revised SHARING Program gives you the necessary resources and flexibility to respond to those needs.

3. A more consistent, responsive, and understandable session structure. As noted earlier, the original SHARING Program offered a variety of formats for its sessions. In the SHARING 9 and 10 manuals, this involved a mix of 2-½-hour, 1-½-hour, and overnight faith-experience models. In SHARING 11/12 there were options for minicourses, daylong "GIFT-Days," and a full weekend retreat.

The initial intent of this variety was sound and positive. The idea was to offer teachers many options and to avoid potential boredom on the part of the students. It was also a response to the demands of my own quite unique job description at the time of the writing of the SHARING Program. For seven years I was director of a five-parish program, and I had to create rather unorthodox class schedules to meet the needs of all five parishes.

Many teachers, to be sure, found this variety refreshing and very effective. But far more teachers, I came to learn, found it confusing, unnecessary, and at times simply unacceptable in their own parish situations. Therefore a great many parishes were forced to rewrite the SHARING session plans into more consistent, conventional formats. In fact, my growing conviction has been that the vast majority of parishes were forced to do so, with only a minority following the SHARING Program precisely as I had designed it.

In the revised SHARING, I have tried to respond to this situation by eliminating the confusing variety of sessions while maintaining my commitment to a unique kind of scheduling at the high school level. I still believe firmly that the traditional one-hour session once a week is completely unworkable at the high school level. More than one hour is required in any given session if any real learning is to take place. Furthermore, high school students simply have too many extracurricular options to be expected to commit one evening a week for religious education classes. By developing a consistent, two-hour time frame for all sessions in the revised SHARING, I think I have opted for a format that will serve far more people more easily and more effectively than did the original SHARING. (Note: Specific scheduling options for SHARING IV can be found in the section titled "Faith Formation: Putting Theory into Practice," pp. 23–28.)

An Overview of the Four-Year Revised SHARING Program

It seems clear to me that those working with any one part of SHARING, or with any one manual, ought to be at least generally aware of the content and progression of the entire four-year curriculum. SHARING is a gradually unfolding program, calling the students at each level to progressively deeper and richer levels of understanding of the Christian message. A teacher working with any one group of students will need to know what has preceded his or her contact with the students as well as what will follow.

I therefore strongly suggest that all those preparing to actually teach the SHARING IV Program reflect carefully on the chart of major themes of the entire four-year program provided here (see pp. 14–15). Think through the progression of material from one level to the next. If you have specific information in mind that you feel all students must have before leaving high school, find where that material is offered in the program. This will alleviate the feeling that you, and you alone, must share all that information. Finally, try to imagine yourself or, perhaps, one of your own children experiencing this program from beginning to end, from SHARING I through SHARING IV. I think you will discover a conviction growing within yourself that this is a well-designed program that you can reasonably expect will achieve its primary goal—the development of a sound foundation for a growing faith relationship between young people and our God.

SHARING IV and the Four-Year Curriculum

The director's manual for the revised SHARING Program provides detailed information on adolescent faith development, an understanding of total youth ministry as it responds to that development, and an extensive explanation of how the revised SHARING can be understood in terms of both. Those looking for an in-depth understanding of how SHARING IV fits into the total curriculum are therefore advised to look to that material in the director's manual. For the needs of the average volunteer teacher, however, this brief introduction to and overview of SHARING IV should suffice.

A quick review of the content and approach of SHARING I, II, and III will help situate SHARING IV within the context of the whole SHARING curriculum. The major goal of the SHARING I program is stated in that manual as follows:

> A popular image in the history of the Church for the process of sharing faith is the planting and nurturing of a seed. Prior to planting the seed, the soil must be prepared, turned over, loosened up if you will. The seed is then planted. But, if

it is to grow, it must be carefully nurtured, watered, protected from the elements, and so on, until it becomes strong enough to fend pretty much on its own. So it is with faith. SHARING I can be understood as a process of "groundbreaking," of opening the students through the building of relationships of trust with the teachers and with one another. It is also a means of "planting the seed," of introducing or reaffirming for the students the very basic proclamation of the Gospel. And, as noted above, this will only take place when students can rub shoulders with adults for whom the faith is alive, vibrant, exciting, real. It is in later levels of the four-year SHARING Program, then, that the students will gradually receive deeper and more formal catechesis.

So SHARING I assumes a certain negativity toward religious education that is common among young adolescents and strives primarily to turn that attitude around. It does so by offering material that is not highly theological, but that is very relational and enjoyable, and which concentrates on the lived experiences of the early adolescent.

SHARING II can be understood as a kind of middle ground, a step between the content of SHARING I and III. The three major themes integrated in the SHARING II program are maturity, sexuality and dating, and Christian morality and moral decision-making. These are areas of obvious importance and interest to adolescents but certainly more sophisticated and challenging than the material in SHARING I. Again, however, SHARING II does not *presume* a developed faith commitment on the part of the students. The program strives, rather, to demonstrate clearly that the faith of Christians is very relevant to the daily lives and concerns of adolescents and that it is, therefore, deserving of serious and sincere reflection.

It is precisely that kind of openness to a serious discussion of Christian faith that is presumed in the SHARING III level of the four-year curriculum. SHARING III concentrates on the very heart of the Christian message by focusing on the three themes of revelation and the Scriptures, the ministry and message of Jesus, and the sacraments. I have to be quick to note that, as is the case throughout SHARING, very creative and enjoyable learning strategies are employed in the treatment of these admittedly challenging themes. There is no attempt to overwhelm the students with advanced theology. At the same time, however, I do not want to minimize the significant increase in sophisticated and intellectually challenging material in SHARING III compared to the earlier manuals in the total program.

Therefore, the first three manuals in the SHARING Program nurture the young people through a developmental period of great growth and change. The students emerge from the challenging stage of early adolescence to that of the relative maturity of senior high school students. They evolve from a stage in which they almost need to be entertained to a time when they are willing and able to reflect upon and discuss the fundamental issues of life. They begin the SHARING Program in ninth grade, typically making a transition between two styles of faith. The thoughtful religious educator, John Westerhoff, claims that junior high school students commonly express a faith style that he has termed "affiliative faith," in which their primary need is to experience a sense of belonging through highly relational kinds of ministry. By the end of their junior year, many young people have become engaged in a whole new style of faith, termed by Westerhoff "searching faith." During this time, the young people have a great need to seriously reflect upon the religious and faith traditions that were offered them as children and to assess whether they will now freely and consciously accept that heritage as adult Catholic Christians.

We must recognize and accept the fact that many of the young people involved in SHARING IV will be engaged in *the transition from* affiliative faith to searching faith. Some individuals, particularly those who have recently experienced effective preparation for the Sacrament of Confirmation, may identify themselves as committed Catholic Christians. Others might remain somewhat tentative, perhaps responsive to further reflection and discussion regarding faith, yet still keeping their options open regarding full commitment to Jesus and the Gospel. Still other young people will display apathy or even antagonism toward the faith. Rarely, however, will the latter individuals be interested in attending a program like SHARING IV. Therefore, the young people most likely to attend the SHARING IV Program will be either quite committed to the faith or open to continuing personal search and serious dialogue about what they believe and value. Having the opportunity, indeed the privilege, to lead a program for young people such as these can be both challenging and exhilarating.

What are we to offer young people who demonstrate these faith characteristics? What do seniors in high school commonly require from the Church if they are to continue to grow as Catholic Christians? The answers to those questions did not come easy to me as I developed the SHARING IV Program. A little background on my experience in designing this material will help you to understand the goals and objectives of SHARING IV as the final level of the four-year SHARING curriculum.

One of the major difficulties I encountered in my writing of SHARING IV was my growing realization that seniors—the likely audience for SHARING IV—require a far different kind of program than I had initially envisioned. I began writing SHARING IV by focusing on the themes traditionally presumed for senior-level religion curriculums—the basic notion of Christian lifestyles followed by more specific discussions of single life, religious vocations, and Christian marriage and family life.

I wrote for approximately three months and found it to be pure drudgery. Quite honestly, the material I was developing left me bored. If I found it boring, I could only imagine what students and their teachers would think of it!

So I scrapped everything I had written and started over. I spent considerable time reading about late adolescent and young adult development. I talked at length with several counselors and teachers of freshman college students, knowing that the vast majority of seniors who will attend SHARING IV will be college-bound. I asked the college teachers and counselors to share with me their experiences with college freshmen. I put these questions to them: When you work with these young people, what do you wish they had already received in their high school years in terms of skills and attitudes? What areas of their life seem to cause them the greatest concern? If you were in my position of developing a religious education program for high school seniors, what would you include in light of what you now know? What helpful resources have you discovered that you can recommend to me? Needless to say, some great conversations came out of these exchanges.

Out of all this reading, conversation, and reflection, a new focus for SHARING IV emerged for me. In many ways, I had to relearn some of the most basic principles of sound educational theory, principles I had somehow forgotten when I became locked into the traditional format. The most basic of these principles is this: People will learn something only if it truly relates to who they are and what their immediate needs are. This is particularly true when people engage in programs on a voluntary basis. If the information does not respond to who they are and what they need, they simply will not participate.

The major problem with the traditional senior themes is that they reflect what we as adults view as essential information for young people. However, the students commonly do not see that information as essential. For example, most of today's seniors do not visualize themselves getting married in the immediate future. Most have not achieved a level of spiritual maturity that leads them to reflect on the qualities of a Christian lifestyle. We have to lead them to reflection on such concerns; we cannot *assume* that the students already care about these matters.

Some adults will argue that many seniors do, in fact, enjoy courses on marriage. However, in evaluating many of these courses, I find that their focus is not strictly on marriage itself. I believe that what makes these courses attractive to seniors is their focus on human relationships, on communication skills, on determining when true love exists between persons, and so on. It is incidental that these themes are discussed within the context of marriage. As you will see, SHARING IV does include all these themes but treats them in an immediate context that will capture the interest of more students.

Given this brief introduction, here are the major components and themes of the SHARING IV manual:

- Seven 2-hour sessions exploring the major developmental tasks of young adults and providing information and skills required to satisfactorily accomplish the tasks. Among these tasks and required skills are: selecting values that will guide one's choices as an adult; learning the skill of effective decision-making; building healthful, mature relationships and achieving intimacy with others; assuming responsibility for one's future faith development

- A weekend retreat (SHARING IV provides both a thoroughly designed retreat that incorporates and expands upon the themes of SHARING IV and a planning guide for leaders and young people who wish to develop their own retreat.)

- A monthlong meditation program in which the young people learn the skills of prayer and meditation that are needed if they are to sustain their spiritual growth after they leave the program.

The chart of major themes on pages 14–15 indicates the specific topics considered in each of the seven 2-hour sessions. As is true throughout the SHARING Program, the content of these sessions is presented with many creative learning strategies, all thoroughly explained in this manual.

A brief review of the chart of major themes reveals that the program format and the components of SHARING IV are quite different than those of previous levels of SHARING. Instead of the sixteen 2-hour sessions offered in SHARING I through III, SHARING IV includes only seven 2-hour sessions. Each level of SHARING includes a retreat component, so users of the earlier levels of SHARING will not be surprised to see retreat options included here as well. However, the monthlong meditation program in SHARING IV is strikingly (perhaps frighteningly!) unique. The rationale for the SHARING IV Program structure and the options in scheduling it are fully explained in the section of this manual entitled "Faith Formation: Putting Theory into Practice," pages 23–28. The meditation program, because of its unique nature, deserves additional comment here.

Novices to youth ministry and adolescent religious education may be somewhat skeptical about young people's interest in prayer and meditation. However, veterans of the ministry—particularly those who have participated in programs like SHARING—know that, when properly guided, young people clearly love to pray. In all my years of work with young people, few things impress them more and receive greater affirmation from them than guided meditations and other creative prayer experiences. In recent years, I have had the opportunity to speak at diocesan and national youth congresses. At a number of these events I have included, in addition to my formal talks, various meditation exercises. When young people write me after such events, they almost invariably comment on how much the prayer meant to them. I have watched as five hundred young poeple in an auditorium remain totally silent and still for twenty minutes or more while I lead them through a meditation. Quite honestly, I have had no more moving and satisfying experiences with young people than these opportunities to share prayer with them.

The meditation program in SHARING IV is geared toward the development of the skills of meditation. The program consists of daily exercises that the young people engage in and then reflect upon, often by writing brief reactions in their journals. On a weekly basis, the participants meet as a group to share the results of their meditation, to learn more prayer skills, and to pray together as a group. I am confident that no dimension of the SHARING Program will nurture more spiritual growth—for both the young people and those adults fortunate enough to lead them—than will this meditation program. I encourage you as strongly as I can to seriously evaluate the program and accept the commitment it demands of both you and the young people. It may well be the greatest gift you will offer them in their four years with the SHARING Program.

The SHARING Director's Manual

I have referred to the director's manual for the revised SHARING Program. It is quite likely that any given parish will require or desire only one copy of that volume, whereas all teachers will need a manual like this one (SHARING I, II, III, or IV) for actually teaching any level of the program. I do encourage you, however, to spend at least a bit of time perusing the director's manual and becoming generally familiar with the information contained there. Then, if or when questions or concerns regarding various dimensions of the entire SHARING Program present themselves, you will at least have a notion of where you might look for some answers. The following overview of the contents will give you an idea of what you will find in the director's manual:

Part 1: Theoretical Foundations of Adolescent Religious Education
1. Total Youth Ministry
2. Adolescent Spirituality: Seeking a God to Call Their Own
3. A Model of Youth Ministry
4. Youth Catechesis in Context

Part 2: The SHARING Curriculum
5. The Curriculum Design of SHARING
6. The Scope and Sequence of SHARING
7. Who Is the Jesus We Are Teaching?
8. How to Understand the Bible
9. Educating for Peace and Justice: Problems and Possibilities

Part 3: Implementing the SHARING Program
10. Introducing the SHARING Program
11. Developing Leaders for SHARING
12. Implementing SHARING: Miscellaneous Questions and Concerns

Part 4: The SHARING Program and Confirmation
13. Confirmation Through History
14. Ten Principles for Designing Confirmation Programs
15. Confirmation and the SHARING Program

Part 5: The SHARING Music Guides
16. Using Rock Music with SHARING
17. Using Religious Music with SHARING

Chart of Major Themes

SHARING I

Components: Sixteen 2-hour sessions and two overnight retreat experiences

Identity
1. Adolescence: a new stage in a new age
2. Identity and self-image
3. Culture and its impact on development

Relating
4. Relating to others; awareness; communication
5. Parent-teen communication

Jesus
6. Faith and religion; images of God
7. Adolescent images of, attitudes toward, and beliefs about Jesus
8. The Gospels: portraits of Jesus
9. The Gospel according to young people; reflecting on the relevance of the Gospel
10. Christian faith: a personal response to and relationship with Jesus

Church
11. The Church as a community of faith
12. Adolescent needs and attitudes regarding the Church
13. Optional meeting on youth ministry with the pastor and/or the parish council
14. The Church as a celebrating community; the sacraments
15. Eucharist: the bread of life
16. Concluding session: summary and party

Overnight retreat themes (two options): (1) a special retreat experience on parent-teen relationships, with parental participation; (2) a retreat integrating the themes of trust, love, sin, God, and prayer

SHARING II

Components: Sixteen 2-hour sessions and an overnight retreat experience

Maturity
1. Becoming a mature person
2. Becoming who and what we are called to be

Sexuality and Dating
3. Introduction to the unit on sexuality and dating
4. Biology of sex (optional)
5. Contemporary society and sexuality
6. Psychology of sexuality; masculinity and femininity
7. Sexuality and dating

Morality and Moral Decision-Making
8. Defining morality; key components in all moralities
9. Human needs and values: foundations of all morality
10. Jesus' vision of being fully human as the foundation of Christian morality
11. Sin, reconciliation, and conversion: growing in Christian morality
12. Critical reflection versus situation ethics
13. Resolving moral conflicts: Christian moral decision-making
14. Christian sexual morality
15. Global moral issues: Christian commitment to justice and peace
16. Becoming the me I want to be: summary of the year and celebration

Overnight retreat themes: Awareness of self, others, and God; the God question; attitudes toward faith and religion; the need for conversion

SHARING III

Components: Sixteen 2-hour sessions and a full weekend retreat experience.

Revelation and the Bible

1. Defining revelation as God's self-disclosure
2. Introduction to the Bible; praying the Scriptures
3. The God of Jews and Christians; evolution of our understanding of God

Jesus and the Gospels

4. Introduction to the unit on Jesus; the historical and social world of Jesus
5. Jesus' mission begins: baptism, temptations, and beginning of public life
6. Kingdom of God: the center of Jesus' message and ministry
7. Parables and miracles of Jesus
8. Jesus' last days: connecting Passover, the Last Supper, the death of Jesus, and our experience of the Eucharist

Death and Dying

9. Death and dying; searching for the meaning of death and the ability to cope with it

Special Section: Adolescent Suicide

10. The Resurrection and Ascension of Jesus: death is conquered; Christ's ongoing presence

Sacraments

11. Jesus and the Church; the Emmaus story and its significance
12. Sacraments and symbols: the need to "see with new eyes"
13. Sacraments of initiation: Baptism, Confirmation, the Eucharist
14. Sacraments of healing: Anointing of the Sick, Reconciliation
15. Sacraments of vocation and commitment: Orders and Matrimony
16. Concluding session; celebration

Weekend retreat themes: Reflecting on our images of Jesus; getting in touch with God; parent-teen relationships; growing in our commitment to Jesus

SHARING IV

Components: Seven 2-hour sessions; a fully designed weekend retreat and a guide for creating one's own retreat; and an intensive thirty-day program in prayer and meditation.

Challenges of Young Adulthood

1. Young adulthood: characteristics and developmental tasks
2. Choosing the dreams and values that will guide me
3. Decision-making skills; Christian discernment

Developing Healthful Relationships

4. Characteristics of healthful relationships
5. Nurturing the skills required for building relationships; resolving conflicts
6. The meaning of and search for intimacy; love, sex, or infatuation: How do I really know?

Faith and the Young Adult

7. Faith development through young adulthood; the process of Christian conversion

Weekend retreat options: A thoroughly designed weekend retreat that expands upon the themes noted above, as well as a planning guide to help the young people and their leaders develop their own retreat.

Learning to Meditate

SHARING IV includes a thirty-day program designed to teach the skills of prayer and meditation, consisting of two major components:

1. With the help of a printed guide, the young people are asked to devote about fifteen minutes a day for four weeks to a series of meditation exercises. They are periodically helped to reflect on the exercises by writing their thoughts in personal journals.
2. Once each week the participants in the program meet with the leaders to share their experience, to learn more about meditation, and to pray together as a group.

A Few Preliminaries

Before turning to the session plans themselves, though, it is important for all teachers of SHARING IV to gain a thorough sense of the foundations of the program, some sound background on the attitudes and developmental characteristics of the young people with whom you will be sharing the material, and finally, some insights into the nature of teaching itself, particularly some practical suggestions on teaching the sessions in this manual. All of that information is provided in Part 1 of this manual. It is usual and understandable that many volunteers as well as professionals will want to get right to the meat of the program—the material you will ultimately be asked to share with the students directly. You may choose to look ahead to that now in Parts 2 and 3 just to satisfy your curiosity! But before teaching any of that material, I urge you to carefully read and reflect upon the following introductory material. Your experience with leading the SHARING IV Program will then be far more comfortable, effective, and therefore fulfilling.

Part 1
New Perspectives on Some Old Questions

"Forming Faith" or "Teaching Religion"

Before getting into the specifics of the SHARING Program, it is essential that you understand the philosophy of religious education behind it—the approach I use in presenting Jesus and his message to students and why I use it. Without that kind of understanding you will lack a focus, a sense of direction and purpose. That lack will not only limit your effectiveness with students but will result in a lot of frustration for you as a teacher.

In this section we will discuss the following points:

- the essential difference between **faith** and **religion;** the effects of that distinction on our understanding of the goals of religious education;
- two possible models of religious education and my preference; a discussion of the goals of this program in light of that preference;
- ramifications of this model of religious education for the format of SHARING; a comment on our role as teachers.

The Distinction Between Faith and Religion

The foundation underlying many of the recent changes in religious education is the distinction we have recognized between the concepts of faith and religion. Often we have treated these two concepts as synonymous, but they are not. It is in the context of this distinction that we define the goals of religious education, the role of the catechist, the content of our programs, and the methodologies we employ.

Very simply stated, faith involves us in a personal relationship with our God. It involves the level on which we meet our God in friendship. It is the level of private prayer, the dimension in which we experience God through nature and through our dealings with others. Faith is private and mysterious because, like all love relationships, it defies description and analysis. Also to some extent our faith is unique to each of us—not because our God is different but because we are. We all "see" God in a different way, we all speak to God from our own personal life experiences, and we relate to God on the level of our greatest needs and desires as individuals.

Religion, on the other hand, is the attempt by people to share and make public their faith relationship with God. Religious expressions of faith are as natural and necessary as physical embraces are to other love relationships. We need to express our inner feelings, we have to give form to our beliefs, and we have to verbalize what we know only too well is "impossible to put into words."

Religious expression in institutional religion happens at the level of creed, code, and cult. It is the attempt to define through doctrinal statements (creed) who our God is and what our relationship to God is all about. Religion also involves the development of a code of ethics, and that code is expressed through special cultic signs, whether they are totem poles or rain dances of certain native American tribes or the sacramental signs of our own Church. By definition, religion cannot completely express human faith in God. That we human beings feel compelled to express our faith, however, is evidenced by all of religious history.

The problem that is so often encountered becomes more clear in this context. We can become so concerned about explaining our religious rituals, doctrines, and moral codes to children that we fail to give witness effectively to our own growing faith relationships with our God. And we often fail as well

19

to guide our students to the development of their own unique faith relationships with God. We therefore end up with many people who see their lives as Christians defined strictly by what they are to *do*—go to Mass, say prayers, follow a code of ethics—and not by what they are to *be*—sons and daughters of the Father, brothers and sisters of Christ, and committed to living a life of love in the Spirit.

We see the results of this development in the so-called "crisis of faith" among many of our young people today. I firmly believe that the crisis is not nearly so much one of faith as it is one of religion. If we ask students why they are turned off or why they do not attend classes, the almost universal response is that they reject not *faith*, but the *religious expressions of faith* that they have been taught. They reject, for example, doctrines that they often do not understand. ("How can you believe in a Christ who is supposed to be three persons?" one student asked me.) They reject rituals that were never explained. They reject laws that to them seem inhuman and cold. On the other hand, if you ask students if they believe in God, most will say yes; if they pray, yes; if they believe they must love, yes.

The point is that we *must* approach our students on the level of Christian faith before we can ever hope to have them "buy" our religion and its implications. Our classes have to become personal and alive; we have to speak to them "where they're at" and in some way communicate the real message of Jesus—that they are loved and are freed by that love, that they are called to become as fully human as Jesus, that their faith is a call and a challenge to a life of service.

Two Models of Religious Education

The distinction between faith and religion clearly implies fundamental changes in our approach to religious education. As we comprehend this distinction, we become involved in a whole new way of viewing our task, our goals shift, and we can more easily define not only *what* we are to do but *how* we are to do it.

In defining where we stand today, it will be helpful to look at two models for religious education—one representing our traditional approach or "the past," the other representing our contemporary perspective. It should be noted that, like all models, the ones provided here have serious drawbacks. They will appear to be overly simplistic—which they are. They will appear to concentrate on extremes—which they do. They will seem to condemn the past while perhaps naively praising our present approach —which, in a sense, they do. With these aspects admitted, the models nevertheless have great benefits in that they help to give us a framework out of which to discuss our present situation.

The models represent two approaches, one of which is primarily concerned with the passing on of religious knowledge; the other is concerned primarily with faith development. Two dimensions are depicted for each approach: the "student focus" (the attitude we have toward our students), and the "program focus" that results from that attitude.

Without going into great detail and again admitting the obvious weaknesses of these models, some comments by way of summary should be made. When the primary focus of our efforts is the teaching of "religion," the student is seen as a blank slate upon which we "write" our understanding of religious truths. This approach is also characterized by what is known as a "two-world view," in which one's existence is understood as being separated into the "vale of tears" of this world and the "hereafter" awaiting us after death.

To endure existence here one must adhere to the law of God. If one does so, salvation is attained. The goal of programs geared toward the student centers on giving him or her this information, "urging" the student to conform to certain practices in order to gain future salvation.

When faith is seen as the primary focus of our efforts, the student is viewed as an individual—unique, free. By leading the students to a realization of their own dignity and worth, a realization of being loved by God is possible. The response to that love is a vision of the unity of life and faith, a realization that one finds God here and now and that one is called to be involved as a co-creator with God in the process of redeeming the world. Programs center around helping students learn and experience—not just *know about*—their selves, God, and the world in which they live. In short, the simple acquisition of facts is seen as secondary to the development of attitudes and values that will shape the students' lives. The adult is seen not so much as a teacher of information but as a witness of the Christian faith that is in him or her. The students perceive the convictions of the adult, evaluate themselves in light of those convictions and, we hope, choose to build a life on faith in Christ.

There are dangers or pitfalls involved in each of these approaches. When the focus of religion is primary, there is a risk that students will see their faith as static, unchanging, ritualistic, threatening, and—consequently—often unappealing. The program that adopts the primary focus of faith, emphasizing as it does the freedom of the individual, risks "losing" students who, in their freedom, choose to reject the message of Christ. There are some who say that this faith-oriented approach naively overestimates the students, their willingness and ability to learn, their maturity. Also, the goal of forming faith rather than simply teaching religion demands considerably more of the teacher. The adult involved in this approach must not only be comfortable with and knowledgeable about his or her faith but also able to enter into a personal relationship with the students, knowing the students' needs and feelings, supporting and encouraging them, struggling with them. Again, some might say this is too much to ask, that although this may be an ideal to be aimed at, we simply do not have enough adults who have the necessary abilities and talents.

The SHARING Approach—And Why

Recognizing only too well the difficulties inherent in an approach based on faith before religion, conscious of the responsibilities it places on the teacher, and occasionally frustrated by the fact that our success is often not objectively measurable, I nevertheless strongly endorse and employ the model of religious education in which faith is primary. And I do so for one simple reason—it's the way Jesus did it! Jesus concerned himself primarily with forming people, not simply *informing* them. He loved, he cajoled, he motivated, he guided. He was totally aware of the freedom and dignity of those he met—he respected them as persons. Many of his followers were drawn to him by the sheer force of his convictions.

Of secondary but great importance is the fact that our previous approach, based strictly on the imparting of knowledge *about* our religion, simply did not work. Though it could be argued that many if not all of our present teachers were raised with that approach and somehow "turned out okay," they did so not necessarily as a result of that system of education but often in spite of it. When I look back over

Two Models of Religious Education

RELIGIOUS KNOWLEDGE (Religion before faith)	FAITH DEVELOPMENT (Faith before religion)
A. Student Focus 1) Receiver 2) Creature 3) Law ("fear of the Lord") 4) Sinner 5) Separation (two-world view) 6) Salvation as goal	**A. Student Focus** 1) Co-learner, co-sharer 2) Co-creator 3) Love (communion, service) 4) "Beloved" 5) Union (one-world view) 6) Salvation as process
B. Program Focus 1) Acquisition of knowledge 2) Factual material (objective) 3) Memorization 4) Content imposed 5) Practices 6) Controlled behavior 7) Teacher-student relationship (hierarchical)	**B. Program Focus** 1) Experiential learning 2) Attitudes, values (subjective) 3) Understanding 4) Content discovered 5) Lifestyle 6) Moral maturity 7) Witness-evaluator relationship (interactive)

my own religious development, I honestly cannot remember a religion class that notably impressed me, even in college. What did impress me, what did change my life, and what did lead me to accept gratefully the gift of faith were *persons*, people committed to Christ and concerned about me as an individual. I don't remember a thing that Sister Fidelis or Sister Estavan taught me in grade school about religion, but I'll never forget *them*. I can't remember the titles of the courses I took from Father Sheets or Father Sullivan in college, but *they* impressed me tremendously with their convictions, their depth of faith. I think all of us can admit to the same kind of experiences, and the lesson behind these experiences is crucial.

Ramifications of the Faith Formation Model for the SHARING Program

Pause here for a moment and briefly reflect on the faith formation model of religious education. Then, take a few minutes to reflect on what you feel are its ramifications. Assuming that you accept the rationale favoring this model, how would you define your own role as a teacher? How would you measure the success or failure of your efforts? How would you handle discipline problems? Would you force students to attend religion programs? What kind of program would *you* design?

One of the advantages of the faith-oriented model of religious education is that it opens up virtually endless possibilities and allows for very creative and innovative approaches. In creating the SHARING Program, I have tried to honestly confront questions such as those posed above. Through this process, I have arrived at a number of personal convictions and assumptions regarding adolescent religious education:

1. Any high school religious education program must be *significantly different* from any other experienced by the students up to that point. This is true largely because of the "negative discovery of self" stage in which students find themselves—a time in development when the past is criticized and often rejected. More on this later.

2. Our programs must be *both* enjoyable and educational. If a program is geared toward the active, pleasurable involvement and participation of the students, they will be much more likely to reach the point where they *want* to come to class.

3. The program must deal with the world as the students see it. Before we can lead them to a realization of the role of faith in their lives, we have to accept them where they are and relate closely with their present needs and perspectives.

4. The approach to discipline must be guided by Christian values and concern. It has been said that we can judge our Christian love by our love for that person whom we love least. The same holds true for discipline within our religious education programs. Our chief concern should be for those who like us least, who are most turned off. Our challenge is to bridge the gap—to enable the most estranged to cooperate not out of fear of reprisal but out of respect for us.

5. We must create an environment for our programs that not only permits but encourages freedom.

6. We do not need adults who want to be "buddies" with the students, but rather those who want to be what they should be—loving, concerned witnesses of faith.

7. The criterion of success *cannot* be the degree to which our students agree with us. If we present the real Christ, we will need to allow for those who will not be able to say yes to him—perhaps out of immaturity, a lack of understanding, or even fear of the implications of a commitment to the vision and values of Jesus.

8. We must realize that we are not the primary educators of our students nor, contrary to popular opinion, are the parents of the students. The primary educator of the students is God. God is not bound, *thank God,* by religion programs, Catholic schools, charismatic movements, Catholicism, or anything else. Let's be open to the reality that those *we* do not reach are not forgotten by God, that our failures may be God's successes, that those who reject us, indeed, may have to do so before they can accept God.

This list of assumptions could be much longer—and probably should be. The point is clear, however: When we discuss "religious education," we are into a whole new ball game. We are not teaching a subject but sharing a person, and all the ground rules are changed because of that fact.

Faith Formation: Putting Theory into Practice

Once we have thought through the ramifications of the faith formation model of religious education, it is relatively easy to discover why so many of our prior efforts to reach high school students have failed. It is, sad to say, not an exaggeration to admit that many of our previous programs missed on all points: We tried to give the wrong message at the wrong time and in an ineffective way to a group of students that, for the most part, did not even show up. We thought we could take a group of high school students, sit them down quietly in a room, throw "facts" at them for a while, and through some unexplainable work of the Spirit, they would eventually catch on to what we were talking about.

We measured our success many times by how quiet and cooperative a group of students happened to be for a given session. We ignored the fact that many were either miles away in their own daydreams or so turned off by what was going on that they simply sat and glared.

By the same token, we thought that if the students acquired a certain body of knowledge *about* their faith, they would automatically become people *of* faith, while more often than not just the opposite result occurred: the more classes they attended, the less attractive the faith became.

We had an almost magical belief in the power of memorization and repetition. That is, if we said the same thing over and over, year after year, somehow it would hit home. With possible variations in vocabulary and terminology, the syllabus for the religion course for my senior year in high school probably was not all that dissimilar to the ones for my fifth- and sixth-grade classes. Such are the pitfalls of programs based simply on the acquisition of religious knowledge rather than on the constantly changing, personal, challenging, and downright exciting development of real faith.

Just how does a teacher go about developing faith in high school students? Or, more accurately stated, how does one design an effective program in which students will be open to developing their own faith —posing significant questions and seeking real answers, willingly taking a look at their own lives, and discovering how Jesus and his message relate to them? Obviously we are confronted with a complex combination of realities, concerns, and questions here. Among them:

- What dimensions of the Gospel are most relevant, meaningful, and therefore important and appealing to high school students?

- Who is our audience? What do these particular students need and how can we best respond to those needs?

- What kind of program should we offer? Where should we offer it? How often should we meet? In other words, how can we best put all this theory into practice?

It is this third point that I wish to discuss in this section. In trying to find answers to all of these questions, I arrived at some basic assumptions upon which I eventually constructed the SHARING Program. I will briefly discuss the main points of each assumption here; the implications of these assumptions will, quite literally, be the subject of the rest of the book.

1. As mentioned briefly before, I believe that in order to reach high school students, **we must provide programs that are significantly different from any program they have experienced up to that**

point. By this I mean different content obviously, but also different methods, different scheduling, different environments—everything.

As we shall see more clearly in the next section, adolescents go through a period in their development aptly called "the negative discovery of self." Simply stated this means that, during the period from about eighth grade to about sophomore year in high school, students often demonstrate a strong rejection of nearly everything they consider "childish." This rejection can appear at times to be all-encompassing and highly unreasonable, but it is a very necessary stage through which the adolescent must pass on the way to eventual adulthood.

During this period the students try to define who they are primarily by reacting negatively against the *past*. They do not clearly know what or who they are, but they can tell you exactly what they are *not*—children! They react against parental discipline, for example, by complaining about being constantly "treated like a child." I can remember when I was in junior high school that it was considered "childish" to be seen riding a bike, so all the "cool" kids either walked or hitchhiked everywhere. Many of my female students mention being embarrassed when their mothers take them shopping for new clothes; they want to go on their own rather than be treated like children. This attitude—which we will discuss again later—has a direct repercussion on our approach to religion classes generally at this age.

Assuming the majority of our high school students have attended some form of religious education, it stands to reason that much of this religious training will also be subject to the negativism of early adolescence. I hardly have to mention this to anyone who has tried teaching religion to this age group—the negative reaction is not exactly hidden! Nor should it be unexpected. What we have to do is to recognize this stage of development and to not only prepare for it but take advantage of it.

How do we do that? Somehow we have to design our high school programs to be obviously distinct from what is offered at earlier ages so that the students will view them as significantly new experiences. To begin with, the content must be not only new but truly relevant to the age group. The structure of the class itself must also be different—no more talking to rows of students for one-hour classes. The schedule has to be different, too; how many years could *you* attend a class once a week for one hour or so before *you* became bored stiff? Furthermore, the environment has to change; the traditional classroom atmosphere cannot help but turn students off. The SHARING Program is structured in an attempt to respond to all these factors.

2. In religious education, we must strive for quality, not quantity. This assumption is most often used to salve the psychological wounds incurred when attendance drops to a new low. "Remember, Jesus started with only twelve," we say, or "The Church cannot continue to play the numbers game!" Not denying the validity of such statements, let's admit that they are often used as a kind of false justification for our own failure to attract students. At the same time, this principle of quality versus quantity can be very valid when applied to time—number of classes, length of sessions, and so on.

I feel that a "one-hour class, once-a-week" program is doomed before it begins. High school students can take up half that time getting their jackets off! Any real depth of learning is impossible. Volunteer catechists struggle, usually unsuccessfully, to be fully prepared with something new each week; by Christmas they are climbing the walls. So we end up with *two* major problems: students who are getting nothing out of the program (and telling you so!) and volunteers who start getting sick every Wednesday evening. Zanzig's motto: One well-planned, successful class is far superior to ten ineffective ones.

3. High school students must be approached as young adults seeking real faith, not as turned-off agnostics (or worse) who want to discuss only premarital sex, parent-teen relationships, and social problems. Many feel that young people are not interested in religion or faith. That is simply not the case. Recent studies indicate that 95 percent of adolescents believe in God, and 87 percent pray to that God. On the other hand, 60 percent feel that organized religion does not play a very important role in their lives.* The figures attest to two realities among adolescents: (*a*) a strong interest in their faith relationships with God, but (*b*) a real disaffection with organized religion. The challenge we face is to speak as representatives of the Church, to the faith development needs of the adolescents. And meeting that challenge is precisely the goal of the SHARING Program.

I do not deny the value and importance of treating "relevant" topics—dating, communication, identity. In fact, these topics form a vital dimension of the SHARING Program. But we are called to Christianize these dimensions of our life, and the only way to do that is to deal with God, Christ, the Church,

---

*Religion in America 1979–1980 (Princeton, NJ: Princeton Religious Research Center, 1980).

Christian morality—in other words, with the real guts of our faith. If God is everything we claim God to be (or, better, everything Jesus tells us God is), then God is precisely what teenagers, like all people, need, want, and are searching for. If we do not respond to *that* need as well as the social needs of our students, we might not lose them in a week, but we will have them bored or frustrated after one year.

4. This last assumption raises an issue that must be confronted. *If* we are to deal directly with the faith needs of our students, and *if* those needs may well require discussion of some pretty "heavy" theology (for instance, the fundamental question of the existence of God or the problem of evil), then *who* is going to do the teaching? Along with the problems of attracting students to a religion program and of devising the program itself, one of the major problems we face is attracting catechists to teach the program. There are a lot of reasons for this: the negative teaching experiences of volunteers who unsuccessfully try to "fight the good fight," misconceptions on the part of many adults about the attitudes of high school students, and probably a fear on the part of many adults to tackle what can be difficult theological topics.

I could not begin to count the number of adults who have told me that, because they have not really worked out their own theology yet, they feel incapable of helping students to do so. Some respond in fear with "My God, what will I tell them if they ask me to prove the existence of God, or explain why innocent children die in war or poverty . . . ?" All my pat answers like "We will train you" or "Just be yourself" do not do much good. And to be honest about it, I do not blame many of these adults for just shaking their heads and walking away. Let's admit it: It *is* tough; it *is* scary; it *does* demand a lot to teach high school students anything, let alone religion! So what do we do?

Assuming that the oft-traveled course—doing nothing—is unacceptable, it seems to me that we have to devise programs that maximize the support given our catechists not only *before* class—through teacher preparation—but actually *in* the classroom with the students. This can be done partially by constructing programs that permit team-teaching, in which individual catechists work very closely with other volunteers both in preparing for and in conducting classes. But I think we also have to have a program structure that readily allows the direct participation of a professional catechist and/or one well-versed in theology. In any given parish, this role at times may be turned over to a professional high school coordinator; more often, however, it will be given to the parish priest. No one denies that our students are seeing less and less of their priests as the number of clergy diminishes, but at the same time no one can expect the priest to be available for teaching one or more nights a week. Therefore I think an effective high school program must be designed to only occasionally involve the parish priest and/or professional religious educator. They should be invited into the classroom a reasonable number of times—not as replacements for the volunteer catechists but as consistent supporters of them.

Implementing SHARING IV

On the basis of the above and other assumptions, the SHARING Program gradually evolved. With this background, we are now able to explore SHARING IV in more detail. In this section, I discuss the following:
- the structure of the program
- scheduling options
- recommended environment for the program
- attracting young people to the program

The Program Structure

Previous levels of the SHARING Program consist of sixteen 2-hour sessions and a retreat. Because of the particular developmental as well as scheduling needs of seniors, SHARING IV is unique in a number of respects. Scheduling options for the program are discussed below. Regarding content, SHARING IV includes the following components:

1. Seven 2-hour sessions: All sessions consist of a variety of learning approaches—group dynamic exercises, discussions, films, input presented by the leader, role-playing—organized in such a way that each session handles a given topic from a number of perspectives, assuring a solid learning experience for the greatest number of participants. Though the seven sessions are well integrated and flow logically from one to the next, each session offers an effective learning experience in and of itself. Therefore, a parish may choose to eliminate one or more sessions if necessary without jeopardizing the success of the entire program.

2. A full weekend retreat experience integrating and expanding upon the major themes of the year:

As explained earlier, SHARING IV provides both a thoroughly designed retreat and a planning guide to help those individuals who wish to develop their own retreat. The designed retreat focuses on the theme of Christian lifestyles, a topic not directly covered during the seven 2-hour sessions.

3. A four-week meditation program: This component of SHARING IV is without question one of the more unique components of the entire four-year curriculum. I described earlier the basic purpose and structure of the meditation program. As you will see in a moment, this component of SHARING IV also responds creatively to the scheduling needs of seniors.

How an individual parish chooses to construct its own program out of these components is, of course, up to the directors and the teachers of the program. I also encourage those leaders to work with representatives of the young people themselves to devise a schedule for the program that responds to the students' needs and wishes. Note that the components of SHARING IV, along with the characteristics described below, assure a program that responds to the assumptions described earlier on pages 23–25.

Characteristics of SHARING IV

1. Participants in this program will quickly realize that the content and methodologies of SHARING IV are substantially different than those of previous levels of the program. The themes treated in the program are clearly relevant to seniors. Furthermore, the young people will quickly realize that the tone of the sessions is different as well—more personal, more intimate. This reflects the assumption that our programs must, as a poet stated, "keep the dew on the rose," that is, remain fresh and alive for the participants.

2. The principle of quality versus quantity is certainly applicable. The SHARING IV Program directly responds to the scheduling conflicts commonly experienced by and with seniors. This feature will become clearer in a moment.

3. The format and schedule of SHARING IV permits greater involvement by the parish priest or the program director. Guest speakers can also be recruited to handle some of the more challenging material.

4. Perhaps most importantly of all, the content and methodologies of SHARING IV effectively respond to the religious developmental characteristics and needs of seniors in high school. The young people grapple with topics that are of special interest to them. Additionally, the intent of the material is not to impose our adult convictions on the young people. Rather, we help the students come to terms with the personal relationships with God that are uniquely theirs. As a result, the program is always relevant and significant for them.

Scheduling for SHARING IV

As indicated above, parishes can use the various components of SHARING IV to construct a schedule that suits their unique needs and desires. However, let me explain what I had in mind regarding scheduling as I developed this material.

In SHARING IV, I have attempted to offer a program design that responds to the unique challenges of the senior year. Seniors are not going to be attracted to any program that requires a long-term commitment. They are often overwhelmed with activities vying for their time and attention. These include, as always, school demands and jobs. In addition, seniors must complete their course of study for graduation, make final decisions and plans regarding college, and get ready for the senior prom and countless graduation activities. We must readily acknowledge and accept the fact that a parish religious education program will not normally be high on the list of priorities.

How can we respond to this situation? You may know that one principle I follow for the scheduling of SHARING I through III is that the students should generally not meet in successive weeks. Those programs seem to work most effectively when students meet only every two or three weeks. This helps to sustain student enthusiasm and allows leaders greater time to effectively prepare for the sessions.

However, in SHARING IV, I suggest that parishes do schedule the seven 2-hour sessions (or whatever sessions are selected from the seven) for successive weeks with no intervals. This is based on the nature of the program as well as the experience of other leaders who have conducted senior programs. My basic rationale for this schedule follows:

- The content and strategies of SHARING IV demand a greater level of openness and sense of trust among the students than do other levels of the SHARING Program. A more intense schedule will help to create and sustain these attitudes.

- The individual sessions of SHARING IV are much more interrelated and complementary than in previous levels of the program. The students must see the connections between sessions, and a more intense schedule will help them do that.

- The typical school schedule of seniors will make an intense, short-term program more attractive than an extended program. For example, the young people will be more likely to attend a program that begins in early October and ends in November than one that stretches throughout their entire first semester.

Implied in this last point is my conviction that the total program should be offered in pieces. That is, all students are invited to attend the seven 2-hour sessions. Then a new invitation goes out to all available students to attend the retreat, followed by a special invitation to everyone to participate in the closing meditation program. Students must feel comfortable in joining any part or all of the program.

A schedule can be devised that responds well to the particular challenges of the senior year, enabling the students who wish to be involved in all parts of the program to attend. For example, consider the following schedule:

- From early October to mid-November, the seven 2-hour sessions are offered.
- The weekend retreat is conducted either before Christmas or in mid-January.
- The meditation program is offered from mid-February to mid-March.

Not only does such a schedule offer breaks between the components, but the entire program is completed early enough in the year so that conflicts with prom and graduation are reduced.

Recommended Environment for SHARING IV

I recommend that *the SHARING IV program be offered in a home environment if at all possible*. For other levels of the SHARING Program, I generally encourage parishes to conduct the program in parish facilities if possible, primarily to maintain the identity of the program as a parish activity rather than one identified with only one person or couple. SHARING IV, however, lends itself well to the more intimate environment of the homes of the leaders for a variety of reasons:

- The character of the program itself is more personal and intimate than that of SHARING I through III.
- The average size of the group of seniors meeting for the program will be, unfortunately but realistically, very small.
- The change of environment for the program also signals in a concrete way the fact that SHARING IV is significantly different from past programs, a positive factor in the recruitment of young people for the program.

One of my basic principles in developing and conducting programs for young people is that we have to keep them guessing—keep our programs changing so that there is always a sense of freshness about them. The most recognizable changes we can make in this regard are in the scheduling and the location for the program. The new approach to both scheduling and location for SHARING IV may be a major factor in attracting young people to the program.

Attracting Young People to the Program

If you asked a hundred parish volunteer teachers or program directors to state their major concern about a religious education program for their seniors, you would likely get one of two responses: the comment "What seniors?" or a blank stare. The greatest challenge you face in conducting SHARING IV is attracting young people to it in the first place. When all is said and done, the best program guided by the world's most gifted teachers will be a miserable failure if no one shows up to experience it.

I will not soft-pedal the depth of the attendance problem. With rare exceptions, parish programs for seniors in the past—where they have existed at all—have had a terrible track record. We need not go into a lengthy discussion of the causes; the explanations range from lack of parental support to conflicts with senior work schedules to lack of effective program materials. To promise that SHARING IV will automatically turn around this situation and attract large numbers of young people would be foolhardy. I truly believe this program can make a significant contribution to eventually resolving this frustrating problem, or I would not have worked so hard on it. The problem has been with us for so long, however, that considerable time and effort will be needed to change the negative perception of senior-level religion courses.

This is pretty depressing talk. Are there no signs of hope, no concrete suggestions on how we might at least *begin* to resolve the situation? As always, I have a few observations:

1. The greatest source of hope we now have for resolving the senior attendance dilemma is the increasing practice of offering senior high school Confirmation programs. Over one-half of the dioceses in the country are now confirming candidates during the sophomore through senior years. These programs—primarily because of strong parental support as well as improved program materials—have, for the most part, been remarkably effective in attracting and positively influencing older high school students.

The implications of successful Confirmation programs for recruitment of SHARING IV participants are clear. If your parish is one that confirms at the senior high school level, concentrate your efforts on sustaining the interest of the young people immediately after the completion of their sacramental preparation. Promote SHARING IV as a natural follow-up to Confirmation for those students confirmed as juniors, and work with the leaders in charge of the Confirmation program to actively support SHARING IV during the time of preparation.

2. What if your parish is not in the position of confirming at the senior high school level? First of all, acknowledge the difficulties you face and set reasonable expectations. If you allow yourself to dream of attracting dozens of young people to the program, you will be setting yourself up for inevitable disappointment, the kind of disappointment that can destroy a program before it ever begins. What constitutes a reasonable expectation? If I were an average-sized parish that had no history of programs for seniors, I might hope to find ten seniors who would be willing to investigate a program if properly invited, and I would expect perhaps five to join such a program after investigating it. Disappointing? Of course—but realistic. In fact, some leaders might suggest that my goals are overly optimistic. I would agree with them—if my main method of promoting the program was an open invitation to all seniors published in the parish bulletin. This leads to my next point.

3. Any recruitment of young people to a senior program must be highly personal in nature. Potential participants must be approached face-to-face, one-on-one with an invitation to at least investigate the program before making a decision about it. They must know that you care about *them*, that the program is for *them*, that it is intended to respond to *their* needs.

4. In order to explain the program to potential participants, I encourage you to have a meeting with them before the start of the program. Make it clear that coming to such a meeting is not a commitment to the program. You only want them to find out what you are attempting to do. If they like what they hear and want to join, wonderful; if they choose not to participate, no hard feelings. Gather in a relaxed environment, but be thoroughly prepared to deliver an attractive presentation on the program. Give information they will want to know before making a decision. (Involving them in decisions about the times and the locations for the meetings is also recommended.) You may be pleasantly surprised to discover that many seniors are looking for a program like SHARING IV. Our task is to get the information about the program to them in an attractive manner.

5. Finally, the best recruitment technique you can have is to provide a good experience for those who decide to participate. They then become ambassadors for your program, talking to their friends, to younger brothers and sisters, and so on. Start small. Concentrate on providing the best program you can to those individuals open to it, and then watch it grow.

A Final Word

In attempting to provide a religious education program for seniors, you are taking on an immense challenge that requires a great investment of your time and energy. At least initially, all your work may seem to pay meager dividends. Low attendance, difficulties in recruiting leaders, lack of parental support, and even disinterest by some parish leaders can sap your energy and drain you of hope.

Yet, does our faith really offer us any alternative but to keep trying? We have been given the responsibility of passing on to future generations the most important and liberating message the world has ever heard. Literally millions of young people hunger to hear and be freed by that message. God bless you as you attempt to share the Good News of love and hope with the young people for whom we care so deeply.

In this section I have discussed the assumptions upon which I feel a high school religious education program must be based and have looked at how the components and characteristics of the SHARING Program respect and reflect those assumptions. We turn now to a discussion of our audience, the young people themselves.

Faith Development and Adolescence: At the Crossroads

I have talked at some length about the origins of the SHARING Program, the educational philosophy that undergirds it, and the basic structure of the program proper. All this information is, of course, essential if we hope to have a firm grasp of the SHARING material and be properly prepared to conduct it. But all this background will serve little purpose if we fail to reflect upon the young people with whom we intend to share the program. Just what is adolescence all about, what are the characteristics we can expect to encounter in the young people and, given those, how are we to teach them? These are the concerns of this section.

Adolescence has often been defined as the transitional period between childhood and adulthood. It seems reasonable, then, that we can fully understand adolescents only when we consider their development as children as well as the characteristics of adulthood toward which they are aspiring. Therefore, in this section I will be taking a bird's-eye view of the entire process of human development and its impact on growth in faith. I will then close the discussion with some reflections on the religious education of adolescents, given this process of development.

From Birth to Age 4: Taking Care of the Basics

The first years of our lives are spent taking care of some pretty basic business—like survival! It is a time when the needs we experience are the most obvious and perhaps the most easily fulfilled: the empty stomach that causes us to literally cry out, the wet diaper that needs to be changed, the sense of fear that needs to be calmed by the warm touch of a loving parent or by an older brother or sister. As these needs are constantly met and as the child experiences healthy growth, there is a gradual development of some sense of independence—the initial experience by the child of being a person apart from the others upon whom he or she has depended so totally. This sense of growing separation and independence is most clearly expressed during the so-called "terrible twos," in the discovery of the word *no* by the toddler, and by what psychologists often call the "first stage of negativity." For the parent with a good sense of humor, this stage can be cute; for others, it can be acutely painful!

It is hard to imagine what we would normally term **religious development** happening during these early years. But even at this stage some foundations for later religious and spiritual growth are being constructed. In many Christian homes, for instance, the child will be introduced to religious symbols during this time—pictures of Jesus on the walls, the crucifix above the bed, and prayers recited by parents and others before meals. Young children will often have their first taste of church life as well: the strange goings-on at Mass as the three-year-old struggles free of his or her parents and attempts to scale the pew, or shouts down the priest during his homily. All of these experiences—including the way parents and others react to them—have a far greater impact on us than we might imagine.

It should also be noted that some psychologists claim that the first three years of life are among the most critical in terms of the development of our self-image, our sense of being loved, and therefore of our gradual ability to reach out to others in love as we grow. The child whose needs are tenderly met at this age will often grow with a sense of security and openness to life. The children tragically subjected to abuse and cruelty in these very early years will often grow to be suspicious, closed, bitter adults who, sadly, often become the kind of parents who will abuse their own children. When one recalls the qualities so often described as central to Christian life—love, joy, peace, kindness, and so on—it is clear that even at this very early stage in development, we all experience things that will greatly affect our religious attitudes later in life.

Ages 4 to 10: Gaining Control of Things

Following the formation of some basic survival skills (feeding oneself, being toilet trained, learning to walk), the child begins a process of gaining further control of the world about him or her. This is initially a matter of achieving some mastery or control over the world of things more than people, and the child accomplishes this through the gradual and continuing development of language and body skills.

Every parent remembers the thrill of the first words a child speaks—not just the emotional kick of hearing the "mama" and "dada" of the toddler, but that magical time when the child truly discovers the wonderful world of words and their meaning. All of a sudden there is an explosion of curiosity and delight as the child begins to understand the world by naming it and therefore gaining some control over it. A baby's constant questions, it seems, are two: "Whaaizzdat?" (the child's version of "What is that?") and "Why?" . . . repeated over and over and over again. These are usually followed by "Meedodat," baby talk for "Let me do that now!" All of life takes on new meaning, including the child's relationships with others. He or she can now meet people on a firmer ground, in simple conversation, in the discovery of different personalities, and so on. As language skills progress through early childhood, they are enhanced gradually by the ability to read, and life becomes even more fascinating. Bedtime stories read by parents at night gradually evolve to quiet times alone, losing oneself in books from the library, in comic books, in books at school that begin to reveal the meaning of the world through words and pictures. A mind is being awakened, and it is a glorious and wondrous time.

It is also during this stage that one begins to master the world of things through the development of body skills. This is expressed in all kinds of ways. The five-year-old child creates forty "masterpieces" a day with crayons and paper, and a milestone is reached when a page out of a coloring book can be completed "without going outside the lines." The eight-year-old catches thirty football passes in a row in the backyard and wins that first big race in the park against all the neighborhood kids. The memorable day arrives when we move from the tricycle to the "two-wheeler." Similar moments are repeated over and over again, from generation to generation, from family to family, across the world. Yet each time they seem somehow very special, because for each of us as individuals, they *are* special. It is the first time *I* colored the page perfectly, the first time *I* caught the pass or won the race, the first time *I* rode the bike without training wheels. And because of that, these are all exciting, even unforgettable, moments for each of us.

Religious Development of Children

What about our religious development during this stage? It too can be a time of discovery, a time of gaining control, a time of mastering the world of religious *things*. And again this is accomplished through the same gradually developing language and body skills. We begin to learn what religious words mean. The priest says, "The Lord be with you," and we learn how to answer him. Some important prayers are memorized, and there is a great sense of pride when we can say the "Our Father" while standing next to our parents at Mass. Slowly the stories about Jesus and his message are learned, many of them sounding at first like the delightful fairy tales and fables told at our bedside at night. We learn how to perform religious actions as well. The sign of the cross is one day made correctly during the mealtime prayer and everyone at the table applauds and offers congratulations. We learn to genuflect and when to sit, stand, and kneel during Mass.

It is usually during this stage that two particularly sacred events occur: First Penance—what we now call the Sacrament of Reconciliation—and first Communion. Many high school students, when asked to identify the moment in their lives when they felt closest to God, when they most sensed the sacred in their lives, will recall their experience of "receiving my first Holy Communion." In many homes the event is celebrated with parties and special new clothes, and commemorated with photos for the family album. Years later, when we stumble across those photos, there is often a sense of sadness along with the fond memory, a sense, perhaps, of having lost the innocent kind of faith represented by the pictures—the slightly embarrassed smile, the fancy clothes, and the parent's arm placed with pride around our shoulders.

One of the frequent religious recollections from childhood is the feeling that, when we are young children, religion seems to provide a lot of answers to questions. It offers occasions when we feel very special and even holy. It may even be enjoyable to attend religion classes when we can learn about God. But for many those feelings of enjoyment and interest do not last. For some people, the very answers that religion once provided now only raise more difficult questions. For some, the feelings of being special and the experiences of "holiness" turn into long periods of loneliness and confusion. For many, it seems, courses in religion become the least interesting part of their education. Why does this happen?

Adolescence: No Longer Just "The Teen Years"

It used to be common to define the stage of development we call adolescence as lasting from about age 12 to age 20, that is, the teen years. There has been a lot of study of this stage of development over the years, and many psychologists now recognize that the "developmental tasks" of adolescents—those things we have to confront and deal with on our way to healthy, mature adulthood—are far too complex to resolve in seven or eight short years. Therefore, some now consider adolescence to last from about age 10 to as late as age 30 and beyond, and to consist of many different stages and processes rather than, for example, simply achieving physical maturity and leaving home. This certainly reveals a refreshing and helpful change in our attitudes, at least from the point of view of eliminating the frightening feeling that we are somehow magically to become full-fledged adults on our eighteenth or twenty-first birthdays! On the other hand, it may be a bit disconcerting to think that we have to deal with the difficult chores of adolescence for eighteen years or more! In any case, let's take a look at what psychologists are now saying about adolescent development, and in particular note the implications of this stage for our religious development and our attitudes about faith.

Ages 10 to 12: A Physical and Emotional Upheaval

Adolescence begins with the tremendous surge in physical and emotional development called **puberty**. This is not the place to detail what occurs at this time and why, but it is fair to summarize it by saying that the body over which one had just begun to gain control goes haywire. There is generally a period of rapid growth that will continue for several years with consequences that can drive parents crazy: new shoes are outgrown in months, food bills skyrocket with the child's appetite, hours are spent locked in the bathroom trying to make oneself presentable to the public.

This kind of physical change cannot help but have strong emotional implications: the horror and self-consciousness that increase with each new pimple; the embarrassment of the kid—a great athlete at age 8—who suddenly finds it difficult to walk on a sidewalk without tripping on each crack; the strong attraction to a person of the opposite sex (who could hardly be tolerated just a few years earlier). Some of these things may one day be looked back upon with a grin and a sense of humor. But at the same time many adults continue to live with permanent emotional scars from this period of their own development—memories of being laughed at, the strong recollection of being unloveable, or the continual fear of rejection by one's peers. It does not eliminate all the pain and heartache to tell people that these are feelings shared by each of us, but it can help to make the pain more bearable.

There seem to be two major religious reactions during this stage of early adolescence. **Some people turn to religion in a more serious way, perhaps as a solution to the problems they are encountering.** A few may even seriously consider the religious life at this time. Religion may even be viewed with an increasing sense of superstition—as, for instance, we begin to bargain with God or to perform religious practices in the hope of forcing God to take care of our problems.

Prayer becomes a more serious affair for some. At a younger age prayer was often primarily a matter of saying prayers at the appropriate times and places. During this stage, however, we may experience prayer as a time for almost begging God to help us out, or perhaps for offering some sacrifice as our end of a bargain: "If I pass this test, God, I will become a priest." "God, if this guy just asks me to go to the dance, I will go to church *every day* for a year." "If only my parents don't find out what happened, God, I will give up candy for six years."

There is nothing wrong with this kind of religious attitude—at least not as experienced by a person in sixth or seventh grade. The problem occurs when people never outgrow this stage and continue to bargain this way with God when they are fifty years old.

The second religious reaction sometimes exhibited during early adolescence is a lack of any interest in religion whatsoever. The personal tasks of dealing with new physical and emotional experiences can be so engrossing that for a while everything else—including religion—may take a back seat. For persons experiencing this, going to Mass seems to be the time for doing some of their most creative daydreaming. Religion classes have all the excitement of a dead battery. This is not always a case of being so turned off or negative about religion that one actively complains about it. It is simply a matter of not really thinking about it at all. There are too many "more important" things in life to deal with. Again, this is neither a good nor a bad attitude necessarily. It is just the way it is. But it will most likely not stay that way for long.

Ages 13 to 15: Clearing the Way for People

Remember the comments about the stage from ages 4 to 10 when the challenge of life was primarily one of gaining control over the world of things through language and body skills? During this stage of development—from ages 13 to 15—that task seems to be almost reversed. All of a sudden the world of things becomes boring. Hobbies that used to hold our attention for hours now no longer even mildly appeal to us. The common cry is "there is nothing to do around here!"—a claim that parents often have a hard time understanding and accepting. ("What do you mean, nothing to do? Take out the garbage!") What the young person is actually saying, however, is that none of the things that might be done seem attractive or exciting anymore.

Speaking of parents, the relationship with them often changes radically during this time. During our early childhood our parents were probably the most important people in the world to us. It did not make much difference what others thought of us as long as our parents still cared. Now that changes. It now seems that our friends become more important to us than our parents—at least in the sense that we will often risk our parents' anger rather than our friends' rejection of us. Now it seems that no matter what our parents say to us and about us, if people our own age do not accept us, we hurt—badly. We find ourselves lashing out at our parents, saying things to them that we would never have dreamed of saying earlier, and then suffering great feelings of guilt because we truly love our parents—even if we cannot tell them that.

All of the experiences that began with puberty—the physical changes, the developing emotions, the self-consciousness—deepen during this stage of development. We begin to grow away from the "gang mentality" that seems so common with grade school children, when we had twenty-five "best friends" and there was always something happening. During the junior high school years we start developing more exclusive friendships—deeper, stronger friendships with fewer people. Though we may often lack compassion at this age (eighth graders, for example, can be extremely cruel to each other), it seems now that when we hurt someone's feelings we almost seem to hurt ourselves as well—we feel a bit guilty, but still find it hard, if not impossible, to apologize.

Time to Move On

As I have mentioned, some psychologists call this stage of adolescent development a time of "negative discovery of self." At some time in our lives each of us has to begin to move away from the simple world of children and from the parents upon whom we have depended totally in order to prepare to live our lives as unique, individual, free, mature persons. That is essentially what is happening here. During roughly the junior high school years, about seventh through ninth grades, we begin to reject the world of children and all that we associate with it—kids' games, dependency upon adults, school, and so on. This is expressed well by another common cry of young people at this age: "I'm not a kid anymore!" The problem is that, at this stage, we are not yet adults either. We are caught between two worlds—childhood and adulthood—and at times it can seem that we are being pulled apart. It can be rough, no question about it. It can also be exciting, exhilarating, and just plain fun. In any case, it is clearly one of the most important of all stages of development, and the way we handle the challenges of this stage often has great impact on what kind of adults we will eventually become.

What about our religious attitudes at this time? **It seems that, for many, during this stage of development religion can appear to be another of those "kids' games" that we react against and perhaps temporarily reject.** Earlier in our development we may have simply been bored by religion and religious practices. For some young people, that boredom may now turn to anger. The religious training and practices that we once accepted and even enjoyed as children now become experiences from our past that no longer appeal to us. In earlier adolescence we may not have thought about religion all that much. Now we may begin to actively question it: Why am I supposed to believe all that "stuff"? What gives other people the right to tell me what is right or wrong? Why do I have to go to church? Why should I listen to what people were saying thousands of years ago? Why should I believe that Jesus was anything more than just a good man? What does all this have to do with my life right now?

It should be clearly stated that this process of gradually rejecting the world of children is as necessary in terms of religion as it is in every other area in our lives. It is just as unhealthy to blindly and unthinkingly accept all religious traditions and teachings as it would be to refuse to grow up, to never leave the homes of our parents, or to refuse to take charge of our lives as mature persons. The hope is that after breaking free from childish dependency upon parents we can eventually grow to meet them on common ground as equals, as friends. This often occurs in young adulthood when we begin to have our own careers and families and thereby gain a whole new appreciation for and love of our parents. The same kind of growth is required if we are to gain religious maturity. In rejecting our childish understandings of religion, we should open ourselves to a more mature and free and conscious personal faith relationship with God. That process can and should begin at the next stage.

Ages 16 to 20: A Time for Weaving Dreams

One of the most encouraging things to say about the process of negative discovery of self, which I just discussed, is that it ends. Although the process is painful and intense for some, it is usually completed in a year or even less. For others the process is actually a relatively simple matter—it just happens with little difficulty or suffering. In either case, there comes a time when any anger or negativity subsides and we get on with the business of building fulfilling lives for ourselves. That next step often involves one of the most exciting and enjoyable phases of personal development—a stage of growth that many will look back upon years later as forming some of the fondest memories in their lives. It is a time of experiencing great potential in our lives, for building visions of exciting futures, a time when we perhaps fall in love for the first time, and a time, it is hoped, when faith and religion can take on a whole new character and appeal.

During our senior high school years—particularly the eleventh and twelfth grades—young people often experience a time of renewed hope and optimism about life in general and about their own lives in particular. This has been characterized by some as a period of "discovering the spirit world." It can be a time for discovering all those realities that touch the interior spirit of each of us. It can be, for instance, a time for experiencing a real sense of brotherhood and sisterhood with all peoples of the world. Ideals like truth, beauty, justice, and peace become more important to us. Many young people will fall in love during this time, but in a way that is much more mature and real than the intense but passing "crushes" of a few years earlier. They will discover the wonder of another human being, the delight of feeling at one with another's heart and mind, the exhilarating feeling of being loved for what one truly is as a person.

These years are a time when all forms of art can be more appreciated and when many young people turn with a new interest to music, to poetry, to film. People begin to come to terms with their future, often by sorting out career opportunities and by trying to imagine the nearly unlimited ways in which to direct their talents. This is sometimes a period when people become more reflective, more able to be alone for extended periods of time, occasionally even yearning for some distance from the people they so recently wanted and needed to be with all the time. While for some young people the difficult tasks and pains of earlier adolescence continue during this stage, for most others this stage of adolescence is one during which they can experience in a new way the wonder and awe of simply being human.

Discovering "The Spirit World"

The implications of this stage for our religious development are perhaps more clear and direct than for any of the earlier stages I have discussed. For many people the "discovery of the spirit world" *does* include a powerful and even profound new appreciation of their personal relationship with God. In some cases this will come about through deep personal experiences—the death of a loved one, the experience of falling in love to the extent that the whole world seems to take on new meaning, and so on. For others the new religious awakening might be the result of a good retreat experience like those offered to young people in many parts of the country: SEARCH retreats, for example, or TEC retreats. For still others this discovery may be the result of simply growing up a bit, taking a new and more mature look at life and its possibilities and challenges.

Regardless of the causes of this new openness to religion and religious experiences, the results are commonly the same—that is, a richer sense of the presence of God in our lives, a greater ability and need to pray, a much deeper sense of compassion for others, or a desire to reach out to others in loving service. In other words, as young adult Christians our faith becomes more truly a part of who we are as persons rather than merely another series of beliefs and practices accepted without question or scrutiny.

It should be understood, however, that this renewed sense of interest in the spirit world seldom if ever entails a return to the childlike acceptance of religious traditions and practices that we discussed earlier. In fact, just the opposite often happens. For some, the discovery of a more personal relationship with God can lead to even greater frustration, anger, or boredom with formal institutional religion. A common example of this would be the case of the young person who feels a deep desire to pray but who also feels that prayer can be more enriching and fulfilling when experienced during a walk in the woods than while sitting in church on a Sunday morning. And parents are often confused and even offended by young people who return from a retreat experience with great religious fervor but who, at the same time, continue to argue with them about their religious practices and beliefs. This is a complex issue, but the main point here is clear: During this stage of development, it is not uncommon for a young person to experience a renewed sense of interest in personal faith while at the same time continuing to have real problems accepting the formal religion he or she was raised with.

Ages 20 to 30: Beginning to Put It All Together

Between ages 20 and 30, most young adults begin to grapple with the process of integrating the idealism and optimism of their late teens with the so-called real world of career choices, decisions about marriage, having children, and so on. These are exceedingly important decisions, and the role that religion will play in all this will vary dramatically from person to person. It is fairly common, however, for religion to remain somewhat in the background, as the pressing major decisions about one's career and lifestyle are confronted and resolved.

A change in this orientation often begins to occur, however, with the birth of the first child. This can have a profound spiritual and religious impact upon a young married couple for two reasons. First, the experience of creating new life and giving birth to it is one of the most spiritually awesome and uplifting of human experiences. Many parents will recall the sense of being in touch in a very real way with the power of God at the moment of delivery of a child. Second, the sense of responsibility and love generated by the birth of a child often motivates parents to reassess their religious practices. They must decide, for example, whether or not to have the child baptized. That decision will often lead to a more active participation in parish life, the decision to attend Mass more frequently than in the past, and so on. These religious practices may not always be fully enjoyed or cherished, but they are recognized as perhaps a necessary part of living in community with others.

Young adulthood—from ages 20 to 30—could perhaps be considered one of the most "romantic" stages of development. This applies of course to the experience of falling in love, making the decision to marry, and then experiencing as a couple the exciting, though occasionally difficult, early years of building a life together. But the sense of romance goes beyond just marriage. There are dreams of selecting and building successful careers—of becoming the company president or the designer and creator of beautiful clothes or great buildings. There is the hope and expectation of raising "the perfect family," one in which the parents remain close friends and the children grow to be lovable and loving. For many people, however, those romantic dreams of young adulthood seem to fade quite quickly.

Ages 30 to 40: Settling Down

As life progresses, there is often a tendency to "settle down" on many levels. For instance, throughout the twenties a person will experiment with several possible occupations or places of employment, but then he or she may recognize the need to "settle down" in a secure job. Maybe there will be several times when the family moves from one home to another or from town to town; eventually there comes a time when a more permanent home is chosen "so that the children can get a good education and build some lasting friendships." There can also be an emotional "settling down" as couples discover that the intense romance of their early marriage seems to be giving way to a more comfortable kind of life together.

Religion, too, can take on an air of "settled" routine, perhaps even becoming simply the fulfillment of an obligation. People find themselves attending Mass just because it is the accepted "thing to do," much like punching the clock at work each day or doing the laundry and cooking the meals. When asked by children why they go to Mass, parents will often respond that "it is not too much to give one hour a week to God"—as if the remaining hours of the week belonged to someone else! Many young people, when asked why they think their parents go to church, will respond that the parents do so "to give us a good example," not necessarily because they are attracted to the experience of the Mass itself.

Interestingly, for quite a number of adults the mid-to-late thirties can also be a time of spiritual renewal or a rediscovery of a sense of vitality in their faith. This renewal may happen in response to a particular event or movement, like a retreat, Marriage Encounter, Cursillo, charismatic renewal, and so on. Or it may simply be a response to the sense of routine that has entered the other dimensions of their lives. For those who experience this renewal, the next stage may be considerably easier to handle.

Ages 40 to 45: "The Crisis of the Limits"

There has been a great deal of talk, writing, and study about this stage in the process of adult development. Basically what seems to happen to many people is this: There comes a point in the lives of adults when it seems that time is running out on their dreams, when it appears that all the things they had hoped for in life are slipping away, when they are confronted with fear of total failure in their lives. Perhaps marriage has become a shaky or boring situation, or they feel that they will never achieve the kind of professional success they had been so certain of years before, or their kids seem to be rejecting them despite all their efforts to be good parents.

For some adults this sense of time running out can lead to almost a panic reaction, the feeling that "if I'm ever going to 'make it' I've got to do something—now!" It is a time when many marriages are severely strained and even broken, when seemingly successful business people quit their jobs to "try something new," when there may be fruitless attempts to somehow recapture the promise of youth. Admittedly this rather depressing picture is not accurate for all people in their forties, but it is the case often enough to be the subject of a great deal of discussion and investigation.

This stage of development has a significant impact in terms of parent-teen relationships. Think for a moment what happens if young married couples have their children when they are in their early twenties. What age will they be when their children reach age 16 or 17? The answer: about forty years old. What are the characteristics we described about the person of sixteen or seventeen? Answer: idealism, optimism, the discovery of life's apparently unlimited potential. Now put the two stages together in the same home. What you end up with is the "generation gap." Adolescents come home bursting with excitement and hope and great dreams to parents who often feel themselves to be running into the wall of human limitations. And the parents' frequent response to the idealism of their children might sound something like this: "Just wait until you grow up. Life is not like you think it is. It's a rough world out there, and you might as well just accept that fact." And the young person walks away depressed or angry or both.

It is very important that young people experiencing this kind of tension in their families try to understand the causes of it, try to be patient with their parents, and try to help their parents get through what for many is a very difficult stage. Young people can do that, oddly enough, by finding ways to say to their parents the very things their parents had to repeatedly say to them as children when they, too, were lonely, frightened, and confused—that they are good, that they are loved and appreciated, that they are needed and cared for. When children express sincere love for their parents, when they speak of their gratitude for what their parents have given them, they give their parents a sense of hope, a sense of fulfillment, and the belief that perhaps they have not failed in life. In other words, there comes a time in our lives when parents turn to their children for help, and when children must take care of their parents' needs—just as parents have taken care of theirs.

One of the most central and challenging spiritual tasks each of us encounters in life is faced in a particularly difficult way by adults experiencing the "crisis of the limits." They are faced with the challenge of accepting themselves as they are—with all their limitations, their weaknesses, their apparent failures. This is what God calls us to and what Jesus reveals to us: the truth that we are loved infinitely and therefore are infinitely loveable—despite all our feelings to the contrary. If we can accept that fact, we can be freed to live life fully and with joy. If we cannot accept that, we are going to remain locked up in our own insecurities and fears. At perhaps no other time—other than at the point of death itself—is self-acceptance more difficult than at this stage of adult development; consequently, this stage of adult development is a critical stage of faith development as well.

Age 45 to Death: Fulfilling Our Potential

If one is able to accept oneself fully despite the challenges and difficulties confronted during the "crisis of the limits," there can be a deep and profound sense of renewal in life, a commitment to develop one's full potential with joy, love, openness to change, and freedom. Perhaps, as an old cliché says it, life *does* "begin at forty," at least in the sense that we can be personally freed from many of our fears and insecurities and simply but happily be who we want and are called to be as persons. We can find new abilities to love in richer ways, because we are now freed from the fear of rejection by others and more able therefore to take risks, to reach out to people. Because of that, we can experience God present in our lives in a much more personal sense. Gradually we recognize the unity of personal faith and institutional religion. We no longer feel the conflicts between our commitment to personal integrity and participation in the life of the faith community— the Church that is perhaps not all that we would hope it to be. Because we are more accepting of ourselves and our limitations, we can now be more accepting of the limitations of others. And as followers of Jesus, we can face the ultimate challenge of life, the ultimate "crisis of the limits"—death— with the hope and conviction that it is really not an end at all, but rather the beginning of a whole new kind of life with God, resurrected life, fullness of life.

Implications for the Religious Education of Adolescents

Having taken our bird's-eye view of the process of human development, what can we say about the challenge of teaching adolescents in light of this development? The following section will deal with the specifics of preparing a session, leading discussions and group activities, and so on. At this point I would like simply to share some random reflections on the religious education of adolescents, keeping in mind all of the characteristics of their development noted above.

1. Effective religious education for adolescents must be fun. I do not mean the belly-laughing, rolling-on-the-floor kind of fun, but simply that a student can leave the class and say he or she really enjoyed being there.

2. The involvement of students must be physical as well as intellectual and emotional. The program must involve the *total* student, recognizing the need for physical outlets for the students' abundant energy, for *safe* and nonthreatening opportunities for emotional experiences, for intellectual stimulation that is responsive to their increasingly inquisitive nature, and for unique approaches to prayer that are responsive to their new sense of the sacred in their lives.

3. The adolescent student cannot be talked *at* but only talked *with*. Though they often have great difficulty expressing their ideas verbally and may at times even refuse to answer straight questions, young people will react strongly against being *preached at*. Therefore SHARING does not contain many formal talks, but rather relies on more informal discussions concerning activities and exercises. Undoubtedly this will be a relief to the teacher reading this book, but do not get the impression that effective discussions require little or no preparation. You will need to prepare almost as fully for a discussion as for a formal talk. More on that later.

4. Adolescents, like all people, cannot relate well to someone who is artificial or phony. In fact, if they sense phoniness in teachers, their rejection will be immediate and total. You do not have to act,

talk, or dress like young people to be accepted by them. Teachers who try these methods will only appear foolish. Just be yourself. If you are scared, tell them so. If you are angry, let them know it and tell them why. If you feel moved, let that be known. They will love and admire you for your openness and honesty and will let themselves be known in return.

5. Never let the students forget who is running the class and what is expected of them as students. They will test you at the outset of the program and throughout the year, so you might as well tell them where you stand right off the bat. And then stick to what you say.

6. The facilities used for the program must be orderly, clean, and obviously ready for the program when the students walk in. First impressions apply as much to places as they do to persons. In both cases they are very important.

7. You must be thoroughly prepared for each moment of the class. You are not fully prepared unless you can enter the room and conduct the class *without* referring to the session plan (though you may want to use brief notes when making presentations). If you more than occasionally read to the students from a text, you are sharing not your own but someone else's ideas, and the students will let you know they do not buy it.

8. Balance discipline with praise. Be positive, not negative. When giving directions to paired students, it is much more effective to say "Try to listen fully to what your partner is saying" than to say "Don't tune out when your partner is speaking to you." Positive discipline will build and reinforce a positive teacher-student relationship: "I am here not as a disciplinarian but because I have something great I want to share with you, and you have something great to offer me. If we cooperate it can be fun being together; if not, you hurt yourself and your friends as much as me."

9. Chronic problems in discipline in which an individual simply does not cooperate should be handled privately. We must avoid an approach to discipline that is based on humiliating an individual in front of his or her peers. Not only will such an approach often backfire, it is simply unchristian!

10. Train yourself through practice to react to groups *as groups* rather than as individuals. This statement will definitely offend some people because it appears to negate past comments about the dignity of the individual or respect for uniqueness. But what I am saying is this: When people gather in a group, they form a community that develops a "personality" all its own, distinct from that of individual members. That is why we can say an athletic team was "flat" on a given night, or a group of students was really "flaky," and so on. It is this *spirit* of the group that you should assess, react to, and control. You are more interested in enabling the overall growth and enrichment of everyone in the program than focusing on selective insights—or shortcomings —of any one person. If you key in on individuals too directly, you will lose your perspective. Theologians call this awareness of group energy "discernment of spirit"—being sensitive to what is happening on a broad level.

Reading and guiding the mood of a group has direct effects on each phase of a given session. If you want to have an effective "fun" exercise, for example, you will try to create a kind of easygoing mood. If you are planning a prayer service, you won't play rock music immediately before it. Throughout the entire program I will be giving hints on how to deal with groups effectively.

I want now to offer some insights into the very practical matters of preparing for a class, leading group discussions, and conducting effective group activities. Those are the concerns of the next section.

Effective Teaching: Making Molehills out of Mountains

Teaching is an art, and like all arts it moves toward perfection only through constant practice, through mistakes, by risking innovations—that is, through plain hard work! This is particularly true when the subject to be taught or shared is faith because, by its very nature, the sharing of faith depends greatly on our ability to share ourselves, our beliefs, values, and attitudes. That kind of ability cannot be programmed. But there are many things that can be done to enable you to share most effectively the faith that is uniquely yours. Session plans can be frightening, and the thought of being responsible for a group of high school students for two hours can be downright terrifying. But this will be much less the case if you have a clear understanding of the nature of the session plans and have a firm grasp of some simple ideas to help make them work.

Because of the convictions stated earlier about adolescents and of how we must approach them, the session plans in this program require an attitude more of sharing than of straight teaching. As mentioned before, you will seldom be asked to "give a talk." You will not have to stand at the front of the room looking like an oracle of truth. On the contrary, you can relax, sit among the students, introduce some activity, exercise, film, or discussion and then simply react appropriately. Sounds easy, right? Well, it *is* easier than you might think—*if* you plan what you are going to do. Discussions can be perhaps the greatest educational tool you will use—or they can be disasters. And films really work with high school students—but first you have to know how to run the projector. That is the reason for the title of this section.

Effective sessions consist of a series of relatively short and apparently simple phases. You introduce a movie and turn on the projector. While the film is running you rethink questions for discussion. You wrap up the discussion, call for a short break, and prepare for the next part. Easy! Sure it is, *if* you think through each step and avoid the molehills that can easily become mountains that sabotage the effectiveness of the session. For instance, what time during the day is your program going to be presented? Will it still be light out? If so, do the windows in the room have drapes—so you can darken the room enough to see the film you are going to show? Do you know where the wall receptacles are? Will you need an adapter for conversion from two-prong to three-prong electrical outlets? Are you going to need an extension cord? And so on.

Here is a classic example of poor planning that I once experienced. See if you can catch the mistake. I was running an overnight for freshmen and working on an evening prayer service on love. We had access to a beautiful chapel in which I had conducted services many times, so there were no problems with familiarity with light switches and whatnot. The plan was to have just the Easter candle burning at the front of the chapel as the students entered (about midnight). They would gather on the floor in silence around the burning candle. After a brief comment on the significance of the Easter candle, we would light a small sand candle from it—one that could be easily handled by the students. Each student would silently hold the candle for a minute or so, reflecting on the meaning of Christ in his or her life, then pass the sand candle to the next student. After everyone had done this (about forty students), the sand candle would be returned to the leader, a closing reading and song would be offered, and we would be done.

Everything was set up, music recorded, candles in place, and we even remembered matches. But the service bombed terribly. Why? Because we did not think it through step-by-step, and we made an absolutely ridiculous blunder that almost blew the whole works. If there are forty students and each one holds the candle for only one minute, that in itself is going to take up forty minutes! The whole service could have taken longer than a Sunday liturgy for five hundred people! And it would have if the leader had not had enough sense to change the whole service in midstream. We saved it and the session ended well, but the mistake was critical.

The point is this: Every session plan offered here is given in great detail, and the reason is simply that the *details make the program work!* The greatest plan in the world will end up a farce if the so-called "Mickey-Mouse stuff" is not planned properly. So in reading the sessions that follow, look for the details and understand them. I will constantly be reminding you of this, especially in cases where I have experienced difficulties myself. The format of the sessions is designed to help you avoid the kinds of mistakes that can ruin a session. I have made almost all the mistakes myself already; if you read carefully you will not have to repeat the same ones. (You can then spend your time more profitably in dealing with the mistakes I did not get around to making!)

Briefly, here is the basic format of each session:

1. Each session is introduced with "Teacher Goals," a brief statement of purpose that should help you focus on the topic immediately. This is followed by "Student Intellectual/Behavioral Objectives"—a formal statement of what you hope the students will gain from the session. Both of these statements not only focus your attention but also offer a means for measuring your effectiveness after class. Did you achieve what you set out to achieve or not, and why? What can you do to improve next time?

2. Next you will find the "Main Ideas." These include, logically enough, the key concepts, goals, and objectives that I hope to get across to the students during the session. The "Main Ideas" often include examples that will prove helpful to you in preparing each session.

3. Following the "Main Ideas" is the detailed session plan itself, that is, the "Procedure" for the session. And remember what I said about details— *they are extremely important!* The sessions are explained with a step-by-step approach. In cases where you will have to make rather involved introductions or closing comments, extensive notes are provided. But it should be clearly noted that these reflect *my* way of handling the material; you will have to paraphrase, rewrite, and plan these to suit yourself.

4. At the end of many of the session plans you will find a list of "Things to Keep in Mind." These are simply hints about various parts of the session that you might find helpful, possible problems you might not foresee, comments on mistakes I may have made, and so on. These may serve as more "molehill makers"!

5. Concluding each session outline, then, are some guidelines "For Evaluation." These are most often questions for reflection regarding each successive phase of the session. In most cases a relatively thorough evaluation of a session can be completed in ten minutes or so. I strongly encourage you to take the time after each session, on your own or with your fellow teachers, to evaluate the session from beginning to end. *Have a notebook available* for recording the results of your evaluation, particularly changes you would recommend making in future attempts to teach the session. This kind of regular evaluation can be invaluable in refining the program to meet the specific needs of your students and teachers.

6. The original SHARING Program often suggested specific music to be used with individual session plans. This proved problematic, as the recommended songs quickly became dated. To deal with this problem we have developed music guides for the revised SHARING. These music guides can be found at the end of the SHARING director's manual. One guide is on the use of rock music, and the other is on the use of religious music with SHARING. Whenever a session in SHARING recommends the use of music, you will be referred to these music guides.

This format for the two-hour sessions in SHARING IV necessarily changes somewhat in the case of the weekend retreat and the four-week meditation program. Nevertheless, the same commitment to thorough guidance reflected in the session plans is maintained in the other components of the program.

I would now like to share a definition of the "successful class" offered in the form of a numbered list that you can use to make sure that you are adequately prepared for each meeting with the young people. Here are my "Ten Commandments for a Successful Session":

1. All participants will be telephoned with a reminder about the session two days ahead of time. Do not rely on bulletin or pulpit announcements. If the students are called earlier than this, they may subsequently forget about the meeting; if they are called later than this, they will not have sufficient time to make plans to come. Note that this is particularly important if you choose *not* to have your sessions in consecutive weeks.

2. The room in which you will conduct the sessions will be thoroughly prepared in advance (the afternoon before an evening session). All group dynamic exercises or photocopied papers will be available where you need them, and pencils will be sharpened. If you do this ahead of time, you can spend the last moments before the session thinking of more important matters—like prayer!

3. *Eventually* every young person who enters the room is called by name by one of the leaders present. This one point can change your entire experience with the program. Nothing will more clearly demonstrate your concern for the young people than this ability to say, "Hi, Dick. Good to see you here!" Playing popular music as the young people arrive is also recommended. This helps break the tension of initial silence and increase the sense of informality.

4. If you are team-teaching with one or more adults, one person assumes primary leadership in calling the group together, starting with prayer, introducing the theme for the session, and so on.

5. All other leaders know exactly what they are to do throughout the session.

6. If there is more than one leader, the transition from one part of the session to the next is planned ahead of time and handled smoothly.

7. The leader is prepared to effectively bring the session to a close with appropriate comments, prayer, and so on.

8. All the young people are thanked—again by name—for attending the session.

9. If necessary, the room is cleaned with the help of the young people.

10. The group leader evaluates how the session went, notes suggested improvements in the session plan, reflects on ways in which he or she might improve the leadership of the session, and so on.

One obvious factor may not need to be mentioned as a formal rule, yet it is the one thing most of us are quite likely to forget because we are too busy with "more important things." I am referring to prayer. If leaders would pause for just a short period of prayer before the young people arrive, the effects on every phase of the session can be tremendous.

Suggestions on Preparing and Delivering Presentations

It has been noted that the session material in SHARING is intentionally designed so that you will seldom be asked to give a formal "talk" to the students. You will not be asked, for example, to stand before your students as an authority figure or to lecture them on some weighty theological topic. (I would not want to do that, so I can't expect you to!) But there are times when you *will* be asked to share some specific information regarding a topic that has been raised for discussion and reflection through a group activity, a film, or whatever. This can be a difficult task, and I do not want to minimize that fact.

I personally suffered through much of my youth and early adulthood with an absolute terror of public speaking, and after years of much practice and hundreds of talks to groups ranging from ten to more than a thousand in number, I still get the dry throat, butterflies, sweaty palms, weak knees—all the usual symptoms. Experts in public speaking will say that such nervous tension is a blessing in disguise, that it gives a sense of vitality and urgency and importance to a presentation that is very attractive to an audience. Nevertheless, you have every right to feel a little nervous before these brief presentations. Such tension is primarily a sign that you care a great deal, not that you are incapable of handling the situation. (It is a sign, in other words, that you are normal!)

I have discovered several helpful hints for preparing and effectively delivering the kind of brief presentation occasionally called for in the SHARING sessions:

1. One key point to remember and gain confidence from is that the essential content of the presentations is always provided in adequate detail in the SHARING session plans. You will therefore not have to do further research or come up with original ideas from scratch. Your task will be to personalize the material—through the use of anecdotes, for example—and to deliver the ideas in a comfortable and casual way.

2. I stress here—and, throughout the SHARING Program, will remind you of—the notion of casual and comfortable presentations. Do not imagine yourself in a position of authoritative teacher, but rather

that of a caring person trying to share some ideas that have personal meaning for you. Your body language should reflect this attitudinal posture. For instance, rather than standing before your students, gather them comfortably about you on the floor for the sharing of the material. Make certain, however, that you are able to make eye contact with each student. If you allow students to sit behind you they will almost inevitably be a distraction to other students . . . and to you.

3. In preparing for the presentation, carefully read and reflect upon the key ideas provided in the session outline. Then ask yourself: How would I share this information with a friend in casual conversation? (Granted, it may seldom be the kind of information you would actually be inclined to share casually with a friend, but use your imagination!)

4. Practice sharing the information in a relaxed way, and do so *out loud* to yourself. If you feel comfortable sharing it with another person or two, so much the better. But the chief purposes of this practice are to hear yourself actually speak the words, to gain a good sense of the pace and timing of your comments, and to find out how much more practice you might need!

5. In the vast majority of those cases when such presentations are suggested in SHARING, the concepts to be shared will be so predictable and so few in number that you should not even need notes to help you out. In fact, it is often the case that sheer common sense would lead you from, say, an activity or film to comments similar to those that I suggest in the session outlines. There may be times, however, when you will want the security of notes, and you should feel free to use them. I encourage you to develop *very brief* notes, the kind that can fit easily on 3-by-5-inch cards. To trigger your recollection of the points you want to make, write down a word or short phrase rather than whole sentences, and then share those points in a conversational rather than rote manner.

6. In those cases when notes are required or desired, I use a very helpful approach that eliminates the sense of delivering a prepared statement from "cheat-sheets." I will often outline the comments I want to make on the chalkboard or newsprint and present them to the students as "the key points I want to share with you at this time." Then I just go through the outline with the students commenting appropriately. This provides me with the guidance I need, offers a visual aid to the students, and even allows me to later return to a particular point easily and clearly.

7. Finally, after delivering the presentation the first time, make notes to yourself regarding how it went, things you would like to change next time, students' responses that might be helpful, and so on. This can prove invaluable in improving the presentations each time you give them.

The time will come (you will have to trust me on this!) when you will actually look forward to these opportunities in teaching. And, as an extra bonus, I find that I have a much better grasp of the material about which I have had to make such presentations. The work that goes into the process of preparing and delivering discussion material can be in itself a valuable learning opportunity.

There are three other dimensions of the SHARING Program that require some explanation before getting into the actual session plans themselves. In all of the sessions I rely heavily on group dynamic exercises and on the discussions following them. These exercises might simply be discussion starters that are photocopied and distributed to the students. Or they might involve props to be used by the teacher in introducing a theme. On occasion the exercise will involve the students physically—for example, having blindfolded students trying to guess certain items in the room, or having "blind" students allow themselves to be led through a maze of thumbtacks! In all these cases not only is it essential to have a feel for the effective use of these exercises and how to direct them, but also you should know some basic techniques for leading discussions. Without effective discussion, the dynamics can degenerate into party games with no purpose or benefit. With good discussion they can become extremely fun activities that lead to a real deepening of awareness about a particular topic. Therefore I offer the following techniques on leading effective group exercises and discussions.

A third component of many SHARING sessions is a film or, less frequently, a filmstrip. The SHARING session outlines provide detailed directions on the use of specific media. I will offer below some general suggestions on their proper use.

Hints on the Effective Use of Group Exercises

1. Make sure you understand thoroughly the purpose for which you are using an exercise. Any

one exercise, of course, can be utilized to bring out a variety of points; be sure you know precisely where you want to go with the experience.

2. Toward that end, try the exercise yourself before conducting it for others. At times this may be difficult, especially in the case of those exercises that demand a group of some size. However, with some imagination and effort one can still experience them. In cases where a duplicated handout will be used, go through each part thoroughly, reacting not only as an individual but as you feel the students themselves may react.

3. Have all materials required for the exercise available and ready for use. Do not let an insufficient number of pencils or some other minor problem ruin the entire exercise.

4. Try to set the appropriate mood for the group *before* introducing the exercise. For example, if your first exercise is going to be loose and intentionally humorous, set the proper tone with a joke or more casual welcoming. If silence during the exercise is critical, begin setting a quiet tone even before conducting it.

5. Explain the directions thoroughly and then *re-explain* them! Adolescents can be staring right at you, seemingly attentive, and be miles away in their own thoughts. When you get the feeling they are somewhere else, say something like "Does everyone know just what I mean? Dave, do you know? How about you, Beth?" More exercises are wasted because of this lack of full communication and comprehension than for any other reason.

6. *However*, do not get trapped by *over*-explaining! Too much information can so influence a group's response that nothing will be gained. For example, you may be conducting an exercise on prejudice. If you tell the group that is what you are doing, they may struggle like mad to prove that they are not prejudiced, and the value of the entire exercise will be lost. Throughout the program I will be reminding you of this.

7. Always stress the need for cooperation and emphasize that nothing will be gained, nor will they have any fun, if students fail to "go along with" the exercise. Ask students to suspend their skepticism and apprehensions and to "give the exercise a chance." Normally students will become progressively more cooperative during the course of the program as they realize how enjoyable it can be. At the beginning of the program, however, you might have to be particularly strong on this.

8. When the purpose of the exercise is to create certain feelings in the group, *time* the exercise in such a way that these feelings are heightened. For example, you might ask each member of the group to get physically "uptight" by curling his or her body into a ball on the floor. The purpose would be to create the feelings of isolation, fear, and anxiety that we experience and cause in other people when we sin. If you allow them to stop the exercise after two minutes, they will experience few if any of the feelings you desire. If you make them hold it for ten minutes, however, the feelings will be very intense. Again the key is to do the exercise yourself when possible to get a "feel" for the correct procedures.

9. Go *immediately* into discussion at the close of the exercise. If you wait too long or allow other conversations to start, you might lose the attention, interest, and cooperation of the group.

10. Finally, *be patient with yourself!* I mentioned earlier the need to practice "getting the feel" for groups of students, "discerning the spirit" of a group, reading their moods. This same kind of practice holds true for the conducting of these exercises. You will learn a great deal from your first experience with an exercise; by the time you have conducted an exercise several times, you will have mastered it, adjusting details to fit your personality, the particular group, the environment in the room, and so forth. Each time you will be more relaxed, you will enjoy the exercises more and more, and your students will continually gain more from the experiences.

Hints on Leading Discussions

1. Do not expect discussion to do what it cannot do or was not intended to do. Discussion must be seen as one part of a much larger learning experience or process.

2. Discussion is primarily a *reaction to* some other stimulus. There must be something real and tangible to discuss.

3. This program is designed in such a way that discussions are always introduced by another stimulus—a group exercise, film, or talk. Remember: The discussion will only be as effective as the activity that motivates it.

4. Discussion only works if the group is interested in—and excited and knowledgeable about—what is to be discussed. For example, one cannot expect a productive discussion by freshmen on the "future of the Church." They're just not interested. Their level of knowledge might only allow a discussion on "Sunday Mass attendance by freshmen."

5. The goal of the discussion must be stated in specific terms in order to give direction to the discussion. For example, rather than saying "What do you think of the film we just viewed?" the leader should say, "Name the three most important points made by the film."

6. Discussions should have a definite time limit —and be stingy! Let the students ask for more time if necessary. The sessions in this program are planned this way, so you should not run out of material for a class.

7. Let each student have a chance to talk, but do not put undue pressure on students who are shy or introspective. You will only drive them away if you do.

8. Do not mistake silence for disinterest. At times students simply will not speak because they are thinking through the question at hand. Though silence can be frustrating and can cause tension, it is often just that very tension that will spark a response later.

9. If the group seems particularly mature or demonstrates a noticeable attitude of cooperation, it is often helpful to let them form their own discussion groups. In this way some initial tensions are dispelled, and the group can get right into the matter at hand. If the group is not cooperative, however, students might have to be assigned to groups. Discussion, almost by definition, will not work well when an uncooperative attitude persists. Some other form of sharing—for instance, a project to work on—might be necessary in such situations.

10. Each group should have a secretary appointed to take notes and report to the larger group. No adult leader should take this role!

11. The adult leader participates *directly* only at the end of the discussion. The leader's role until that time is to stimulate, to ask questions, and to request clarification. At the end the leader's own ideas and attitudes can be offered by way of a summary. If the leader gives direct input too readily, he or she can become the focus of the discussion, someone to whom the students are always looking for information.

12. Always close discussions with a summary of the points raised in order to highlight the main issues discussed.

Hints on Using the Films Recommended in SHARING

Another key dimension in a number of SHARING sessions is film—most often 16-mm motion pictures, and less frequently filmstrips. Many guides for the use of such media state that the most difficult tasks involved in their use are (a) choosing the right film or filmstrip for the occasion and (b) effectively handling the introduction and discussion of the material. The SHARING Program provides most of the direction you will need for these two tasks:

- All of the films used in the program have been very carefully selected to respond to both the subject matter at hand and the needs and characteristics of your audience, the young people.

- Every film or filmstrip is clearly situated in the session plans, with suggested introductory comments or exercises that are intended to heighten the interest and attentiveness of the students.

- All of the films or filmstrips recommended in SHARING—with the exception of a few that are intended to be reflective pieces used as part of prayer services—are accompanied by specific discussion questions or directions for other activities that are designed to help students and teachers gain the most benefit from experiencing the material.

Therefore, most of the hard work that might go into the use of film has been done for you already in SHARING. But there are, in addition, a few very practical hints that I would like to share that will assure you of a successful and therefore satisfying experience with the films and filmstrips recommended in the program:

1. Make certain that the proper equipment will be available to you when you need it.

2. Set up and test your equipment, making sure that it is in good working order and that you know how to use it properly. As much as possible, lower the risk of possible equipment failure. With film and filmstrip projectors, the most frequent problems that

occur are with the projection lamp and/or the exciter bulb. Make sure these are both working properly and that you have spares available in case they are needed.

3. Check to make sure extension cords are available if needed, and that you have adapters if necessary to convert three-prong plugs to fit two-prong receptacles. Test the lighting in the room, making certain that the room can be sufficiently darkened for viewing. Make sure that the wall receptacle in which you plug your projector is not turned off when the light switch is turned off!

4. Arrange the room for easy and comfortable viewing by all who attend. I often find that placing the screen in a corner works best, almost forcing the students to gather in a semicircle around the screen. This avoids the possibility of students sitting on the sides where their view is limited or where they might distract others.

5. Set the screen and projector as high as possible, thereby avoiding the distraction of students' heads or hands interfering with the projection of the film on the screen. Make certain as well that the sound on the film or filmstrip is adjusted properly for the room you are in. If you listen to the soundtrack while previewing the film alone, you will almost certainly have to turn the volume up when sharing the film with a group. Many film projectors have a portable speaker as well as the built-in one. When available, set the portable speaker in front of the audience.

6. Prior to showing the film, set up the projector and check all parts. Frame the picture on the screen and focus it as the numbers on the film lead are projected. Run the film through the projector to the beginning of the film, and then stop the projector at that point. It will then be ready to run when you need it.

7. *Never* leave the projector running without supervision.

8. Even with the films and filmstrips recommended in SHARING, *always preview the material before using it.* Make certain, in light of your own viewing of it, that you are comfortable with the introduction and follow-up material suggested in the session outline. Feel free to adapt as desired. It is as important to *personalize* your use of the films and filmstrips as it is the rest of the SHARING material.

9. When introducing the film or filmstrip, do not overexplain it. The film or filmstrip itself is your medium, and a too lengthy introduction can detract from its effectiveness. As one film guide puts it—not too subtly—the person who introduces a film should know how to "stand up, speak up, and shut up!"

There is one final point that should be discussed before moving on to the actual session plans for SHARING IV. (I promise, this *is* the final point!) After all we have said about preparing for the sessions, and after all the guidelines for leading discussions and group exercises, it must be acknowledged that the ultimate key for the successful teaching of the SHARING material is *you*, the group leader. All the great session plans in the world cannot ensure a successful program unless the students are relating to a mature and caring adult for whom the faith is alive and growing. The implications of this fact are explored in the next section.

The Teacher as a Witness of Faith

A Relational Approach

A central focus of the SHARING Program, and in a real way the philosophical and theological foundation for all we try to share here, is the conviction that faith is not simply an intellectual assent to a body of doctrines and dogmas. Rather, Christian faith is essentially and primarily a developing personal response in love by the believer to the unconditional love of God as revealed in Jesus. The implications of this relatively recent shift in our thinking are truly extensive. They affect those of us involved in the educational ministry of the Church on all levels:

1. A relational, rather than academic, approach to faith dramatically affects the way we view the student. If faith is viewed as a body of truths, the student is merely called upon to memorize those truths and to make some intellectual commitment to them. If faith is primarily relational, the student must be viewed as a unique individual who enters freely into a growing, changing relationship with God.

2. A relational approach to faith affects in many ways the content of religion courses, but it affects even more the pedagogical approach to that content. The content must be in touch with the lived experience of the student. Anything less than this makes real learning (as distinct from the simple accumulation of knowledge) impossible. Educational methodologies must be varied and responsive to the many levels of need and experience. Faith as a system of truths can be taught from the basis of intellectual inquiry; faith as a personal relationship must involve the whole person—intellectually, emotionally, spiritually, even physically.

3. An academic approach to faith necessarily emphasizes the academic qualifications of the teacher. With such an approach the "good teacher" is one who: (a) knows theology and (b) has the skills required to share that knowledge. In the case of a relational concept of faith, the "good teacher" is one who: (a) knows theology, (b) is personally involved in the development of his or her own faith, and (c) makes a commitment to enter into the shared experience of faith with the student.

These implications are intentionally simplified here for the sake of clarity. In reality, there can be a wedding of the two approaches—a healthy blend of both the academic and relational dimensions of faith. It is precisely such a blend that this program seeks to provide. Nevertheless, it should be clearly stated that the approach used in SHARING is primarily the relational approach. Academic knowledge is required to shed light on the personal experience of faith, but without that foundation of personal faith, academic knowledge is often unappealing and fruitless.

Witnesses of Faith

So faith is more than an intellectual commitment to a set of beliefs, doctrines, or religious practices. It is a developing response in love to the love of God. In the same sense we must recognize that we are called to be more than teachers of religion, if by that we mean teachers of our creed, codes, and religious traditions. We are ultimately called to be sharers of faith as well, and the implications of this are far-reaching.

It has been said—and perceptively so—that faith is not taught, it is *caught*. The seed of faith is indeed a gift of God planted in the hearts of people. Yet, that seed must be nourished and nurtured if it is to grow. Parents have the primary responsibility to provide such care and support. But the teacher of religion courses, because of the close association he or she has as a formal representative of the faith, is in a particularly strong position to influence the faith development of the students. This is even more true when the students are adolescents who are often reacting against their past in the attempt to establish personal identity. At this age, the teacher can be one who is often looked to for help in making the transition from childhood to adulthood.

The recognition of the religion teacher as a witness of faith poses some definite and perhaps disconcerting questions for the conscientious teacher: How can I as an individual best present myself as a person of faith? To what degree can I share my own religious doubts and questions with the students? Am I primarily a representative of Catholic tradition or a witness to my own personal faith convictions—and what do I do if the two are not in agreement? These are terribly difficult—and extremely important—questions.

We do not have the space to fully pursue the answers to these questions here, nor is that the purpose of this manual. But it is important to clearly state several principles or realities that should be remembered as the teacher of religion strives to be a witness of faith:

1. If faith involves a developing love relationship between a person and God, it is clear that the experience of that relationship will be unique to each person. Though we can say that we share the *same* faith in the sense of a mutual commitment to Jesus and his message, it is also true that each of us experiences the reality and implications of that commitment in *unique* and *personal* ways.

2. Because of this, it can be rightly said that each of us, as individual Christians, reflects in a very special and personal way the creative power and wisdom of our God. You do this differently than I, and you reveal a facet or dimension of God that no other person in the history of the world or in its future will be able to reveal. This is precisely the foundation for the incredible sense of human dignity that is so much a part of the message of Jesus.

3. One of the chief functions of a Church is to facilitate the sharing of personal faith among the members and to provide opportunities to celebrate such personal experiences communally. If the Church is to fulfill its purpose and its promise, therefore, it will only do so to the degree that individual Christians can openly and honestly share their own "faith-stories," their own unique and personal experiences of the revelation of God in and through their lives.

4. The only way our young people will comprehend this dimension of Christian faith is to observe it in the lives of adult Christians. Young people need to see the faith lived and proclaimed in a personal way in the witness of parents and teachers and in the communal expressions of the faith community.

To clarify the importance of this kind of personal sharing, recall, if you can, those teachers in your own experience who particularly impressed you, who made a real impact on your life. Recall as well your experiences of effective public speakers—the kind of speakers, for example, who can capture the attention of a large audience. Go back over those moments in a formal talk or presentation when the audience became especially quiet and attentive. And, most importantly of all, recall your own most fulfilling and exciting moments as a teacher. In all these cases it is very likely that there was a personal sharing between the teacher and the students or between the audience and the speaker. As soon as it is clear that a person is sharing more than facts and figures—that is, more than "book knowledge"—as soon as it is clear that one is sharing one's self rather than simply one's ideas, the entire relationship takes on a different tone, and effective communication becomes possible. The good teacher is above all a master communicator, and what he or she communicates most is a person—him or her *self*. "What you are speaks so loudly, I cannot hear what you are saying."

Suggestions for Effective Storytelling

Though our religious education is obviously based on revealed truths, the faith that we attempt to share can only be conveyed through our own convictions, our own personalities, our own lives. No teacher of religion will be effective until he or she can somehow share his or her own "story," the way in which he or she has had to come to terms with faith. The following suggestions are intended to help the teacher effectively share unique life experiences in the relatively formal educational settings employed in the SHARING Program.

1. Your stories must have a very clear lesson and purpose. In planning your sessions, always start from your intended *conclusion*—the point you want to teach—and then "back up" from there. What have you personally experienced that relates to that point?

2. As you begin to share your story, identify the experience as one probably shared by and therefore relevant to your audience, that is, as something worth listening to. This need not be done elaborately and will normally happen naturally, but it is important.

3. Lead up to your story logically, and have it fit in with the rest of your plan for the class. If it is presented out of context, it will lose its impact.

4. Give your story time to develop. The details are vital! Do not forget to describe the atmosphere, the location, the people you were with—all the things that made it important to you in the first place.

5. Clearly state the lesson to be learned at the conclusion of your story, unless it is so evident that such explanation is unnecessary. With young people, it is better not to presume that they got the point.

6. The "tone" of your story should fit the overall purpose of the session being taught and create the attitudes you need for whatever follows. For example, you will not want to tell a knee-slapping humorous story prior to prayer.

7. Always make explicit the *feeling* level of your story. Good stories touch the heart, not just the mind.

8. In looking for stories in your life, you must get so in touch with your own experience that others can "touch" it. Your stories must flow from your life honestly, sincerely. Any phoniness will be detected and promptly rejected. God speaks in your real, everyday life, not in artificiality. Implied in this is the fact that the successful storyteller will always be a person of prayer, sensitive to the ongoing revelation of God in his or her personal life.

9. *Practice your stories!* Good stories can be told a hundred times—and should be. Usually, if a story does not go over well, it simply needs better telling. Try different approaches, expressions, and so on. This is not a threat to spontaneity but rather a courtesy to those who are listening.

10. Paradoxically, the story or stories that are most difficult, personally, for you to share are probably the ones you need to share the most. This does *not* mean that you should pour out your deepest secrets to your students. But if you are confiding totally in some person close to you, you can more freely share other elements of your story with young people. Total openness with one special person can lead to freedom with many.

:
Part 2
Seven 2-Hour Sessions

Session 1

The Next Challenge: Moving into Adulthood

Teacher Goals

To effectively introduce the program for the year; to help the students reflect upon their major concerns and needs as they leave high school and enter the next stage of young adult development.

Student Intellectual/Behavioral Objectives

That the young persons begin the program with a positive attitude; that they grow in their willingness to explore and dialogue about the major concerns of young adults.

Main Ideas

The first session of any program is a particularly important one. Initial impressions can permanently influence the experience of the entire program for both the leaders and the young people. This certainly has been the case for all previous levels of the SHARING Program. Presumably, the students who have had previous experience with SHARING have a positive impression of the program and are now interested in investigating SHARING IV. That initial level of interest or openness on their part should reduce the tension that often accompanies the first session of a program. Yet factors peculiar to the SHARING IV program make this first session somewhat unique and particularly significant.

One of the unique factors of the SHARING IV program is the likely posture of the students. We can assume that, as seniors, the students will only attend a program if they want to. Parental support for attendance at religious education programs is minimal at this point. The vast majority of the young people will have been confirmed by this time, so the personal desire or the parental encouragement to receive the sacrament is no longer present to motivate them. Also, they have all kinds of opportunities to gather with their friends in environments that are less demanding and perhaps more fun than a formal education program. (Remember, just two or three years ago they might have attended a parish program merely as a way to get out of the house.) The students will be investigating participation in SHARING IV with a curiosity about whether the program will respond to their felt needs. If they begin to believe that the program will not, the young people will probably choose not to participate.

A second factor that makes this initial session of SHARING IV particularly significant is the nature of the program itself. Though the entire SHARING Program is committed to the educational principle that learning must actively engage the students in the process—as opposed to simply giving them the facts—SHARING IV suggests a learning environment that is unique, even for the SHARING Program. Although SHARING I through III were clearly committed to actively involving the young people, the teacher played the primary roles of presenter of information and facilitator of reflection upon that information. The students were not expected to take leadership roles in those programs. In a certain sense, the teacher bore the major responsibility of initiating and maintaining student interest, of drawing the young people out of themselves, and of holding their attention through careful and creative guidance of the programs' lessons.

SHARING IV, on the other hand, moves beyond the model of education in which the teacher shares a predetermined body of knowledge with receptive students. In SHARING IV, the young persons' concerns, interests—indeed their very lives—are the content of the program. The students are asked to assume greater personal responsibility for the program. The adult leader (the title *teacher* is avoided) in SHARING IV continues to play the role of facilitator of reflection, but often that reflection is upon the lives of the young people themselves rather than upon a predetermined body of information. It is hoped that what evolves through the course of the SHARING IV program is a support group of peers who are gathered and guided by an adult friend. This is different than the notion of a class of students who are expected to learn material presented by an authoritative teacher.

Session 1 of SHARING IV is particularly important, then, because it establishes this unique learning environment for the program. Naturally, the adult leader must still assume a strong leadership position in this session, but he or she should make it clear to the young people that one goal of the program is to gradually reduce the leader's role while increasing the students' active involvement and leadership. The entire SHARING IV program is designed in such a way that it *can* succeed even when the young people do not take strong leadership roles. However, the adult leader must emphasize that the more the young people take over the program, the more enjoyable and helpful it will be for them.

In addition to establishing a relationship of shared responsibility, session 1 also introduces the young people to the major themes of the program and initiates the personal reflection and the dialogue that are primary ingredients of the remaining sessions. This reflection and dialogue are accomplished through nonthreatening exercises, an evocative film, and the leader's presentation of a few major concepts. By the end of this session, the young people will be inclined to freely choose participation in the program because they will recognize that it is a program designed to respond to their felt needs. If that choice is accomplished, this will truly have been a successful first session.

Finally, a comment about the use of the film for this session: I suggested in the introduction that SHARING IV might best be conducted in the homes of the adult leaders. This presents a problem when a film is part of a session plan and when there is more than one group scheduled to meet in different homes at the same time. There are two basic options to consider: (1) the groups can meet on different evenings, or (2) the groups can meet together for the session. The latter alternative seems reasonable for session 1. During this first session of the year, introducing all the participating students to one another and to the adult leader benefits the program. This introduction gives everyone involved a sense of being part of a broader, parish-based program rather than being isolated in individual groups. Such a large-group gathering can also facilitate the initial formation of the smaller groups and the assignments of their leaders. The individual home-centered groups can then begin functioning at the next session.

Procedure

A. Welcome and Introduction (10–20 minutes)

Note: The allotted time for this introduction depends on whether a barrier breaker is used.

1. Introduce yourself to the young people. You may already know many of them. If so, you will be able to move quickly into the session. If you are meeting in your home, you naturally will offer a brief welcome and introduction to the young people as they arrive for the session. If you do not know the students through previous contacts, you might begin by briefly describing your family, your work, and why you chose to become involved in the program.

2. Offer a brief introduction to the program, noting the following:

a. **The major theme of the program,** namely, reflection upon, discussion of, and preparation for the major developmental tasks that confront young people as they leave mid-adolescence and enter into young adulthood. These tasks include (1) choosing the values that will guide the young people; (2) evolving a dream that will provide a sense of direction for their lives; (3) honing the skills that will make it possible for them to enter into and maintain intimacy with others; and (4) for some, choosing one person with whom to build a permanent relationship. All these tasks and others will be discussed during the SHARING IV program.

b. **The schedule for the year,** perhaps including a printed list of dates and times for all the sessions.

c. **The possibility of a retreat,** perhaps one that will largely be created by the young people if they so wish. (Note that a fuller discussion of the retreat will be part of session 2.)

d. **The change in the nature of the program,** from the teacher-student character of past programs to that of a support group of friends reflecting together, guided by an adult leader. Mention that this may be the last religious education program that they will experience, at least in the sense of a formally structured program developed and guided by others. In the near future, the young people will have to assume personal responsibility for their faith formation, and one goal of this program is to give them the tools with which to do that effectively.

3. At this point, ask the young people to introduce themselves, if necessary. To ease the introductions, you may want to use one of the barrier breakers suggested below. If the students already know one another quite well, feel free to skip this part of the session, thereby freeing up additional time for other activities.

Optional barrier breakers

Name game: Gather the group in a circle and have one person introduce himself or herself with his or her first name and an adjective that has the same first letter as the first name (e.g., serious Sue, terrific Tom, vivacious Vivian). The next person in the group repeats the adjective-name of the first person and then adds his or her own adjective-name. The third person repeats the first two adjective-names and then adds his or her own. This continues until the last person in the group attempts to say everyone's adjective-name prior to giving his or her own. If individuals have difficulty along the way, be quick to offer clues to avoid embarrassment. Consider breaking into groups of ten or so if there are more than twenty participants.

Famous name charades: Before the participants gather, prepare a series of stick-on name tags with the names of famous persons. They can be biblical characters, current movie stars, athletes, or other celebrities.

Divide the large group into groups of four. Have the group members briefly introduce themselves to one another, if necessary. Then place a celebrity name tag on the back of one person in each small group. The person then stands in front of the small group and turns around slowly so that the members of the group can see the name tag.

In silence, the group members act out the celebrity until the person with the name tag guesses who he or she is. Remember, there can be no talking. All clues must be given without words.

When the person guesses correctly, encourage a round of applause. Then place a different name tag on another person and repeat the exercise. (Note: Depending on the number of students involved and their performance of this activity, it can take longer than the allotted time. Be prepared to adjust the schedule accordingly, should you choose this activity.)

Sentence completions: One of the easiest ways to get people talking to one another is to provide a list of open-ended sentences and then have participants complete and explain them to others. Before the session, prepare individual slips of paper with partial sentences like those suggested below. Fold the papers so they cannot be read. Divide the large group into small groups. Ask each small group to form a circle. Place the slips of paper in the centers of the circles on the floor. Ask each person to state his or her name, randomly select a piece of paper, read it to the group, and then spontaneously complete the sentence on the paper. You can create humorous statements, but avoid anything that might embarrass a participant. The following are some possibilities:

- My favorite season of the year is . . .
- My favorite subject in school is . . .
- My favorite pastime is . . .
- My favorite rock group is . . .
- If I could live at any other time in history, I would choose . . .
- If I could throw caution to the winds, I would like to . . .
- If I dressed up for a masquerade ball, I would go as . . .
- If I would describe my personal life right now in terms of a garden, I would be a . . .

B. Film: *Solo* (15 minutes; with introduction, 20 minutes)

1. Synopsis: This film is a stunning, highly evocative, and deeply moving visual experience. See "Things to Keep in Mind" at the end of this session for rental information. A promotional piece on the film describes it this way:

> A lone mountain climber sets out in the misty predawn to climb his mountain, up past thundering waterfalls, along thin crevasses, across glaciers and snow fields, clinging to sheer rock face, feeling for a handhold on an overhanging rock, swinging joyfully from a rope above the world that most of us inhabit. The soundtrack is composed of music, waterfalls, wind and other natural sounds—and silence. An exhilarating film that emphasizes the positive aspects of human aloneness, individual accomplishment and spiritual achievement.

In the context of this session, we are going to use the film as an allegory of the struggle for both personal development and spiritual growth. To effectively make this connection, it is important that the film be properly introduced.

2. Introduce the film: Have the film prepared for viewing before the group arrives. In a home environment, this might demand setting up the film in a room other than the one in which you initially meet. As you gather the group to view the film, ask if anyone could offer a definition for the word *allegory*. Can anyone give an example of an allegory? After inviting the students' responses, provide the following introduction to the film:

An *allegory* is an art form—a painting, a piece of music, a film, or a play—in which symbolic characters or events are used to represent the deeper meanings of life. *The Wizard of Oz* and *Alice in Wonderland* are classic examples of allegories. Within these fanciful stories we can discover many profound insights about human nature and the meaning of existence.

At this time I'd like us to view a film that can be understood as a striking allegory for the great adventure we call life. It's such a wonderful film that I'd like to run it more than once, just enjoying it the first time and then reflecting on it carefully later. However, time doesn't allow us to do that, so I ask you to view the film this first time with a reflective and thoughtful attitude. While allowing the film to touch you emotionally, continually ask yourself these questions: How might this film symbolize the journey to self-understanding? What might this particular scene mean in terms of my own life experience? Are there times in my life when I have felt the way this man must feel at this point in the film? What facet of the journey of life might this part of the film symbolize?

After we've seen the film, we'll try to share some of the thoughts that strike you. So, as we begin to watch the film, look upon it as an allegory of your own life.

3. Show the film.

C. Discussion of the Film (30 minutes)

See Student Handout 1–A following this session outline. Also, allow 20 minutes for the discussion in dyads and 10 minutes for the large-group summation.

1. The initial strategy used for discussing the film is formally called a dyadic encounter. This means that the group will be asked to divide into couples and discuss the film in a structured way. The intent of this approach in this case is twofold: (a) to analyze the film and its meaning; (b) to engage the young people in some relatively intense dialogue early in the program, creating the sense of personal sharing that is desirable in the SHARING IV program.

2. Small discussion booklets must be prepared before the session, one for each participant. Use Student Handout 1–A, "Discussion Booklet for the Film *Solo*," to make the booklets. (Photocopy masters for all the student handouts are found at the end of this manual, unless noted otherwise.) Simply reproduce enough copies of the master for your group, cut the pages along the lines as indicated, assemble according to the numbers in the corner of each section, and staple the sections together in the upper left-hand corner. Each page in the booklet presents a point for discussion—at times a partial sentence to be completed, at other times a direct question, and so on. There are eight such items for discussion, that is, eight one-sided pages in the booklet.

3. Ask the students to divide into couples, preferably joining with someone they do not know well. If there is an uneven number of participants, the leader may be a partner to one of the young people. (An option would be to make one group a triad, but that group would necessarily take more time to complete the assignment than would the dyads.) When the students are in their dyads, tell them that you are going to distribute discussion booklets, but that they are not to read through them at this time. Then pass out the booklets, one to each person.

4. Explain the following guidelines for the discussion:

a. One of the persons in each dyad begins with just the first page of his or her booklet, mentally completes the sentence on it, and then states it out loud. Then the partner does the same thing. When they are done with the first page, they move to the second page and follow the directions on it, this time reversing who answers first so that the same person does not always have to start. They continue in this fashion until the entire booklet is completed.

b. Though the items for discussion in this exercise are not threatening, the participants may refuse to respond to any item at any time they wish. In such cases, however, their partners can still respond to that item if they want to.

c. There is a limited amount of time to be spent on this discussion (about 15 minutes), so the participants should move quickly through the booklet. Each person will be able to spend about one minute responding to each item in the booklet.

5. Depending on the size of the group and the amount of available space, you may be able to provide separate space for each couple. If the students must remain in one room, ask only that they speak quietly to avoid disturbing the conversations of others. A comment on the time limit: The time allowed for this exercise is intentionally limited. The desire is to keep the session moving but to avoid pressuring the students too much this early in the program. However, you may find that their discussions are going so well that you choose not to interrupt them. In previous levels of the SHARING Program, I recommended sticking closely to the schedule and making adjustments reluctantly. In SHARING IV, however, we are using a different educational dynamic. We want the students to assume more leadership for the sessions, even if it means that some planned activities will have to be dropped. Trust your judgment on this—or better, let the young people know that you trust *their* judgment. Announce when time is up, but offer them the chance to discuss further if they are finding it enjoyable and fruitful. When the majority of dyads are ready to end their discussion, gather them together for large-group discussion.

6. Large-group discussion (10 minutes): When all the participants are gathered together, review the results of their discussion as dyads, concentrating on the following general items:

a. What were some of the words you heard describing the present stage of life in terms of the allegory of mountain climbing? (Note any responses that seem to be common or that appear to characterize this stage of development in a particularly important way.)

b. What did you discover about the experience of aloneness in life? Was anything mentioned about facing many of life's challenges alone? Is there a difference between loneliness and solitude? If so, how would you describe the difference?

c. How did you interpret the gesture of the mountain climber catching and then releasing a toad?

d. What are the major risks that people your age confront?

e. How did you summarize the basic meaning of the film?

7. Close the discussion appropriately, thanking the students for their cooperation.

D. Break with Simple Refreshments
(10 minutes)

E. Guided Reflection on Concerns of Young Adulthood (15 minutes)

1. Give each of the young people a 3-by-5-inch card and a pencil. Then ask them to get in a relaxed position—reclining on the floor or sitting with their backs up against a wall or chair for support—whatever position allows them to be comfortable. Next, tell them to take a few deep breaths, slowly inhaling through their nostrils, holding their breath a moment, and then slowly exhaling through their mouths. With each breath they should try to imagine that all their tensions, distractions, and concerns are leaving them. Invite them to close their eyes if they find that doing so helps them to concentrate.

2. Now ask the students to try to imagine themselves five years from now. They should make a strong effort to actually *see* themselves: How might their appearance differ from what they look like now? Are they dressed casually or professionally? Are they larger? thinner? Allow them a moment or two to get in touch with the image of their future selves.

3. Next, tell the students that you are going to slowly mention various facets of their lives and that you want them to briefly reflect on each facet *as they imagine they will be experiencing it five years from now*. Ask them to be as imaginative as they can, but to try as well to respond reasonably, keeping their images of the future in line with their present situations, their talents, their personalities, and so on. They will *not* be asked to share their response with others. Once again, they should attempt to actually see themselves in their minds in the life situations that you mention. After sharing these directions, slowly mention each of the following situations, pausing briefly (about 30–60 seconds) after each one to allow time for reflection:

a. **It is possible that five years from now you will either be working or beginning graduate school. Which will you be doing? If working, what kind of job do you think you will have? If going to school, what do you think you might be studying?** (Pause.)

b. **You are now probably living at home with your family. In five years, that will likely not be the case. Try to imagine where you might be living, with whom, and how you might be relating at that time with your present family members. That is, will you be living near your family? Will you be close to them emotionally? socially?** (Pause.)

c. **Try now to imagine yourself in terms of your primary personal relationship five years from now. Do you see yourself as married or single? If married, is the person to whom you are married someone you now know? If so, does she or he look any different than now? If you do not imagine yourself as being married, do you envision yourself having a serious romantic relationship with someone at that time? Imagine when you might choose to marry. How old would you likely be?** (Pause.)

d. **Try to imagine yourself five years from now in terms of faith and religion. Do you see yourself as involved in formal, institutional religion? For example, can you imagine yourself as an adult member of a parish? Will you be attending church regularly? Regarding your personal faith relationship with God, do you feel that five years from now you will be praying, discussing matters of faith with others, and so on?** (Pause.)

e. **Finally, the most difficult facet to imagine: Try to visualize your face as it might appear five years from now. Look into your own eyes. Do you appear to be happy? Do your eyes reflect fulfillment as a person? Do you seem to be experiencing satisfying relationships with others? Do you look as though you are in charge of your life and on your way to a happy adulthood?** (Pause.)

4. After leading the young people through these reflective questions, ask them to open their eyes and to relax for just a moment, perhaps allowing them to talk with the other students for a few seconds about the experience. Then quickly move to the next step in the process.

5. The students' imaginary trip into the future has likely raised all sorts of concerns, questions, and maybe even fears about the major tasks that they will confront over the next five years. Ask them to quickly jot down on their 3-by-5-inch card those concerns or issues that confront them as they look toward the immediate future. Resist giving them examples to avoid prejudicing their responses. However, if they insist that you give them a clearer sense of what you are looking for here, use this example:

One of the things you were asked to think about was the possibility of being married five years from now. That possibility raises all kinds of concerns and issues, the most obvious being, How does one decide whom to marry? How does a person know when love is real? Every one of the facets you were asked to reflect upon raises questions like these. Try to list them on your card. The five areas we thought about included these facets of life: (*a*) school or work, (*b*) relationship with family, (*c*) primary relationship in life, whether married or single, (*d*) faith and religion, (*e*) happiness and fulfillment as an adult. What concerns and issues does each of these areas present to you?

F. Discussion of the Developmental Tasks of Young Adults (10–20 minutes, time permitting)

See Student Handout 1–B following this session outline.

1. You will have to be quite flexible regarding the use of time as you near the end of this session. There are a number of variables involved that have affected the amount of time left at this point: whether or not you needed barrier breakers, and if so, how long they took to complete; how vocal and animated the group is at this first meeting; and so on. That is why such a broad range of time is suggested for this part of the session, anywhere from 10–20 minutes. (The experienced teacher knows that 10 minutes can be an eternity.) There are two ways to approach this portion of the session, depending on the available time and knowing that you will want to save at least 5 minutes for a closing prayer:

a. If time is tight (15 minutes or less until the end of the session), I suggest that you simply brainstorm the concerns and issues that the young people listed on their cards. When doing this, use a chalkboard or newsprint to record the responses so that all the participants can see them, and place a checkmark behind points that are repeated during the brainstorming. Then conclude the brainstorming by briefly noting how many, if not all, of the concerns and issues listed are going to be discussed during this program. Then move to the closing prayer as described below.

b. If your available time is less tight (20 minutes or more), do the brainstorming and recording as described above, but then follow with the brief presentation of concepts explained in point 2 below. From that, move on to the closing prayer.

2. Optional presentation by leader: Begin this presentation with the following description of Arthur Chickering's work:

Arthur Chickering is a researcher in the area of young adult development. He has developed a model of the way college students experience personal development, and his work has been influential in the way colleges and universities deal with their students. (See "Things to Keep in Mind" for resources on Chickering's work.) **Although his work has centered on young adult development as it is expressed in the college environment, much of his model also pertains to those who choose not to attend college.**

Chickering has identified seven "vectors," or dimensions, of personal development that occur in young adulthood. Other researchers have modified or expanded his work to include ten basic developmental tasks for young adults. We can only list these dimensions here, but as we go through them quickly, let's see if the concerns and issues you have written on your cards fit into this list.

At this point, reveal a poster or a sheet of newsprint on which you have previously printed the following list of young adult tasks. (Following each task, as it is stated here, is a brief description that you need not include on your chart.) This list is also available on Student Handout 1–B, "Ten Tasks for Young Adults," which you can reproduce in advance and distribute to the students at this time. It is preferred, however, that you also use the chart so that all the students can see the information unfold, rather than simply read through the handout with the students. The information is reinforced by examining it on the chart as well as giving the students the handout version to take home with them. These are the ten developmental tasks of young adults:

- **Becoming Competent:** I must acquire the working knowledge and skills I need to begin to accomplish the other developmental tasks of young adulthood; I must enhance my self-esteem by growing in the knowledge that I can "get things done."

- **Achieving Autonomy:** I must gradually grow from a sense of *dependence* upon others (e.g., parents) to greater *independence* (often really a change to dependency upon peers rather than on parents) to a more mature sense of *interdependence*. I must learn to sustain myself without the constant approval of and reliance upon others, while recognizing and accepting that I am a person in relationship with, and therefore somewhat responsible for the good of, others.

- **Developing and Implementing Values:** Out of all the values that have been presented to me by parents, school, church, and so on, I must personally choose a set of values that will give guidance and meaning to my life.
- **Forming a Personal Identity:** One definition of *identity* is "a stable sense of who I am that is confirmed by the people in my life who are important to me." One's sense of identity, therefore, has both personal and social dimensions. I must achieve a sense of integrity between how I see myself and how significant others see me. I must become comfortable with who I am, not needing to wear masks or to act phony with others.
- **Integrating Sexuality into Life:** Sex offers an important kind of intimacy with others, but in our culture it can be difficult to integrate one's sexuality into one's total identity in a healthful way. Some individuals try to solve the "problem" of sex by overemphasizing it, while others try to minimize its importance and thereby fail to develop a vital dimension of a mature personality. During young adulthood, I am challenged to develop values regarding sexuality and sexual expression that can be integrated comfortably into my entire value system.
- **Making Friends and Developing Intimacy:** Growing as a person requires the capacity for intimacy with others that goes beyond sexuality and romance. As I become more secure with my own identity, I grow in my ability to relate to and become friends with people who differ from me. My relationships are increasingly characterized by trust, interdependency rather than dependency, the capacity for forgiveness, and the sense that I do not lose my own identity when joining with others in the commitment of friendship.
- **Loving and Making a Commitment to Another Person:** Many, though not all, young adults will also confront the task of making decisions about marriage, a unique and profound expression of friendship and intimacy. Though I may not, in fact, choose to marry during these years, I am challenged to grow in the personal traits and capacities that will make a possible future marriage satisfying and successful.
- **Making Initial Job and Career Choices:** Daniel Levinson, in a book titled *The Seasons of a Man's Life* (New York: Alfred A. Knopf, 1978), states:

    One of the great paradoxes of human development is that we are required to make crucial choices before we have the knowledge, judgment and self-understanding to choose wisely. Yet, if we put off these choices until we feel truly ready, the delay may produce other and greater costs. This is especially true of the two great choices of early adulthood: occupation and marriage. (P. 102)

    What skills and knowledge can I learn now that will help me successfully make some of the initial decisions I must make during the next few years about my future career and life work?

- **Becoming an Active Community Member and Citizen:** Some individuals may resist the notion that we have a personal responsibility to contribute our talents to benefit our local, national, and global communities. For many people in today's society, young adulthood can be a time for "getting mine and letting others fend for themselves." As Christians, we recognize that we are a human family called to serve one another. How can I develop the skills to do this, and how do I balance my need for developing intimate relationships and preparing for a personal career with the need and desire to serve the broader good of humanity?
- **Learning How to Use Leisure Time:** In light of the values that I have chosen for my life, how can I best use the growing amount of leisure time that I will experience in my life? During the young adult years, I may well set a pattern for use of leisure time that will last for the rest of my life. Will I spend that time in front of a television or in finding ways to continually grow as a person?

3. Again, your available time will dictate to what degree you can discuss any or all of the developmental tasks of young adulthood. Whatever your time limits, comment on the relationship of these tasks to the SHARING IV discussion topics:

Certainly we cannot discuss all of these issues in our limited time, nor can we hope to thoroughly discuss any one of them to the depth we would like. During this program, however, we will spend as much time as we have to reflect upon and discuss with one another the challenges that you face in the next years of your life.

G. Closing Prayer (5–10 minutes)

See Student Handout 1–C following this session outline.

1. The closing prayer includes four components: (*a*) a call to prayer by the adult leader, (*b*) a brief reading, (*c*) the distribution of symbolic plants if you wish, and (d) a closing reading recited by the entire group. The time for prayer is most easily reduced by eliminating the distribution of plants and restricting yourself solely to the recitation of specific prayers. The plant symbol, however, can become meaningful for participants, and you are encouraged to include it if possible. One suggestion: If time is tight, consider delaying the brief presentation of Chickering's young adult developmental tasks until session 2, giving yourself a bit more time for this prayer experience.

2. Two brief prayers—actually, one reflective reading and one formal prayer—are included here. At the end of this session outline, you will find a two-page handout (Student Handout 1–C, "Keepsake Prayers"), with each page containing one prayer. Photocopy these pages back-to-back on one sheet. Cut the page apart, laminate the sections, and you will have four prayer cards, with the prayers back-to-back. Lamination will allow you to use the cards repeatedly throughout the year, as well as to give them to the young people as a keepsake at the conclusion of the program. Inexpensive, coin-operated laminating machines can now be found at many supermarkets as well as at commercial print shops. Even if you choose not to prepare such cards, you can still use the prayer and the reading for this service.

3. **Call to prayer:** The adult leader simply concludes the previous discussion by asking all the participants to gather closely together for a moment of prayer to close the first session. Call for a moment of silence, asking everyone to ponder the marvelous reality that, in their midst at this very moment, there is a God who loves each person passionately and unconditionally. When you are sure that all the participants have become centered and prepared for prayer, proceed.

4. **A reflective reading:** At this time, distribute the sheet or card with the reading and prayer. Share the selection by John Powell, "This Is Who I Am." Note: This can be read by the adult leader, by one of the youth, or even by the group in unison. It is important that it be read *well*. If you wish to have a young person read it, be sure to share it with him or her early in the session—perhaps during the break—so that it can be properly prepared.

5. **Distribution of plants:** We are all aware of the value—indeed, the necessity—of symbols in life, physical expressions of realities and truths that are so profound that they defy description and discussion. I want to offer here a symbol of personal development and growth that can be experienced in both an individual and a communal way with the members of the group.

I suggest that you consider purchasing a small, potted plant for each young person. (See "Things to Keep in Mind" for specific suggestions.) At this point, explain the value of symbols in life, and mention that you want to have a shared symbol of the process of human growth and development that will be the focus of your time together during this program. Then give each youth one of the potted plants with a blank piece of tape or paper attached on which they can quickly print their names. You may wish to pass a small watering can or pitcher, asking each person to gently water their plant with this *communal water*—another wonderful symbolic gesture. Mention that the plants will be kept together to be used as a changing, growing symbol at each meeting of the group. Each person will be given his or her plant at the end of the program. Depending on the size of the group, this ritual might take only a few minutes but should have strong impact, particularly if it is done reverently and prayerfully.

6. **Closing communal reading:** Close the prayer service by asking all the participants to join in reciting the prayer "You Have Great Plans for Me" (Student Handout 1–C). I suggest that this become a regularly recited prayer at each meeting. The prayer was written by the staff of the Vocation Center of the Archdiocese of Saint Paul–Minneapolis.

Things to Keep in Mind

Regarding the Film *Solo*

The film *Solo* can be rented from Mass Media Ministries, 2116 North Charles Street, Baltimore, Maryland 21216. Phone 301-727-3270. The rental fee at the time of this writing was $20. Remember always to order films far in advance of your actual show date, preferably six weeks or more. Also, check your diocesan resource center and local public libraries before ordering the film from commercial distributors.

Regarding the Work of Arthur Chickering

If you are interested in further studying Arthur Chickering's work on young adult development, I recommend the following two resources:

Egan, Gerard, and Michael A. Cowan. *Moving into Adulthood: Themes and Variations in Self-Directed Development for Effective Living.* Belmont, CA: Brooks/Cole Publishing Co., 1980. (See pp. 32–37 for an overview and adaptation of Chickering's theory. The entire book then devotes individual chapters to a systematic process of reflection on each developmental task. This book was among the most helpful of those I used in developing the SHARING IV manual.)

Knefelkamp, Lee, Carole Widick, and Clyde A. Parker, eds. *Applying New Developmental Findings.* San Francisco: Jossey-Bass, 1978. (See the article titled "Arthur Chickering's Vectors of Development," pp. 19–34.)

Regarding the Use of Plants During the Prayer Service

Your decision regarding symbolic plants for the prayer service may be largely influenced by your geographic location. I suggest that you consult a local nursery for advice. In my case, the recommended plant was a green houseplant called Fittonia. To be perfectly honest about it, I did not find the plant particularly attractive; however, it did what was promised—it grew quickly enough so that there was a recognizable change on a week-by-week basis. If you are sure that your young people will stay with you throughout the year—including the retreat and meditation program—you may even consider giving them seeds to plant as part of the prayer service. The symbolic value will be stronger than with a plant, but the time for recognizable growth would obviously be greatly extended beyond what will be true for established plants. Experiment and let me know of your experience; I'll then share the results with readers of **SHARING News.**

Regarding the Use of Prayer Cards

If you decide to prepare laminated prayer cards for the program, I suggest that you collect them at the end of each session. Many of the young people will forget to bring them regularly to the sessions. The cards can then be given to them at the end of the program.

For Evaluation

1. Reflect on the general feel of the session and the group's response to the session. Did the young people seem to respond positively to the description of the content and approach of the year's program? Can you foresee any potential problems that might occur, given the makeup of the group and the goals of the program? How might you address those problems?

2. Did the film and its discussion go well? Was the dyadic encounter strategy effective with your group? If not, how might you adapt this in the future?

3. Guided reflection activities require a proper introduction and a good sense of pacing that only comes with practice. What did you learn from your experience with the guided reflection on the concerns of young adults? Would you now change any part of your guidance of it? Record your suggested changes in your notebook for future reference.

4. In your discussion of the developmental tasks of young adults, were the young people able to identify and articulate their major concerns for the next five years of their lives? If you used Chickering's theory, did the students find it helpful? Finally, were there any insights you gained from this discussion that might be helpful to you in directing the rest of the program?

5. Review your experience with the closing prayer and note any changes you want to make for the future.

6. Were the "Teacher Goals" and "Student Intellectual/Behavioral Objectives" for this session achieved?

STUDENT HANDOUT 1-A

Discussion Booklet for the Film *Solo*

1

It seems to me that growing as a person is a lot like climbing a mountain because . . .

2

Sometimes mountain climbing can be fun and exciting, while at other times it can be scary, risky, thrilling, peaceful, prayerful, painful. Comparing my life to the process of climbing a mountain, I would describe my present stage in life as . . .

3

At times, individual experiences in life can be viewed as mountains in themselves—difficult challenges we must face and, it is hoped, endure, conquer, or grow through. In the last five years, one of the most difficult mountains I had to climb was when . . .

4

At this point, tell your partner as much as you feel comfortable sharing about the mountain climbing experience you just identified. Possible points to consider include, Who were the significant people involved? What exactly happened? How did you first react to the situation? What made it such a challenge?

The Next Challenge: Moving into Adulthood

5

The name of the film is *Solo,* referring to the fact that the climber in the film accomplishes his task all alone. In what sense must each of us face the major challenges of life alone? Is that good or bad?

6

How would you interpret the significance of the mountain climber finding, protecting, and later releasing the small toad? What might that symbolize about life?

7

If our lives are to be exciting and fulfilling— even just plain fun—it seems that we have to be willing to take some risks. Either that, or we spend all our time on the ground in fear and boredom and never climb the mountains in life.
At this point in my life, the greatest risks I probably have to take are . . .

8

If I were asked to sum up the main message of the film, I think it is that . . .

Reproduction permission is granted if you wish to make copies for classroom use.
The photocopy master for this handout is found at the back of this manual.

STUDENT HANDOUT 1-B

Ten Tasks for Young Adults

The following developmental tasks have been identified by researchers as the primary challenges facing young adults who are striving for maturity and fulfillment as persons. The tasks are stated here as personal decisions or commitments in order to affirm the fact that success in each area is indeed attainable.

1. Becoming Competent: As a young adult, I will acquire a belief in my ability to "get things done," a sense that I can handle all the other tasks that I will face in the next few years.

2. Achieving Autonomy: I am a person who chooses to be in relationships with others, but I do not depend on the approval of other people to sustain me. I freely choose interdependency; I reject total dependency upon others.

3. Developing and Implementing Values: I will personally choose a set of values that will give guidance and meaning to my life.

4. Forming a Personal Identity: I will strive to rid myself of the masks that I wear. People who encounter me will meet the **real** me, not an artificial role that I assume.

5. Integrating Sexuality into Life: I will develop values regarding sexuality and sexual expression that reflect my total value system and that support my goal of living with moral and personal integrity.

6. Making Friends and Developing Intimacy: I will strive to develop the friendship skills that allow me to be trustful, open, forgiving, and nurturing in my relationships with others.

7. Loving and Making a Commitment to Another Person: Should my life bring me to the point of choosing a permanent relationship with another person, I will have developed the maturity and personal integrity necessary to make it a lifelong relationship of caring, interdependency, and true intimacy.

8. Making Initial Job and Career Choices: In the years ahead, I will test and slowly refine my career choice. My life's work will reflect my values and contribute to my sense of personal integrity.

9. Becoming an Active Community Member and Citizen: Knowing that my primary concern in the next few years is the development of my personal and interpersonal skills, I resist the notion that I am responsible only to myself. I am a member of a community, and I will seek ways to share my gifts and skills with others.

10. Learning How to Use Leisure Time: I will learn to use my leisure time as an invitation to **re-creation**—that is, for "re-creating" myself—rather than allowing my free time to be a wasted opportunity to grow.

Reproduction permission is granted if you wish to make copies for classroom use.
The photocopy master for this handout is found at the back of this manual.

Keepsake Prayers — STUDENT HANDOUT 1-C

This Is Who I Am

My person is *not* a little hard core inside of me, a fully-formed statue that is real and authentic, permanent and fixed. If I am anything as a person, it is what I . . .
- think
- judge
- feel
- value
- honor
- esteem
- love
- hate
- fear
- desire
- hope for
- believe in
- and am committed to.

These are the things that define my person, and they are constantly in process, in the process of change. In other words, if you knew me yesterday, please do not think that it is the same person you are meeting today. I have experienced more of life, I have encountered new depths in those I love, I have suffered and prayed, and I am different.

Approach me, then, with a sense of wonder, study my face and hands and voice for the signs of change—for it is certain that I have changed.

Adapted from John Powell, SJ

This Is Who I Am

My person is *not* a little hard core inside of me, a fully-formed statue that is real and authentic, permanent and fixed. If I am anything as a person, it is what I . . .
- think
- judge
- feel
- value
- honor
- esteem
- love
- hate
- fear
- desire
- hope for
- believe in
- and am committed to.

These are the things that define my person, and they are constantly in process, in the process of change. In other words, if you knew me yesterday, please do not think that it is the same person you are meeting today. I have experienced more of life, I have encountered new depths in those I love, I have suffered and prayed, and I am different.

Approach me, then, with a sense of wonder, study my face and hands and voice for the signs of change—for it is certain that I have changed.

Adapted from John Powell, SJ

This Is Who I Am

My person is *not* a little hard core inside of me, a fully-formed statue that is real and authentic, permanent and fixed. If I am anything as a person, it is what I . . .
- think
- judge
- feel
- value
- honor
- esteem
- love
- hate
- fear
- desire
- hope for
- believe in
- and am committed to.

These are the things that define my person, and they are constantly in process, in the process of change. In other words, if you knew me yesterday, please do not think that it is the same person you are meeting today. I have experienced more of life, I have encountered new depths in those I love, I have suffered and prayed, and I am different.

Approach me, then, with a sense of wonder, study my face and hands and voice for the signs of change—for it is certain that I have changed.

Adapted from John Powell, SJ

This Is Who I Am

My person is *not* a little hard core inside of me, a fully-formed statue that is real and authentic, permanent and fixed. If I am anything as a person, it is what I . . .
- think
- judge
- feel
- value
- honor
- esteem
- love
- hate
- fear
- desire
- hope for
- believe in
- and am committed to.

These are the things that define my person, and they are constantly in process, in the process of change. In other words, if you knew me yesterday, please do not think that it is the same person you are meeting today. I have experienced more of life, I have encountered new depths in those I love, I have suffered and prayed, and I am different.

Approach me, then, with a sense of wonder, study my face and hands and voice for the signs of change—for it is certain that I have changed.

Adapted from John Powell, SJ

You Have Great Plans for Me

Lord, I know you love me
    and have great plans for me.
But sometimes I am overwhelmed
    by the thought of my future.
It's scary, Lord!
Show me how to walk forward one day at a time.
May I take heart while I search openly,
    learn about all the choices I face,
    listen to others for advice,
    and pay attention
    to my own feelings.
By doing these things may I hear your call
    to a lifestyle and a career
    that will let me love
    as only I can,
    and let me serve others
    with the special gifts
    that you have given me.
Lord, thank you for the hope you have in me.
Amen.

            Adapted from the Vocation Center
            Archdiocese of Saint Paul-Minneapolis

Reproduction permission is granted if you wish to make copies for classroom use. The photocopy master for this handout is found at the back of this manual.

Session 2

The Future Is in My Hands: Turning Dreams into Realities

Teacher Goals

To awaken the young people to the possibility of creating their own future rather than simply accepting the future as something that happens to them; to help them begin to shape a dream that will guide them; to reflect on the Christian dream of the kingdom of God.

Student Intellectual/Behavioral Objectives

That the young people begin to view their future as something over which they have at least some control and for which they must assume responsibility; that they view their futures as hopeful and challenging; that they reflect on their own future in terms of Christian faith.

Main Ideas

In session 1, we helped the young people focus on the developmental tasks that challenge them as they move into young adulthood. One of the primary intents of that session was to convince the students that this program will cover material that is of high interest to them. Now that we have identified our major theme for the program and have raised student interest and enthusiasm, we can begin a structured discussion of some of the individual tasks and issues that confront the young people at this stage of their development.

There is a popular adage that states, If you don't know where you're going, it's very hard to get there. This session concerns helping the young people decide on where they want to go with their life. Given the limits of time, we obviously cannot help each student systematically work through his or her own options for the future. Nevertheless, we can strongly promote the notion that the young people have something to say about what they will become.

Having some say about one's own future may seem so self-evident as to not warrant a full session in a program already strapped for time. The fact is, though, that a major problem for many young adults today is an apathy derived from feeling helpless about their own futures. As we shall discuss in more detail in the next session, psychologists and sociologists speak today of a phenomenon among young people termed *option shock*. The basic notion is that, on virtually every level of their lives, young people are confronted with so many choices, so many possibilities, that they shut down—they avoid the burdens of decision-making by allowing life to happen to them rather than taking personal charge of it.

Adults may initially envy the apparent freedom of today's youth. Many adults tend to look at today's youth with the conviction that young people have been relieved of many of the past social conventions and expectations and are freer to create lifestyles than previous generations.

Young people today do experience greater freedom than many of us adults did. However, what we see as freedom, many of them experience as the unbearable burden of infinite choices. Nothing comes easily. Many of us grew up with a sexual morality that we now feel, perhaps justifiably, was Victorian and oppressive. Today's youth, on the other hand, are confronted with a sexuality without apparent guidelines. For example, as youths the thought of abortion may never have entered our mind, whereas most young people today personally know someone who has actually had an abortion. When we fell in love, marriage and children were the only tolerable options. When today's youth fall in love, they face choices ranging from living together before marriage to whether or when to have a family. The range of occupational choices has also expanded dramatically in recent decades, each choice presenting further options for training and education. The examples could go on and on.

In sessions 2 and 3 of SHARING IV, we will be addressing this option difficulty of today's young adults. In session 2, we will take the long view of the future by introducing what some people call a dream—a vision of life that points to the future and helps focus on the questions individuals must confront if they are to take charge of who and what they become. After guiding the young people through a process of reflection on the goals they would like to set for their lives, we will conclude with a prayer experience. This prayer calls to mind the Christian dream—the vision of the kingdom of God proclaimed by Jesus—and the values, summarized in the Beatitudes, that will make that dream a reality.

In session 3, we will take the short view of the future. The discussion centers on the day in, day out struggle to pursue one's dream in a time of option shock. That session will present a concrete, practical process of decision-making that will help the young people deal with the many difficult choices confronting them—whether to attend college, how to select a potential career, how to resolve difficulties in personal relationships, and so on.

It should be noted here that the topic of values is implicit in all of the discussions in sessions 2 and 3. A separate discussion on the nature and role of values in personal development, on deciding what values will guide one's decision-making, and so on, would be very apropos at this point in the program. However, there simply is not enough time to include it within the confines of the proposed SHARING IV schedule. It should also be mentioned that the SHARING II manual contains two sessions on values discussed in terms of Christian morality. (See SHARING II, sessions 9 and 10.) Should you wish to include some discussion of values at this point, you might refer to that material. Reading or rereading that material might also be helpful preparation for you in leading discussions during these two sessions of SHARING IV.

Special note: In the SHARING IV Program, I offer the option of having the young people develop their own retreat rather than providing them with a prepackaged one. The necessary steps in planning the retreat include organizing a planning team, a group of student volunteers who work under the direction of the adult leader. The planning team handles all the details involved in organizing and conducting the retreat. *If you intend to conduct a student-planned retreat, it is essential that you begin preparation at this point in the program.* The section of the SHARING IV manual covering the retreat and its development begins on page 000. You will need to thoroughly review that material before this session and then briefly explain the process to the students as part of the comments before the closing prayer. Ask for volunteers to serve on the planning team, noting that others can join later if they want to think about it for a week or two. Then meet with the volunteers after this session, using the guidelines given on page 00.

Procedure

A. Welcome and Opening Prayer
(10–15 minutes, depending on size of group)

1. I suggest that you establish an opening prayer ritual, a pattern for opening the sessions that comes to be expected, and even looked forward to, by the young people. Rituals have an intriguing power to give a group a sense of shared meaning and solidarity. We mistakenly believe that young people are always demanding something new and different, perhaps based on their common complaint, "the Mass is the same thing over and over again." Young people, though, like all of us, truly need and enjoy ritual. Their lives are loaded with it—from their "in" language to the school song at athletic events. Try changing the menu at a major holiday family meal and see who complains most loudly!

2. The prayer ritual that I propose includes two elements introduced in the closing prayer of session 1—the plants that were given to the young people and the reading by John Powell. In addition, I suggest that you ask each individual to identify one way in which they feel they have grown as a person during the previous week.

3. Prepare the setting for the prayer ritual before the participants' arrival. It would be helpful, but not essential, to conduct this and other prayer experiences in a room other than the one in which the rest of the session takes place. The gesture of moving to and from that room for prayer will heighten the students' awareness of the special nature of that sacred time together.

If the group size allows it (ten students or fewer), arrange the symbolic plants in a circular fashion on the floor, two feet apart from each other. In the center of the circle, place an attractive pitcher of water, one or two large candles, and perhaps a Bible. (In the SHARING III Program, the Bible is formally installed in the room and then used regularly in each session. Using and displaying the same Bible may help the students relate and connect SHARING III experiences with those of SHARING IV.) If possible, dim the lights for prayer.

4. When all the young people have arrived, invite them to gather for prayer and ask them to sit on the floor behind their plant. (If some members of the group are absent, allow their spaces to remain empty and visible; that is, do not remove their plants. Simply mention that those individuals are still part of the group and that they should be remembered in prayer at this time. If someone is repeatedly absent or chooses to drop out of the group, their plant can be removed as part of a future prayer experience. This should be done without criticism or condemnation and simply as an acknowledgment that the person has chosen not to remain with the group.) Distribute the prayer cards containing the reading from John Powell used in session 1.

5. Light the candle to signal the beginning of prayer. Then share the sign of the cross and offer a brief spontaneous prayer of your own, perhaps thanking God for the opportunity to again gather as a group of people committed to supporting and caring for one another. An opening song, either recorded or sung, is optional. See the SHARING music guides in the program director's manual for suggested songs.

6. Recall for the young people the symbol of the plant, a reminder of the ongoing process of human growth and development throughout the program. Tell them that you would like to share a ritual involving the plants that will be used to begin all future sessions. Call for a moment of silence during which the participants should think of one thing that happened in the preceding week that helped them to become better people—more caring, happy, thoughtful. It might have been a conversation with a friend, a book or an article that they read, a scene from nature that impressed them, a letter, or anything else that they feel in some way helped to make them more human. Note that the purpose of sharing an insight about personal growth is not just a filler for the prayer ritual. It is hoped that this practice will continually affirm in a prayerful way the reality we want to stress strongly in this session: that we are people capable of constant growth and change (even more capable than the symbolic plants we possess), and that we can and should assume personal responsibility for guiding that growth in the direction of our dream.

Explain that, after all the students have thought in silence for a moment, one young person should take the pitcher of water from the middle of the circle and slowly water his or her plant. While doing so, the person names the event that he or she has experienced, using the following simple formula: "Lord, for (*name the life-enhancing experience*), I thank you." The pitcher is then passed to the person to the right, who repeats the ritual. Continue in this fashion until all the participants have had their turn.

Note well: Make it clear, especially this first time, that it is not necessary for the young people to say something out loud if they do not wish to. They can simply water their plants and say the prayers silently. However, encourage them to share if they can, so that all the participants might recognize the many ways in which an individual can grow and so that everyone might thank God for what each person has experienced. When it becomes clear that the ritual is simple and nonthreatening, even the reluctant individuals should gradually participate in future sessions.

7. Next, ask the students to slowly recite in unison the selection from John Powell, noting that it, too, speaks of the growing and constantly changing nature of human life. End the ritual with a brief, spontaneous prayer of your own and the sign of the cross. The students can keep their prayer cards until the end of the session. If necessary or desirable, blow out the candle before moving to the area where you will continue with the session.

B. Leader Input: Finding a Dream to Guide Us
(5–10 minutes)

Note: The time allotment depends on whether you need to include a comment on Arthur Chickering's work.

Share the following thoughts in a relaxed, conversational manner:

At our first session together, we talked quite a lot about the tasks that you face as you enter young adulthood. Using the film about the mountain climber, we reflected on the many challenges that we confront in life and how we often must face those alone. You spent some time imagining your life five years from now and identified some of the common concerns of your age-group. We then briefly looked at a list of those young adult tasks as they have been identified by one theorist, Arthur Chickering. (Include a brief summary of Chickering's work here if you could not do so in session 1, perhaps using Student Handout 1–B from that session to guide you.) We concluded our first session with a prayer experience on the theme of accepting and enthusiastically embracing the challenges that await us, trusting that our God is with us.

Beginning with this session, and then continuing on throughout the remainder of this program, I want to discuss some of the young adult tasks that you face, exploring together ways in which each of you can successfully and enjoyably navigate your way through this time of your life. Each of us must grasp an important point implied in that metaphor of navigation: Though life throws a lot of events at us over which we have no control, we can still decide how we are going to respond to life; we can take charge of who we are and what we are to become. If that were not the case, if life just happened to us and we had no control at all, there would be no sense in gathering like this. We could just sit in front of the television and wait for the next event to happen to us. It is possible, though, to assume a vital measure of control over our lives, and only in doing so can we find any real fulfillment as persons.

Abraham Maslow, a United States psychologist (1908–1970) who did a lot of work in human needs and motivation, suggested that most people set their sights too low in life or fail to develop the skills they need to achieve the worthwhile goals that they have set. He has an interesting term for this characteristic, calling it the *psychopathology of the average.* Maslow said that many people suffer from the sickness of accepting the average as their standard for living. I don't want that to happen to you. Certainly Jesus had something else in mind when he spoke of what it means to be human!

What does it take to keep us from settling for the average in life? Some theorists suggest that each of us, particularly during young adulthood, has to develop a *dream.* By this dream, they don't mean just a fantasy or a casual daydream. Rather, they mean a vision of what we want to become so that we have something reasonably clear to strive for in our life. This dream is more than pure fantasy, yet perhaps not as fully thought out as a specific plan for our life. It is eloquently reflected in Martin Luther King, Jr.'s, famous speech "I Have a Dream."

King's vision of life was real enough to him—and to many of us as well—to generate excitement and enthusiasm. Like King, each of us must find a dream that can give our life meaning and direction.

Our personal dream comes from a variety of sources: It comes, in part, from within us, as a response to our own internal longings, abilities, talents, motives, and fears. Our dream is also a product of our interactions with people who have been influential, either positively or negatively, in our lives. We may be influenced, for example, by a very loving and generous uncle or by a grandmother who was ruthless and only concerned with accumulating money. Finally, our dream arises out of our social settings, both past and present. Someone raised in a ghetto and stung by poverty may build an entire dream on getting out of the ghetto and succeeding in society.

It may be too early in your life for your dream to have taken a clear shape. You may have bits and pieces of it, hints about those things you think will bring you fulfillment and happiness. Perhaps you've not consciously considered the future or the shape that your life will take—though most people your age spend some time playing with all the possibilities the future holds for them. The point I wish to make in this session is that a dream—a vision of what your life can be—is important to your future happiness and deserves your time and attention.

It has been said that if we don't know where we're going, we'll have a hard time getting there. That may sound funny, but it's loaded with wisdom. I want to spend some time together building and reflecting on the dream that will give meaning and direction to your life. We will begin with an activity that you can do on your own, in quiet reflection. Quiet time alone isn't boring when we're spending it thinking about ourselves. Then we'll share our ideas with one another for the rest of the session.

C. Two Optional Self-reflection Exercises
(30 minutes, including group discussion)

See Student Handout 2–A following this session outline.

At this point, give the young people a brief period of private reflection on the dreams that are likely already taking shape in their life. Two exercises are suggested for this, and you can select either one or both. One of the two may appeal to you more, and you can offer it to all the students. Another option is to split the group in two and ask each half to take one of the two exercises. If you choose to use both, it may take more time and you will have to adjust the schedule for the rest of the session accordingly.

The two activities offered in this session are adapted from the work of Sidney B. Simon. The original version of these activities can be found in his book *Meeting Yourself Halfway* (Niles, IL: Argus Communications, 1974. See pp. 1–4.) The book includes thirty-one helpful exercises, nearly all of which relate directly to many of the themes in SHARING IV. I considered including one of these activities for each of the sessions in this program as optional take-home activities (not *homework*). However, I resisted this, primarily because I wanted to avoid the notion of homework. If your group is interested in additional self-reflection, consider having the students choose activities from Simon's book to complete on their own.

Option 1: Lifeline

This activity includes reflection on the potentially grim reality that all of us are going to die. The focus of the activity is not on the inevitability of death but rather on the insights into life that the acknowledgment of death provokes.

1. Give each student (or all those selected to complete this particular exercise) a piece of paper and a pencil. Then give them the following directions:

a. Draw a line across your paper, and place a dot at each end of the line. The dot at the left represents your birthday. Write the date of your birth above that dot. The dot at the right of the line represents your death. Above that dot, write your best guess of the number of years you expect to live. You can base your guess on intuition, the average life span of your past family members, and so on. After writing above the dot the number of years that you expect to live, write the estimated date of your death *under* the dot on the right end of the line.

b. Now place a dot that represents your present age between your birth and estimated date of death. Write today's date above the new dot. Reflect for a moment on the relative span of years between those you have already lived and those presumably yet to come. (Assuming that many of the students, if not all, are projecting reasonably long lives, they will see that only a relatively small amount of the precious gift of life has been used up, that each of them has a long span of time in which to define and then live out their dreams.)

2. Ask the students to complete the next part of the activity on their own in quiet reflection. If your

house or facility allows it, give them the freedom to move to places where they can find some privacy for 10–15 minutes. When they find their place, they should do two things:

a. **To the left of today's date on the lifeline, write down a few simple words about what you feel are your major attributes or accomplishments in life to this point.** (By way of example, they might write "good student," "loyal friend," or "sense of humor.")

b. **To the right of today's date, write some things that you would like to accomplish before you die.** (These need not be—indeed, should not be—based on the expectations of other people or on what society deems "success." Tell the students to note accomplishments that will bring them personal fulfillment and happiness in life *as they define those qualities for themselves.*)

3. Assure the students that no one will see what they write on their paper; it is a completely private exercise. Give them 10 minutes on their own, check on their progress, and then give them an additional 5 minutes if they need it. When time is up, gather the students for a brief discussion of the activity. Emphasize that their notes are personal and need not be shared—unless, of course, someone wishes to share what he or she wrote. Invite such sharing, and afterward, lead a brief discussion on the activity in general, using directive questions such as the following:

- Why is it difficult for some people to acknowledge the reality of inevitable death in our life?
- What are some benefits of realizing and accepting the reality of death?
- Were any of those benefits reflected in the exercise you just completed? Can you give some examples?
- This exercise was intended to give you a sense of your dream, your personal vision of what will make your life meaningful. Can anyone give examples of how the exercise did that for him or her?
- Try to identify any major insight into life that you gained from this activity.

Option 2: Rest in Peace

This activity also uses reflection on death as a stimulus for getting in touch with the meaning of life. Rather than using a lifeline to do so, it uses the graphic image of gravestones.

1. Give each student a copy of Student Handout 2–A, "Rest in Peace." The handout is self-explanatory. On the gravestone on the left side of the handout, the young people are to write the current date and then complete their obituary as they might read if they were to die today. On the right side, they are to write the date ten years from now (that is, after they have presumedly completed most of the tasks of young adulthood that you have been discussing) and then complete their obituary as they think they might read at that time. Give them 15–20 minutes to complete this private reflection.

2. When you have gathered them back together, lead a brief discussion, using the bulleted questions listed under number 3 of option 1.

D. Break (10 minutes)

E. Exercise: The Dream of a Lifetime (45 minutes)

See Student Handout 2–B following this session outline.

1. Student Handout 2–B, "The Dream of a Lifetime," provides the materials needed for this exercise. Make one copy of the handout for each student in your group. Then cut each handout into a set of individual slips of paper by cutting along the dotted lines. Separate the last slip, the large one entitled "I Have a Dream," from the other eighteen smaller ones, and keep it from the students until the time indicated in the directions below. Bind together the eighteen slips that contain the life goals, using a rubber band or paper clip.

2. Give each young person one set of the slips of paper containing the life goals. Then make the following comments:

The directions for this exercise are simple, but their execution may be difficult. The slips of paper you've just received contain eighteen different life goals—simple statements of possible major goals in life that you may want to include in your dream for a fulfilling, happy life. Simply organize them in front of you on the floor in terms of their importance to *you*. Place the highest ranked goal at the top of your list, the second highest below it, all the way down to the goal with the least importance to you, which will be placed at the bottom of the row of slips. You will have to make some difficult decisions along the way, but do the best you can.

***Please note this important point:* You are to rank the items as honestly as you can in terms of**

what you truly believe will make you happy and fulfilled in life. There are no *right* answers to this exercise, no order in which you *should* rank them. Everyone's list will be different. The point of the exercise is to help you shape your dream, not to test you. You will have 10–15 minutes to complete this part of the exercise; then I will give you further directions.

3. Allow the students to separate from one another so that they can work without others knowing how they are ranking their items. Give them 10 minutes to work, then circulate among them with the "I Have a Dream" slips of paper. Give one of these larger slips to the students who have completed their ranking, explaining that they are to follow the directions indicated on the slip. If some students need more time to complete the ranking, give them another 5 minutes before asking them to complete the next step.

The large slip of paper asks the young people to look at the top four life goals they have identified in their ranking and, with those four goals, to construct a statement of their own dream similar to Martin Luther King, Jr.'s, famous speech "I Have a Dream." They are not expected to be as eloquent as Dr. King, though they can express their life goals poetically if they wish. In any case, they have just 10 minutes for this part of the exercise; then they will be called back to the group.

4. When you have gathered the young people back together, explain that values clarification studies show that a primary indicator of the true values in our lives is a willingness to publicly affirm them, to let others know what those values are. Emphasize, however, that you also want to respect the students' privacy in this matter and that no one has to share their dream if they do not want to. Then invite those students who wish to do so to read their dream to the group. Do not evaluate what they share; simply listen to each dream, perhaps offer a compliment, and then move on to another dream.

Be alert to the need for an additional 15 minutes after the dream sharing if you are to complete the session as described below. You may have to move directly from the sharing of dreams to the closing comments and prayer.

5. *If* time permits (e.g., if few of the young people are willing to share their stated dreams), discuss the activity in a general way along the following lines:

a. **Was it easy or difficult to decide which of the life goals should be ranked as the first four or five? For those who found it difficult, what does that say to you? For those who found it quite easy, what does that say to you?**

b. **Did anyone find that two or more goals seemed to be in conflict with each other—that is, where achieving one goal implied giving up another? Can you offer any examples?** (After students have a chance to respond, make the following comment:) **In the real world, this conflict of values is at the heart of many personal and even international conflicts. For example, achieving world peace may include limiting the freedoms of individuals. An individual may want to achieve a sense of accomplishment in life but will have to give up a so-called comfortable life in order to do so. In our society, many individuals appear to achieve a comfortable life at the expense of their self-respect or inner harmony. Part of the task of building a dream is to develop a master plan that sorts out and integrates these life goals so that they are both in harmony with one another and attainable.**

c. Next, have the students define the notion of living the good life or, put more simply, achieving happiness in life. You may have to clarify this by suggesting they try, in light of the activity, to complete the following sentence: "For me, being happy means . . ." The response implied by this exercise would be something like this: "Being happy means making decisions and always acting in life in accord with my goals, choosing those things that are in harmony with my goals, and avoiding those actions, attitudes, or beliefs that are in conflict with what I want to be in life."

6. Close the activity with your own statement about achieving happiness in life. Sum up the ultimate purpose of taking on the admittedly difficult task of articulating the dreams we wish to guide us: that this is the only way that we can avoid the "psychopathology of the average," of passively allowing life to happen to us; that we must identify what we want out of life and then live according to that vision if we hope to find real happiness.

F. Closing Comments Before Prayer
(5 minutes)

1. Inform the students that the next session covers one of the major skills needed for achieving our dreams—namely, the ability to make good decisions as we move through life. As they enter into the next stage of their life, the young people will be confronted by some of the most important and difficult decisions that they will ever have to make—

decisions about lifestyles, careers, personal relationships—all of which will have lifelong effects on the pursuit of their dream. In session 3, the discussion includes concrete strategies for making those decisions, if not more easily, at least with a better chance of achieving satisfying results.

2. Explain the retreat planning process to the students and ask for volunteers for the planning team.

G. Closing Prayer (10–15 minutes, depending on components selected)

See Student Handout 2-C following this session outline.

1. This closing prayer centers on two of the fundamental elements in what could be called the Christian dream, the vision of life proclaimed and lived by Jesus. Those two elements are Jesus' proclamation of the kingdom of God and his teaching of the Beatitudes, those qualities of the human heart that will make the kingdom of God a reality. The prayer service involves many of the young people as readers and requires that each student have a copy of Student Handout 2-C, "Prayer Service: The Dream of Jesus."

You can divide the responsibility for the readings any way you wish. You can involve a few students who are comfortable with public reading, or you can ask each student in the group to do just a short reading—perhaps one of the Beatitudes with its brief descriptive statement. If you involve all the students, a way to prepare the readings is to use a highlighter pen and highlight different statements on each copy of the prayer handout. Students then read in order the section highlighted on their individual handout. This has the attractive effect of the separate readings jumping around the room during the service. Use whatever approach best serves your need or preference. (Note: Some of the readings include a parenthetical statement of their source for copyright purposes. Tell the readers that they do not have to include those citations when they read their section.)

You may wish to also include musical selections in the service (e.g., at the beginning of the service, after the reading from Mark's Gospel on the kingdom, or at the end of the service). Available time will dictate how much music you choose to include. See the SHARING music guides in the director's manual, particularly the one for religious music, for suggested songs.

2. Gather the young people in the space that you are using for prayer. Light some candles as a sign of the beginning of prayer. Introduce the service by sharing the following thoughts:

We have spent our time together this evening reflecting on the dream that each of us is seeking, that vision of life that we feel will lead us to personal fulfillment and happiness. As Christians, we know that Jesus clearly had his own vision of the meaning of life, one so powerful and central that he was willing to die rather than deny it. He summarized his own dream by calling it "the kingdom of God." We discussed this at some length in the SHARING III Program when we defined Jesus' understanding of the kingdom this way: The kingdom of God is made real when God's passionate and unconditional love reigns over the hearts of people, and as a consequence of that, a new social order takes root in the world, one based on the love of persons for one another. (For a thorough discussion of the kingdom of God, see SHARING III, pp. 103–107.)

Jesus also talked at length about the qualities of the human heart that are required if the vision of the kingdom is to become a reality. We have a beautiful summary of those qualities in what we call the Beatitudes. The Beatitudes are part of that marvelous collection of Jesus' sayings and teachings in Matthew's Gospel called the Sermon on the Mount. In this prayer service, we are going to center on these words of Jesus. We will first listen to a reading on the kingdom of God. Next, we will pause for silent prayer (and, perhaps, listen to a song). **We will then respond to the reading by doing a shared reading of the Beatitudes, each one followed by a brief comment taken from the writings of saints, scriptural scholars, or theologians.**

In preparation for the prayer, let's make the sign of the cross together. Now, listen again to the words of Jesus, spoken nearly two thousand years ago, words that can still speak to us today—in fact, *must* be heard today if there is to be any hope of a world in which our dreams can become realities.

The leader or a prepared student now reads the passage from Mark's Gospel, included on the handout for this prayer service. After the reading, pause for a moment of silent prayer or music.

3. At this point, begin the shared reading of the Beatitudes as presented on the prayer service handout. If you wish, you can incorporate music, silence, or your comments. At the conclusion of the service, simply close with the sign of the cross and extinguish the candles.

Things to Keep in Mind

Regarding the Closing Prayer Experience

You may wish to incorporate into your prayer experience a recording of Martin Luther King's famous speech "I Have a Dream," certainly one of the most moving and memorable public statements of recent times. The speech is available on each of three cassette tapes produced by Motown Records: *I Have a Dream, Free at Last,* and *March on Washington.* The tapes are available from Tower Records, Department 9B, 2525 Jones Street, San Francisco, CA 94133. Phone 415-885-0500. The price of each tape at the time of this writing was $3.99. You may also check with your local or diocesan libraries before ordering to see if they have the recording. Also note that this speech was suggested for use in session 15 of SHARING II. The leader of that program in your parish may have already purchased the recorded speech. If you choose to use this speech during this session, time may become a problem for you. Consider dropping the reading about the kingdom and replacing it with Dr. King's speech. Then use the Beatitude reading as a response.

For Evaluation

1. Review your experience of the opening prayer ritual. Do you feel that the ritual will be effective if repeated as a regular feature of your sessions? Why or why not? Adjust the service as you wish to have it better meet the needs of your group.

2. Evaluate your use of the optional self-reflection activities, the lifeline and gravestone exercises. If you used both, did one work better than the other? Might you want to use just that one in the future? If you used one of the two, schedule a future use of the other one so that you can compare the results. Note your reactions to both in your notebook.

3. The "Dream of a Lifetime" exercise requires considerable private, personal reflection by the students. Were the young people able to handle this reflection well? If there were difficulties with it, try to identify their causes and note possible alternatives.

4. The closing prayer experience is an unusual one for the SHARING Program, requiring much more reading than is normally the case. It is hoped that this approach will succeed precisely because it is unique, but it does require the ability to read well publicly. Evaluate your experience with the service. Are there ways in which it could be improved? Would it help to select readers in advance and have them rephrase their part? Note your thoughts in your notebook.

5. Were the "Teacher Goals" and "Student Intellectual Behavioral/Objectives" for this session achieved?

STUDENT HANDOUT 2-A

Rest in Peace

RIP

Here lies _____
who died this day, _____.
The deceased is survived by _____
_____.
At the time of death, the deceased was best known for _____
_____.
He or she will be remembered by _____
for _____.
The deceased always hoped that he or she _____
_____.
As it turned out, _____.
Those wishing to honor the memory of the deceased, should
_____.
On his or her deathbed, the final words of the deceased were
_____.

REST IN PEACE

RIP

Here lies _____
who died this day, _____.
The deceased is survived by _____
_____.
At the time of death, the deceased was best known for _____
_____.
He or she will be remembered by _____
for _____.
The deceased always hoped that he or she _____
_____.
As it turned out, _____.
Those wishing to honor the memory of the deceased, should
_____.
On his or her deathbed, the final words of the deceased were
_____.

REST IN PEACE

Reproduction permission is granted if you wish to make copies for classroom use.
The photocopy master for this handout is found at the back of this manual.

STUDENT HANDOUT 2–B

The Dream of a Lifetime

Note to the leader: The following are statements of eighteen possible life goals. Make one copy of the handout for each student in your group. Then divide them into individual slips of paper by cutting along the dotted lines. Bind the individual slips together with clips or rubber bands in separate packets, each containing all eighteen life goals. Give each student a full packet. Note the large slip of paper at the end titled "I Have a Dream." Distribute that slip to the young people only **after** they have completed their work with the life goals, as described in the directions for this activity given in the session plan.

A COMFORTABLE LIFE, a prosperous life

AN EXCITING LIFE, a stimulating, active life

A SENSE OF ACCOMPLISHMENT, lasting contribution

A WORLD AT PEACE, free of war and conflict

A WORLD OF BEAUTY, beauty of nature and the arts

EQUALITY, equal opportunity for all

FAMILY SECURITY, taking care of loved ones

FREEDOM, independence, free choice

HAPPINESS, contentedness

INNER HARMONY, freedom from inner conflict

MATURE LOVE, sexual and spiritual intimacy

NATIONAL SECURITY, protection from attack

PLEASURE, an enjoyable, leisurely life

SALVATION, saved, eternal life

SELF-RESPECT, self-esteem

SOCIAL RECOGNITION, respect, admiration

TRUE FRIENDSHIP, close companionship

WISDOM, a mature understanding of life

I Have a Dream

Now take your highest rated life goals—using at least the top four of them—and below write a statement of your dream, modeled somewhat on the form of Martin Luther King, Jr's, famous statement of his own vision.

I _____ have a dream, that one day _____.

I have a dream, that _____
_____.

I have a dream, that _____
_____.

I have a dream, that _____
_____.

Reproduction permission is granted if you wish to make copies for classroom use.
The photocopy master for this handout is found at the back of this manual.

The Future Is in My Hands: Turning Dreams into Realities

STUDENT HANDOUT 2-C

Prayer Service: The Dream of Jesus

Reader 1: A reading from the Gospel of Mark:

One of the scribes . . . put a further question to him, "Which is the first of all the commandments?" Jesus replied, "This is the first: Listen, Israel, the Lord our God is the one, only Lord, and you must love the Lord your God with all your heart, with all your soul, with all your mind and with all your strength. The second is this: You must love your neighbour as yourself. There is no commandment greater than these." The scribe said to him, "Well spoken, Master; what you have said is true, that he is one and there is no other. To love him with all your heart, with all your understanding and strength, and to love your neighbour as yourself, this is far more important than any burnt offering or sacrifice." Jesus, seeing how wisely he had spoken, said, "You are not far from the kingdom of God." (Mark 12:28–34)

Leader: Let us now respond to Jesus' call to help build up the kingdom of God through love of God and neighbor by prayerfully reading and reflecting on the Beatitudes, Jesus' wonderful description of the hearts of those people who will be called "blessed."

Reader 2: Blessed are the poor in spirit, for theirs is the kingdom of God.

The spirit of poverty consists . . . in seeing the universe and everything in it (ourselves included) as held in existence from moment to moment by nothing save God's continuing will to hold it there and . . . in setting our hearts upon God and loving Him above all things. (John Wu)

Reader 3: Blessed are the meek, the gentle, for they shall have the earth for their heritage.

A first step to inner gentleness is thus to gratefully love myself as a unique gift and to admit and accept my weakness. Gentleness with self is possible only when I recognize and "own" all the vulnerability of the treasure I am. I must be able to look at myself with a forgiving eye. (Adrian van Kaam)

Reader 4: Blessed are those who mourn, for they shall be comforted.

When things go well it is possible to live for years on the surface of things; but when sorrow comes a person is driven to the deep things of life, and, if one accepts it aright, a new strength and beauty enter into one's soul. (William Barclay)

Reader 5: Blessed are those who hunger and thirst for justice, for they shall be filled.

Maybe our children, our husband, our wife are not hungry, are not naked, are not homeless. But are you sure there is no one there who feels unwanted, unloved? Let us look straight into our own families. For love begins at home. We don't have to think of numbers. We can love one person at a time, serve one person at a time. (Mother Teresa)

Reader 6: Blessed are the merciful, for they shall receive mercy.

Be kind and merciful. Let no one ever come to you without coming away better and happier. Be the living expression of God's kindness: kindness in your face, kindness in your eyes, kindness in your smile, kindness in your warm greeting. . . . To the children, to the poor, to all who suffer and are lonely, give always a happy smile; give them not only your care, but also your heart. (Mother Teresa)

Reader 7: Blessed are those who are persecuted for the cause of right; theirs is the kingdom of heaven.

It is not likely that death awaits us because of our loyalty to the Christian faith. But . . . mockery awaits the person who practices Christian love and forgiveness. . . . Christ still needs his witnesses; he needs those who are prepared, not so much to die for him as to live for him. (William Barclay)

Reader 8: Blessed are the single-hearted, for they shall see God.

Persons [who are pure in heart] have no weapon in their hands, no defensive wall around their heart. They open their arms to embrace, knowing that one may be crucified when his or her arms are open, but unable to approach others in any other manner. (Anthony Padovano)

Reader 9: Blessed are the peacemakers, for they shall be called the children of God.

We all long for heaven where God is, but we have it in our power to be in heaven with him at this very moment. But being happy with him now means: loving as he loves, helping as he helps, giving as he gives, serving as he serves. . . . (Mother Teresa)

Leader: Lord, we pray that the Spirit of Jesus will find a home in our hearts, so that we may be witnesses of God's love to all who meet us. We ask this in the name of Jesus, whom we believe to be alive and with each of us at this moment and always.

All: Amen.

Reproduction permission is granted if you wish to make copies for classroom use.
The photocopy master for this handout is found at the back of this manual.

Session 3

Choices: Deciding How to Decide

Teacher Goals

To awaken the young people to the need for effective decision-making skills as they approach the developmental tasks of young adulthood; to introduce them to such skills; to clarify the contribution that Christian faith can make to sound decision-making.

Student Intellectual/Behavioral Objectives

That the young people acknowledge the need for strong decision-making skills and begin to identify and develop such skills; that they gain a rudimentary sense of Christian discernment as a faith-informed approach to decision-making.

Main Ideas

In the "Main Ideas" section of session 2, I noted that psychologists and sociologists speak of the relatively new phenomenon *option shock*, which young adults experience to a particularly intense degree. Today's youth, like the generations before them, face challenging decisions in all the major facets of human life—careers, families, lifestyles, and so on. The big difference is that today each of these facets hold innumerable options from which to choose, certainly far more than were offered to previous generations. When we add decisions about sexuality, drug abuse, and more, it becomes increasingly clear what option shock is all about. People confronted with such tension-producing options—especially people who lack the experience and the skills with which to choose their options in a healthful way—attempt to escape these difficult situations by simply not making any decision at all. Hence, option shock.

We who try to nurture the personal and faith development of young people cannot substantially change the world in which they live. Young people necessarily face difficult situations. What we can and must do is provide them with the skills they need to handle their world creatively and healthfully. We have accomplished part of that task by awakening our groups to the challenges they face as they experience young adulthood. Having done that, we will try in this session to provide them with some of the decision-making skills that they will need as they confront the issues of careers, lifestyles, and relationships head-on.

Although there is no magic formula for effective decision-making, the literature on the subject shows that a common approach to making sound decisions has emerged over the years. This session will introduce a decision-making process that incorporates the major principles emerging from the literature. We will then apply those principles to an artificial—but, it is hoped, realistic—case study of a difficult situation that the group will create. Allowing the group to create its own case study will ensure a discussion that is relevant to them. A brief comment and a prayer experience on the nature of Christian discernment closes the session.

Without a doubt, mature Christians should make critical decisions in their lives in a manner unique from that of people for whom the Christian faith is unknown or meaningless. You might even wonder why this entire session does not concentrate solely on Christian discernment and leave to others the secular approaches to the subject. Actually, I had to ask myself the same question in developing this material. Here are a few of my reasons for centering the session on good decision-making rather than on Christian discernment.

First, it strikes me that many young people, particularly those exposed to a fundamentalist bent, might misunderstand the very nature of Christian discernment. They may see it as simply turning their lives over to God, allowing the Spirit to somehow guide them in their choices and trusting that whatever happens as a result of those choices is God's will. Others might use essentially the same approach by just praying for God's guidance and then trusting that, whatever choices they make and whatever their effects, they are in tune with the will of God. When taken to an extreme, this approach strikes me as a kind of baptized option shock, a cop-out on personal responsibility in the name of faith in God. People using these approaches may not necessarily be living their life for God; they may, in fact, be trying to let God live their life for them so that they won't have to take responsibility for the difficult decisions that mature living demands.

Second, the issue of readiness on the part of the young people in our groups must be considered. Presumedly, we are not dealing with people whose faith is fully formed and already a central core in their lives. We *are* trying to nurture such faith, but we cannot presuppose its existence in our young people. Discernment is a skill that comes with depth of faith. It could be irrelevant to those for whom Christian commitment is still an option to consider rather than an embraced reality.

Finally, the Incarnation of Jesus has taught us that the human and the divine are inextricably interwoven and wed to each other, not at war. The SHARING Program is committed to the notions that the sacred can be found in and through the secular and that one of our chief responsibilities as Christians is to see all reality through the eyes of faith. In this case, we can take an apparently secular approach to decision-making and share it within the context of our own Christian values, beliefs, and practices. In fact, it can be reasonably argued that whenever a committed Christian follows the decision-making process suggested here, he or she *will* be involved in the process of Christian discernment because his or her own Christian values will permeate and influence each step of the process.

Enough of this heady theologizing. (I just can't resist sometimes!) One final comment about the methodology involved in this session: Much of this session takes the form of a *guided conversation* rather than a clearly identifiable series of exercises and activities that is characteristic of most of the other sessions in the program. Much of this session relies on an exchange of ideas between the young people and the adult leader; that is, the leader asks a question or poses a thought for reflection, the group responds, and then the next step of the session *grows out of* that response. So you will have to be a bit more flexible and spontaneous in directing this session than is normally the case. However, as usual, the directions provided are so thorough that you should have no difficulty.

Procedure

A. Welcome and Opening Prayer (10–15 minutes, depending on size of group)

For the opening prayer, repeat the ritual described in session 2, perhaps adjusting it as decided in your response to evaluation question 1 in that session.

B. Guided Discussion on the Need for Effective Decision-making Skills (about 30 minutes)

1. This discussion activity is a clear example of the unique nature of this session, as mentioned in the "Main Ideas" above. As the adult leader, you are asked to guide the young people in a logical, step-by-step fashion to a recognition of the great need for sound decision-making skills as they confront the challenges of young adulthood.

The quality or depth of the discussion will vary from group to group, so it is a little difficult to project the amount of time this discussion will take. You will have to be somewhat flexible in your guidance of the session. The time allowed here, in keeping with past practice in SHARING, is quite tight, assuring you that you will not be faced with excess time at the end of the session. If your group is particularly talkative and animated, you will have to restrict this discussion or be prepared to cut back later in the session. Because this discussion is intended primarily as an introductory one, I encourage you to take no more than 35–40 minutes so that the important information to be shared later in the session is not left out.

2. **Leader comment:** Before presenting the following material, be sure to read and then reflect carefully on the major points provided. Paraphrase the material in your own words and deliver it in a conversational style. Avoid dwelling on details that would make your presentation sound preachy or artificial.

So far in our discussions we've considered two major themes: In the first session, we talked about the major tasks that you face as you enter into your twenties, including decisions about personal relationships, lifestyles, and careers. Though these issues can be downright frightening on some levels, I hope that you look forward to facing them with a sense of excitement and enthusiasm.

In our last session, we talked about the importance of creating for yourself a "dream," or vision, of what you want your life to be like—with the conviction that if you don't know where you're going, you'll have a hard time getting there. I'm reminded of a scene in *Alice's Adventures in Wonderland.* **When Alice was deciding where to go, she asked the Cheshire cat,**

> "Would you tell me, please, which way I ought to go from here?"
>
> "That depends a good deal on where you want to get to," said the Cat.
>
> "I don't much care where—" said Alice.
>
> "Then, it doesn't matter which way you go," said the Cat.

All of what we have been talking about—as well as all those topics that we will discuss during this program—will be interesting and valuable only to people who care about where they're going in life. I presume that you care or you wouldn't be giving up your leisure time to be here. However, it's important to point out how central to this discussion your own level of caring is. A lot of hard work will go into the pursuit of your dream, especially if that dream includes high ideals and deeply held values. It won't be easy to move toward your dream, but it will be worth all the effort.

A second presumption—one that's closely related to the conviction that you care about your future—is that you want to have reasonable control over that future, that you want to take charge of your life and assume responsibility for who you are and who you will become. This presumption may seem obvious, but it's important to state it clearly and consciously. Once you acknowledge that you want to take responsibility for your life and determine how it will unfold, you will begin to recognize the central importance of our discussion this evening.

In this session, we will be talking about the essential skill of making good decisions. A "good decision" is somewhat relative, because what will be a good decision for me may not be a good one for you. For the sake of definition, let's say that *a* *good decision is basically one that brings with it satisfying results.* Now, in light of our discussion in the last session, let's take that definition one step further. We can then say that *a good decision is one that is in touch with and reflects your dream and that moves you closer to the attainment of that dream.* Keep in mind also that good dreams are relative; your dream is most likely not my dream. What is true for all of us, though, is that we all want to make decisions that move us closer to our dream.

A quick example: If my dream includes a commitment to relationships that are based on personal integrity and mutual respect, a good decision in my life at this point is one aimed at building these kinds of relationships. I can't hope to use people for my own pleasure at age twenty and then count on having a satisfying relationship when I'm thirty. I can grow and change, of course, and simply luck out. However, my chances of attaining my dream are greatly enhanced if I develop ways of thinking and behaving now that are in tune with that dream.

Another example: Perhaps one part of my dream is that I want to be successful professionally. This future success will likely demand that I decide now to make the sacrifices necessary for doing well in school. Or, maybe I am committed to being a good parent to my future children. If so, I will have to begin now to develop the skills that will make that possible, skills such as learning to listen well or to empathize with the feelings of others.

All of this implies that we have to learn to make good decisions in all areas of our life, whether they are decisions about future careers, values we will hold, difficult moral issues, or even what we eat and drink (presuming one part of our dream is to have a healthy body). So this session deals with what goes into making good, dream-achieving decisions.

3. At this point, pass out a pencil and a small piece of paper or an index card to each young person. Tell them to spend a few minutes in quiet reflection on the last five years of their life. Ask them to try to list five major decisions they made during that time. Describe a *major decision* as being any decision that they remember that long. It is not important that it be earth-shattering or that anyone else would think of it as particularly significant. All that matters is that it be a difficult decision that they clearly remember working through, either on their own or with the help of others. Evidence of such a decision would be the recollection of having asked the agonizing question, "What am I going to do?" in reaction to a situation in their life. Finally, note that *they will not have to share their list with the group.*

It is possible that after giving these directions you will not have to explain any further. It is best if you can avoid offering examples that might skew their responses. If, however, the students indicate a need for examples, offer one or more of the following situations:

- deciding whether to smoke, be it tobacco or marijuana
- deciding what school they would attend
- deciding with whom they would live after their parents divorced
- deciding about sexual behavior
- deciding whether to join or drop out of a sport or other extracurricular activity

Once the students understand the directions, give them several minutes to reflect and to note briefly their five decisions on their cards, using only a word or two for each to help them recall the situations. When all the students have finished, move on to the next step.

4. Point out that there are many different ways to make decisions. Some ways are effective, consistently bringing about satisfying results, while other ways lead to problems. Then, using a sheet of poster paper, newsprint, or perhaps a portable blackboard, show the young people a list of the following optional approaches to decision-making. You need only list the words given in bold-faced type, *including the numbers that precede each;* the brief description of each approach can be provided orally as you work your way down the list.

Approaches to decision-making

1. **Impulsive approach:** giving little thought or examination to the decision at hand; merely taking the first alternative that presents itself
2. **Fatalistic approach:** leaving it all up to fate; the "what will be, will be" approach
3. **Compliant approach:** letting someone else decide for you; just following someone else's plan for you
4. **Delaying approach:** postponing thought or action and simply refusing to make a decision; similar to the fatalistic approach
5. **Agonizing strategy:** getting lost in all the data and possibilities and becoming too bewildered to act
6. **Planning approach:** using a thoughtful conscious process of reflection to work out a decision that is satisfying; involves weighing the facts, both cognitively and emotionally

7. **Intuitive approach:** trusting only your feelings to make the right choices rather than relying on investigation and critical reflection
8. **Wish approach:** opting for the most desirable outcome without regard to the risks involved; based on what you want rather than on the probabilities involved
9. **Safe approach:** based on considered alternatives, choosing the one that appears most likely to bring success; presupposes that some consideration has been given to alternatives
10. **Escape approach:** operating out of fear of the worst rather than commitment to the best; based on avoiding bad results rather than on choosing good ones

5. Having provided the list of possible approaches—and keeping it posted so that it can be seen by the group—ask the young people to again look at their list of major decisions made during the last five years. Now, as best they can, they should write a number behind each decision that indicates which decision-making approach they remember using in each situation. When their approach in any one situation seems to have been a hybrid—that is, one that involves more than one of the approaches—they should choose the one approach that seemed most influential or most evident in each situation. This activity should only take a couple of minutes.

6. The next step may seem a bit awkward, but it is the easiest and quickest way to tabulate the results of this exercise and to make a point that will serve to introduce the remainder of the session. While going through the list of approaches one at a time, ask the young people to hold up the fingers of one hand, indicating the number of times that they used each approach in their decision-making. For example, persons using the impulsive approach twice in their five situations would hold up two fingers. When all hands are raised, simply count the number of fingers held up and indicate that count next to the listed approach. Repeat this process until all the approaches have been tabulated.

7. Now review the results of the tabulation, commenting on interesting results and patterns that emerge. Concentrate particularly on the extremes, that is, those strategies that are used most and those that are seldom, if ever, used. The approaches requiring the least amount of effort might be the most popular—for example, the impulsive or delaying strategies. Conversely, the approach with the highest possibility of success and the one that we will be promoting—the planning approach—may well be one of those that was rarely used. If time allows, you may want to pursue further some of the results, discussing why some approaches are common and others are not.

8. Close the discussion by summarizing the main point of this exercise as follows:

We are faced with countless decisions in life—some major, some relatively minor. Many of these decisions have a direct bearing on whether we will ever achieve our dreams, whether we will ever find fulfillment and happiness. Yet, the startling reality is that most of us never learn how to make good decisions. Most people learn to read and write, to add and multiply, to feed and clothe themselves. Too many people apparently never learn the skill that is as important as any of the other basic skills we need for survival.

We cannot hope to learn all there is to learn about good decision-making in this short session, but we will learn some strategies that you can begin to appreciate and practice in your lives. After all, decision-making requires practice just like any other skill. In fact, that's the only way to improve this skill.

C. Activity: Creating a Case Study (5 minutes)

See Student Handout 3-A following this session outline.

1. In this exercise, the young people select a particular topic and create a pertinent situation to which they will later apply the decision-making process advocated in this session. This approach can be difficult for some groups, while others will respond enthusiastically and creatively. You will already have a good sense of the character or personality of your group and will know rather intuitively whether this approach will work. If, after reading this strategy, you decide that it is risky, you can opt for the alternative approach explained under number 7 below.

2. Tell the students that you want them to create a difficult but realistic situation commonly confronted by young adults—one that calls for a decision. Then they will discuss the application of a recommended process of decision-making. Creating their own situation will assure them that this discussion will be relevant to them.

3. To begin, ask the students to simply call out general topics of concern to young adults, issues or problems they will likely encounter in the next five years that will require sound decision-making skills. One example is deciding whether to attend college.

Another example is deciding which college to attend. Having offered these examples, ask the group to call out other likely situations. Use a piece of poster paper or newsprint and a large felt-tipped marker to write down the suggestions as they are made.

4. Place the list of situations so that they can be seen by all, and ask the group to choose one of these situations for further discussion. If necessary, use a simple majority vote to determine the topic.

5. The young people should now construct an imaginary case study involving the chosen topic. Provide them with copies of Student Handout 3–A, "Guidelines for Creating Your Story." If your group has more than ten participants, you may want to break it into smaller groups of six or eight members. Ask one person in each group to act as secretary, making notes of their discussion directly on the handout. Read the directions with the students, making sure that they understand what they are to do. Given the restrictions of time and the nature of this activity, it is suggested that you combine it with the break for this session.

6. Break for refreshments and work on the assignment. If you have more than one group you will have to separate the groups so that they can discuss without distraction. Encourage the young people to work quickly.

7. **Optional approach:** If you feel that your group will not be able to handle the assignment given above, consider this alternative. Reflect on your own life and identify a particularly perplexing situation—one in which making a decision required much struggle. Then, recount the situation with all the detail necessary for the young people to fully grasp your dilemma. Your account should minimally contain information related to all the questions stated on the handout.

Note: Be careful not to select a dilemma in which the solution you chose is obvious, for example, your choice of career or marriage partner. You want to be able to challenge the young people to think through the story in terms of the decision-making principles shared later. Reveal your response *only after* they have stated their proposed solution.

D. Break and Discussion (15 minutes)

Circulate among the participants during the discussion activity, offering suggestions if requested. If you opted for sharing a story from your own life, you may invite the young people to discuss alternate responses to your dilemma as a topic of conversation during this break, but that is not essential to the success of the activity.

E. Presentation of a Process for Making Good Decisions (5 minutes)

See Student Handout 3–B following this session outline.

1. Before discussing the specific situation, either created by the participants or provided by you, present the decision-making process described here and also on Student Handout 3–B, "A Step-by-Step Decision-making Process." Distribute a copy of the handout to each student.

2. Introduce the handout in this way:

Here is an outline of a decision-making process that reflects the kind of step-by-step approach that authorities on decision-making agree leads to the most effective and satisfying decisions. I admit that this will seem artificial at first. You may not be able to imagine yourselves using such a formal process. The fact is that this is actually a graphic description of the process that most people use many times a day without thinking about it.

Remember back to this morning when you had to decide what to wear today. Look at the decision-making process diagram and think of your decision about what to wear:

a. **First of all, you *identified the problem to be resolved*. In this case, that was easy: "What shall I wear today?" In many cases, this first step is not nearly so easy.**

b. **You then *gathered information*. You probably checked the weather to determine what kind of clothing would be appropriate. You looked through the closet and dresser to see what was available (and probably felt irritated if your favorite blouse or shirt wasn't clean).**

c. **Then you *identified options*. You could choose between various styles, different colors, more or less casual, and so on. You may have even gone so far as to actually lay out various outfits on your bed so that you could get a good look at them in comparison to one another.**

d. **Next, you *weighed the evidence*, checking out each possible outfit in terms of the weather, your mood, and who you were going to be seeing during the day.**

e. **Finally, you had to *choose from the options*. You picked the outfit you wanted and, it is hoped, neatly put away all the others.**

f. **Then you *took action*—you put on the clothes.**

Choices: Deciding How to Decide 85

g. Finally, you probably *reviewed your decision* by looking into the mirror and evaluating how you looked, no doubt stunned by the attractiveness of the person in the mirror.

What is suggested here is that we can use this same, commonsense process when confronting some of the major decisions of life, decisions that will have a lot more impact than the clothes we wear. It's ironic that we may spend such concentrated, thoughtful time on items like our wardrobe but make other major decisions—like the friends we'll have, what we value in life, even decisions about careers and marriage partners—by resorting to many of the less effective ways of decision-making identified earlier in this session. Then we wonder why so many people seem to have messed up lives! Now let's apply this process to the imaginary situation we created on the handout.

F. Application of the Decision-making Process to the Case Study (20–30 minutes)

1. The time allowed for this discussion needs to be flexible. If more than one group created an imaginary situation, you will have to begin by having each small group present their story and then have the large group select one as the case study. If only one group created a story, that story will have to be read or retold as you begin your discussion. On the other hand, if you as the leader shared one of your own dilemmas, you will be able to move directly into the application of the decision-making process. Finally, the complexity of the issue at hand and the ability of the group to discuss will affect the amount of time required. You should, however, restrict the discussion to 30 minutes, allowing time for the information on discernment and for the closing prayer. That restriction of time will determine the extent to which you can discuss each step of the process.

2. As time permits, ask the group to comment on each of the seven steps of the decision-making process as they relate to the selected case study. (To enhance the discussion with a visual aid, prepare the seven steps of the process on newsprint or a chalkboard, and as the discussion goes on, jot in the parts of the story next to the steps of the process to which they best relate.) Encourage the young people to be as creative and thoughtful as possible. Play the devil's advocate, if necessary, to provoke further thought and discussion. Point out as you go along that some steps will be more difficult than others, that some may be handled quickly while others may take a long time, and so on.

3. When the time limit is approached, ask the group for a final decision on what should be done in this particular situation as a result of using the process of decision-making. If you opted to share a dilemma of your own, let them arrive at their recommended solution, and then share the decision that you actually made. Comment on whether or not you employed a process similar to this one, whether or not the results were satisfying, and so on. This kind of personal storytelling by the adult leader can dramatically affect the relationship between the leader and the young people.

4. Close the discussion, noting that the young people should not infer that life's difficult decisions are going to be made easy by a process such as the one just completed. Making choices can be hard work, no matter what approach is used. However, this systematic, thoughtful approach *can* help in making good decisions that are satisfying—decisions that help us attain our dreams. Those aren't bad dividends for the work invested.

G. Introduction to the Closing Prayer: The Meaning of Christian Discernment (5 minutes)

1. At this point, lead the young people to your designated prayer area, if you have one. Tell them that there is another dimension to making good decisions, a component of the process that only believing Christians can include. Yet this dimension may be the most important element in making decisions that truly move us toward our dreams.

2. Comment as follows:

Writers on the topics of spirituality and what is called "spiritual direction"—personal counseling in which a director or guide helps an individual handle his or her relationship with God—often address the need for Christians to develop the skill of *Christian discernment.* Such discernment includes the ability to make decisions in life within the context of Christian faith. In one sense, Christian discernment might be understood as adding another step or two to the process of decision-making that we have discussed in this session. For instance, the person who is truly committed to living his or her life in harmony with God might begin the process of decision-making by praying for an openness to God's guidance and a willingness to trust in God's loving presence as he or she works through a difficult time of life.

Another possible step might come later in the process. One might look at all the alternatives that

have been identified in response to a certain situation and then ask: "How might Jesus respond in this situation? Which of the alternatives best fits my understanding of what God is calling me to be in life? Which decision will have the most life-giving effects for *all* people involved, not just for me?"

Spiritual direction and the personal counseling it includes offers another dimension to Christian decision-making or discernment. There are times in our lives when the decisions we have to make are so difficult or so important that we shouldn't try to make them completely on our own. Sometimes we get so close to our problems, so wrapped up in the details of our dilemmas, that we have a hard time sorting out our thoughts and feelings. Then we need the help of others. We can go to all kinds of people for advice, of course, and we should feel free to seek out help from anyone who can offer it to us. For Christian discernment, however, we need to look to people with mature Christian faith —people so in touch with Christ that they will help us see his hand at work in our life. Some people even hire spiritual directors, people who will guide them in spiritual life by meeting with them on a regular basis for prayerful reflection on the experiences of life.

What I would like to close with here is not just more talk about decision-making and Christian discernment, but rather a prayerful experience of one way we can add Christian discernment to our own process of making personal decisions. You may have already experienced exercises like "prayer trips" or "guided fantasy meditations," and if so, you know how helpful these can be in our attempts to pray. What we will experience now is a variation on these exercises that you can use specifically for applying Christian discernment when you have tough decisions to make.

H. Guided Meditation and Closing Prayer
(15 minutes)

1. Begin by asking the young people to each find a place in the room where they can assume a relaxed position. Suggest that they recline on their back if space permits, gently folding their hands on their stomach or resting them at their sides on the floor. Advise them not to get into positions that will quickly become uncomfortable or force them to move (e.g., they should not put their hands behind their heads as they recline). If the students choose to sit up, ask them to do so with their back as straight as possible, legs lightly crossed, and perhaps cupping their hands on their laps with the palms opened and directed upward in a gesture of openness to God.

Tell the students that prayer is a listening, a receptivity, even an emptiness, to the presence of God, and that the exercises they will be doing are helps to making themselves available to God who desires to communicate with us.

2. Next, lead the students through a brief series of breathing exercises that can help them become "centered." The basic technique is to use controlled breathing to relax the body and focus the mind. Ask the young people to close their eyes, gently letting the lids fall, not squeezing their eyes tightly shut. Then they are to inhale through their nose, drawing air deeply into their lungs. They should hold their breath for a moment, and then slowly and quietly exhale through their mouth. As the students do this, they should imagine that all physical, emotional, and mental tension is released from their body. With each breath, they become more relaxed, muscles lose their tightness, and their mind begins to clear of distractions. Allow a couple of minutes for this exercise, using plenty of silence, so that all of the students become relaxed and centered.

3. Now ask the young people to each spend a minute or so identifying a situation in their life with which they are having a hard time coping. It may be a situation demanding a decision and they are not sure which choice to make. Or it could be a situation over which they have no power, a situation that they suffer but cannot change. The students should attempt to get in touch with the situation emotionally, allowing the feelings caused by the problem to be felt at this time.

4. The young people should now imagine themselves alone at their favorite place, that special spot where they can get in touch with themselves and their God and feel at peace. It might be on a hillside, a lakeshore, a bridge over a bubbling creek, or maybe the roof of a building in a busy city. They should try to place themselves there now.

5. Next, the young people are to imagine that Jesus is approaching them at their favorite place. They look into his eyes, and he into theirs. They greet each other as friends. Jesus tells them to explain their problem to him, that he cares and wants to help.

6. Ask the students to imagine Jesus responding to their situation as they have pictured it. What does he say? What does his voice sound like as he speaks to them? What do they feel inside as his healing words and loving kindness touch their heart? You may want to play some reflective music at this point in the prayer.

7. Now ask the young people to imagine Jesus departing from them. They are once again all alone in their favorite place. How do they feel now? What have they decided to do, if anything, about their difficult situation? Then ask them slowly to return to the present and open their eyes.

8. Briefly comment that this kind of prayerful reflection on problems can be extremely helpful. One way for the students to learn this approach to meditation is to record the directions on a tape and then use the tape to guide themselves through the process step-by-step. Encourage the young people to practice this technique. Tell them that they will be participating in more guided meditations during the rest of the course.

9. Finally, you may want to close the prayer by distributing the prayer cards used earlier in the program. Ask the group to say together the prayer "You Have Great Plans for Me."

For Evaluation

1. Review your experience with the opening prayer ritual. Do you think that this will be effective as a regular feature of your sessions? How might you change it, if at all, based on your experience in this session?

2. As noted in the "Main Ideas" section, this session calls for a guided discussion approach more than other sessions have. The early part of the session included student reflection on past decisions, the leader's presentation of strategies for decision-making, and evaluation of the students' past decisions in terms of those approaches. How would you evaluate the student response to that part of the session? Were the students able to identify key decisions in their life? Did the various approaches to decision-making make sense to them? How might you improve your use of this material?

3. Evaluate your choice of either having the young people create their own story or providing a story from your own life. Do you now wish you had chosen the alternative approach? Why? If so, note this in your notebook so that you can try the other approach next time.

4. Perhaps the most difficult phase of this session is when the young people are asked to apply the seven-step decision-making process to the selected story. Were your students able to do this? If not, can you identify the difficulty and suggest ways to correct it in the future?

5. Review your experience with the closing guided meditation, noting improvements for directing it.

6. Were the "Teacher Goals" and "Student Intellectual/Behavioral Objectives" for this session achieved?

STUDENT HANDOUT 3-A

Guidelines for Creating Your Story

You are to create a story or situation in which a decision needs to be made, centered on the topic for discussion chosen by the group. Your story should include as many details as you can provide in the time allowed (about 15 minutes). You can be creative, even humorous if you wish, perhaps presenting your story in the form of a summary of a soap opera script or a letter to "Dear Abby." Or you can make your story serious, perhaps retelling a true situation with which you are familiar. You should answer the following questions to some degree in your story:

- Who are the people involved? Be specific, giving the characters' names.
- Precisely what is the character's dilemma or problem? Remember, this should reflect the topic chosen by the group.
- Close your story with a direct question that sums up the situation and clearly presents all the issues at hand. This question will be the focus of the decision-making process that the group will explore later.

Notes on your story:

_____
_____
_____
_____
_____
_____
_____
_____
_____
_____
_____
_____
_____
_____
_____

Reproduction permission is granted if you wish to make copies for classroom use.
The photocopy master for this handout is found at the back of this manual.

Choices: Deciding How to Decide

STUDENT HANDOUT 3-B

A Step-by-Step Decision-making Process

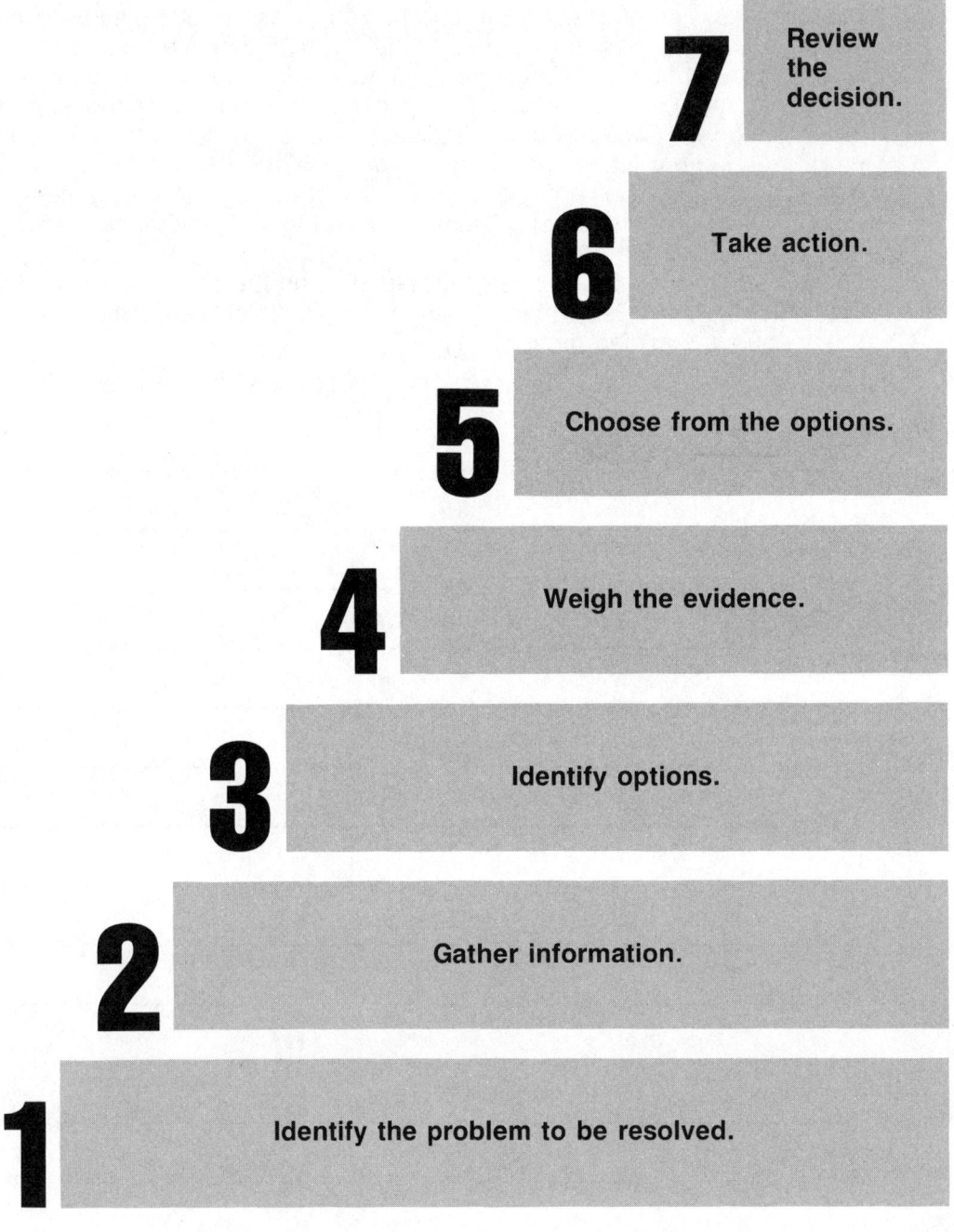

7 Review the decision.
6 Take action.
5 Choose from the options.
4 Weigh the evidence.
3 Identify options.
2 Gather information.
1 Identify the problem to be resolved.

Reproduction permission is granted if you wish to make copies for classroom use.
The photocopy master for this handout is found at the back of this manual.

Session 4

Connections: Building Healthful Relationships

Teacher Goals

To introduce the three-session unit on relationships; to help the young people reflect on and discuss the various kinds and characteristics of human relationships; to help the young people begin to come to terms with the impact of negative or hurtful relationships from their pasts.

Student Intellectual/Behavioral Objectives

That the young people seriously reflect upon the natures and characteristics of their present relationships; that they identify the qualities and skills that are essential to the development of healthful relationships; that they begin to feel comfortable in sharing their thoughts and feelings about these issues with other people in the group.

Main Ideas

With this session, we begin a three-session unit on personal relationships. Late adolescents and young adults are commonly caught up in the complex world of personal relationships, often to such an extent that concerns, thoughts, and questions about relationships dominate their lives: How can I develop and sustain caring relationships? Can I trust other people? Will I ever escape my feeling of loneliness? How do I know when I am in love? Do I want to get married or remain single? How do I break free from the confines of my family without hurting other family members or myself? How do I express my maturing sexuality in ways that are healthful and satisfying? Such questions—and all the feelings that go with them—are at the very center of the lives of most young adults.

If SHARING IV is to meet the needs of young adults, we must deal with their experiences and questions about personal relationships, and we must do so with openness, honesty, sensitivity, and gentleness. In developing this material, my most difficult and often frustrating challenge was to grapple with this complex subject within the time limits of a parish program like SHARING. The list of possible areas for discussion and reflection appeared endless, and each potential theme seemed to demand hours of session time. It quickly became clear that I had to take a deep breath, grit my teeth, and accept the following facts:

- Within the time limits of a parish program, we cannot hope to accomplish as much as we would like to or as much as we know the young people need in regard to personal relationships.
- We *can* introduce a number of basic insights, concepts, and principles that will enhance young peoples' chances for achieving satisfying personal relationships in the future.

Even after accepting these obvious realities, I struggled a great deal to settle on the central themes for these sessions and then to create effective strategies with which to explore those themes. Here is what I finally decided to include in these sessions:

- This first session in the unit of three introduces the young people to the subject of relationships. The participants in session 4 identify the various kinds of relationships that people experience, reflecting on the distinctions between relationships of acquaintanceship, friendship, and intimacy. The students then consider their prior experiences with various relationships, attempting to identify characteristics common to satisfying relationships and those common to destructive relationships. Finally, in a closing prayer experience, the group reflects on the need to heal the hurts of their past relationships if they are to move into future relationships positively and with hope.
- In session 5, the participants consider some of the skills needed to build healthful and satisfying relationships. The overarching theme of session 5 is interpersonal communication. The treatment of that theme includes discussion of the skills of active listening and empathy on the one hand and self-disclosure on the other. Basic principles of communication are reviewed, and these are then applied by role-playing some common interpersonal conflict situations in which young adults might find themselves.
- Session 6 concludes the unit on relationships with a discussion of intimacy—what it involves, how it is achieved, and what is needed to nurture it in relationships. In that session, the participants focus on the narrow but common concern of many young adults—How do I know when I am in love? What is the relationship and difference between love and infatuation? Although marriage per se is not discussed at length, much of the session touches upon some of the pivotal issues surrounding the choice of a marriage partner.

With the themes of the three sessions in this unit on relationships identified, we now need to consider learning strategies. In developing learning strategies, I always begin by asking myself: At what stage are the young people in regard to this theme? What are their likely attitudes toward it? On what assumptions or presumptions can I base the learning strategies for this material? In short, What is the starting point of this group? The basic principle here is that the starting point of the potential learner directly affects and even dictates the kinds of learning strategies one can employ in teaching. For example, the higher the interest or motivation on the part of the learner, the more direct and demanding the teaching style can be. If the learner is only reluctantly dealing with the material, then the learning strategies have to be far more motivational and engaging.

My underlying presumptions in developing the three sessions on relationships are the following:

- that the young people are profoundly interested in the theme of human relationships and little effort is required to pique their interest in it

- that the young people already have had experiences with most, if not all, of the issues raised in these sessions, and that they can be invited to draw upon and share these experiences with other participants
- that the young people have achieved a degree of maturity that enables them to articulate their experiences and associated feelings, and that they have a desire to share their experiences and their feelings with other people

If these presumptions are accurate, the primary strategies of these sessions must focus on individual, personal reflection as well as on serious group discussion. These sessions do include a number of individual reflection activities and group exercises, some excellent films, and inventive and appealing prayer experiences. However, the success of these sessions will rise or fall with the quality of the personal reflection and group discussion that those strategies generate.

To a certain extent, the emphasis on reflection and dialogue is true of *all* the sessions in SHARING, but never more so than here. This is so much the case that I make this recommendation: If your group shows extreme enthusiasm for discussing a certain point or issue during any of these sessions, feel free to allow the discussion to play itself out, even if that means abbreviating, delaying, or altogether skipping some information included in the session plans. Allow the young people to focus on the concerns that are truly important to them. If they learn the skill and experience the sheer enjoyment of open communication about sensitive issues, this unit on relationships will be a success.

Procedure

A. Welcome and Opening Prayer
(10–15 minutes, depending on size of group)

Begin the session with the prayer ritual described in session 2, adjusting it as desired based on your previous experience.

B. Introductory Comments by the Leader
(5 minutes)

Briefly review the major themes of the first three sessions, and then introduce this unit on relationships by sharing the following comments:

1. In our first session, we identified the major tasks confronting you as you enter the period of young adulthood. In the second session, we reflected on the need to develop what we called a dream, a personal vision of the shape you would like your life to take. The development of such a guiding dream is necessary if you are to avoid simply wandering aimlessly through life, hoping to luck out in the quest for happiness. In our last session, we explored a practical process for making the kinds of personal decisions that can lead, in concrete ways, to the attainment of your dream.

2. The first three sessions serve as a solid foundation as we now move into reflection and discussion on the theme of the next unit. This theme is personal relationships, perhaps the most significant concern of people in general and, in a special way, of young adults like you. It is significant that four out of the ten major developmental tasks of young adults that we identified earlier in this program deal directly with human relationships:

- *forming a personal identity,* **which involves having your sense of self affirmed by the significant people in your life**
- *integrating sexuality into life*
- *making friends and developing a capacity for intimacy with others*
- *loving and making a commitment to another person*

To a great extent, many of the central challenges that you face as young adults are bound to the relationships you have with other people.

3. Personal relationships, especially love relationships, are also a common and central component in the dreams that people evolve for their life. Consider this intriguing fact: A person's dream might include acquiring a successful career in business or attaining a certain level of income. She or he no doubt expects that reaching such goals requires tremendous effort, education, and plain hard work and thinks nothing of accepting such demands as reasonable. However, somehow the notion of finding and nurturing a caring, loving relationship—the very heart of the dream for many people—is simply taken for granted. We hope and pray that we'll get lucky in our relationships, but we don't often recognize the fact that loving another person also requires hard work, knowledge, practice, and commitment. Curious, isn't it?

4. Our discussion of the decision-making process has pointed out that the most difficult and

significant decisions people make seem to involve their relationships with other people. Perhaps you've already experienced the need for good decision-making skills in relationships with the other sex—whom to ask out, how to resolve conflicts when they arise, how to heal or even end relationships that become difficult. Perhaps you've experienced the need for good decision-making skills in your other relationships—such as relationships with friends, teachers, coaches, your parents, and so on. So we see that the themes we've already talked about have direct implications for our personal relationships.

5. We are going to spend this session as well as the next two sessions exploring this complex topic of personal relationships. However, because of limited time, we can touch upon only a few of the significant issues that are involved in this theme:

- In this session, we'll identify the different kinds of relationships that we experience in life, explore the qualities that are required in healthful, satisfying relationships, and reflect on the need to heal hurts that might be left over from some of our earlier relationships—hurts that can cripple our capacity for forming new relationships in the present and future.

- In our next session, we'll talk about communication as the binding force of all personal relationships. We'll review basic principles of effective communication, and then we'll apply those principles to common conflict situations experienced by young adults.

- Then, in the third session of this unit on personal relationships, we'll discuss the theme of intimacy, which includes the notion of determining in our romantic relationships whether we are involved in infatuation or real love.

6. So we've got a lot of ground to cover in a short time. Because of the nature of these sessions, I want to point out the need for two requirements of each of you that will determine how enjoyable and fruitful these sessions will be for all of us:

- First, these sessions will demand that you seriously reflect upon your own life and what it has taught you about human relationships to this point. I'll be using a number of strategies to help you do that—for example, printed reflection guides that you'll be asked to complete on your own. I'll be counting on you to enter into these exercises as sincerely and fully as you can, all the time guaranteeing that you'll never be asked to reveal anything about yourself that you do not want to reveal to others.

- The second thing I will ask of you in these sessions is a serious commitment to enter fully into group activities and discussions. As I said, you'll never be asked to share things about your experience that you do not want to share. However, you'll often be invited to share your ideas, your opinions, and your beliefs about human relationships. You'll also be asked to listen respectfully and with a caring heart to the ideas and feelings of other people in the group.

If everyone in the group makes a strong effort in these two areas—personal reflection and group sharing—these next three sessions we have together may be the most useful and enjoyable of all the sessions in our entire high school program.

7. At this point, ask if there are any questions or observations. Then move into the next part of the session.

C. Demonstration and Discussion on the Nature of Personal Relationships (10–20 minutes)

1. This introductory demonstration initially may seem somewhat confusing and demanding. However, by following the directions carefully and practicing it a couple of times before class, you will find that it is a quite simple and creative way to stimulate initial reflection and discussion on the theme of relationships.

2. Before the session, prepare for this activity as specified below.

a. Gather the following materials:
   1) a cardboard box, anywhere from 18" to 24" square at the top and bottom (make sure that either the top or the bottom of the box is plain, clean, and without large creases or overlapping panels)
   2) a dozen large paper clips
   3) eight or ten rubber bands of various sizes, from short, thin ones to long, heavy bands
   4) six or eight thumbtacks
   5) a large washer, the kind used with large screws or bolts and preferably at least an inch in diameter

b. Attach paper clips to both ends of each rubber band.

c. Next, attach five or six of the rubber bands to the washer, using the paper clips.

d. On the clean side of the box, while keeping the washer in the middle of the box, stretch the rubber bands in various directions. Attach the free ends of most of the rubber bands to the box by sticking thumbtacks through the paper clips and into the box. The effect should resemble that of a hub with spokes; however, because each rubber band is a different size, the resulting shape will not be that of a wheel. You may find that this part of the process works most easily if the washer itself is initially attached to the center of the box with a thumbtack, but that tack is removed once the rubber bands have been secured. This will leave the washer freely suspended by the rubber bands.

e. Finally, connect the remaining outside paper clips with other rubber bands, indicating that there can be relationships or connections that are independent of the washer at the center of the model.

3. After introducing the session, gather the group about you, and place the prepared box in front of you so that all of the students can see it. Begin by asking the group, **"In light of what I've already said, will anyone try to analyze or describe what this model is intended to symbolize?"** Allow some time for silence while the students look over the model. They can also feel free to chat among themselves as they try to decipher the meaning of the model. Do not judge any of their responses.

4. If the group has difficulty getting started or maintaining their interpretations of the model, help them along with leading questions such as the following:

a. **What do you think the washer at the center of the model represents?** (Because this is a religious education program, some will automatically assume that the washer represents God or Jesus. The proper response is "a person" or, more specifically, "me." If they do not arrive at this conclusion, ask **"What do you think the model represents if I tell you that the washer symbolizes the individual or you as a person?"**)

b. **What do the rubber bands represent?** (See the comment below for the proper interpretation, but do not share it with the young people at this point. Rather, encourage them to first come up with their own understanding of the model.)

c. **Why are some rubber bands thin and others thick and strong? What might this reflect?**

d. **Watch what happens when I pull on one of the rubber bands or disconnect one at either end.** (Demonstrate this by actually pulling on various bands or disconnecting one or two of them by removing their connecting thumbtacks.) **What might this represent?**

e. **What might be indicated by the fact that some rubber bands are linked to each other but not to the washer?**

5. Leader comment: After the young people have offered their interpretations of the model, conclude this demonstration with comments similar to the following:

The model represents the fact that each of us is connected to the world outside us through our personal relationships. Human beings are social animals; we cannot survive or grow in healthful ways independent of other people. Our relationships take on all kinds of characteristics. Some of our relationships with others are strong and influential. This is commonly the case with family members or best friends. The model represents such relationships with the strong, heavy bands. Other relationships are relatively weak and fragile, as with the many people with whom we will never be more than acquaintances.

In some cases, the people with whom we have relationships share relationships with one another. This might be true in our families, in the school community, or in the work place. Such clusters of people can become social networks or cultural groups that can exert great influence on our life.

We can't help but be affected by what goes on in our relationships with other people. When I pulled on one rubber band or removed one from the model, the washer at the center—indeed, the entire model—was affected, sometimes dramatically and at other times only a little. If we argue with our best friend, the argument can put a strain on every other relationship we have. If one of our relationships becomes stronger, or if one of our weak connections grows into a strong connection, it can strengthen the entire network of relationships that makes up our life. On the other hand, it might happen that one relationship becomes so strong and overpowering that it dominates our life and weakens, or even breaks, our connections with others. Can anyone offer an example of when this might happen?

The major point of this little exercise is this: We can never fully understand ourselves as persons or assume significant control of our life without understanding and directing our personal relationships with others. That's why we're devoting so much of this program to a discussion of this area of our life.

D. Reflecting on the Varieties of Relationships
(25 minutes)

See Student Handout 4–A following this session outline.

1. At this point, distribute pencils and copies of Student Handout 4–A, "Reflecting on My Relationships."

2. When all of the students have received a pencil and a handout, explain the directions as follows:

a. **The concentric circles on the handout represent the various kinds of relationships we experience in our life. Many of the people we know in life remain simply acquaintances. Other people become friends. Still others might become what we call intimates, people to whom we feel especially close. The word** *intimate* **is often used to refer to sexual or romantic relationships with persons of the other sex, but it actually refers to deep friendships with anyone. The purpose of this activity is to help us recognize the different qualities or characteristics of these various kinds of relationships. What distinguishes one from the others?**

b. **I want to begin this activity by having each of you work alone for a few minutes.** (If your facility permits it, you may want to allow the students to move to different parts of the building for this part of the activity, but that is not essential to its effectiveness.) **First, take a minute or so and, in each of the circles on the handout, write the names of a few people who come to your mind as representative acquaintances, friends, or intimates. Then, at the bottom of the page, under each heading list five characteristics, actions, attitudes—whatever comes to your mind—regarding each of those three types of relationships. I can only give you 5 minutes or so for this, so work quickly. You will** *not* **have to share the names of the people you write on the paper, but I will ask you to share the descriptive words you write at the bottom of the page.**

3. Allow the young people to separate from one another for their work on this part of the activity. Give them 5 minutes, and then ask if they need more time. Realize that they will certainly have some difficulty with this, especially in distinguishing between friends and intimates. The purpose of the activity is to arrive at these insights, not to begin with them, so encourage the students to keep trying. After 7 or 8 minutes have elapsed, call the young people back together.

4. Have available a chalkboard or poster paper or newsprint attached to a wall. A few inches down from the top of the board or paper, write the headings "Acquaintances," "Friends," and "Intimates" in three columns. You may want to ask one of the young people to act as a recorder. Then brainstorm with the group, having them call out all the responses they came up with for each of the three kinds of relationships. Write all of the responses under the appropriate headings. When a particular point is repeated, simply put a checkmark after it rather than writing it again.

5. After all the responses have been listed, comment on any surprise insights, common patterns that emerged from the private reflection, difficulties that the students experienced in doing the activity, and so on.

6. Conclude the activity by sharing the following insights:

a. **We can gain some understanding of the variety and quality of our relationships by thinking of them as part of a continuum.** (At this point, draw an arrow across the top of the board or paper from left to right, that is, from "Acquaintanceship" to "Intimacy.") **At one end of the continuum, we have acquaintances. These are people we know casually. We may know their name, feel comfortable in their presence, even participate in sports or other activities with them, and yet not socialize with or feel particularly close to them.** (For each of the three categories, feel free to draw from the group's list of characteristics to illustrate these points.)

b. **At the other end of the continuum, we have people with whom we share a feeling of intimacy. There is a deep bonding with such people, a sense of openness and trust, honesty and warmth. Because such relationships take a lot of time, work, and more than a little luck, we normally have only a few people in our life who we consider intimates. That shouldn't make us sad but, rather, grateful for those people.**

c. **It is possible for two people to move along the continuum from acquaintanceship through friendship to intimacy. On the other hand, some people might remain acquaintances or friends, never reaching the level of intimacy. It is important to note that** *not all relationships need to have intimacy as their goal.* **Each kind of relationship has value and worth in itself.**

d. Before class, prepare a sheet of poster paper or newsprint with the following list of characteristics of friendship and intimacy

Friendship
- firm loyalty
- strong, mutual support
- shared view of the world

Intimacy
- firm loyalty
- strong, mutual support
- shared view of the world
- deep, mutual self-disclosure
- shared vulnerability

At this point, tape the list of characteristics to the wall or board.

e. Comment on the list as follows:

Probably one of the hardest parts of this activity is distinguishing between friendship and intimacy. We know from experience that there is a difference here; we most commonly reflect it by speaking of being "just friends" with some people and "best or special friends" with others. Here is one way to distinguish between friendship and intimacy. (Now, simply read through the list, pointing out those characteristics that are common to both types of relationships and those that differentiate them. You might briefly define the more complex terms as follows:)

- *A shared view of the world* means that two people have a common understanding of the basic meaning of life.
- *Mutual self-disclosure* refers to the willingness and ability for two people to reveal to one another their deepest feelings, fears, thoughts, and dreams.
- *Shared vulnerability* is, in a sense, a result or expression of mutual self-disclosure; it is the sense of risk or openness to potential pain that one accepts in an intimate relationship with another person. The more we open ourselves to someone, the greater the risk we take.

f. **Therefore, intimacy includes all the qualities of friendship, but it goes beyond them. Why is knowledge about intimacy important? Psychologists and others—among them, many writers in spirituality—believe that we can only attain fulfillment as persons if we develop our capacity for intimacy. In a couple of weeks, we will be exploring the specific meaning of intimacy in greater depth. In this session, we'll continue to reflect on personal relationships in general by considering what we have learned about them from our own experiences.**

E. **Break** (10 minutes)

F. **Activity: Creating a Best-seller on Personal Relationships** (30 minutes)

1. After the break is over, introduce the second part of this session with the following points:

Personal relationships and all the questions and concerns surrounding them have become a big business. Take a look at a list of best-selling books, for example. It seems that every week there is another book published on learning to love, attracting the other sex, overcoming personal problems, or recovering from bad relationships. (At this point, you may want to read the latest list of the top ten nonfiction books. Such lists are regularly published in most newspapers and many national magazines.) **The larger newspapers now publish advice columns addressing human relationships.** (If you wish, page through a newspaper and identify such columns, including Ann Landers, Dear Abby, Miss Manners, and the many others that address personal development or interpersonal relations.) **During the last two decades, there has been a tremendous increase in the number of counseling centers, educational programs, and other services whose primary product is promised improvement of the participants' or buyers' personal life.**

2. **In a certain sense, this increased interest in consciousness-raising may be a healthy sign of our progress as people. The fact that people are concerned about improving the personal and interpersonal dimensions of their lives is encouraging. However, why do we need so-called experts to tell us how to accept ourselves or how to get along with one another? Doesn't it seem that a lot of the ingredients required for stable relationships are simply a matter of common sense?**

3. **The point is that we probably know a lot more about personal relationships than we think we do. If we try to live our life reflectively—that is, being aware of what's really going on in our life and willing to spend some time mulling over the lessons of our own experiences—we can become our own experts, our own gurus, our own counselors and guides.**

4. **To illustrate our own capacity for directing our relationships, we're now going to develop a table of contents for a guaranteed best-selling book on how to form satisfying personal relationships. To get us started, I already have the title of the book we're going to create:** *Now You're Cookin'!: A Recipe for Great Personal Relationships.* **Cookbooks are**

Connections: Building Healthful Relationships

also big sellers, so we'll grab their audience too! (At this point, present a sheet of poster paper with this book title at the top of the paper, followed by the name of your parish youth group or class, thereby identifying the young people as the authors of the book. Under the group's name, print the heading "List of Ingredients," instead of the usual "Table of Contents.")

5. Next, give each young person in the group five small pieces of paper or index cards. They should still have the pencils distributed earlier; if not, redistribute them. Then ask the group to sit together in a rather tight circle on the floor. (If you have more than eight people in the group, you may want to create two or more circles.)

6. Now ask the students to close their eyes, quiet themselves, and relax for a moment. After a brief pause, ask them to picture in their mind a person with whom they have experienced a happy, satisfying, enriching relationship. It could be a parent, best friend, relative, teacher—anyone. It is only important that the thought of the person elicits within them a feeling of happiness or gratitude. Ask them to spend just a moment concentrating on that person and the relationship that they have experienced with that individual.

7. After pausing briefly, ask the students to try to find words that capture some of the things about the relationship that have made it so special. The words could relate to personal qualities of the person about whom they are thinking, things they have shared together that have been meaningful, characteristics about the person for which they are most grateful, the way in which they relate, and so on. Whenever the students think of a word or brief phrase, they are to *print* it on one of the cards and then place the card *face down* on the floor in the middle of the group. They are to write only one word or phrase on each card. Ask them to keep doing this until they have used all five of their cards. When it appears that most students have completed the exercise, allow them another 30 seconds or so, and then call an end to this part of the activity. Avoid embarrassing anyone who may have had a difficult time coming up with five responses.

8. Next, tell the group that the cards need to be collected, shuffled, and organized into chapter titles for their best-seller. Ask one of the students to collect and shuffle the cards. Then she or he should turn one card over at a time in the middle of the group, reading off each word or phrase as it is revealed. The group should then work together to gather the cards into piles according to identical or similar content. For example, all cards referring to trust as a major quality of healthy relationships should be placed in one pile, all those related to humor in another, and so on. As the leader, feel free throughout this part of the activity to comment on the content of the cards as they are turned over. If the meaning of a particular card is self-evident, you can simply affirm the fact that it represents a vital ingredient in healthy relationships. If the meaning is unclear or particularly insightful or clever, invite the group to comment on its meaning.

9. Then ask the students to look at all the themes or concepts reflected in the individual piles of cards. Are there any major ingredients for healthy relationships that seem to be missing? If so, the students can add them at this point.

10. Now ask the young people to quickly arrange the piles of cards in the sequence in which they would like them to appear in the book. They should not spend a great deal of time discussing this. Rather, acknowledge that there are many ways to mix the ingredients, and tell them to simply prepare a logical sequence of themes.

11. When the students have prepared their sequence of themes, announce that it is now time to finalize the "List of Ingredients" for their recipe on human relationships. Ask them to pick a catchy phrase that captures the main point of each of their piles of cards, expressing each with some of the jargon of recipes. For instance, "Stir in a Cup of Humor" or "Beat Thoroughly with Some Difficult Experiences." As each phrase or chapter title is agreed upon, someone in the group, using a felt-tipped marker, should print it in the proper order on the poster paper that has the book title at the top. The result will be a thorough outline for their best-seller on personal relationships.

12. Close this activity by sharing the following thoughts:

It's clear that the members of this group already know a great deal about what it takes to nurture successful relationships. When you identified the ingredients, you were actually pinpointing the kinds of principles or characteristics that need to be part of all satisfying relationships. If you compared your book outline with the tables of contents of many of the best-sellers, you may be surprised to see how knowledgeable you already are! The key to developing healthy relationships, of course, is to live out the principles that you identified in this exercise, rather than to simply list them or even to write a book about them. In the next session, we will spend more time reflecting on the major skills that

we will require if we are to initiate and sustain satisfying relationships in our lives. At this point, we want to move to our closing prayer.

G. Closing Prayer (two options, depending on available time)

1. As was noted in the "Main Ideas" section for this session, the leaders of SHARING IV have to be quite flexible in their guidance of this program. If your group is particularly comfortable and talkative, you may find that little or no time for prayer remains at the end of this session. I suggest that you have available copies of the prayers distributed during the first session. If time is severely restricted, simply lead the group in reading one of the prayers. The prayer "You Have Great Plans for Me" is appropriate for this session. If time permits, first take a moment for silent reflection. Then allow the participants to offer any intentions they have, and conclude with the group reading of the prayer.

On the other hand, you may find that significant time remains at the end of this session. If the session plan unfolds as it is outlined, you will have 15 minutes for this closing prayer. In that case, close with the optional prayer service described below.

2. For this prayer experience, you will need the following materials:

a. one small piece of paper for each group member (the index cards used for the previous activity would be fine)
b. pencils
c. a metal bowl lined with foil
d. one large candle, one taper or small candle, and matches
e. a Bible
f. the reading by Doris Donnelly quoted below
g. an appropriate recorded song (see the SHARING music guides in the SHARING director's manual for suggestions)

3. Place the Bible, the reading, and the tape recorder or record player near you. Call the group members to prayer by gathering them in a circle. Place the foil-lined bowl, the matches, and the two candles in the middle of the circle. Distribute the pieces of paper and pencils. Then light the large candle and set it next to the bowl.

4. Lead the participants in making the sign of the cross. Then read Romans 12:14–21. This scriptural reading describes the attitude of forgiveness that we are to have toward those who have hurt us.

5. Comment on the reading as follows:

This evening we have talked about the qualities and attitudes required for happy and satisfying relationships. In all of our lives, however, we also experience sad, hurtful, and destructive relationships. In fact, one of the most difficult tasks we face if we hope to grow as loving, caring people is that of getting over the bad experiences we've had. It's hard to trust people if we've been betrayed in the past. It takes great courage to risk being open with others if we've been ridiculed for such openness in other relationships. Sometimes we carry deep anger and resentment, even hatred, within our hearts that cripples our relationships with others. The scriptural reading we have just heard addresses our need to heal these past hurts if we are to grow as persons.

Many times it's hard to find the motivation to forgive those persons who have brought pain into our life. However, reflect on these facts: The anger or resentment or hatred we might feel toward another person may or may not affect that person, but for certain it cripples us: it destroys us. It eats away at our capacity for joy in life and makes us bitter, unhappy people. It is heroic to forgive others out of concern for them, but at times we are incapable of that kind of heroism. In those cases, we can let go of the anger and hurt within us for our own sakes so that we can get on with our life instead of living in a painful past.

6. Listen to a story told by one young man in Nashville during a workshop on forgiveness a couple years ago:

> **Two months before [the workshop, the young man's] father had died. The young man had only sketchy memories of his father, who had abandoned the family when the boy was six years old. The boy and his mother skimped and lived on the brink of poverty until the son could take on a job and support them both. Then, word came through distant acquaintances that the father had died. For fourteen consecutive nights after hearing the news, the young man had tortured dreams about his father until one night when the son said this prayer before he fell asleep:**
>
> > **"Dear Lord in heaven, my father is in pain. He is living in his death with a heavy burden of guilt for the hardship he inflicted on my mom and me. He wasn't much of a father, Lord, but I forgive him.**
> >
> > **"Dad, I forgive you. It's O.K. Maybe you couldn't help what you did. I don't know, but I forgive you, Dad. I want you to rest in peace."**
>
> **And the dreams about his father stopped that very night.** (Doris Donnelly, *Putting Forgiveness into Practice* [Allen, TX: Argus Communications, 1982], p. 50)

7. Forgiving others who have hurt us is not easy, but it is essential if we are to grow as persons. Pause for a moment now, and think of one person who has hurt you in your life. As the story suggests, the person you choose need not be someone who is now alive; the power of forgiveness can extend beyond the grave to heal our memories. Bring the hurt, the pain, the anger, or the hatred into your heart and your mind right now. (Pause in silence for a moment.)

8. Now, on your piece of paper, write a brief statement that describes the person you're thinking about and the pain that that individual has brought to your life. You may want to write only the person's name. Maybe you want to write a sentence or two directly to that person. Or perhaps you'd like to write something in the form of a prayer to God: for example, "Dear God, please take away the anger and the hurt from my heart." No one will ever see what you write on your paper. Spend just a minute or two doing this.

9. When the students are finished, tell them that you are going to invite them to symbolically rid themselves of their past hurts. Ask them to look briefly at their paper and then to slowly tear the papers into several pieces. They should then slowly and quietly drop the torn papers into the bowl. Allow a minute or two for them to do so.

10. When all the papers are in the bowl, tell the participants that the lighted candle is a symbol of Jesus, the one who, more than any other, taught us the healing power of forgiveness of enemies. Take the small candle or taper and light it from the larger candle. Then use the smaller candle to light the papers in the foil-lined bowl. Invite the young people to pray silently and to see the burning papers as symbols of the purifying and cleansing of their past hurts. You may want to play a song at this time.

11. Close the service by asking the young people to join hands and to say the Lord's Prayer together. Note that one line of the prayer directly states the need to forgive those who have hurt us. Then make the sign of the cross and extinguish the large candle's flame.

For Evaluation

1. Begin your evaluation of the session by reflecting on the flow of the material, the response of the young people to individual activities, and so on. Are there any major changes in the session plan that are clearly required?

2. The session plan acknowledges the potential difficulty with time, that is, the possible lack of time, given the amount of material included in the plan. Was this a problem for you? Do you have any immediate ideas on how that might be rectified in the future? Note such changes in your notebook.

3. Did your use of the box model of human relationships seem to be an effective way to introduce this session? If not, do you think the problem lies with the activity itself or with your guidance of it? How might your use of this model be improved in the future?

4. Did the activity on the varieties of relationships clearly identify and convey to the young people the distinctions between acquaintanceships, friendships, and intimate relationships? In the discussion of this material, did the young people make comments or raise issues that should be reacted to in the next two sessions of this unit on relationships?

5. Evaluate the activity on creating a best-selling book about personal relationships. Did the strategy itself spark the interest and discussion of the group? Was there sufficient time to complete the activity? If not, how might you adjust this activity or this session's schedule in the future?

6. Did you have time to use the prayer service on forgiveness? If not, consider how it might be used in session 6, which discusses intimacy. If you were able to use the prayer service, what was your impression of the group's response to the prayer? Occasionally, such prayer experiences can have considerable impact on individuals. Is there an apparent need to follow up with any of the young people in the group, based on their response to the prayer?

7. Were the "Teacher Goals" and "Student Intellectual/Behavioral Objectives" for this session achieved?

STUDENT HANDOUT 4-A

Reflecting on My Relationships

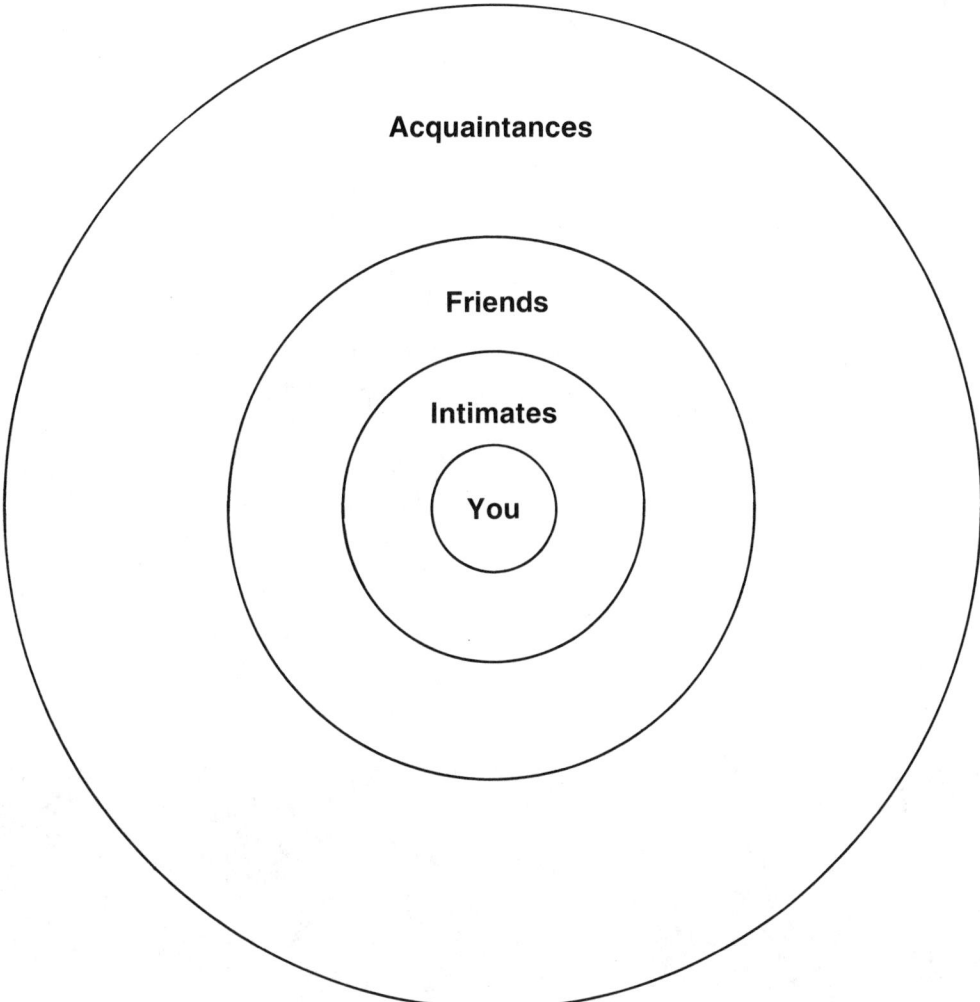

On the lines below, list characteristics, actions, attitudes—whatever comes to your mind—regarding each type of personal relationship identified in the circles above.

Acquaintances	Friends	Intimates
_____	_____	_____
_____	_____	_____
_____	_____	_____
_____	_____	_____
_____	_____	_____
_____	_____	_____

Reproduction permission is granted if you wish to make copies for classroom use.
The photocopy master for this handout is found at the back of this manual.

Connections: Building Healthful Relationships

Session 5

Communication: The Tie That Binds All Relationships

Teacher Goals

To awaken the young people to the need for effective communication in personal relationships; to help them reflect on key principles of communication; to challenge them to apply such principles to concrete life situations.

Student Intellectual/Behavioral Objectives

That the young people reflect on the role and characteristics of communication in their personal relationships; that they evaluate their own communication skills; that they recognize the need to practice the skills of effective communication in their personal relationships.

Main Ideas

Session 4, the first of a three-session unit, introduced the theme of personal relationships and approached it from a broad perspective. We identified various kinds of relationships and then asked the young people to reflect on the basic ingredients required for positive, satisfying relationships. The session concluded with a prayer service on the need to heal the hurts of the past.

In this session, we are going to discuss a few of the more specific, practical skills needed to nurture healthy relationships in our lives. The umbrella theme under which this material is gathered is *communication*. As indicated in the "Main Ideas" section of session 4, in this unit on personal relationships we are continually confronted with the complexity of the issues involved and the limitations of time. The theme of personal relationships is complex and daunting. One might also argue that the subtheme of human communication is no less challenging. In preparing to develop this material, I reviewed dozens of books on communication between persons. Many of those books acknowledged that only a surface treatment of the topic could be made in a single book. Yet we have only a single session of two hours! What to do?

We will simply introduce the young people to the basic principles and skills involved in effective communication and encourage them to reflect on their abilities and needs in this area. Then, through reflection on some concrete situations that require strong communication skills, we will attempt to increase the young peoples' awareness of the value of such skills in their interpersonal relationships. It is hoped that this session will prompt the young people to continually develop their own communication skills.

For the purposes of this session, the following four aspects of effective communication are identified and discussed:
- the commitment to care as the foundation of all communication
- open and honest self-expression and active listening as primary ingredients of effective communication
- practical guidelines for effective communication
- conflict situations as opportunities to grow in interpersonal relationships

The first half of the session consists of input from the leader, an enjoyable simulation activity, and an exercise in guided imagery. These three components are designed to introduce major concepts and principles related to the four aspects of communication noted above. In the second half of the session, the young people role-play assigned conflict situations in order to explore the practical applications of these communication principles in life experiences.

This session is active and entertaining but also requires thoughtful preparation and practice by the leader. When reading through this session plan, try to imagine the strategies unfolding in a step-by-step fashion. Keep the young people and their different personalities in mind as you reflect on each step in the session, perhaps noting any adjustments that you feel are necessary, given the makeup of your group. This kind of careful preparation will ensure a successful and enjoyable session.

Procedure

A. Welcome and Opening Prayer
(10–15 minutes, depending on the size of the group)

Once again begin the session with the prayer ritual described in session 2, adjusting it as needed based on previous experience.

B. Introductory Comments by the Leader
(5 minutes)

1. Briefly review the themes of session 4: the three levels of personal relationships that we experience, the qualities of satisfying relationships that we can identify from our own experiences, and the need to heal the hurts of the past to be able to build healthy relationships in the present and future. Then introduce this session with comments similar to those that follow. Prepare and present these ideas in your own words and as informally as possible.

2. **In this session, we will concentrate on a critical factor in all satisfying relationships, one without which no relationship of any depth is possible. That factor is communication. By communication I mean the ability of both parties involved in a relationship to effectively share their thoughts, feelings, and values with each other. In a sense, communication can be understood as the glue of successful relationships. Good communication holds people together, binds them together in mind and heart, and gives their relationship the strength it**

needs to weather inevitable difficulties and conflicts. When people cease to communicate effectively, their relationship eventually becomes shaky and weak and will usually crumble under stress.

3. During this session, we will reflect on and discuss just four of the aspects of the complex process of interpersonal communication (you may want to have these listed on the chalkboard or on newsprint):

- the commitment to care that is the foundation of all communication
- the central communication skills of self-expression and active listening, which allow us to truly understand the verbal and nonverbal messages that are such important features of all personal communication
- the general guidelines for guaranteeing good communication between people
- the skill of effectively coping with conflict situations that will inevitably arise in any relationship

4. We cannot study at length any one of these four aspects of communication. Even if I just stood here and lectured on these four aspects I could only introduce, and neither you nor I want me to give a lecture! However, by participating in three interesting activities and then reflecting briefly on the insights gained from them, we can at least begin to look at these important facets of personal relationships.

5. As we begin this session, I'd like to share a couple of thoughts about the first of the four aspects of communication—that is, the commitment to care. Commitment to care is the foundation of all communication. This aspect of communication may seem so self-evident that we may be inclined to ignore it or take it for granted. Yet it is absolutely vital that we acknowledge this reality about human relationships: All satisfying and growing relationships demand a commitment to the hard work of communication, a commitment that is strong enough to weather the tough times that are part of every relationship. *Such a strong commitment can only exist if it is rooted in a deep sense of caring for the well-being of the other.* However, the commitment to care is not totally selfless. When we reach out to others with a caring heart, we also tend to our own need to be of value to others. At times the work of sustaining relationships through care and effective communication will be extremely trying and challenging, even when our own self-interest is at stake.

6. One popular author on human relationships, John Powell, suggests that a person has to have the following attitude about the hard work of communication:

I am determined to work at this, to give it all I've got. This commitment is unconditional: no fine print in the contract, no "ifs" or "buts" or time limits. I will work at it when it is easy and when it is difficult. I will try to tell you who I am. And I will listen to learn who you are. I will do this when I feel like it and even when I don't feel like it. I promise to hang in there with you even when the child in me would rather play games, pout, or punish you. I promise to hang in there even when I feel like quitting. Together we will work at sharing until we have built strong lines of communication. Only then can we experience the personal fulfillment that comes with effective communication. [John Powell and Loretta Brady, *Will the Real Me Please Stand Up?* (Allen, TX: Argus Communications, 1985), p. 18]

7. It is reasonable to ask why one should care about an effort that seems to promise so much hard work and frustration. The shortest and perhaps most accurate response is simply this: We need strong relationships and a sense of intimacy with others in order to be happy as persons, and we simply cannot achieve and sustain such relationships without caring about how we communicate with others. As we've noted before, it is curious that we would not hesitate to prepare for a career that promises financial security. Neither do we hesitate to make such a commitment in order to achieve excellence in athletics or in academics or to master a favorite musical instrument. However, none of those things will supplant the need for satisfying personal relationships in our life. So the commitment to care as an aspect of communication promises all sorts of dividends that make it a reasonable investment.

8. From this point on in our discussion of human relationships, we will assume that you share this commitment to care for others, but we will try not to take that commitment for granted. From time to time, we simply may have to repeat the fact that at the very foundation of all efforts to build relationships with others is an attitude of care and concern for oneself and others. To put it another, perhaps more familiar way: We are committed to love one another and to treat other people as we would like them to treat us. We may learn once again that the teachings of Jesus are not just poetic

or uplifting; they are, to a great degree, sheer common sense rooted in human need and are constantly affirmed by life experiences.

C. A Simulation Game on Communication
(30 minutes)

1. This enjoyable activity provides insight into two pivotal elements in effective communication: the need for one party to accurately express what she or he is thinking or feeling, and the ability of the other party to listen attentively and imaginatively to what is being expressed.

2. Though all the young people will participate in the activity, you will need three volunteers to act as presenters. Tell the group that the role of the volunteers will be somewhat similar to that of the leader in a game of charades. Then ask for three volunteers.

3. Distribute three pieces of paper and a pencil to each participant. The paper should be at least 8½-by-11 inches. If there are no hard surfaces available on which to write, stiffer paper, such as construction or poster paper, would be preferred. Felt-tipped markers for the volunteers would be helpful but are not required.

4. Now take one of the three volunteers aside for a moment and give him or her this assignment. On a sheet of paper, the volunteer should draw the following four shapes in any size and arrange them in any configuration as long as the four do not intersect with one another: a square, a circle, a triangle, and a rectangle. This should be done very quickly.

5. Ask the rest of the group members to each take one piece of paper and a pencil and to prepare to draw something at the direction of the first volunteer. Then ask the volunteer to turn his or her back to the group and begin describing what is on the paper without naming the shapes. The group members should listen to the volunteer's descriptions as carefully as possible and try as best as they can to reproduce on their papers what he or she is describing. The students are not allowed to ask any questions or to discuss their drawings with one another.

6. When the volunteer has completed the description of the drawing, ask the group members to hold up their drawings. Compare the results with the original drawing of the volunteer. Without getting into a long discussion or an evaluation of individual drawings, identify the drawing that comes closest to that of the volunteer as well as the one that seems least like the original. Feel free to do this in a humorous manner, maintaining the game-like character of the activity.

7. Now ask the second of your three volunteers to repeat the process by drawing a different design using the same four shapes. When he or she is ready to describe the drawing to the group, however, the volunteer should be allowed to face the group and to use hand gestures in describing his or her drawing. The group members still may not ask any questions of the volunteer or discuss with one another. When the group has completed this round, again compare results. Note whether the drawings of the group more commonly coincide with that of the volunteer in this case than in the first instance.

8. Then ask for the third volunteer to repeat the exercise. While he or she is describing the drawing in this case, the group is permitted to ask questions of the volunteer. Once again, compare results. Presumedly, each successive experience will demonstrate significant improvement in the ability of the group to accurately reproduce the drawings of the volunteers. In fact, nearly everyone in the group may correctly reproduce the drawing of the third volunteer.

9. Follow up on the exercise by discussing the experience from the perspectives of both the volunteer presenters and the group members, using questions like the following:

a. **In regard to the presentations or descriptions made by the volunteers, what significant differences can you identify from one to the next? That is, what did the second volunteer do that the first one didn't, and what did the third volunteer do that neither the first nor the second did? How much did these differences contribute to the effectiveness of each volunteer's communication? Can you relate any of these factors to everyday kinds of communication?** Your goal here is to have the group clearly identify some of the specific components of effective communication. For example, call to their attention the importance of a conscious effort by the volunteers to describe their drawings in great detail, the remarkable value of nonverbal communication such as hand gestures, and so on. Note that in everyday communication between people, nonverbal signals such as facial expression and body posture can be so strong as to overwhelm the verbal message. In cases when one senses a conflict between what is being said and what is being expressed nonverbally, one often feels a kind of distrust or suspicion about a person.

b. **What skills and attitudes were required as you attempted to reproduce the drawings of the volunteers? In what ways do we require these skills in our day-to-day experiences with interpersonal communication?** Urge the young people to respond as specifically as possible to these questions. Your primary goal is to have them identify the need to listen attentively and with imagination, as when they tried to see in their mind's eye exactly what the volunteers were describing. When this point has been made, associate the need for *empathy* in human communication, the ability to see reality through the eyes of others, to "walk a mile in their shoes," as the saying goes. This struggle to enter into the hearts and minds of others is at the very center of good communication.

c. For the volunteers: **If you were asked to do this exercise over again or to advise others on how best to do this, what advice would you give?**

d. For the other group members: **If you were to instruct another group on how best to accomplish their task in this exercise, what advice would you give?**

10. *Optional step in this discussion:* You may end the discussion of the activity at this point if you feel that the group has clearly understood the major lessons. If, however, you feel the group has not fully made the connections between this activity and the common forms of communication, expand the discussion by asking the group to state three guidelines for effective communication for both parties involved in communication:

a. **Identify three guidelines for individuals who are trying to communicate an idea, feeling, value, or other information to another person.** Examples: The one attempting to communicate must fully describe what he or she is feeling or thinking. He or she must consciously use nonverbal signals or gestures that enhance or help convey what is being communicated. He or she must be sensitive to the ability of the listener to understand what is being conveyed.

b. **Identify three guidelines for individuals who are trying to receive or understand what is being communicated by another person.** Examples: One must listen to the total message that is being conveyed. One must try to see through the eyes of the other. One must ask for clarification whenever necessary.

11. Close the activity and discussion with this point:

We just completed a relatively simple game in which the image of a few simple shapes of various sizes was all that was being conveyed from one person to the group members. Yet we discovered how challenging that communication was. How much more challenging, then, is the task of learning to communicate such complex realities as feelings, dreams, values, beliefs, and attitudes. No wonder people have a hard time getting along sometimes!

We can make a giant leap forward in our ability to build strong relationships if we just acknowledge and accept the difficulties involved and the degree of commitment such relationships require. If we accept the reality that personal relationships can be complex and complicated, we will set more realistic expectations for others as well as for ourselves. We will become more patient with one another, more sensitive, more understanding, less judgmental, less frustrated, and less angry. We'll have a better shot at achieving satisfying and happy relationships because of these attitudes.

D. Guided Imagery Exercise: Becoming the Communicator I Would Like to Be (20 minutes)

See Student Handout 5–A following this session outline.

1. The following exercise is based on the book quoted above, *Will the Real Me Please Stand Up?* by John Powell and Loretta Brady. The book offers twenty-five guidelines for good communication, all presented in an anecdotal, almost folksy style. I recommend your becoming familiar with the book, both for your own background and as a possible resource to offer those young people in your group who are interested enough in the topic of communication to want to read about it.

I have created a handout titled "Imagining Myself as a Communicator" (Student Handout 5–A) from the twenty-five guidelines found in *Will the Real Me Please Stand Up?* It contains a guided imagery exercise for use with groups or by individuals. With a group, the exercise starts with a relaxation and centering activity with which your group should now be quite familiar. Following the centering activity, slowly read one of the statements from the handout. Then ask the students to imagine themselves possessing the characteristic or quality identified by the statement. Pause for about 30 seconds to allow the imaging to take place. Repeat this pattern for each of the statements.

This exercise is intended to achieve at least two objectives. It introduces a useful meditation technique to the young people that can be used outside of the course. The exercise also allows us to summarize a great many principles of communication in a brief time.

The directions that follow include an introduction, a suggested relaxation technique, and conclusion to the exercise. Note that the handout used for the exercise is to be distributed to interested young people at the end of the session for individual use only. Have copies available for those who wish to take them.

2. Introductory comment: **Nathaniel Hawthorne, a great nineteenth-century American writer, once wrote a story called "The Great Stone Face." In the story, a little boy spends a great deal of his time admiring a face that he sees etched in stone on the side of a mountain. When the boy becomes an adult, he discovers that the face is his own. The boy had become that which he had admired.**

The insight into human nature explored in Hawthorne's story is one each of us must reflect on. To a great extent, we become what we admire, we take on the qualities of the ideals we reach for, we imitate those people who model what we would like to become. It stands to reason, then, that the more noble and uplifting the ideals and models we choose, the more fully we will grow as human beings.

We are going to share an exercise that is based on this principle. Earlier in this session, I quoted from the book entitled *Will the Real Me Please Stand Up?* **That book offers twenty-five guidelines for effective communication.** (If you have the book available, you might show it to the group at this time.) **In the exercise we are going to experience, many of the principles of communication identified in that book have been rephrased into statements directly related to the attitudes and values that we must have if we are to become effective communicators. I will lead you through some relaxation exercises to help you calm your mind and focus your attention. Then I'll read one of the statements and pause while you try to imagine yourself possessing the characteristics reflected in each statement. See yourself actually taking on the qualities required for effective communication between people. Remember, you will become that which you imagine yourself to be.**

3. At this point, spend a few minutes helping the students to quiet themselves, to relax, and to focus their attention. If space permits and the floor is carpeted, invite them to stretch out on the floor. They need to assume positions that they can maintain for some time. This means avoiding hands behind their heads, which will quickly become cramped, legs crossed in uncomfortable ways, and so on. For most, the best approach is to lie flat on their back, arms at the sides, body limp, and eyes closed.

4. Next, ask the students to concentrate on their breathing for a moment, with the intent of making their breathing deep and steady and relaxing. They should fill their lungs completely by breathing in through the nose, hold the breath for a moment, and then slowly exhale through the mouth. With each breath, they are to imagine their body becoming more and more relaxed, as if all tension and stress is being slowly and peacefully blown out of their body with each breath they exhale.

5. If you wish to take the time, it is also helpful to spend a few minutes relaxing the body from toes to head. Suggest that the students concentrate on one part of the body, become conscious of it by tightening the muscles in that area, and then consciously allow that part of the body to relax. The common order for this step of the process would be feet, legs, hands, arms, torso, and then finally the head.

6. Once the group members have become relaxed and focused, make a statement like the following: **I want you now to picture yourself in your mind. Try to see yourself so vividly that you can look into your own eyes. See yourself dressed in a way that is totally comfortable and natural for you. Imagine yourself, strange as it may seem at first, all alone with yourself. As I now read the statements, try to hear yourself saying them. Watch the expression on your face as you begin to reflect the attitudes and values conveyed by each statement. See yourself actually possessing the qualities identified by each statement. I will pause briefly after each statement to give you a chance to imagine the qualities mentioned as being your own. Let's begin.**

7. At this point, slowly and in a relaxing voice, read the statements from Student Handout 5–A. Pause for just 30 seconds or so after reading each statement. This will allow you to go through the list in about 15 minutes.

8. After you have read the list of statements, tell the students that they should take one more look at themselves in light of the experience. Do they look different in any way? Can they imagine themselves taking on these qualities and characteristics? Would they not be happier if they, in fact, could do so?

Then ask them to rejoin the group by opening their eyes and sitting up.

9. There is no need to discuss the activity at length. You might simply ask the young people if they enjoyed it, what they liked or did not like about it, and so on. Then point out to them that many people routinely practice this kind of exercise with great benefits. At this time, distribute the handouts to those who are interested in keeping one for themselves.

E. Break with Preparation for Role-playing (20 minutes)

See Student Handout 5–B following this session outline.

1. Tell the group that time is so short for this session that you would like to combine the break with preparation for another activity. Ask them to count off into groups of three. (Note: If your group is larger than fifteen, you may want to make some groups larger than three. However, the larger groups should then receive role-playing assignments from the options provided that allow for more than three participants.)

2. After the young people have formed their groups, announce that they will be doing some role-playing after the break and that the groups are to use the refreshment break to prepare for their particular assignments. Each of the situations involves a common communication dilemma or conflict. After they have received their assignment, the students are to find a place in the house or facility to practice their role-playing. The situations are relatively simple and straightforward, normally involving only a narrator, who is to explain the situation to the audience, and two characters, who are to act out the situation for the large group.

3. Point out that for each role-playing situation, the students are to do two things:

a. After the narrator has explained the situation, the players are to first act out at least one improper or poor way to respond to the situation. The negative response should be a common one, not one so absurd or fanciful that people could not relate to it. If the students wish, they can offer more than one such negative response but should keep them brief. They certainly need not avoid humor but should try to make a legitimate point about communication.

b. After the negative response has been presented, the narrator should announce that the proper way to handle the situation will now be role-played. This scene should illustrate how one committed to caring relationships and to the principles of effective communication might deal with the situation.

4. *Note well:* Tell the young people that they are *not* to role-play the situation that is described by the narrator but only the possible *responses* to the situation. This is why the role-plays should not take too long to either prepare or present.

5. Tell the students that after each role-play, the others in the large group will be asked to evaluate the role-plays, especially discussing whether the positive response suggested for each situation was a good one, whether there might be other approaches that would be more fruitful, and so on. The limits of time, however, will force you to keep the discussion to a minimum.

6. Give the young people a chance to ask questions. Then distribute the role-play situations. (Feel free to create other situations if you wish.) Simply make a photocopy of Student Handout 5–B and cut it into individual assignments. Fold each assignment and put all of them into a hat or a small box. Ask one person from each group to choose one of the papers. Then the students are to pick up some refreshments and gather in their groups to practice their role-plays. They should be ready to return in fifteen minutes. (Note: If some groups have more than three members, you will have to assign appropriate situations to them rather than allowing them a random choice.)

F. Performance of Role-plays (25 minutes)

1. Call the groups back together for the performances of their role-plays. You will have to be somewhat flexible on the timing of this, depending on the flow of the earlier part of the session and the actual amount of time remaining. Reserve 5 minutes of the total remaining time for final comments and perhaps a closing prayer. Try to allow at least 3 to 5 minutes for each role-play and the discussion of it. This may seem brief, but the role-play situations are simple, and discussion on each should be short and to the point.

2. Begin the role-plays. If it is clear that the groups are taking a largely humorous approach to the activity, enjoy it with them. Great lessons can be learned while belly laughing! Invite comments on each situation, concentrating on the positive response as it was portrayed and inviting suggestions on optional ways that one might handle similar

situations in a positive way. Encourage applause after each group has presented its role-play.

3. Close the activity by noting that communication skills are among the most practical skills people can develop. The role-plays illustrate the variety of situations in life that demand a sensitivity to the needs of others, the ability to express one's thoughts and feelings, and the talent for listening to both the words and feelings of people. Granted, it is hard work, but the outcome of more satisfying personal relationships justifies the effort.

G. Closing Prayer

It is quite possible that at the end of this session there will be little time left for a closing group prayer. You may wish to offer a brief spontaneous prayer of your own. For example, "Dear God, we thank you for the gift of this time together, for the conversation, support, insights, and laughter that we share with each other. May we have the courage and strength to share these gifts with all whom we meet. We ask this in Jesus' name. Amen."

For Evaluation

1. Evaluate your experience with the simulation game on communication. Did the young people enjoy the activity? Were they able to gain the insights about communication that the activity is intended to show? How might you change the activity, given your experience with it?

2. The guided imagery exercise in this session is difficult to evaluate. By its very nature, much of what is attempted through the exercise happens inside the participants and is not discussed at length. You will have to judge the effectiveness of this exercise on the basis of (*a*) the group's apparent openness to the activity; (*b*) their immediate response to it; and (*c*) whether they showed interest in the handout when it was offered to them. On these bases, how would you evaluate the exercise?

3. Regarding the role-playing activity, did it work to combine the refreshment break with preparation of the role-play situations? If not, how might you better handle this, given the time limits? Did the young people enter into and enjoy the activity? Were helpful insights into the process of communication gained from the role-plays and the discussion of them? Finally, was there sufficient time available for this activity? If not, how might you adjust your use of this activity in the future?

4. Were the "Teacher Goals" and "Student Intellectual/Behavioral Objectives" for this session achieved?

STUDENT HANDOUT 5-A

Imagining Myself as a Communicator

Directions: Find a place where you can be alone and left undisturbed. Assume a comfortable position that you can maintain for a reasonable length of time. Spend a few minutes relaxing your body and focusing your attention by using the breathing exercises practiced in group sessions. Then slowly and deliberately read each of the following affirmations. After reading each one, pause briefly and try to imagine yourself possessing the quality or characteristic reflected in the statement. Do this on a regular basis (twice a week or more) until the attitudes imagined become part of you and the way you act.

- I am fully committed to the hard work of communicating with others. I will work at it even when the results are frustrating or difficult to see.

- I believe that I am a gift to be offered to others and that all people I meet are gifts offered to me.

- I am determined to be completely honest with myself. I try to stay in touch with my thoughts and feelings, their origins, and their expression. If I am to be honest with others, I must first be honest with myself.

- I am fully responsible for all my actions and reactions. I blame no one and no thing for how I behave or for what I feel.

- I try always to speak the truth that is within me. I also respect the truth that is within others. I do not impose what I believe upon others, nor do I try to interpret the beliefs of others to suit my needs or desires.

- In communicating with others, I share my feelings as well as my thoughts. I do so with gentleness and sensitivity, not out of a desire to satisfy my own emotional needs or to manipulate others.

- I am willing to be open and honest with my thoughts and feelings even when rejection or ridicule by others is possible. To grow, I must be open to some pain in life.

- I am deeply grateful for all who love and care for me, and I let them know of my gratitude.

- When others approach me, I try to focus on their thoughts, feelings, and needs rather than on my own. I try always to be truly present and available to those I meet.

- I accept others just the way they are, without judging who they are or demanding that they become what I would like them to be.

- I avoid judging the intentions and motives of others. I recognize that people are complicated, and I resist the arrogant attitude that people are exactly what I believe them to be.

- When others attempt to share themselves with me, I try to see and feel the world through their eyes and heart. I try to understand their experience of life, not interpret their life in terms of my own experiences.

- I try to fully understand what others are sharing with me. When I am not sure if I understand, I always ask them to explain or clarify what they mean so that I do not falsely judge them.

- When others ask for my advice, I offer suggestions and honest opinions but never orders or directions. Only they can decide what is right for them.

- In a culture that fills our time with electronic sights and sounds and endless ways to waste time, I am committed to spending quality time with friends and loved ones.

- I recognize that many thoughts and feelings are better expressed with a touch of the hand or a hug than with words. I do not invade the privacy of others but touch them with tenderness and sensitivity.

- As one who is fully human, I make mistakes and hurt those I love. When I do so, I quickly apologize and ask their forgiveness.

- When I sense a problem in my communication with someone, I quickly seek the source of the problem and try to correct it. I do not allow small problems to grow into big ones through my neglect or denial.

- When a communication problem arises that is beyond my power to solve, I seek the advice and help of those who can provide it.

- In all my efforts at communication—in all my attempts to share my own thoughts and feelings and in my struggles to be attentive and accepting of those of others—my motive and guide is love.

- Finally, as one who believes in the presence of a loving God within all loving relationships, I regularly pray for God's guidance as I try to communicate with others.

STUDENT HANDOUT 5-B

Assignments for Role-playing

You have a good friend whose father has recently died unexpectedly. The friend has been out of school for several days and has just returned to school. You see this friend in the hall after school. What do you say or do?

In preparing this role-play, one person should be a narrator who explains the above scene to the rest of the group. The others in your small group are then to role-play two scenes:
1. an improper or poor way to respond in this situation
2. a proper or positive way to respond in this situation
You have just 15 minutes to prepare your role-play.

Your brother or sister has just had a big fight with your parents. He or she had made some plans for next Saturday but has just found out from your parents that they had already made commitments for the family without remembering to tell the kids. Your sibling has yelled at your folks and stomped up the stairs and into your bedroom, where he or she begins to grumble about how unfair the whole situation is. What do you do or say?

In preparing this role-play, one person should be a narrator who explains the above scene to the rest of the group. The others in your small group are then to role-play two scenes:
1. an improper or poor way to respond in this situation
2. a proper or positive way to respond in this situation
You have just 15 minutes to prepare your role-play.

One of your grandparents is dying of cancer. The illness has been lengthy, requiring many visits by family members, and your relatives have been taking turns visiting the grandparent in the hospital. When you are taking your turn, you find that your grandparent is particularly depressed and begins to talk of regrets about life and fears of death. What do you say or do?

In preparing this role-play, one person should be a narrator who explains the above scene to the rest of the group. The others in your small group are then to role-play two scenes:
1. an improper or poor way to respond in this situation
2. a proper or positive way to respond in this situation
You have just 15 minutes to prepare your role-play.

You are at a birthday party, and everyone is having a good time. However, one of your friends seems to be down and getting more depressed by the minute. Just when the birthday cake is being presented and everyone starts to sing the birthday song, your friend mumbles something and, near tears, runs out of the room. The party seems to come to a halt, and everyone feels very uncomfortable. You leave to find your friend and find him or her sitting on the steps. What do you say or do?

In preparing this role-play, one person should be a narrator who explains the above scene to the rest of the group. The others in your small group are then to role-play two scenes:
1. an improper or poor way to respond in this situation
2. a proper or positive way to respond in this situation
You have just 15 minutes to prepare your role-play.

You are at a dance, and you have told your parents that you will be home by midnight. At 11:30 P.M., one of your friends shows up and he or she obviously has been drinking heavily. The friend wants to talk to you about "something very serious." You spend over an hour with your friend, who manages to spill some liquor on you while you talk. You finally arrive home after 1:00 A.M., smelling of liquor, your angry parents waiting for you. What do you say or do?

In preparing this role-play, one person should be a narrator who explains the above scene to the rest of the group. The others in your small group are then to role-play two scenes:
1. an improper or poor way to respond in this situation
2. a proper or positive way to respond in this situation
You have just 15 minutes to prepare your role-play.

You have been going steady with the same person for nearly two years. Recently, you have been feeling less and less enthusiastic about the relationship and have been trying to find some way to break up without hurting the person. Just as you are ready to bring up the subject, the person suggests that the two of you get married. Obviously, she or he has had no inkling of what you have been feeling. What do you say or do?

In preparing this role-play, one person should be a narrator who explains the above scene to the rest of the group. The others in your small group are then to role-play two scenes:
1. an improper or poor way to respond in this situation
2. a proper or positive way to respond in this situation
You have just 15 minutes to prepare your role-play.

Session 6

The Search for Intimacy: A Risk Worth Taking

Teacher Goals

To help the young people reflect on their personal need for intimate relationships; to explore healthful ways to achieve intimacy with others; to present criteria for determining when one is truly in love rather than merely infatuated with another person.

Student Intellectual/Behavioral Objectives

That the young people comprehend the nature and characteristics of true intimacy; that they reflect on and dialogue with others about their need for intimacy; that they develop the ability to determine when a romantic relationship reflects authentic intimacy or simply infatuation.

Main Ideas

This session is, in a word, loaded. It is loaded in terms of content, some of which is quite heavy. It is loaded with educational strategies that can provoke considerable response from the young people. Your greatest difficulty with this session, particularly if your group has matured and the young people are willing and able to share openly and freely, will be to fit it all in. That problem is preferred, to be sure, to running short of material, but it can be almost as disconcerting.

Two things explain the packed quality of this session. First, we are exploring two rich, distinct, yet complementary themes in this session—the characteristics of human intimacy and the distinction between love and infatuation. Either of the two themes deserves at least a full session, if not more, but time simply does not permit that. So we must join them together in this session of our unit on personal relationships.

Second, young adults have a high interest in the themes of this session. You may well find, therefore, that the students want to just keep talking about certain points raised during the session. This is, of course, a delightful problem, one many teachers would pay to have! Nevertheless, you should be aware of this possibility as you reflect on and prepare for this session.

What does this mean for you in your preparation for this session? First, read through the session plan imaginatively, trying to project as best as you can how your group will react to each part of the session, given their past response to materials and strategies. For example, you may find that some questions or concerns raised by individuals in previous sessions are addressed in this session. If so, you may want to spend more time on one part of the plan than what I suggest. Feel free, as always, to follow your instincts in adapting the session as necessary.

Second, be prepared to drop the confidential self-test on love and infatuation if your discussion of the film is lively and longer than the schedule allows. The self-test is not required for effective discussion of the theme of love versus infatuation, but it can serve as a helpful option if the discussion of the film is restrained and brief.

Third, the session plan suggests that the closing prayer service of session 4 can be used with this session if you were not able to use it earlier. If you feel uncertain about your group's ability to discuss the session material at length, be prepared to use the longer prayer experience.

Both major themes of this session—intimacy and the distinction between love and infatuation—are rich and complex. I recommend two major strategies to pursue these themes: the twenty-minute film *A Question of Intimacy* and a discussion activity on love and infatuation based on research done by Dr. Ray Short.

Note well: As background for your preparation of this session, I am including in this "Main Ideas" section extensive notes on both the film and Dr. Short's material. By first reading and reflecting on this information, you will better be able to thoroughly understand the session plan itself. Therefore, this "Main Ideas" section will be unusually long, and the session plan itself will be comparatively short. The session plan is written with the presumption that you are familiar with the information given in this "Main Ideas" section.

Notes on the Film *A Question of Intimacy*

See "Things to Keep in Mind" at the end of this session for film rental information and for an alternative use of this film summary.

Given the central importance of the film *A Question of Intimacy* in this session, I am providing a thorough summary of the content of the film, including comments of the narrator and the film's subjects. This summary will be helpful to you in your preparation of this session and offers insights that will be valuable in your teaching of this session.

Introduction

The narrator of the film *A Question of Intimacy*, Christian author and lecturer Keith Miller, introduces himself and explains the origins of this film. Miller's travels have led him to recognize the apparent universal hunger among people for intimacy with others, and he has explored the phenomenon in great depth.

In his exploration of the need for intimacy, Miller noticed that, along with the incredible hunger for it, many of us experience a fear, almost a terror, of entering an intimate human relationship. This fear is something we do not want to talk about, especially the degree of fear that we experience. The sad reality, the paradox, is that this fear of intimacy keeps us from achieving intimacy and therefore locks us into an isolation that we yearn to escape.

Miller spent a day with a group of people sharing, on a deep level, their experiences, joys, and fears about intimacy with others. The film shows the highlights of that encounter.

Brainstorming on the meaning of intimacy

The film shows a word association game played by the people in the group—about ten young adults—as they attempt to define intimacy. Terms that are suggested include *security, closeness, fear, sense of belonging and being loved, knowing something special about oneself, ultimate trust, overall acceptance of one another,* and *vulnerability to rejection.*

Miller suggests that intimacy is a human drive similar to hunger, a drive that comes from loneliness and prompts us into relationships with one another. The problem is that we are all afraid of the drive toward intimacy and the pain that can accompany it. Unfortunately, according to Miller, "intimacy and pain come through the same doorway, so that if we block the pain, we block the intimacy."

We also have an anxiety that covers up the pain of loneliness like a fog so that we feel fear in our lives but we don't know of what—we just feel afraid generally. Miller's goal for the group is to "pull back the anxiety so that we can see what our fears are, so that we can face them and overcome them."

Discussion of fears

A young man in the group says that one of his biggest fears is that of not being known. He recounts the experience of making a phone call, saying "Hi, this is Drew" (which, he notes, is an unusual name), and having the other party say "Who?" He experiences a fear in the pit of his stomach whenever he picks up the phone.

Another man says that he fears he will be awkward in expressing affection. This lack of self-confidence makes him afraid to initiate expressions of intimacy.

Miller interjects that there is an issue here of identifying the source of our security. We can seek it inside ourselves (e.g., through therapy or the self-understanding that I really am okay as a person) or outside of ourselves. For Miller, the source of security in his life comes from the belief that God accepts him as he is. Therefore, if a particular relationship in which he is interested does not work out as he had hoped, he can still feel that he is okay.

A young woman suggests that the cause of her insecurity is her upbringing and its emphasis on the fact that a person cannot be close to someone until married.

Another woman says that she has a great fear of not being accepted when she behaves as she wants to behave in a relationship.

Still another young woman fears the lack of permanence in an intimate relationship; she fears that the relationship will not last and that the intimacy will be taken away. She wants a guarantee that the intimacy will always be there and that she will be safe to trust in the relationship.

Someone then suggests that, based on past experience, we often reject new opportunities for intimacy: "Because it didn't work out before, it probably won't work out this time." So we build walls around ourselves, and then the fear becomes one of never being able to take the walls down.

Defenses against intimacy

Playing off of the above points, Miller talks about the fact that we all have developed particular defenses against the fears that we experience. He suggests that there are basically two kinds of people:

- "Skunks" have defenses ready when people get too close (they might use humor or heavy talk to keep people at a distance).
- "Turtles" withdraw and hide out to such a degree that you almost feel you have to bang on their shells to get them to "come out."

Miller goes on to say, "Unfortunately, skunks and turtles almost always marry each other!"

Others pick up on Miller's comments. One woman says that, based on her experience of a failed marriage, people go into marriage acting in certain ways, hoping that there will be some kind of payoff for their behavior: "I'll do all these things, hoping that you'll fill my needs." She apparently feels badly because she wants to be rewarded for her efforts in relationships rather than entering them with a selfless attitude.

Miller uses the woman's viewpoint to discuss the defense mechanism of repression identified by Freud. Miller suggests that we can think of our conscious minds as movie screens. We sense a thought or feeling coming up on the screen that we cannot tolerate or do not want to acknowledge and we repress it. However, the repressed thought or feeling is like a beach ball that we try to hold under water. It takes tremendous energy to keep the ball under water. We deny that such things (like wanting a payoff from relationships) are within us, and we push them further into our unconscious. But the further down we push them, the more energy it takes to hold them there. Something has to eventually give somewhere. When the repressed thought or feeling finally comes to the surface, like the submerged beach ball, it often will come out at an inappropriate angle and will hit anyone in the way. So when we finally get angry, for example, we get *too* mad and often hurt those who are not at fault. If we could just let the thought or feeling come to the surface when it first starts to emerge, it would still be part of our lives but would not be out of control.

Another participant voices the fear of becoming intimate, revealing something of our deepest self, and then having that used against us later. This is a fear of betrayal.

Another woman suggests that she has a fear of losing control of the relationship. She ends up imagining all sorts of things that are not part of the relationship but serve as reasons to terminate it. Then she goes through terrible pain. Miller suggests that this is what is known in psychology as *approach-avoidance*. We are afraid of being rejected, so we reject people first. We draw people into a relationship (approach) and then reject them (avoid). This tactic is also called sabotaging a relationship.

How does one achieve intimacy?

Miller then offers a helpful summary of recent psychoanalytic theories. He states that psychoanalysts have come to believe that people are like chickens in eggs. There are two basic ways to get inside the eggs and let the chickens out, that is, ways to get people out of their shells:

- One way is like using a hammer to break the egg. This school of thought involves gestalt and T-group methods. The basic technique involved here is to invite people to say anything they want to say about another person in the context of so-called truth sessions. The problem with this approach, says Miller, is that you end up with a lot of bruised chickens or chickens who come out of their shells before they are ready to deal with the realities of life.

- The other psychoanalytic approach is to create an atmosphere of trust by sharing yourself with others rather than by analyzing them. When you share yourself, you do not threaten others, and they can "peck on their own shell and come out at their own speed."

On the other hand, Miller cautions that some people seem to have a "vomit theory of honesty" (not a happy image here!), in which they believe sharing one's self means "spilling their guts" so to speak. It might make the one doing it feel good, but it doesn't do much for the recipient. Spilling one's guts can have the same inhibiting effect that analyzing has.

A young man comments that the problem with intimacy is that previous experiences can inflict wounds so deep that we become gun-shy about opening ourselves to another person. In response, Miller says that there is no other way to start intimacy than for one person to start risking. How? We begin by practicing in a group of friends in which we find we have support, and based on that experience, we can then go out and try to relate with other individuals. We can then come back to our support group and tell our friends what happened. No other way exists to initiate intimacy than for someone to take the first vulnerable step. Our problem is that we are always waiting for the other person to take the risk!

A woman says that her fear now is that when she feels attracted to someone, she is going to make a mistake and get hurt. Miller responds that part of this problem is that many people have a fixation on looking for a mate. If we meet someone who is looking for more out of a relationship than we want to give, we get scared off. Miller says that he made a major leap forward in his life when he stopped looking for a mate and started tending to his own identity. Constant evaluation of others as potential mates puts too much pressure on both parties. If we instead tend to becoming the kind of persons that we want to be, others will look at us and say, "This person knows what he or she is all about," and mutual attraction, if it is to happen at all, will take care of itself. The appropriate question is not, Is this the right mate for me? The proper questions are, Who am I? What can I do to grow as a person? What can I offer others?

Another woman describes the difficult problem of having healthy relationships with people who are seeking romantic intimacy. In these cases she backs off because she is afraid that any expression of affection will send the wrong signals or that her motives will be misinterpreted. She fears becoming a cold person, rather than a warm one, because of this. Her comments lead to the discussion of commitment and the fear of it. The fear of commitment, of course, forces us to back away from the intimacy that can bring us fulfillment as persons.

Miller asks the question, "What do we need in order to instigate openness to intimacy and then maintain it?" He then answers that we need one of two things:

- We must feel good inside ourselves.
- We need a security beyond the relationship.

Again, Miller makes the point that he began to feel good about himself when he began to feel that God felt good about him. He also had a regular support group that he met with frequently, friends who would occasionally remind him of his goodness despite his failures. "You've got to have someone who loves you if you fail," he says. He concludes the film by asking, "Will your source of security be religious faith, therapy, a relationship? You've got to have something, because you can't do it alone."

Notes on Distinctions Between Love and Infatuation

I am indebted in this session to the work of Dr. Ray Short, a professor of sociology at the University of Wisconsin-Platteville and a popular lecturer on love and marriage. Several years ago, Dr. Short, who is also a Methodist minister, made a presentation at a convention that I attended. In his presentation, Short summarized what he had discovered about love and infatuation during a long search through the literature of the social sciences.

One of the primary goals of Short's research, writing, and speaking has been to help young people avoid weak or failed marriages by making better decisions about marriage partners in the first place. A major key to such good decisions, according to Short, is to be able to distinguish between infatuation and a love that can last. His conclusions serve as the primary source of the information you will find in this session. Short is the source of the information; I am responsible for the strategies for conveying it.

Short has also written a number of popular books. His most popular is titled *Sex, Love, or Infatuation: How Can I Really Know?* (Minneapolis: Augsburg Publishing, 1978). The book offers a detailed discussion of the information found in this session. I encourage you to not only read the book but to recommend it to your young people as well. Though written for a slightly younger audience, many young adults will find the information enlightening and helpful.

I will summarize Dr. Short's major points here as I did above for the film. This summary is sufficient for understanding the discussion exercise on love and infatuation in this session. I am also including several interesting statistics, insights, and anecdotes that you may find helpful in working with this material.

General background

Research has found that one-half of all adolescents believe that they are "in love," that is, involved in a romantic relationship, *right now*. On the average, people have seven or eight romantic relationships before they marry. They also average more than one romantic relationship *after* they marry. Short quickly points out here that a minority of people have a lot of extramarital relationships, thereby skewing the statistic. The majority of married people have no extramarital romantic relationships.

More than nine out of ten people marry at least once. One out of three of first marriages end in divorce and three percent more in separation. Fifteen to twenty percent stay together for the sake of the children, because of religious convictions, and so on, but they do not experience marital happiness. If all of these figures are combined, an individual getting married today will have no more than a fifty-fifty chance of experiencing marital happiness. This is a rather chilling picture, to say the least.

Consider these statistics also: If one marries when still a teen, the odds for a successful marriage are one in four. For a woman, the odds of a successful marriage are three times better if she marries between the ages of twenty-two and twenty-five than if she marries as a teen. One recommendation is immediately apparent to Short and others: The longer one waits for marriage, the better the odds for success.

Perplexity of the problem

Short identifies four factors that have combined to lead to this tragedy of failed marital relationships:

- There is the age-old myth that says that a person knows in his or her heart when the right person comes along. The research is clear, says Short: "You cannot trust your heart alone in choosing a marital partner."
- The media continue to propagate an idealized, totally inaccurate understanding of romantic love and sex.
- Religious institutions have failed to provide sufficient help to their members in the area of marital relationships.
- The social sciences have contributed very little research in the area of love and the art of sustaining love relationships.

What is needed, according to Short, is some means by which people—especially young adults—can evaluate their romantic relationships on the basis of concrete, verifiable, understandable principles. He has developed such a means, he claims, by identifying fourteen clues that people can look to for guidance in determining whether they are involved in a true love relationship that will last or in a relationship of infatuation that will end in three years or less. The clues are all based on sound research and can be statistically verified.

Before identifying his fourteen clues, Short cautions against three "false clues" that can mislead one in this matter:

- strong feelings
- a "gnawing need for nearness"
- a "powerful pull to passion"

All three of these characteristics can be found in either infatuation or love relationships, so they cannot be relied upon as clues. However, Short says that there are fourteen other clues that can be relied upon *if they are taken together*. These are not ranked in any priority of importance. The key issue is *how many* of the clues fall on the right side of the equation when judging a relationship. For example, Short would not recommend marriage to anyone unless they could add up their responses on the love side of the equation and get at least a total of eleven positive responses out of the fourteen. This will become clearer in light of the reflection guide that I have developed for this material.

Prescription for solving the problem

Here are Short's fourteen clues. Each begins with a question, which is then followed by two responses. The first response to the question reflects what is true in a relationship based on infatuation. The second response to each question shows how a love relationship is characterized in terms of the question's focus. When helpful, I have added a brief comment to clarify some points in this discussion.

1. What is the major attraction of the persons to each other?

a. In infatuation, the primary attraction is what Short calls *the physical equipment*—which should require little explanation!

b. In a love relationship, each person will be attracted to *the total personality* of the other.

2. How many different things attract the persons to each other?

a. In infatuation, only a few things will attract the persons to each other, but often with such intensity that they are unaware of how little they share.

b. In a love relationship, many different attributes attract the parties to each other.

3. How does the relationship start?

a. In infatuation, the relationship likely begins very fast, characterized by the popular notion of "love at first sight." Short says that it is absolutely impossible to have love at first sight but that it is common to experience infatuation at first sight.

b. Love relationships tend to develop slowly over time.

4. How does the relationship end?

a. In a relationship based on infatuation, the relationship will normally die out as quickly as it began. There may be some temporary pain and pining, but normally within weeks or a couple months, a person begins to question what he or she ever saw in the other.

b. In love, the relationship will stand the test of time. If, for some reason, the love relationship must end, the pain may linger for years and, in fact, a person may never fully recover from the loss.

An interesting point to raise on this topic: Research shows that most relationships based on infatuation last *two years or less, unless the couple also shares a satisfying sex life*. A satisfying sex life can be such a strong influence in the relationship that it may help the couple stay together for three to five years before separating, *but such relationships will always end*. According to Short, this research makes a strong argument against premarital sex—that premarital sex totally skews one's judgment of the other and can lead to tragic consequences. He also suggests, based on this research, that people should not decide to marry unless they have been courting or engaged for two years, and longer if they are sexually active. To do otherwise is to invite a failed marriage.

5. How consistent are the levels of interest in each other?

a. In infatuation, interest comes and goes with almost daily fluctuations, vacillating between total interest, boredom, and even dislike for each other.

b. In love, the level or intensity of interest may tend to level out but will be constant.

6. How do the partners see each other?

a. In infatuation, the other is seen ideally, as faultless. One has an inability to see that the other has any weaknesses or problems. Psychologists call this "idealization of the other."

b. In love relationships, the faults of the other are recognized but accepted.

7. How does the relationship affect one's relationships with other people?

a. In infatuation, the universe of the person narrows down to just this one individual. Other friends and family members are often ignored or excluded. In the words of the song, "I only have eyes for you."

b. When real love is present, all of one's relationships are enhanced and enriched.

8. How do the parties react to physical separation over a period of time?

a. In relationships based on infatuation, Short says, "Absence truly makes the heart grow fonder . . . for someone else!" Distance and separation kill infatuation because it is so shallow to begin with.

b. In love, distance and time can be survived, and the relationship may actually grow stronger despite it.

9. What about quarreling between the persons involved?

a. In infatuation, quarrels and arguments tend to increase in both number and severity.

b. In love, this is reversed to the point that some people in love may legitimately claim that they have not argued in years. They find other ways to handle their disagreements and conflicts.

10. How do friends evaluate and react to the relationship?

a. In infatuation, friends of one party will often not care for his or her partner. Short points out that people become friends primarily because of many shared interests, common concerns, tastes, and so on. In infatuation, as we have noted, common interests are relatively few. It stands to reason that one's friends would see this and not feel attracted to the other party. One common response of a friend might be, "I just don't understand what she sees in him."

b. In the case of love, however, one's good friends often grow to care deeply for the other party. Why? Because, again, they all share many common interests and personality traits.

11. What are the effects of the relationships on the personalities of those involved?

a. People who are deeply infatuated are commonly disorganized, absent-minded, confused, spacey.

b. In love, one's life becomes more organized, better structured, and so on. Friends and others will be inclined to say things like, "Jane really got her act together after meeting John."

12. How do the parties feel and think about each other when not consciously choosing their reaction?

a. Infatuated people will commonly speak in terms of "he" or "she" and "I." Short suggests, for example, that in talking about a date one might say, "He picked me up at eight. And I was dressed in this way. And then he brought me to that place, where I did such-and-such."

b. By contrast, people in love will naturally and unconsciously speak in terms of "we" or "us."

13. What is the person's attitude toward his or her own needs?

a. In infatuation, one is primarily concerned about the satisfaction of one's own needs and speaks in terms of the other's ability to respond to those. The emphasis is on what is good for me, on taking, on selfishness.

b. When truly in love, one is primarily concerned about the needs of the other and will be willing to submerge his or her own needs to satisfy those of the other. The emphasis is toward selflessness.

Short says that this may be the clue that, of all fourteen, most clearly identifies true love. He suggests that one can ask oneself this related question: Do I love the other person so much that I want him or her to be happy *even if I am not the one who can make him or her so?* That is, would I rather have him or her happy with another person than unhappy with me? That is the truest test of love.

14. How is jealousy expressed in the relationship?

a. In infatuation, one will commonly speak of being "insanely jealous" of the other.

b. In love, one not only is generally not jealous but actually desires to share the loved one with other people so that they too can experience the gift that she or he is. One wants the other to grow and be fulfilled as a person in his or her own right.

As you have seen, there is a great deal of information in these "Main Ideas." The session plan, though, thoroughly explains how it all is to be shared with your group.

Procedure

A. Welcome and Opening Prayer (up to 15 minutes, depending on size of group)

Begin the session with the ritual described in session 2, adjusting it as needed, based on previous experience.

B. Introductory Comments by the Leader
(5 minutes)

1. Briefly review the themes already treated in this unit on human relationships:

- the variety of relationships experienced in life
- the qualities of satisfying relationships
- communication as the binding force of all relationships
- resolving conflicts in relationships through the use of good communication skills

2. Then comment along the following lines:

When all these themes are taken together, they point us toward the deepest, most satisfying relationships we can experience in life—relationships of intimacy. They are those rare relationships in our life that are characterized by true openness and trust, free self-expression and deep caring, and profound levels of communication. Because of the very nature of these intimate relationships, we will experience relatively few of them in life. For one thing, they take a lot of time to develop and then nurture. Also, there is a certain sense of giftedness experienced with such relationships, a feeling that we have been blessed by the other's presence through no power of our own. In other words, one often has the feeling of "just lucking out" when he or she discovers such an intimate relationship with another person.

3. However, a problem can result from the attitude of lucking out with relationships. If we allow ourselves to believe that good relationships are just a matter of luck, we will have no motivation to actively choose and develop them. The fact is, without at all denying that deep friendships are a gift, we can do a great deal to increase our chances of both developing and sustaining such relationships. It is no accident or just good luck that some people have more close friends than others. Nor is it just bad luck that so many people seem to go through life alone and miserable. It is not just luck that makes some marriages delightful and others disastrous. We *can* exert control over having successful intimate relationships in our life.

4. This session is going to be devoted to reflection on and discussion about intimacy and a related theme, the distinction between love and infatuation. These are vitally important issues for all people, of course, but never more important than at your stage of life. As young adults, you soon will be making some of the most important decisions about personal relationships that you will ever make. In the cultural situation of our times, such decisions can be downright terrifying.

5. At this point, I suggest that you illustrate the importance of this session and its themes. Offer a few of Dr. Ray Short's statistics of the success rate of marriages, provided in the "Main Ideas" section.

6. **The obvious question before us is, How can we increase our chances of making good decisions in future relationships? Such decisions are not restricted to those about marriage. Don't think that because your current plans for the immediate future do not include marriage that this discussion of intimacy, love, and infatuation has no meaning for you. We all need intimate relationships in order to grow as persons, whether we marry or not. Priests and religious need such relationships as much as anyone else. Remember what we said about this earlier: Intimacy doesn't necessarily include genital sexual expression. It is true that our main focus in this session will be on romantic relationships, primarily because this is such a common concern for young adults. However, much of what I have to say about intimacy applies to all close personal relationships.**

7. This session will include a fine film on intimacy, a discussion of it, and a discussion exercise on the differences between love and infatuation. We won't be getting so personal in this that you will be asked to reveal things about your private, personal relationships. However, we will be talking about sensitive issues that require a commitment to share what we believe and feel as well as great sensitivity to the thoughts and feelings of one another. As noted in our last session, these qualities are always required if communication is to take place. So I ask that you try even more than usual in this session to think seriously, to share your thoughts and feelings, and to listen attentively when others are sharing theirs.

C. Film: *A Question of Intimacy* (20 minutes)

Prepare the projector and screen in advance. The film begins with an introduction delivered by Keith Miller, so there is no need to say much about the film itself by way of introduction. Simply say something like this:

We're going to begin this session with an insightful film about intimacy—what it is, why people have such difficulty achieving it, how we can nurture it in our life. This film is different than any other film we have used during the SHARING Program. For one thing, it is quite demanding in that the topic is a complicated one, approached head-on, with mostly young adults doing the talking. There is no entertaining story line, no wonderful cinematography, no actors giving stunning performances. You will see people just like yourself, though a little older, talking from their hearts about a profoundly important subject.

So this is a film that must be closely listened to as well as viewed. Try to enter personally into the discussion by the people in the film. Pretend that you are a participant. What would you say in response to some of the questions raised? How would you react to the comments of various people? With whom would you agree or disagree? What would you want to say that no one seems to be saying? After the film, we will have the chance to express our own thoughts and opinions. Having said this, start the projector.

D. Discussion Activity on Intimacy (30 minutes total: 5 minutes in small groups; 25 minutes in large-group discussion)

See Student Handout 6–A following this session outline.

1. After showing the film, tell the group that the film offers so many insights and topics for discussion that one cannot simply say, "What do you think?" and expect the conversation to go well. Tell them that you want to begin the discussion with a brief activity to help focus thoughts in an ordered way.

2. This activity is based on a series of eight questions. The discussion of the questions will lead the group through a review of the major points raised in the film. Break the large group into eight small groups. If you have fewer than eight students in your group, you will have to eliminate some questions for this part of the activity; you can then interject those questions on your own during the large-group discussion.

3. Student Handout 6–A provides the discussion questions for the small groups. Simply cut a copy of that handout into individual slips for distribution to the groups. You could have the students randomly choose slips out of a box or hat. Each group will also need one pencil for taking notes. The assignments are self-explanatory. Tell the students that they have only 5 minutes for this part of the activity, so they must work quite quickly, brainstorming their responses to the questions on their slip of paper.

4. After 5 minutes, call the young people back together. The assigned slips of paper are numbered, and the numbers follow the order in which the issues are discussed in the film. Therefore, ask the group assigned the first question to share their thoughts first, then invite those assigned the second question to respond next, and so on through the last question. After each small group has stated its thoughts, invite reactions from the rest of the young people. Do they agree or disagree? Do they have anything to add? In this way, you will thoroughly discuss the entire film.

5. The allotted time for this discussion of the film is just 30 minutes, and that includes both small-group brainstorming and large-group sharing. This permits only 3 minutes of discussion on any one question. Obviously, that is very tight—though, at times, 3 minutes can seem like an eternity! If the group appears to be enthusiastically engaged in discussion, allow the discussion to flow and make the time adjustment later in the session. If the discussion of the film goes quickly, do not panic. Plenty of material is provided to fill the available time.

Note: If you choose not to use the film, see "Things to Keep in Mind" at the end of this session for an alternative approach to this session.

E. Break (10 minutes)

F. Love or Infatuation? A Confidential Self-test (15 minutes)

See Student Handout 6–B following this session outline.

1. As noted earlier, you may have time for this optional self-test only if your discussion of the film is shorter than the allotted 30 minutes. Have it available in case you need it. If you do not use it during the session, you might give it to the young people at the end of the session and suggest that they share the self-test with friends or the person with whom they are "going steady." The intent is to have the students reflect privately on the meaning of love and infatuation before a large-group discussion on the theme. Given the high interest in the subject, mature students are willing to spend considerable time in this kind of guided, individual reflection.

2. Distribute to each student a pencil and a copy of Student Handout 6–B, "Love or Infatuation? A Confidential Self-test." Read the directions on the handout, and make sure that the young people understand them. Emphasize that they will later compare

their answers to the results of research that has been done on this topic. As Dr. Joyce Brothers and other newspaper columnists have discovered, people love to compare their personal opinions about human relationships to those of the "experts."

3. You can be quite flexible with regard to the time allotted for this activity. Your major concentration of time should be on the next activity—the large-group sharing on this theme. You will want at least 30 minutes for that discussion and another 5 minutes or so for a closing prayer. Therefore, if time is tight, you may want to encourage the students to work quite quickly on their confidential self-test. If time is not a great concern, you can allow them to work at a more relaxed pace. Trust your intuition on this. If you feel that some are becoming bored while others are working diligently, try to motivate the latter to work more quickly.

G. Discussion Activity: Sex, Love, or Infatuation—How Can I Really Know?
(30 minutes minimum)

See Student Handout 6–C following this session outline.

1. Use Student Handout 6–C, "Is It Love or Infatuation?" for this discussion activity. One copy of the handout can serve a group of fourteen or fewer people; make additional copies if your group is larger than that. Prepare enough copies of the handout for all the students if you choose to give them each a copy at the end of the exercise.

2. If your group did *not* use the confidential self-test, you will need to cut up the copy of the handout into individual slips of paper, with one question and its answers on each slip. If your group *did* use the self-test, you will only need one copy of the handout to use as an answer sheet for yourself.

3. If your group used the confidential self-test, the transition to this activity will be quite simple. After all the students have completed the self-test and have regathered, tell them that you now want to review their responses and compare them to the information about love and infatuation gathered by researchers. Remind them that you are respecting their privacy on this; they are asked to share only what they are comfortable sharing. Then simply go through the self-test one question at a time, and ask anyone who is interested to share their response. Ask the group to come to a general concensus on how each question should be answered. Then, only *after* the group has arrived at its conclusion, reveal the results of the researchers. In cases where the young people's answers have been close to that of the researchers, commend them on their insight. If significant differences between the two are apparent, discuss the differences to the degree that you feel it beneficial or interesting.

4. If your group did *not* use the self-test, conduct this activity as follows:

a. Explain to the group that you have discovered research by social scientists on the distinctions between love and infatuation. As young adults who will be making terribly important decisions about marriage in the near future, it is absolutely vital that they be able to distinguish between love that will endure and the kind of infatuation that will last only a short time. This discussion is intended to help them make such distinctions.

b. Tell the young people that a great deal of what we know of human relationships is common sense based on past experience. We do not need doctoral degrees to know what makes people tick. To demonstrate this, you will have them answer some key questions about love and infatuation. Only one person in the group will have the answer based on social research. After some discussion, the right answer will be shared and compared to that offered by the group.

c. At this point, gather the group into a tight circle on the floor. (If the group is larger than fourteen, you will need more than one circle. The number in each of these groups can be whatever you wish, given the size of your group.)

d. In the center of the group, drop the fourteen slips of paper cut from the handout. These should be folded so that their contents cannot be seen. Tell the students that each slip of paper contains a question related to romantic relationships. They are to respond to the question in two ways:

- **First, how would one know when a couple is involved in infatuation regarding the question?**
- **Second, how would one determine when a couple is experiencing a true love relationship regarding the focus of the question?**

e. When these directions are clear, ask for a volunteer to randomly choose one of the slips of paper and to read *only the question in the left-hand column*. Open the question for discussion by the group on the two responses requested. Then have the volunteer share the results of the research summarized in the second and third columns, pointing out that these deal with the characteristics of infatuation and love respectively. When general agreement is apparent, ask another volunteer to randomly choose another slip and proceed as before. If significant disagreement exists, feel free to discuss a point at greater length, making sure that enough time is available to complete the activity.

5. If you prepared copies of the handout for each student, distribute them at the end of the activity.

H. Closing Prayer (two options, depending on available time)

1. Even more so than in other sessions, predicting the flow of time in this session is difficult. In SHARING IV, we are committed to having the young people control the depth of discussion and the time spent on individual points. Guesswork is necessarily involved in predicting the amount of time needed, so you will need optional approaches to this closing prayer.

2. The first option is dependent upon your experience with the last session. Session 4 also offered two options to the closing prayer, given available time. One of the options was a somewhat involved prayer service on healing the hurts of the past. *If you were not able to use the service at that time, and if* in preparing for this session you expect to have the time available here, I suggest that you prepare to use the prayer service in this session.

The prayer service will require the leader to offer a brief transitional statement along the following lines:

We have been discussing intimacy, and early in the session we talked of the kinds of fears that can keep us from pursuing intimate relationships with others. Of all of the fears that we experience, perhaps the most crippling is that rooted in the memory of bad past experiences. If we've been hurt in the past—and we all have been—it's hard to move into the future with hope and openness. So we must try to come to terms with the past hurts, to heal them in order to open ourselves to the possibility of future relationships. That is the focus of our closing prayer experience.

Then conduct the service as described in session 4.

3. If time is tight, you may have to opt for just a brief spontaneous prayer of your own. Or, if you want a prayer experience with a length that falls somewhere between the extensive and brief ones, consider incorporating into your closing prayer the lovely reading offered below. The reading relates well to the self-esteem that is required if one is to have the courage to reach out to others. Many songs in the SHARING music guides, located in the director's manual, also relate to the themes of this session and could be incorporated into your closing prayer.

Celebrate You!

Celebrate you!
   You are worth celebrating.
   You are worth everything.
   You are unique.
In the whole world there is only one you.
There is only one person with
   your talents
   your experiences
   your gifts.
No one can take your place.

God created only one you, precious in his sight.
You have immense potential
   to love
   to care
   to create
   to grow
   to sacrifice
   If you believe in yourself.

It doesn't matter your age, or your color, or whether your parents loved you or not. (Maybe they wanted to but couldn't.) Let that go. It belongs in the past. You belong to the *now.*

It doesn't matter what you have been, the wrong you've done, the mistakes you've made, the people you've hurt.

You are forgiven. You are accepted. You are OK.
   You are loved in spite of yourself.
   So love yourself, and nourish the seeds within you.

Celebrate you!

Begin *now.* Start anew. Give yourself a new birth.
   Today!
   You are you, and that is all you need to be.
   You are temporary. Here today and gone tomorrow.
   But today . . .
   Today can be a new beginning, a new thing, a new life.

You cannot deserve this new life.
   It is given freely.
   That is the miracle called God,
   So celebrate the miracle
   and celebrate you!

Things to Keep in Mind

Regarding the film *A Question of Intimacy*

The film can be rented for $35.00 from Mass Media Ministries, 2116 North Charles Street, Baltimore, Maryland 21218. Phone 301-727-3270. Be sure to rent the film well in advance of your scheduled show date.

For a variety of reasons, you may decide not to use the film *A Question of Intimacy*, which is a major component of this session. What can you do in such a situation?

I noted a number of times that this session is loaded with content and stimulating educational strategies. The leaders who *do* choose to use the film may find that they have too much material and end up cutting some of it; those who choose *not* to use the film on intimacy, therefore, will be able to expand their discussion on love versus infatuation to fill the available time. It will be possible to incorporate some of the meanings of intimacy into this discussion. Consider the following suggestions in conducting this session without the use of the film.

1. Include the confidential self-test on love and infatuation that is identified as optional in the session plan. As noted in the directions for that activity, the time allotted for it is quite flexible. If you do not use the film, allow the students a relaxed period of time for completing the self-test.

2. For the discussion activity "Sex, Love, or Infatuation: How Can I Really Know?" I indicated that a *minimum* of 30 minutes is to be devoted to the discussion. Feel free to expand the time frame for this discussion, simply by allowing the young people to pursue the many avenues for further discussion opened up by the activity.

3. The "Main Ideas" section of this session plan provides a great deal of information about intimacy as it is discussed in the film. Read that information thoroughly before teaching the session, reflecting on those points that might relate most directly to the love versus infatuation discussion activity. You will then be able to interject these ideas into that activity, provoking more discussion among the young people.

4. Finally, plan on using all of the components suggested for the closing prayer experience.

The fact that I have included the film *A Question of Intimacy* in this session plan indicates how highly I regard it, and I encourage you to share it with your young people if at all possible. However, I hope that these suggestions on how to conduct the session without the film will allay the fears of the leaders who are unable to arrange use of the film.

For Evaluation

1. From your experience with the film, do you now feel that it required the disciplined approach to discussion recommended in the session plan? Would a more open-ended approach have better served your young people?

2. If you used the confidential self-test, did it appear to hold the interest of your young people while they worked on it alone, and did its use then result in an effective large-group discussion? If not, note the possibility of dropping the self-test in your future use of this session.

3. One of my major concerns in developing this session was the restricted time allowed for the large-group discussion of love and infatuation. Given your experience, do you feel that the discussion activity requires more time than was allowed for it? Could you make a decision at this time on which elements of the plan you would shorten or drop altogether to accommodate a lengthier discussion?

4. How did you choose to handle the closing prayer? Would you now want to close the session in a different manner? Note this in your notebook.

5. Were the "Teacher Goals" and "Student Intellectual/Behavioral Objectives" for this session achieved?

STUDENT HANDOUT 6-A

Small-Group Discussion Assignments for
A Question of Intimacy

---

1. The film suggests several words or phrases that are related to the meaning of intimacy:

   security, closeness, fear, sense of belonging and being loved, knowing something special about oneself, ultimate trust, overall acceptance of another, vulnerability to rejection

   Your assignment is this: Using these or other words of your own choosing, develop a one-sentence definition of intimacy. You may write it on the back of this paper.

---

2. Keith Miller, the narrator of the film, says at one point, "Unfortunately, intimacy and pain come through the same doorway, so that if we block the pain, we block the intimacy." Identify three kinds or examples of pain associated with intimacy to which he might have been referring. Jot your answers on the back of this paper.

---

3. Below are listed all of the fears associated with intimacy that are identified by members of the group in the film. Rank these fears in terms of which are most prevalent or strong **for people your age.** Do so by putting number 1 in front of the most common fear for your age-group, number 2 in front of the second most common, and so on, for each fear. Be prepared to explain your top choices.

   ____ fear of not being known or recognized
   ____ fear of being awkward in expressing affection
   ____ fear based on one's upbringing, in which one has been told to "save intimacy for marriage"
   ____ fear of being rejected when one reveals his or her real self
   ____ fear that, after risking intimacy, the relationship won't last
   ____ fear based on past failures
   ____ fear of revealing something about oneself that will be used against you later
   ____ fear of losing control of the relationship

---

4. The narrator of the film suggests that there are basically two kinds of people:

   a. "skunks" find ways to keep people at a distance
   b. "turtles" withdraw into a shell to hide from people

   He goes on to say, "Unfortunately, skunks and turtles almost always marry each other!"
   From your experience, do you believe that "opposites attract one another" in human relationships? If so, why do you think this happens? Do you agree with the narrator when he claims this is "unfortunate"? Why or why not?

---

5. Using the image of a chicken in an egg, Miller summarizes two schools of thought about helping people to "come out of their shells" to reveal their true selves:
   a. We can use a hammer to break open their shells.
   b. We can surround them with a warm, caring environment and let them break out of their own shells.

   Give examples of how this imagery relates to human relationships. Why does Miller suggest that the second approach has the better chance of leading to intimacy?

6. Miller suggests that ultimately there is only one way for two people to initiate an intimate relationship: Someone has to take the risk to make it happen. Give three reasons of your own that such a risk seems worth taking:

   a. _____

   b. _____

   c. _____

7. One woman in the film suggests that a major problem in establishing intimate relationships with the opposite sex is having one's intentions misunderstood. A person might want to be a caring friend but can be misunderstood as wanting a romantic, sexual relationship. Is this a common concern of young adults? How might one overcome this problem without withdrawing or hiding from people?

8. Miller states twice that we need a sense of personal security before we can reach out to others in intimate relationships. He says we can find such security in two ways: We can look within ourselves and count on our own resources. Or we can look outside ourselves—to psychotherapy, support groups, religious faith, and so on. Do you agree with him that faith in God can provide the security one needs to seek intimacy? Why or why not?

STUDENT HANDOUT 6-B

Love or Infatuation?
A Confidential Self-test

Directions: In preparation for a discussion on determining whether one is in a true love relationship or merely infatuated with another person, you are asked to complete this confidential self-test. **No one will see what you write, and you will not be asked to share with anyone anything you write on this paper that you do not wish to share.** This is only intended to spark your interest in and focus your attention on this complex issue.

Look at the three columns of boxes below. In the first column is a series of questions regarding romantic relationships. You are to do the following:
- In the second column across from each question, jot down a few words that summarize the characteristic response to the question when people are infatuated with one another;
- In the third column, briefly summarize a likely response to the question when a person is truly in love.

Later in the session, answers to these questions will be provided that are based on social scientists' research on love and marriage. You will be able to check your opinions and intuitions against "the facts" as the research has determined them.

Regarding the questions below	. . . when one is infatuated?	. . . when one is truly in love?
What is the major attraction between the persons . . .		
How many different things attract them to each other . . .		
How did the relationship begin . . .		
How will the relationship end, if at all . . .		
How consistent are their levels of interest in each other . . .		

Reproduction permission is granted if you wish to make copies for classroom use.
The photocopy master for this handout is found at the back of this manual.

Regarding the questions below	. . . when one is infatuated?	. . . when one is truly in love?
How does one react to the other's faults and weaknesses . . .		
How does their relationship with each other affect their relationships with others . . .		
How do they react to distance of time or space away from each other . . .		
How frequent and severe are their arguments or quarrels . . .		
How do one's friends respond to the other person and to the relationship . . .		
How does the relationship affect their personalities as individuals . . .		
How does each refer to the other in casual speech . . .		
What is a person's attitude toward his or her own needs . . .		
In what ways, if at all, is jealousy of the other expressed in the relationship . . .		

The Search for Intimacy: A Risk Worth Taking

STUDENT HANDOUT 6-C

Is It Love or Infatuation?

The following chart summarizes the results of research done by social scientists on the phenomena of love and infatuation. In the left-hand column are key questions, the answers to which can serve as clues as to whether one is involved in a relationship based on infatuation or on love. The middle and right-hand columns indicate responses reflective of relationships of infatuation or love, respectively.

Clearly, romantic personal relationships are so complex in reality that they cannot be easily evaluated and judged. However, one sociologist—Dr. Ray Short, the originator of this material—suggests that before deciding to marry, a couple should be able to answer positively to at least eleven of the fourteen responses in the right-hand column. Or, on the negative side, if a couple agrees with five or more of the responses listed in the middle column, they are likely involved in a relationship of infatuation and should avoid or delay a decision to get married.

Regarding the questions below	...when one is infatuated?	...when one is truly in love?
What is the major attraction between the persons...	The major attraction is physical appearance.	The major attraction is the total personality.
How many different things attract them to each other...	Only a few things attract one to the other.	One finds many things attractive in the other.
How did the relationship begin...	The relationship began very fast; "love at first sight."	The relationship grew more slowly, steadily.
How will the relationship end, if at all...	The relationship will end as it began—fast.	The relationship will stand the test of time.
How consistent are their levels of interest in each other...	The interest will come and go, and will be uneven and unreliable.	Interest will have fewer peaks and valleys, and will be more consistent.

Regarding the following question . . .	. . . when one is infatuated?	. . . when one is truly in love?
How does one react to the other's faults and weaknesses . . .	The other's faults are never seen; the person is idealized.	The faults and weaknesses are recognized but accepted.
How does their relationship with each other affect their relationships with others . . .	The universe narrows to this relationship; all others are excluded.	All other relationships are enhanced and enriched.
How do they react to distance of time or space away from each other . . .	Distance and time apart kills the relationship.	The two may actually grow closer when separated; they can overcome it.
How frequent and severe are their arguments or quarrels . . .	Arguments become more frequent and increase in intensity.	Arguments lessen as they find better ways to resolve conflict.
How do one's friends respond to the other person and to the relationship . . .	One's friends tend not to like the other; they have differing interests.	Friends support and affirm the relationship; they share interests.
How does the relationship affect their personalities as individuals . . .	Persons become disorganized, forgetful, spacey.	Persons become more organized, structured, together.
How does each refer to the other in casual speech . . .	Tends to speak as "he and I" or "she and I."	Begins to refer to selves as "we" or "us."
What is a person's attitude toward his or her own needs . . .	Emphasis will be on satisfying one's own needs.	Emphasis will be on the needs of the other.

Regarding the following question . . .	. . . when one is infatuated?	. . . when one is truly in love?
In what ways, if at all, is jealousy of the other expressed in the relationship . . .	One tends to speak of being "insanely" jealous.	Little or no jealousy exists; one desires to share loved one with others.

Session 7

Faith and the Young Adult: Seeking Intimacy with God

Teacher Goals

To help the young people reflect on and begin to prepare for the faith development tasks and challenges they confront as young adults; to provide them with a sense of hope in their ability to cope with those tasks and challenges; to invite them to participate in the next phase of this program.

Student Intellectual/Behavioral Objectives

That the young people identify those areas of their life that require their attention and nurturing if they are to grow in their Catholic Christian faith; that they begin to set concrete goals for their future faith development; that they seriously consider joining the next phase of this program.

Main Ideas

In this session, the last of the two-hour sessions of SHARING IV, the focus is directly on the future faith development of the young adults in your group. Certainly all of the other sessions have included a faith dimension. For example, all the sessions have included opening and closing prayers as well as references to the significance of Christian faith in regard to the session topics. However, in this session we will directly address the unique faith development tasks that will soon confront the young people.

What is so unique about faith development through the young adult years? To some extent, the faith characteristics common for seniors in high school will simply continue on during the next several years. Protestant religious educator John Westerhoff calls the style of faith typical to middle to late adolescence as "searching faith." From about the sophomore year of high school through at least the mid-twenties, young people go through a process of evaluating and weighing a commitment to the religious tradition introduced to them in childhood. Much of what they have learned and experienced during childhood has to be reassessed in terms of their maturing cognitive abilities and in light of their life experience to this point. The decision they face is whether they want to freely adopt and personally claim as their own the faith tradition that has been handed on to them by others.

As noted, searching faith is typical of middle to late adolescence. What is unique to young adults is the common fact that as they leave high school and move on to college or employment, they will be experiencing searching faith without the support of family and parish. The majority will soon be leaving their home and often their community. For most, the days when parish representatives such as yourself would take the initiative and invite them to a religion-oriented program are over. The schools they go to may have chaplains or Newman Center programs, but it will be up to them as individuals to take advantage of such opportunities. The reality is that for the vast majority of the young people in your program, this will be their last formal religious education unless they consciously choose otherwise. They may even have to initiate such programs themselves.

The primary focus of this session is to alert the young people to the character of their future religious development and to help them prepare for the faith challenges they face as young adults. The context in which we will discuss their future faith life will be the concepts of Christian spirituality and conversion. The session is heavily dependent on two short presentations by the leader and concentrated discussion by the young people. Yet the session dynamically moves back and forth from input to discussion and includes effective strategies for promoting group discussion.

Special note: Depending on how you organize your use of SHARING IV and on how the young people respond to it, this may or may not be your final session with them. Though the retreat options follow the sessions in the program manual, you may opt to conduct the retreat early in the year or not at all. Similarly, you may or may not be using the meditation program as part of your total program. Consequently, this session has the flavor of a conclusion, of coming to the end of the program. Time is allotted in the session plan for announcing future program opportunities if there are any available. In any case, you may have to slightly adjust some of the tone and content of this session depending on the schedule for the year.

Due to the centrality of the themes of Christian spirituality and conversion in this session, some information about these two themes is offered here. Read these notes over carefully because they will be your major resource for the comments that you will be asked to share in this session. Like session 6, this session includes an extensive "Main Ideas" section and then relatively brief directions in the procedure section.

Christian Spirituality: Living by the Spirit of Jesus

Throughout the SHARING Program, Christian faith has consistently been defined as a personal love relationship with God, the God who is revealed to us in and through the life, death, and Resurrection of Jesus. As a love relationship with God, religious faith, if it is to achieve depth, demands the kind of hard work required in loving. As a love relationship, faith is an art that requires a willingness to learn from personal experience, a sensitivity to the many ways God is revealed in life, a desire to make daily efforts at community building, and creativity in responding to God's revelation.

The art of living one's faith in God in unique, individual ways is called *personal spirituality*. Each person develops a personal spirituality according to his or her own needs, abilities, and background. A person's spirituality is Christian when it centers on and responds to the life and message of Jesus as revealed in the Gospel. Christian spirituality is living by the Spirit of Jesus.

Throughout the Gospels, we see that Jesus himself was led by the Spirit. He promised to send a Spirit who would lead people to truth, and then he shared that Spirit at Pentecost. The signs of the presence of that Spirit are identified in Saint Paul's letter to the Galatians: "The fruit of the Spirit is love, joy, peace, patience, kindness, goodness, trustfulness, gentleness and self-control" (Gal. 5:22). How does a Christian learn to live by the Spirit? That is, how can someone gain the openness, sensitivity, strength, and creativity to follow the impulses of that Spirit in daily life?

If Christians are to continually grow in their ability to respond to God in the Spirit of Jesus, they must take on the following four tasks:

1. Christians must constantly seek better knowledge of the meaning and message of Jesus.
2. Christians must grow in personal prayer to sustain and strengthen their faith.
3. Christians must seek and participate in the community of faith to gain support and encouragement from other believers.
4. Christians must reach out in loving service to the people around them.

These four tasks—centered on knowledge, prayer, community, and service—are at the heart of Christian spirituality. A few comments about each of these tasks may be helpful for discussing them with the young people in your group.

Growing in knowledge of Jesus' life and message

A growing love relationship of any kind requires a constantly growing understanding between the people involved. Whereas initial knowledge of a person is necessary for making a commitment of love, that love in turn often drives a person to seek more understanding of the loved one.

The same is true about faith in God: A basic knowledge about Jesus and his message is required before the personal decision about faith can be made. Yet after that decision has been made, an almost unquenchable thirst for more knowledge develops. To whom or to what sources does the Christian turn for more information?

To this point in their life, the young people have been provided with most of their information about the Gospel of Jesus. It has come from their parents, from formal religious education programs sponsored by their parish, and from the experience of communal worship, particularly from hearing the Gospel proclaimed and explained in the liturgy. A minority may have sought out information on their own by private reading of the Scriptures. Some may have developed personal, caring relationships with people of faith who have shared their spiritual journey with the young people. Mainly, however, it would seem that parents, parish religious education, and communal worship have been ready-made sources for their information about Jesus and the Good News he proclaimed.

As the young people now move forward into young adulthood, what new sources of growing understanding about the Gospel will be available to them? What kind of initiative and discipline will be required of them if their level of understanding is not to stagnate as they leave behind home and home parish?

Deepening knowledge through prayer

For a long time in the history of the Catholic Church, Christian faith was viewed as an assent to truth, that is, an intellectual acceptance of the teachings of Jesus. The Church now teaches that such a view of faith in God is too narrow, too restricted to the intellectual level of a person. Christian faith is much more than an understanding of and agreement with truth. If faith in God were only that, a person's ability to grow in faith would be mainly dependent upon his or her level of intelligence. Nothing could be further from the truth.

Believers need to learn and accept as much truth about God as possible, but if faith remains on the level of the intellect, it is not faith in its fullest sense. Faith in God must go much deeper than the mind. It must touch the depths of the heart and become a person-to-person relationship. The usual way that faith lives and grows at this level is through the experience of prayer.

Prayer is often thought about in the restricted sense of talking to God or saying prayers—as if prayer is simply a matter of repeating words in the hope that someone out there is listening to them. Thinking of prayer in a larger and more personal sense can help to improve our appreciation of it.

Contemporary writings often refer to prayer as communication in a relationship of love. The word *communication* indicates that prayer is not a one-way process in which a person simply talks to God. Rather, *communication* implies that what is shared in prayer is a two-way exchange, or dialogue. In a prayerful dialogue, the person shares his or her thoughts and feelings but also receives some feedback—that is, some kind of response from God. How does this happen?

While keeping in mind that God's ways are not always our human ways, the answer has much to do with the fact that the communication within prayer takes place within a relationship of love. People in love communicate in all sorts of ways, not just with words. Many times, in fact, words seem almost to get in the way of communication between friends. For example, many of us have had the experience of simply sitting for a long time in the presence of a friend without saying a thing. We might listen to music together, take a long walk in silence, or sit quietly by a lakeshore or on a hill, sharing a beautiful view. Does communication take place in such situations? Sure it does; we leave these encounters with friends feeling refreshed and also feeling closer and more trustful than before.

Prayer works in a similar way. Some kinds of prayer do not require words, yet they are fulfilling dialogues rather than monologues. For example, teachers of spirituality would identify the experience of contemplation as somewhat akin to sitting silently with a friend.

The young people who have participated in a good portion of the SHARING Program have experienced a wide variety of approaches to prayer, and they have probably grown in this dimension of their life. Soon, however, they are going to be leaving the program. How will they sustain their prayer life?

Participation in the community of believers

The third dimension of Christian spirituality is the practice of joining with others in the community of faith. Jesus taught that faith in God is not just a one-on-one relationship. In other words, Christian faith is not a matter of each believer living in isolation, pursuing only a private relationship with God. Faith is ultimately a communal experience—that is, an experience that must be shared with others if it is to mature. That is precisely why the Church exists.

Consequently, participation in community is necessary for Christian spirituality for two main reasons:

- The message of God's love promotes a sense of celebration. The believer has a desire to reach out to others in joy. When something great happens to us, we want to have a party, to get all the gang together to share our good fortune. This urge to celebrate God's blessings is one of the impulses for participating in the Church, the community of faith.

- The actual living out of the message of Jesus can be difficult. Trying to be all we can, trying to care for others, can be plain hard work, which cannot be done without the help of others who share our convictions. So the encouragement and support of other believers is vital.

The parish has been the primary faith community of the young people to this point in their life. More specifically, the parish may have sponsored a youth group of which the young people felt very much a part and to which they felt deeply committed. In the near future, the young people will likely be leaving these supportive communities behind, at least temporarily. Where will they go to find the kind of communal experience that is required if their spirituality is to be sustained?

Reaching out to others in service

Mature Christian spirituality demands that believers care for more than their own happiness and that of their local community. Indeed, the entire thrust of the message of Jesus is that Christians must use their talents to reach out to the whole world—a world that desperately needs the healing touch of love.

Too many Christians feel responsible only for themselves and their own development. They figure that if they avoid doing bad things, they have done all that is asked of them. This simply is not the case. Christian spirituality is more than avoiding the bad. Rather, it is a matter of doing the good by stretching beyond one's own interests to help others. This attitude of service includes a sincere concern that all people be treated with justice. Everyone must do as much as possible to alleviate the monumental problem of world hunger, for example, and to work toward the time when the world can truly live at peace.

Confronting the worldwide problems of justice and peace is an awesome task. These issues can seem so tough that many people, regardless of age, have a tremendous sense of powerlessness in the face of them. The result can be feelings of frustration and despair. This is a major reason that Christians seek the support of a caring community as they devote themselves to efforts on behalf of justice and peace. Such feelings can be particularly strong for adolescents and young adults, who are also caught up in struggles concerning identity and relationships.

How might these young people continue to make service a part of their spirituality as they leave their parish and its programs? How might they avoid the common spiritual trap of seeking satisfaction of their personal needs while forgetting or ignoring the gospel call to help the needy and the suffering?

The first half of this session includes a discussion activity designed to engage the young people in reflection on and discussion of these four tasks and questions about their future spiritual development.

The second major theme of the session, Christian

conversion, also requires some background for the leader. The following information should be helpful.

Christian Conversion: Turning Toward the Lord

One of the most striking features of Jesus' preaching was his call for a radical change in the lives of those who would be his followers. For instance, early in Mark's Gospel, we find this statement: "After John [the Baptist] had been arrested, Jesus went into Galilee. There he proclaimed the gospel from God saying, 'The time is fulfilled, and the kingdom of God is close at hand. Repent, and believe the gospel'" (Mark 1:14–15).

The Greek word that Mark used for "repent"—*metanoia*—literally means to "turn around" or to change one's direction. This turning around refers to a deeply personal change of direction—that is, a change of heart or a change of mind. Jesus taught that if people are to fully experience the kingdom of God, they must not only see God within themselves but also within others. In Christian theology, this change of heart and mind is called conversion.

Different Christian churches understand conversion in different ways. If you have watched some of the preachers on Sunday morning television programs, for example, you have heard conversion described as a dramatic, emotional moment in the believers' lives when they "accepted Jesus as their Lord and Savior." Or perhaps at the door of your home or even in a public place, someone has asked you directly, "Have you been saved? Have you turned your life over to Jesus?" Some Christians can even provide a specific date and time when they "asked Jesus into their heart."

Certainly God can touch the minds and hearts of people in dramatic and deeply moving personal experiences. However, most Christians do not experience this kind of conversion. The long-standing Catholic perception of conversion is that it is a gradual, lifelong process in which the person of faith turns to God as the center of his or her life. This process can be filled with many twists and turns, with hopeful leaps forward and fearful steps backward, with moments of intense closeness to God and times of deep loneliness and confusion.

In the Catholic tradition, therefore, conversion is understood as similar to the process of human development in all other stages of life. That is, each of us must grow through childhood, adolescence, and years of adulthood before we can achieve full maturity. In the same way, only gradually do people choose, freely and consciously, to live out a faith in Jesus.

Some people have suggested that Christian conversions have a common pattern. I have evolved my own understanding of this common pattern, one that can be expressed graphically as follows:

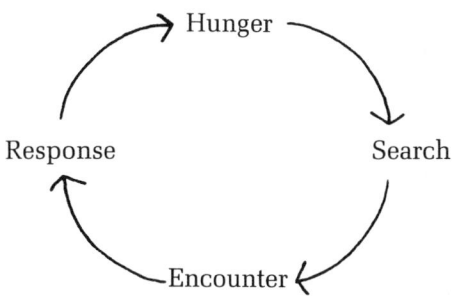

This model of the conversion process identifies four steps in the process that seem to have a cyclic movement in the lives of believers:

1. All growth in faith appears to be motivated by some experience of what I call "hunger." We experience within ourselves an emptiness, a need for meaning, deep confusion, loneliness—the hunger can take many forms. Within this hunger there is an overriding yearning for something more, something that can satisfy our deepest needs.

2. The experience of hunger necessarily leads to a search for what will satisfy it. The nature of the search will be directly related to the kind of hunger involved. For example, if the hunger is for an intellectual grasp of the meaning of one's life, the search may well be a disciplined, cognitive activity often identified in discussions of conversion as "the search for truth." On the other hand, one might experience the hunger as the need for personal intimacy. In that case, the search might take various forms: A misguided search, for instance, might include sexual promiscuity. Or, more positively, the search for intimacy could be a search for more authentic and deeper friendships.

3. Christian faith leads us to the conviction that whenever one is engaged in an honest search for truth—whether that takes an intellectual form or otherwise—God will inevitably be encountered in the midst of or at the end of that search. How God is actually encountered will vary from person to person and from one experience to another. Commonly, the encounter with God takes place within other personal love relationships. When we are truly loved by another human person, the reality of God's presence can become very tangible. That is one reason why Saint John could say that "God is love, and whoever remains in love remains in God and God in him" (1 John 4:16). One can almost be loved into a profound encounter with God.

4. God's offer of love is always an invitation. God never forces people to respond. Accordingly, every encounter with God demands a free response on the part of the individual. That response, like the search, can take many forms. It may be a simple matter of acknowledging the presence of God and deciding to follow the Gospel more enthusiastically. On the other hand, the response may be difficult and challenging, perhaps requiring a dramatic change of lifestyle. By the same token, one's response to God may result in exhilaration, joy, even euphoria, or in a fear about the possible consequences. What is certain is that whatever the immediate effects of the response may be, the sense of hunger will soon return, often with a different appetite. The process of conversion once again repeats its cycle.

The image of conversion in this model is a cyclic one. A more accurate or richer image would be that of a descending spiral, reflecting the fact that a person never stays at the same level of relationship with God. With each successive cycle, faith and relationship with God grows deeper and deeper. The hunger may become sharper and the search more intense, but faith and relationship also become more substantive, more mature. Moved by the deeper hunger, the believer searches more directly for God's presence at the center of his or her life, now heartened in the search by previous encounters with God. The encounters with God take on greater intimacy, and the response becomes more passionate. The cycle of growth continues. This is the marvelous journey of faith.

What does this understanding of conversion have to offer the young people in your group? My intent is that it will provide them with a hopeful context in which to view their future spiritual development. In this session, the young people will reflect on the hungers that are peculiar to young adults and will weigh alternate directions their search may take. They will do this with the conviction—if not with a personal conviction, with the promise of the Gospel—that God will inevitably be encountered in the search. In embracing the journey that is Christian conversion, they will be saying yes to all that God has in store for them as they leave our programs and pursue on their own a relationship of intimacy with God. In the closing prayer for this session, we express together, in the words of Dag Hammarskjold, the sentiment that I hope sums up the attitudes of the young people at this time: "For all that has been, thanks! For all that will be, yes!"

Procedure

A. Welcome and Opening Prayer (up to 15 minutes, depending on size of group)

Begin the session with the prayer ritual as it has evolved throughout previous sessions. Note that if you have been using the individual plants as symbols during this ritual, the plants will be formally presented to the young people during the closing prayer for this session.

B. Introductory Comments by the Leader (5 to 10 minutes)

1. Prepare an introductory presentation for this session based on the notes on Christian spirituality from the "Main Ideas" section. Note that throughout this course we have been discussing themes such as developing a dream for the future, making difficult choices, and learning how to develop satisfying personal relationships. All of these themes apply directly to our spiritual development as Christians. Just as a personal relationship with another person can be one of acquaintanceship, friendship, or intimacy, so it is with our God. Should we choose to commit to a relationship of true intimacy with God, we will have to work as hard on that as on marriage or any other intimate relationship.

2. You may wish to use a chalkboard or newsprint for listing the four dimensions of spirituality: growing knowledge of Jesus, deepening prayer life, participation in community, and service to others. Such a visual aid will help both your presentation and the young people's comprehension. Illustrating each point with an insight or an anecdote based on your personal experience will also help to bring the information to life for the group.

3. The session plan allows 5 to 10 minutes for this presentation. If you wish to keep it brief, a simple listing and short explanation of each of the four dimensions of spirituality will be sufficient. If you wish to present the information with anecdotes, try to keep them short and to the point so as not to extend beyond 10 minutes.

C. Discussion Activity: Growing in Spirituality as a Young Adult (30 minutes)

1. The purpose of this activity is to have the young people discuss the ways in which they as young adults might grow in the four areas of spirituality identified in the introductory presentation. Making such decisions on their own—rather

than having leaders supply them with predetermined ideas or advice—is necessary if they are to view this material as relevant and achievable in the real world.

2. Before the session, prepare four large (4-by-6-inch) index cards with one of the following four statements typed or printed at the top of each:

a. **On this card, identify specific questions or concerns you have regarding** *the ability of young adults to continue to grow in their understanding of Jesus and the Gospel after they leave the parish and its formal religious education programs.* **Your task is simply to state the problems confronting young adults in this area of their spirituality, not to propose solutions to those problems. You have 5 minutes.**

b. **On this card, identify specific questions or concerns you have regarding** *the ability of young adults to continue to grow in their prayer life after they leave the parish and its formal religious education programs.* **Your task is simply to state the problems confronting young adults in this area of their spirituality, not to propose solutions to those problems. You have 5 minutes.**

c. **On this card, identify specific questions or concerns you have regarding** *the ability of young adults to continue to be part of the community of faith after they leave the parish and its formal religious education programs.* **Your task is simply to state the problems confronting young adults in this area of their spirituality, not to propose solutions to those problems. You have 5 minutes.**

d. **On this card, identify specific questions or concerns you have regarding** *the ability of young adults to engage in Christian service to others after they leave the parish and its formal religious education programs.* **Your task is simply to state the problems confronting young adults in this area of their spirituality, not to propose solutions to those problems. You have 5 minutes.**

3. Divide the large group into four small groups. After giving the introductory comments, tell the young people that you want them to help one another come up with ideas on how, as young adults, they might creatively meet the challenge of developing their spirituality. The first step is to have them identify the particular concerns and problems of young adults associated with each of the four dimensions of spirituality. To accomplish this, give each of the four groups one of the cards and its assignment, along with a pencil for note-taking. Ask each group to select a secretary. After the group discusses the problems or concerns called for by the assignment, the secretary is to briefly summarize the responses in writing on the cards. Emphasize that the groups have 5 minutes to complete the assignment on the card.

4. The students may request a little more time than the 5 minutes allotted. If so, permit just a couple more minutes, but ask them to work quickly. When the students are done, collect the cards. Then redistribute the cards to the groups, making sure that no group receives its own card. Now the groups are to discuss the cards they have been given. Their new task is to propose three concrete solutions to the problems summarized on their cards. Their solutions to the problems should also be briefly summarized in writing on the cards. Ask them to be as practical as possible, offering advice they believe is reasonable for young adults. They have just 10 minutes for this part of the activity.

5. When time is up, gather the young people together. Each group secretary should first read the assignment on the card and then state the problems identified by the previous group. Then the secretaries share with the large group their group's suggested solutions to those problems. After each of these reports, open the discussion to reactions and further comments by the rest of the young people. Feel free to contribute your own observations, but do so primarily by way of closing comments for each of the four reports.

6. Close the activity with appropriate observations of your own. That is, commend the young people if you feel that they have creatively responded to the assignment and have come up with sound advice about the spiritual growth of young adults. If the discussion indicated a lack of such advice, or if it is clear that they have few thoughts about how to nurture their future spirituality, call this to their attention. You need not minimize or sugarcoat the situation. It is vital that the young people become conscious of this need and awakened to the requirement of effort on their part if their spiritual life is not to stagnate after they leave the program.

D. Break (10 minutes)

E. Leader Presentation on Christian Conversion (up to 15 minutes, depending on degree of personal sharing)

1. Present to the young people the basic understanding of Christian conversion explained in the

"Main Ideas" section. Be prepared to describe the process of conversion in a step-by-step fashion, drawing the cyclic model of conversion on the chalkboard or newsprint as you present it.

2. A flexible time frame is indicated for this presentation. The basic information about conversion might be shared in as little as 5 minutes. If you opt for such a brief approach, adjust the time allotted for other parts of the session accordingly. However, I encourage you to expand the presentation with personal anecdotes. Such personal sharing may be easier in this presentation than in the first one and, as always, personal storytelling will greatly enliven the presentation.

F. Discussion Activity: Searching for Satisfaction of the Hungers of Young Adulthood (20 minutes)

1. After your presentation on the cyclic process of conversion, ask the young people if any parts of the process seem to be more pressing or typical for young adults than for other age-groups. After noting their responses, make the following comment:

Although the entire process of conversion is going on at all times within each of us, it does seem that at certain stages of development, some dimensions of the process take center stage. Many would suggest, for instance, that during the period of adolescence, the experiences of hunger and search predominate. Adolescence seems to be more a time for asking the questions about life than it is a time for discovering the answers. After all, it is hard to come up with answers before the questions have been asked. If adolescence is the time for questions, then two questions seem paramount:

a. Just what are the major hungers experienced by young adults today?

b. Where and in what ways can young people search for responses to those hungers, responses that have a good chance of leading to satisfying results—and encounters with God—rather than to disappointment or worse?

2. Be prepared at this time to redistribute a handout used in the first session of this program, Student Handout 1–B, entitled "Ten Tasks for Young Adults." Ask the students if the handout looks familiar to them and briefly note its origin for anyone who was not at the first session.

3. Suggest that one reasonable way to identify the major hungers of young adults is to look once again at their key developmental tasks. Remind the students again of the basic meaning of hunger as understood in the context of conversion—that it is a strong interior sense of need, of looking for more in life, of experiencing a kind of emptiness within oneself. Then ask this question: **When looking at the list of the ten tasks of young adults, do any of them strike you as undertakings in which you might experience that sense of need, of emptiness, of looking for more?** Allow a couple of minutes for responses, and offer the opportunity for others to agree or disagree when someone in the group makes a suggestion. Have a pen or pencil handy to check off on your copy of the handout those tasks that the students identify as including hungers. The students might acknowledge that *all* of the tasks could be identified as involving hungers. If they do so, ask them to choose the three tasks that they think will likely provoke the deepest hunger in their life.

4. Note that one key to happiness in life, and in the process of conversion as well, is to search for that which has the best chance of satisfying the hungers of life. We are constantly confronted with tough choices, a fact that we explored in session 3 of this program. For every hunger we experience, we can choose positive, life-affirming, fulfilling responses, or we can choose negative, destructive, death-dealing responses.

5. At this point, randomly select any one of the tasks identified as strongly relating to the experience of hunger in the young people's life. Then brainstorm with the group in this manner:

a. Try to think of three negative ways to try to satisfy this hunger, that is, common responses that some individuals might choose that ultimately produce negative effects.

b. Then try to come up with three positive ways to respond to this hunger, that is, responses that can enrich and enhance the life of the person.

Carry this discussion as long as time permits, having decided in advance the time needed for your closing prayer experience.

6. When available time is spent, sum up the discussion with comments such as these:

The process of conversion to the Lord, like that of life itself, is a matter of continually making life-affirming choices when confronted with many options. At times the best option will be fairly clear, and your decision will be an easy one. At other times all of the available options will seem painful and difficult, and your decision may come only grudgingly after a few sleepless nights. In all cases,

if your heart is set on truth, if your goal is to be a person of integrity and honesty, if your commitment is to the dream that you have chosen for your life, then you can be assured that God is with you in your search—with you on your journey every step of the way. That is why we adults who care for you so much can be filled with hope and gratitude as you move away from us in pursuit of your dream. You go with God and with our prayers.

G. Announcements About Future Programs (5 minutes)

If you are providing the retreat, the meditation program, or other options following this session, make all relevant announcements about those programs at this time. If appropriate, you may wish to sign up interested students for participation in a future program.

H. Closing Prayer (flexible, depending on time available and optional elements selected)

1. If the maximum time suggested for each element of the session plan is used, 15 minutes should still be available for the closing prayer. This time of prayer, because it may well be the last prayer you will share with the group in this intimate context, should be given central importance in your planning for the session. I encourage you to plan the prayer carefully, note the time it requires, and then monitor the time used during the session to save time for the prayer.

2. The prayer service suggested here provides a number of elements, any of which can be included or dropped at your discretion. The elements are the following:

a. a short Jewish story

b. a ritual presentation of the plants that were given to the young people during the first session of the program

c. an invitation for individual young people to offer prayers of petition or thanksgiving

d. the popular reading "Footprints"

e. a shared recitation of the Our Father

f. music of your choice

The suggestions below represent one way in which these elements might be organized. Again, feel free to adjust the service as you wish.

3. Call the young people to prayer by gathering them in a comfortable setting, perhaps the one regularly used for prayer in past sessions. Remind them that this may be the last opportunity you will have to pray as a group and that you have much to be grateful for as you now thank God for the time you have had together. Then invite them to join you in making the sign of the cross as a sign of the group's unity.

4. Consider sharing the following Jewish story. Though you are free to read it to the group, virtually any story takes on added power if it can be told directly. Practice both reading and telling the story before deciding how you will present it. Introduce the story in this way:

Many profound religious truths have been passed on from one generation to another through the telling of stories. Here is a marvelous Jewish story that reflects the themes we have been discussing this evening:

Long, long ago, a desperately poor man yearned to escape the agony of his wretched existence. He dreamed of a magical, heavenly city far away where all his pain would be dispelled and all his wishes fulfilled.

One day, with some fear but also with great hope, the poor man decided to go in search of the magical city of his dreams. With little regret, he kissed his wife and children good-bye, left his miserable home, and began his journey.

The man walked all morning and through the heat of midday. Near nightfall, he decided to stop. He ate a crust of bread, said his prayers to Yahweh, and prepared to sleep. In his simple innocence he took off his shoes and placed them directly in the middle of the path on which he had been walking, carefully pointing the shoes in the direction he had been traveling. In this way he felt sure that the next day he would begin his walk in the proper direction toward the magical city of his dreams.

While the poor man slept, a practical joker passed by the spot and came upon the shoes on the path. The joker turned the shoes around so that they were now pointing back toward the direction from which the poor man had come. When he awoke the next morning, the man thanked Yahweh for the gift of a new day, ate another crust of bread, and resumed his trek to the heavenly city of his dreams.

The man walked throughout the morning and through the heat of midday. Finally, as evening fell, he looked off into the distance, and his heart leapt as he saw the skyline of the magical city. The city was not nearly as large as he had expected. In fact, it seemed vaguely familiar. Yet with great expectation the man passed through the gates. As he walked through the city he came upon a street that looked strangely like the one on which he used to live. He walked down the street, and he came upon a house that looked very much like the one he had left. He knocked on the door of the home, greeted with great affection the woman and children who lived there, and lived happily ever after in the heavenly city of his dreams.

5. If you wish and time permits, invite the young people to interpret the story. Then comment on its meaning as follows:

Like all great stories, this one has many layers of meaning. On one level, it suggests that we will find the deepest kind of happiness not in dreaming of faraway places but in accepting and treasuring life as we experience it each day. A popular poster expresses this message in its inscription, Bloom where you are planted.

Another meaning is that each of us needs a joker in our life—that is, someone who can almost literally turn us around in our tracks when we stray in the wrong direction in our search for meaning and happiness. For many people, Jesus has served as this joker in the night in that his life and message can turn people around and head them in the direction of happiness. Perhaps in some small way we have been jokers to one another during our time together . . . probably in more ways than one!

Finally, the major point of the story as it relates to this evening's session is this: You will soon be taking a major step in your journey. It is the step away from your homes, your parish community, and in many cases, from your friends. This can be an exciting, though occasionally scary, time. Remember two things as you move out on this leg of your journey: First, we will always be with one another in prayer and love. Second, the greatest journey in life is not the one that takes us from here to somewhere else but the one that takes us deep within ourselves. That journey toward self-discovery, when taken with honesty and a search for truth, will inevitably lead us to our true home, that is, to our God.

6. At this point, offer the opportunity for the young people to say what is on their mind and in their heart as this phase of the program comes to a close. You may make this an open exchange of comments or offer this as a time for prayers of petition or thanksgiving. If you choose the latter, invite the young people to pray in gratitude for what has been shared or in hope for the future. A suggested response to be said by everyone at the end of each intention or prayer is this wonderful quote from Dag Hammarskjöld: "For all that has been, thanks! For all that will be, yes!"

Special note: If you have been using the plants as a symbol in your opening prayer ritual, you will want to formally present them to the young people during this session. Suggest that they now take the plants home and continue to care for them as an ongoing reminder of what you have shared together as a group. I recommend that you do this as part of these closing prayers of thanksgiving or petition. One approach would be to formally present the plants one at a time to each of the young people. When each person receives the plant, he or she could be invited to respond by offering a prayer. Again, the entire group would then respond with the Hammarskjöld quote.

7. For a closing reflection, consider the popular reading "Footprints." The reading ties in beautifully with the journey theme of this prayer service.

One night a man had a dream. He dreamed he was walking along the beach with the Lord. Across the sky flashed scenes from his life. For each scene, he noticed two sets of footprints in the sand, one belonging to him, the other to the Lord.

When the last scene of his life flashed before him, he looked back at the footprints in the sand. He noticed that many times along the path of his life there was only one set of footprints. He also noticed that it happened at the very lowest and saddest times in his life.

This really bothered the man, and he questioned the Lord about it. "Lord, you said that once I decided to follow you, you would walk with me all the way. Yet I have noticed that during the most troublesome times in my life, there is only one set of footprints. I don't understand why, when I needed you the most, you would leave me."

The Lord replied, "My precious, precious child, I love you and would never leave you. During your times of trial and suffering, when you see only one set of footprints, it was then that I carried you."

8. You may wish to end the prayer service by having everyone join hands for a communal recitation of the Our Father.

9. In addition to all of the above elements, consider including music with your closing prayer. For suggestions, see the SHARING music guides in the SHARING Program director's manual.

For Evaluation

1. This session offers a great deal of flexibility in the time allowed for each element of the session plan. Evaluate the session in terms of the flow of time. Are there elements you would now want to cut back on or eliminate altogether? Do some elements warrant more time than was permitted? Make notes of your assessments.

2. The session is characterized by an unusually heavy concentration on teacher input and group discussion, dictated by the themes of the session. Were the young people able to handle this approach? If not, how might you adjust your approach to the session in the future?

3. Evaluate the presentations you gave as the leader. In what ways were they effective? How might they be improved?

4. Review your approach to the closing prayer service. Eliminate or add optional elements based on your experience this time.

5. Were the "Teacher Goals" and "Student Intellectual/Behavioral Objectives" for this session achieved?

Part 3
SHARING IV
Weekend Retreat Program

SHARING IV
Designed Retreat

Introduction

Each level of the SHARING Program includes either an overnight or a weekend retreat experience. My earliest involvement in youth ministry over twenty years ago was with youth retreats, and I have been convinced ever since that a retreat is an essential component of any effective program for young people. This is so true that, if I had to make a choice, I would choose a retreat over any other kind of program. Some leaders in youth ministry—notably, Michael Warren—suggest that the youth retreat should be adopted as *the* primary model for youth catechesis.

A retreat appears to be particularly appropriate and beneficial as part of the SHARING IV Program. The seven 2-hour sessions of SHARING IV culminate with the theme of the faith development and spirituality of young adults, and the next major component of the program is a month-long meditation program. Furthermore, the methodologies of SHARING IV have centered on prayerful reflection and serious dialogue, both characteristics of many youth retreats. Finally, the young people involved in SHARING IV, given their natural desire to reflect on the past years of high school and to look forward, perhaps anxiously, to the future, will find the opportunity to attend a retreat quite attractive. For all these reasons, I strongly urge you to consider incorporating a retreat into your SHARING IV schedule.

As an aside, note that you need not offer the components of SHARING IV in the order suggested here. It is not essential that the schedule begin with the seven 2-hour sessions, followed by the retreat at midyear, and then conclude with the meditation program. Under some circumstances, you may wish to begin with the retreat. Also, you may choose not to offer the meditation program at all, at least not if this is your initial year with the program. You may even wish to offer more than one retreat. Nevertheless, the order suggested above is a reasonable and effective one.

One more general comment before getting into the specifics of the SHARING IV retreat options: The first three manuals of the SHARING Program—SHARING I, II, and III—each include an introductory essay on youth retreats. The essay provides information on such points as the basic structure of youth retreats, appropriate numbers of participants, facilities, and so on. I decided that such information was not required in SHARING IV. If such basic issues are a concern to you, however, you may find it helpful to review that introductory material.

In all the previous levels of SHARING, I provided a thoroughly detailed plan for conducting each retreat. In SHARING IV, two options are offered:

- a designed retreat, in this case a weekend model that will sum up and expand upon the major themes of SHARING IV
- a retreat planning guide, to help each parish design its own retreat

By the fourth level of the program, your young people will likely have had enough experience with retreats to be highly motivated not only to attend one but to work together in developing one. Those who have already experienced the seven 2-hour sessions should also have a good sense of the themes that they would like to pursue on their retreat. Furthermore, their increased maturity should equip them for appreciating and handling the coordinated effort that goes into creating and conducting a retreat program. Finally, the experience of working together on and assuming leadership of such a program may well be the highlight of the young people's time together.

The designed retreat is presented first, followed by the planning guide. This arrangement suggests that though you may decide to design your own retreat using the planning guide, reading through the designed retreat will be a big help in using the guide.

A Topical Overview of the Retreat Schedule

Friday Evening

6:45	Team members arrive and make final preparations.
7:30	Young people arrive. Registration.
8:00	Orientation.
8:20	Overview of the theme for the retreat.
8:30	Optional icebreaker and team-building exercises.
9:30	Break.
9:45	Dyadic encounter activity.
11:15	Night prayer.
11:30	Announcements and free time.
1:00	Lights out.

Saturday

8:00	Rising.
8:30	Morning prayer.
8:45	Breakfast.
9:30	Discussion of dyadic encounter activity.
9:55	Stretch break.
10:00	Discussion activity: "Dreaming of the Good Life."
11:30	Free time.
12:00	Lunch.
12:30	Extended free time and recreation.
2:00	Panel discussion on lifestyles.
5:00	Free time.
5:30	Dinner.
6:30	Free time.
7:00	Guest speaker on marriage.
9:00	Break.
9:15	Journal writing activity: "A Letter to Myself."
10:00	Evening prayer.
10:30	Relaxation and recreation.
1:00	Lights out.

Sunday

8:00	Rising.
8:30	Morning prayer.
8:45	Breakfast.
9:15	Cleanup and packing.
9:45	Closing presentation: "Signposts for the Journey of Life."
10:15	Break.
10:30	Group preparation for the liturgy.
10:45	Private, personal preparation for the liturgy: "A Letter to God."
11:15	Liturgy.
12:00	Closing lunch.

Directing the SHARING IV Designed Retreat

This section provides a detailed plan for a SHARING IV weekend retreat. The entire schedule overview given in the previous section is detailed here to provide the kind of information that you need either to fully understand the retreat program or to conduct it yourself. This section does not provide such details as the preparation of facilities or menus for the meals simply because these will vary greatly depending on budget and available facilities. Meals can be kept simple, and the preparation of facilities should be dictated by the needs of the program and common sense; for example, separate and supervised dormitories, a comfortable room for discussion, and so on. Additional guidelines for making these kinds of provisions can be found in the next section, "Retreat Planning Guide," on pages 170–176.

Note also that many of the ideas, principles, and suggestions made in Part 1 of this book are applicable for directing retreats, especially the chapter entitled "Effective Teaching: Making Molehills Out of Mountains" on pages 38–44. Suggestions on conducting effective group dynamics and leading discussions, the description of a "successful class," and so on, all relate to the proper conducting of the retreat. By the same token, if you have guided the entire SHARING IV Program, by now you have probably found that many of these practices have become second nature to you, in which case you certainly have a head start toward leading a successful retreat.

Leaders can assume that, for the SHARING IV retreat, only rather mature and serious young people will participate. They will probably come with an attitude of openness and cooperation. Most of them will have participated in the seven 2-hour sessions that constitute the first half of the program. Many of these people will be consciously confronting the challenges of young adulthood that await them as they leave high school.

For all these reasons, this SHARING IV retreat is designed to be particularly reflective and rather low-key when compared to the other retreats in the SHARING Program. The intent is to have the young people experience a peaceful, prayerful sharing with peers about issues of primary importance at this time of their life. Considerable time is devoted to reflection upon and discussion of optional lifestyles, a topic that was not treated directly in the seven 2-hour sessions. Where previous retreats in the SHARING Program may have offered a group activity, this retreat calls for direct input by a team leader or guest speaker, followed by a period of personal reflection and then group discussion. The moments of prayer in this retreat are intentionally subdued and reflective. All of these characteristics of the retreat are based on the starting point of the young people.

Detailed Schedule for the Designed Weekend Retreat

Friday Evening

6:45 Team members arrive ahead of young people. Check the facilities, make any final preparations that are necessary, and gather for the final team prayer before the young people arrive.

7:30 Young people arrive. Registration. Give the students name tags that are to be worn throughout the entire program. (An exception can be made if all the participants already know one another's names.) Assign the young people to either rooms or cots in the dormitory areas, offering any specific direction that is required. Collect the fees at this time, if necessary.

8:00 Orientation. The orientation to the program should include the following:

1. Explain the physical setup of the building, the location of lavatories, and so on.
2. Specify off-limit areas, if any: dormitories of the opposite sex at specified times, kitchen area, others.
3. Explain the importance of wearing the name tags (if needed) and also the importance of staying in assigned rooms or cots during sleeping hours, in case of emergency.
4. Encourage all the participants to help keep the facilities clean.
5. Specify restrictions on smoking and on the use of equipment (for example, a telephone or a record player).
6. Clearly state that anyone found with beer, liquor, pot, or other drugs will be immediately sent home to parents (and stick with this rule—no exceptions!).
7. Point out the need for trust and mutual respect. If these are present, laws become unnecessary.
8. Ask for any questions on rules or other matters.
9. Introduce the team members. Also, small discussion groups may have to be formed at this time, depending on your choice of optional icebreakers or team-building activities described below. If required here, small group formation can be most easily accomplished by having the entire group stand in a circle, with boys and girls alternating. Then have them count off by the number of the groups you desire. Try to have seven or eight retreatants in each group.

8:20 Overview of the theme for the retreat. At this point, provide the young people with a brief overview of the retreat as follows:

Many of you have attended previous retreats in our high school program, and you know how much fun they can be. This retreat will be enjoyable as well, but perhaps in a different way.

You are at a crossroad in your life right now. You are ending one major period in your life—high school and, for some, maybe even your contact with formal education—and you are entering a new and exciting time of changes and challenges, young adulthood. I want our time together during this retreat to speak to and reflect on many of the thoughts and feelings that you now likely experience. We're going to be talking about some serious topics: the values that will guide you in the future; the lifestyle options and decisions that face you; and the role that Christian faith can play in your life during the coming years.

Also, though we intend to have a good time together, the plan for this retreat is a bit more serious than in past retreats. There will be time for private reflection and prayer. Our discussions will

require a sincere commitment to share and to listen. To make this work, you need to be not somber but serious, not pious but prayerful, not reserved but reflective. If we are successful, you may leave on Sunday feeling, and even saying, two things: (1) "This wasn't as much fun as past retreats," and (2) "This is the best and most meaningful retreat I've been on."

After sharing these comments, announce a short break. Ask the students to gather in a specified place when called.

8:30 Optional icebreaker and team-building exercises. Several options for icebreakers and team-building activities are offered below. If the participants of the retreat already know one another well, some icebreakers can seem artificial and unnecessary. However, if the young people come from different parishes or are not familiar with one another or with the retreat team, you might want to include one or more of these activities at this point. The activities will help dissipate some of the initial discomfort and tension common in groups as they begin a program of this kind. Select the activities based on your assessment of the starting point of your group.

As indicated in the directions below, some of these activities can serve the secondary purpose of forming the small discussion groups required during the retreat. If the option you select does not do so, you will have to include small-group formation as part of the orientation to that option.

The suggested schedule provides one hour for these activities. Feel free to adjust the time as you see fit.

For optional activities, look first to the SHARING III weekend retreat, pages 214–228. That program offers several barrier breakers and team-building activities from which to choose. Choose from any options not used before.

Below are two additional suggestions for icebreaking or team-building activities. Feel free to create your own variations of any of these activities. The primary intent is to get people mingling, chatting, introducing each other, and so on, in order to help the group members relax.

Option 1: Name the mystery person

This is a good activity if the group members already have some familiarity with one another and you wish only to warm them up at the start of the program. If your group has more than twelve members, consider breaking it into smaller groups for this activity. These same groupings may be used as small discussion groups for the retreat.

Give each participant a pencil and a piece of paper with the following questions printed on it:

a. **One color that represents my basic personality is . . .**

b. **If I could be any animal in the world, I would be a . . .**

c. **A well-known song that captures my philosophy of life is . . .**

d. **If I could be a car, I would want to be a . . .**

e. **If I were a musical instrument in an orchestra, most of my friends would say that I would be a . . .**

Everyone is to print answers to the questions on the paper as truthfully and accurately as possible.

When all the participants have completed the paper, ask them to fold the papers and drop them in a box or basket placed in the middle of the group. Then ask one person in the group to select one of the papers and to read the responses to the rest of the group. At that point, everyone tries to guess who wrote the answers. When they come to some consensus, they ask the person they have agreed upon if he or she is in fact the originator of the answers. The person asked must respond honestly. If the group has guessed wrong, they try again until they have correctly identified the correct person. Then the activity is repeated, each time with a different person selecting and reading a paper.

Note that this activity will work only if most of the participants already have had some previous association with one another. Note also that, as the game progresses and people are identified, the task becomes increasingly easy. This makes the game move very fast toward the end. So, if it appears to be moving slowly initially, do not be overly concerned.

Option 2: What a frightening thought!

See Student Handout A following this retreat outline.

This activity is based on a study that was done some years ago that attempted to identify the most common fears of people. In the activity, small groups attempt to rank a list of fears in the order in which they believe the fears were most frequently named by survey respondents. This is a great discussion starter, and it is effective whether or not the participants know each other before the retreat. The activity has the additional benefit of helping to form the small discussion groups. Directions for the activity follow.

1. Form small discussion groups of a workable size and with a reasonable balance of boys and girls.

2. When the groups are formed, distribute pencils and copies of Student Handout A, "What a Frightening Thought!"

3. Read the directions of the handout to the group, making sure that all members understand what they are to do. Emphasize that one goal of the activity is to learn to dialogue and work together as a group. The students should therefore avoid simply seeking a majority vote on each item. Rather, they should discuss the reasons behind their rankings and try to persuade one another based on reason and logic.

4. Feel free to choose a time frame for the activity that suits your schedule. Recognize, however, that insufficient time for the consensus-seeking will virtually force the groups into the kind of majority voting you wish to avoid. A reasonable time frame for the activity would include about 5 minutes for individual ranking, a minimum of 25–30 minutes for group consensus-seeking, and an additional 15 minutes for scoring and further discussion as a large group.

5. Below is the ranking of human fears determined by a survey. It serves as the answer sheet for this activity. Though perhaps interesting, the primary intent of the activity is not to determine who is the winner but to get the young people talking to one another as they begin the retreat. The source of the information used in this activity is *A Handbook of Structured Experiences for Human Relations Training*, volume 3, edited by J. Willam Pfeiffer and John E. Jones (San Diego: University Associates, 1979, pp. 60 and 64).

Survey results: The most commonly experienced human fears, in order, are (identical numbers indicate ties):
1. speaking before a group
2. heights
3. insects and bugs
3. financial problems
3. deep water
6. sickness
6. death
8. flying
9. loneliness
10. dogs
11. driving or riding in a car
12. darkness
12. elevators
14. escalators

6. Bring the activity to a close by noting the primary lessons of the exercise—the importance of personal sharing, careful listening, and cooperation to effectively work together as a group, one of the requirements for a successful and satisfying retreat.

9:30 Break. You may wish to offer just a simple beverage, knowing that more snacks will be available after night prayer.

9:45 Dyadic encounter activity. See Student Handout B following this retreat outline. This activity is intended to set the tone of personal reflection and relaxed but rather deep sharing that is to characterize this retreat for high school seniors. The term *dyadic encounter* simply refers to an activity that involves two people sharing with each other.

This type of activity will be familiar to you and to the young people if you led them in the first of the 2-hour sessions in SHARING IV. A similar style of discussion was used in that session to study the film titled *Solo*. Repetition of this technique is intentional. It is hoped that a familiar activity will help the young people feel more comfortable in the setting of the retreat. In this case, many of the points for discussion are more personal than those in the discussion of the film—not personally threatening but more focused on the young people's personal experiences, relationships, and so on.

Assigning a specific time frame to this activity is difficult. The time required or requested by your group will vary dramatically, depending on their familiarity with one another, the level of intimacy they may have achieved through their time together during the year, their individual personalities and temperaments, even the weather. One person using this activity with freshman college students told me it lasted five hours! (Don't panic—we have ways to avoid that here.)

Given the flexible nature of this activity, the only other activity scheduled for this evening is night prayer. This gives you considerable freedom to adjust the activity as you see fit. My recommendation, reflected in this schedule, is to allow a minimum of 90 minutes for this activity. At that time, check to see if the dyads want to continue. If so, allow another 30 minutes. If not, gather the young people immediately for night prayer. Note that, following night prayer, they will also have some free time for relaxation and further sharing if they wish. Directions for guiding the activity follow.

1. Create the booklet required for this activity with Student Handout B, "Dyadic Encounter Guide."

The booklet consists of sixteen small pages, each of which is numbered on the handout. The handout is to be photocopied and then cut up into the small pages as indicated by the dotted lines. The small pages are then appropriately collated and stapled together in the upper left-hand corner. You may wish to add a cover of colored paper to the booklet. You will need one booklet for each member of the group, so photocopy at least that number. It is always a good idea to have extra handouts available.

2. In introducing the activity, remind the young people that a primary theme of the year's program is the search for healthful and satisfying personal relationships.

It is a sad reality that many people are dying of loneliness. They desperately want to experience intimacy with others, but they don't have either the understanding or the skills needed. Earlier in this program, we identified communication skills as the binding force of all relationships. This activity, to which we will devote considerable time this evening of the retreat, is intended to give us good insights into the ingredients necessary for good communication between persons. The activity will also give each of us insights into ourselves—our self-image, our ability to share with others, and so on.

3. Distribute a booklet to each person, telling them not to open the booklets until they are told to do so. When all the students have received a booklet, give the following directions:

a. **Right now, I would like you to pair up for this activity. Though you can choose your partner, please find someone whom you do not know well. You can choose a partner of either the same or the other sex.** (Note: In the case of an odd number of retreatants, one of the team members will have to join the activity. He or she should seek either a particularly shy young person—who might well be threatened by the activity—or one who is particularly self-possessed, one who would be comfortable working with an adult on this activity. Allow the young people several minutes to find their partners. Then continue the directions as follows.)

b. **In a moment, I will ask you to go as couples anywhere you wish in the building.** (For this activity, I suggest that restricted areas such as dormitories be opened to the couples.) **Find a place where you can be alone, where you can talk without interruption or distraction.**

c. **When you find your quiet place, open to the first page of your booklets. You'll find the first part of a sentence that each person should complete orally for the other. When you both have verbally completed the sentence, comment on or ask questions about each other's response. You do not have to do any writing during this activity. After you have discussed the item on the first page, turn to the second page and read what you find there. Again, each person should respond to the item and discuss the responses. Then turn to the next page and continue in that way until you are called back to the large group. *We have no set time for this activity.* It will last as long as most of you want it to last.**

d. **Keep the following rules in mind for this activity:**
   1) **Both people in your dyad must respond to the item on each page of the booklet. It is up to you to determine *how much* you wish to say, but you must say something. None of the items are embarrassing or highly personal.**
   2) **However, the goal is *not* to get through the entire booklet; the only goal for the activity is to achieve good conversation and communication with your partner. So if you want to talk for 20 minutes about the item on page 1, go ahead. The booklet is not a test but simply an aid to stimulate good conversation.**
   3) **There is no pressure to complete the booklet, so feel free to ask your partner for more details about any of the responses. For example, if someone says something that you'd like to hear more about, feel free to ask him or her to tell you more. However, remember two things: (*a*) You can only ask questions of the other person that you would be willing to answer yourself; (*b*) the other person always has the right to refuse to give more information if that is his or her desire.**

e. **I'll be checking with you later to see how you're doing. When it appears that all of you have gone about as far as you can with the activity, we will gather for our closing evening prayer. However, we'll come back to this experience tomorrow morning, when we'll try to determine the lessons it has taught us. So try to be conscious of how you react to the activity, what you learn from it, and what you might be able to share with the rest of us later.**

4. At this point, send the couples off to begin their conversations. As noted above, I suggest that you allow a minimum of 90 minutes for their conversations. This may seem extremely long. Trust your own judgment, but remember that the intent of the exercise is to have the young people grapple

with both the joys and the frustrations of interpersonal communication. If given sufficient time, the students will be forced to deal with the challenge of maintaining conversation when it begins to lag or go stale. They will experience significant personal sharing as well as active listening. They will realize that true communication—rather than shallow chit-chat—takes commitment and effort. For a fortunate few, they may actually experience the start of a new and meaningful relationship with another person. All of these are lessons and gifts worth the investment of time.

5. When you feel it is appropriate, check with the couples to see how they are doing. If the majority ask for more time, give them another 30 minutes and then check with them again. When you determine it is time to end the activity, call the young people together for night prayer.

11:15 Night prayer. As noted in the earlier discussion of the theme for this retreat, the goal is to achieve a sense of a peaceful, prayerful, even intimate sharing among faithful friends during this retreat. Toward that end, I try to avoid efforts to wow the students with special effects or elaborate rituals. This is especially the case in prayer and the liturgy. This is not a condemnation of highly imaginative and involved prayer services; such experiences are at times totally appropriate and, in fact, appear in other parts of this and other SHARING manuals. However, for this retreat I suggest that you set a more intimate tone to the prayer. This can be achieved through a proper use of silence, a prayerful reading of the Scriptures, a subtle and reflective use of music, both spontaneous and communal prayer, and so on.

Nonetheless, this subdued approach to prayer requires the same careful planning, preparation, and practice required by the more involved prayer services included in the SHARING Program. As a leader of such prayer, you must try to gain a deep sense of the tone or spirit of the prayer and imagine how best to prepare a physical environment that will promote that spirit. Practice scriptural and other readings, working on the pacing and the vocal inflection that will make the readings come alive for the young people. If you choose to use music, select it carefully and be particularly sensitive to the volume at which you play it.

The best suggestion I can give you is to assume a personal role during this prayer, not of a leader of prayer, but as one truly *praying with* the young people. Prepare the prayer as you would want it to be to truly touch your own heart; it will, in turn, touch the hearts of those with whom you share it. Therefore, view what follows as the way I would guide this prayer, and feel free to adapt it to meet your needs and tastes.

1. Properly prepare the room where you will conduct the night prayer. I suggest: low lighting, perhaps only candlelight; furniture, if any, arranged in such a way that everyone will be encouraged to gather closely together; an open Bible placed in a central location, perhaps also with candles nearby; quiet, instrumental music playing as the young people gather. See the SHARING music guides in the director's manual for music suggestions. Both the rock music and the religious music guides suggest instrumental pieces that would be appropriate for this prayer.

2. As the young people enter the room, invite them to gather closely together. You might allow the music to play softly throughout the service. When all the participants have gathered, simply ask them to become quiet and to center on the reality that they are in the presence of a holy and loving God. Allow a couple minutes of quite reflection as they become centered.

3. Then share the following thoughts in your own words:

You have just spent considerable time getting to know one person. This may have been the most involved and challenging conversation you've had in a long time. We'll talk more about the experience tomorrow morning, but at this time we want to focus on what it means to be truly known, truly understood, truly cared for by another person.

The Hebrew Scriptures tell us that God calls each of us by name. (At this point, I suggest that you read the following passage directly from your Bible. The Jerusalem Bible version given here is intended to help you understand the prayer service. However, it is much more effective to read from the Bible itself than from a manual such as this.)

> **Do not be afraid [God says to each of us], for I have redeemed you;**
> **I have called you by your name, you are mine.**
> **Should you pass through the waters, I shall be with you;**
> **or through rivers, they will not swallow you up.**
> **Should you walk through fire, you will not suffer,**
> **and the flame will not burn you.**
> **For I am Yahweh, your God.** (Isaiah 43:1–2)

What a beautifully poetic way to say the words that all of us long to hear from someone in our

SHARING IV Designed Retreat   153

lives—that "I am always here, loving you totally. Don't be afraid."

4. The fear that most of us carry with us is that people will love us only if we measure up to their standards, only if we fit their image of what we should be. So we hide ourselves from one another, playing games, being phony, fearing embarrassment should people find out who we truly are inside. The more we hide, the less able we are to create the kind of relationships that we so desperately hunger for. So we live with a painful paradox: we continually run away from the very thing we need to make us happy.

5. When it comes to God, however, we can't run away. Nor should we want to. God is a relentless lover, one who never stops trying to achieve intimacy with us. Consider this awesome reality: God knows every single facet of our being—every past action, every thought, every fear, every desire, every evil as well as every loving thought we have had—and God still loves us passionately. What a gift! In God, and only in God, can we find the perfect kind of intimate relationship we yearn to experience with others. It is only in God that our deepest needs will be totally satisfied.

6. After all your sharing with one another during the last hour or two, we shall close our evening together by reflecting on this perfect love that God has for each of us. I want you to get in a relaxed position, perhaps close your eyes, and simply listen to the word of God for a few minutes. Listen to the words as if they were coming from your own heart. Hear yourself say them to God. After each verse, I will pause for a moment to allow you to reflect.

7. Now prayerfully read Psalm 139:1–18. Again, the passage is given here for your convenience, but you should read it from your Bible. Note that verses 19–24 of the psalm should not be read. Pause prayerfully after each verse for at least 30 seconds. Consider allowing the quiet music to continue as you share the reading. You may want to remind the young people that the Hebrew name for God was Yahweh, and tell them that this reading may be nearly 3000 years old.

> **Yahweh, you examine me and know me,**
> **you know when I sit, when I rise,**
> **you understand my thoughts from afar.**
> **You watch when I walk or lie down,**
> **you know every detail of my conduct.** (Pause.)

> **A word is not yet on my tongue**
> **before you, Yahweh, know all about it.**
> **You fence me in, behind and in front,**
> **you have laid your hand upon me.**
> **Such amazing knowledge is beyond me,**
> **a height to which I cannot attain.** (Pause.)

> **Where shall I go to escape your spirit?**
> **Where shall I flee from your presence?**
> **If I scale the heavens you are there,**
> **if I lie flat in Sheol, there you are.** (Pause.)

> **If I speed away on the wings of dawn,**
> **if I dwell beyond the ocean,**
> **even there your hand will be guiding me,**
> **your right hand holding me fast.** (Pause.)

> **I will say, "Let the darkness cover me,**
> **and the night wrap itself around me,"**
> **even darkness to you is not dark,**
> **and night is as clear as the day.** (Pause.)

> **You created my inmost self,**
> **Knit me together in my mother's womb.**
> **For so many marvels I thank you;**
> **a wonder am I, and all your works are wonders.**
> (Pause.)

> **You knew me through and through,**
> **my being held no secrets from you,**
> **when I was being formed in secret,**
> **textured in the depths of the earth.** (Pause.)

> **Your eyes could see my embryo,**
> **In your book all my days were inscribed,**
> **every one that was fixed is there.** (Pause.)

> **How hard for me to grasp your thoughts,**
> **how many, God, there are!**
> **If I count them, they are more than the grains**
> **of sand;**
> **if I come to an end, I am still with you.** (Pause.)

8. After the reading, tell the group that one purpose of this retreat is to help the participants grow in our relationship with this wonderful God. Invite them to share any intentions or prayers they might be feeling at this point as they close their first evening together. On occasion I have passed lighted sand candles around the room during such opportunities for personal prayer, inviting people to pray privately or out loud as they hold the candle briefly. If you choose to do so, make sure you have two candles so that someone has a candle and is ready to pray while the other candle is being passed.

9. Close the prayer by joining hands for a shared recitation of the Our Father.

11:30 Announcements and free time. After the close of prayer, remind the participants that morning prayer is at 8:30 A.M. Make announcements regarding available refreshments, options during free time, the time for lights out, and so on. I always have available various party games, cards, and other activities for those who enjoy them. Refreshments can be simple but plentiful. Stress the importance of a good night's sleep, and ask for the students' cooperation.

1:00 Lights out. Time is approximate, depending on how the evening unfolds. I would not, however, recommend extending it beyond 1:30.

Saturday

8:00 Rising. If you have a sound system that allows it, consider waking the young people with music, perhaps the music used during Friday night's prayer.

8:30 Morning prayer. Greet the young people as they gather for prayer. Spend a couple minutes having them freely describe what their life is typically like from the time they awake in the morning until they leave for school. Most will admit that they are either in a complete fog for a while or, more likely, they feel hurried, pressured, anxious. Tell them you want the group to experience the sense of peace that can come from just a few moments of quiet, reflective time with God before getting caught up in the events of the day.

1. Begin by having the young people focus on the fact that we are held constantly in the loving care of God. Recall the theme of the psalm from Friday's evening prayer. Have the participants close their eyes, steady their breathing, and relax in the sense of God's sure care. You might play an appropriate song from the SHARING music guides.

2. Tell the young people that, when we grow in our intimacy with God, we grow as well in a vision of the world and our role in it that can bring meaning and purpose to our life. Years ago, one person attempted to describe such a vision, and he expressed it in a statement he called "Desiderata," meaning those things that are to be desired in life. Invite the group to listen to his thoughts.

3. At this point, share "Desiderata" with the young people. It is offered here in print, but it also became popular in the early 1970s as a recorded song performed by Les Crane and his orchestra. That version was produced by Warner Brothers, and the 45 RPM recording was numbered 7520. A more recent recording of "Desiderata" is included as part of an album titled *You Bring Out the Best in Me*, performed by Kamahl and produced by PHI Recording Company. The record number is 6603001. These records may no longer be available in some areas, but this information might help you locate the recordings through specialty record shops or distributors. Contact your local music distributor for help in ordering the record or cassette tape of the album.

If you can locate the recorded version, it can be used periodically throughout the retreat, particularly during prayer or liturgy. You may also wish to have this reading printed on a card to be distributed to the young people as a memento of the retreat.

Desiderata

Go placidly amid the noise and the haste, and remember what peace there may be in silence. As far as possible without surrender be on good terms with all persons. Speak your truth quietly and clearly; and listen to others, even the dull and ignorant; they too have their story.

Avoid loud and aggressive persons, they are vexatious to the spirit. If you compare yourself with others you may become vain and bitter; for always there will be greater and lesser persons than yourself. Enjoy your achievements as well as your plans.

Keep interested in your own career, however humble; it is a real possession in the changing fortunes of time. Exercise caution in your business affairs; for the world is full of trickery. But let this not blind you to what virtue there is; many persons strive for high ideals; and everywhere life is full of heroism.

Be yourself. Especially do not feign affection. Neither be cynical about love; for in the face of all aridity and disenchantment it is perennial as the grass.

Take kindly the counsel of the years, gracefully surrendering the things of youth. Nurture strength of spirit to shield you in sudden misfortune. But do not distress yourself with imaginings. Many fears are born of fatigue and loneliness. Beyond a wholesome discipline, be gentle with yourself.

You are a child of the universe no less than the trees and the stars; you have a right to be here. And whether or not it is clear to you, no doubt the universe is unfolding as it should.

Therefore be at peace with God, whatever you conceive Him to be. And whatever your labors and aspirations, in the noisy confusion of life keep peace with your soul.

With all its sham, drudgery and broken dreams, it is still a beautiful world. Be cheerful.

Strive to be happy. (Copyright © 1927 by Max Ehrmann. All rights reserved. Copyright renewed 1954 by Bertha K. Ehrmann. Reprinted by permission of Robert L. Bell, Melrose, MA 02176.)

4. After the reading or song, invite the young people to offer intentions for the day. Ask the group to respond to each intention with an appropriate response, for example, "Lord, we dedicate this day to you," or "Lord, lead us to your truth."

5. Conclude the intentions and the morning prayer with a personal prayer of your own.

8:45 Breakfast. Young people eat this meal quickly—in about 10 minutes. This schedule allows time for clean up, the use of lavatories, and so on.

9:30 Discussion of dyadic encounter activity.

1. Tell the group that you wish to take a few minutes this morning to reflect upon and discuss some of the lessons of the discussion activity from last evening.

The activity is helpful and enjoyable simply as a way to break the ice at the start of a program such as this. It also offers some insights into life and interpersonal communication that can help us throughout our life. I want us to try to identify some of those lessons this morning.

2. Begin the discussion by asking some or all of the following questions and inviting responses.

a. **Can you identify the various feelings that you experienced during the activity? For example, did you at any time feel afraid, offended, judgmental, threatened? Or did you feel trusted, secure, affirmed, enriched?**

b. **As best you can remember, which questions or statements did you find particularly difficult to respond to? Can you explain why?**

c. **Did you notice a change in your relationship with your partner during the course of the activity? Can you describe that?**

d. **Can you think of any questions that were not part of the exercise that you wish had been included, that is, are there things you now wish that you had been able to discuss with your partner?**

e. **Out of all the questions or statements in the activity, which did you find the most embarrassing? Why?**

3. After this general discussion of the activity, try to draw from the young people some insights about interpersonal communication that they gained from the activity. State that you would now like them to identify five basic guidelines for interpersonal communication based on this activity. Write the following sentence stem on a chalkboard or newsprint: "If a person wishes to experience true communication with another, he or she must . . ." Ask the young people to complete that sentence orally, as a way to identify and express the five guidelines.

4. When a person offers a suggested guideline, write it on the chalkboard or newsprint, and ask him or her to give an example from the dyadic encounter that illustrates the guideline. Feel free to invite group reactions to each suggested guideline. When all the suggestions are given, sort out the five that seem to best represent them all. Have the group amend them to everyone's satisfaction. Record the five guidelines on newsprint, and post it where all the participants can see it.

9:55 Stretch break.

10:00 Discussion activity: "Dreaming of the Good Life."

1. Introduce this activity along the following lines:

Earlier this year, we spent one session of the program talking about the need for each person to develop what we called a dream, a vision of life as he or she would like to experience it. (For details, see session 2 of SHARING IV, "The Future Is in My Hands: Turning Dreams into Realities," pp. 66–79.) **We noted in that session how Martin Luther King, Jr., articulated his dream in one of the most famous speeches in history. Then, during this morning's prayer, we listened to another person's vision of the meaning of life in the reading titled "Desiderata," meaning "those things that are to be desired in life."**

2. This morning I would like you to work together as a group to develop your own community "Desiderata," your vision of the meaning of life and the qualities needed to live life fully. This is no easy task; it will require a great deal of thought, discussion, and cooperation. Yet, particularly at this stage in your life, it would be hard to think of a more important use of your time and energy.

3. The activity will unfold in the following way throughout the morning:

a. **You will first work as individuals, privately completing a brief reflection activity.**

b. Then you will gather in your small groups, with each group assigned the task of discussing and articulating one facet of the vision that you wish to guide you in life.

c. Next, all the small groups will be brought back together to share the results of their discussions and to then work together to combine those results into one coherent statement—your "Desiderata."

4. To set a time frame for this activity, a number of variables must be taken into account: the number of participants, the nature of their individual personalities and how they work together as a group, and the retreat environment. For example, if the retreat environment is a scenic setting that offers a peaceful and prayerful walk outdoors you might extend the time for private, personal reflection. If, on the other hand, your retreat setting is rather cold and institutional—a school building, for instance—you might abbreviate the private part of the activity. The schedule provided here calls for a rather intense 90 minutes for the entire activity, followed by some time for relaxation before lunch. This is designed with a rather sterile environment in mind. If your facilities are stimulating, feel free to extend this activity considerably, perhaps even delaying lunch until 12:30.

5. Begin the activity by distributing pencils and copies of a handout titled, "Creating a Life Worth Living—A Guide for Personal Reflection." *You will have to create this handout yourself.* Include on it the directions plus the number of the suggested statements given below that equals the number of small groups. This will later allow you to assign one of these statements to each of the small groups. You can design and embellish your handout as you wish. The following is just an example using five statements or areas of concern. This will be sufficient for the majority of retreat groups. If you have more small groups than this, create additional statements as needed. Again, decide the amount of time you wish to allow for this private, personal reflection.

Creating a Life Worth Living: A Guide for Personal Reflection

Directions: Respond in writing to each of the following sentence stems. You do not need to respond in complete sentences. You *will* be asked to share the content of your responses, but do not worry at this time about the way in which you state your beliefs or feelings. You have (insert the number of minutes you wish to allow for this part of the activity).

- **When I think of how people relate to and take care of the earth and its resources, I believe we must . . .** (Leave space for writing.)
- **In their relationships with others, I believe people must . . .** (space)
- **In choosing and pursuing a career, I want to be sure to . . .** (space)
- **When living out their personal faith in God, I believe people must . . .** (space)
- **The attitude that I hope to always have toward myself as a person is . . .** (space)

6. At the determined time, gather the individuals into their small groups. Assign each group the task of coming to a consensus and a completion for one of the statements on the personal reflection guide. The groups are to try to express their ideas and convictions as clearly and poetically as possible, in keeping with the style of "Desiderata." Ask each group to choose a recorder to take notes. Provide the recorders with some scrap paper, two sheets of newsprint or poster paper, and a felt-tipped marker. Ask them to print the final group statement in such a way that it can later be seen and read by the entire group. Again, determine the amount of time you wish to allow for this, though I suggest 20 minutes as a minimum for this phase of the activity.

7. Call the small groups together and have their respective recorders share the results of their discussion. Do this in the order given by the sample personal reflection guide provided above, that is, starting with the statement about the earth and its resources, then the one on personal relationships, and so on. Allow the entire group to react to and suggest changes in each statement. As each one is changed and approved by the majority, tape the final statement to the wall so all can see it.

8. Ask for a volunteer or two who would be willing to write out a final version of the group's total "Desiderata" during the free time after lunch. Provide the volunteer with poster paper and various colored felt-tipped markers. The poster that the volunteer creates can then be taped to the wall of the area used for prayer. If the quality of the content is good, you might create a card of the final statement to be sent to the retreatants after the retreat.

11:30 Free time.

12:00 Lunch.

12:30 Extended free time and recreation. Some free time for relaxation and recreation is helpful during a youth retreat. Group activities such as volleyball or softball games are effective ways to build a spirit of community among the participants, as well as to allow the young people to blow off steam. You might consider offering such activities at this time.

Remember, however, that the purpose and intended mood of this retreat differs somewhat from the norm. Promote an attitude of quiet personal reflection and peaceful, prayerful sharing. Reflect on ways to achieve such a mood, given the physical environment of your retreat. For example, if you use a facility with an attractive nature setting, take full advantage of that. Allow time for quiet walks alone or in small groups. If such opportunities are not available, you will need to provide structured recreation during this time. Keep in mind that certain types of recreation call for taking showers. Adjust your schedule accordingly.

2:00 Panel discussion on lifestyles. This entire afternoon of the retreat is devoted to a discussion of lifestyles. Four lifestyles are to be discussed—priesthood, religious life, marriage, and the single life. The basic approach is to have representative individuals make brief presentations on each lifestyle, followed by a panel discussion in which all the guest speakers participate. The time frame of three hours may initially seem too long. However, when that time frame is broken into four separate presentations, a panel discussion, and a number of brief breaks, it will not appear so daunting. The following are some suggestions on organizing the presentations and the panel discussion:

1. I recommend that you invite fairly young people to represent the four lifestyles to be discussed —for example, a rather recently ordained priest or professed religious and a couple married, say, less than five years. The exception here might be the representative single person. A person in his or her late twenties may simply be delaying marriage. You will want to find someone who has already made a long-term commitment to the single lifestyle.

The recommendation to recruit younger people for the panel is not to be construed as age discrimination. Rather, it is in keeping with the primary focus of the afternoon, which is not so much centered on the unique nature of each lifestyle but on *the process of decision-making* that each person experienced as he or she worked out a life choice. The retreat participants will more readily identify with younger representatives of the lifestyles, persons who just recently made their decisions. Such people will reflect the process of decision-making in a period of what session 3 of SHARING IV called "option shock." Their younger age will, in this context, enhance their credibility.

2. Provide the persons representing each lifestyle with information about the format of the afternoon. They will have about 20 minutes in which to share their reflections on their lifestyle and, more importantly, on their experience of coming to a decision regarding it. Emphasize that, given the limits of time, extensive discussions about the specifics of their lifestyle will not be possible. They should not say a lot about this in their prepared comments.

3. Ask each guest speaker to prepare remarks in response to the following directions:

a. Provide *brief* biographical data that will give the retreatants some sense of your personal history before making your lifestyle choice.

b. Describe what initially attracted you to your chosen lifestyle.

c. Explain any fears or misgivings that accompanied the decision regarding your lifestyle.

d. If you consulted others for guidance in making the decision, describe who the people were and the roles that they played in your decision-making.

e. If your situation had characteristics that you view as particularly unique, describe them. Explain how helpful or applicable your experience might be for others.

f. In reviewing the decision that you made, describe what you now see as things you wished you had known before. Give any advice based on your experience that you would like to share with the retreatants.

Ask the speakers to restrict their comments to about 20 minutes.

4. Gather the retreatants in the most comfortable room available, one that lends itself to relaxed sharing. Explain to them the nature of the afternoon along the following lines:

Throughout our program this year, we have discussed many facets of young adulthood—the developmental tasks that you face and the kinds of skills you will need in order to cope with them. Perhaps the most challenging task most young adults face is making initial—maybe even permanent—choices about their adult lifestyle. This will include, of course, decisions about possible careers, where to live, and so on. Yet the most difficult and

far-reaching decisions young adults face revolve around what Christians traditionally call their *vocation.*

We in the Church commonly think of a vocation as a call to the priesthood or to the religious life as a professed sister or brother. The fact is that marriage is also a vocation, as is the single life. All of these lifestyles offer opportunities for individuals to live out their unique relationship with God. Each lifestyle also provides avenues for service to others, as people share their unique talents and gifts.

We are going to devote the entire afternoon to sharing and discussing lifestyle options that are open to you. Within the Catholic Christian tradition, four options are commonly identified: the single life, marriage, the life of a professed religious brother or sister, and the priesthood. You may already feel quite convinced of the lifestyle you wish to follow. It isn't the intent of this discussion to promote one lifestyle over the others, or to in any way try to influence your choice. This is, rather, a matter of helping you make an informed choice by considering all the options available to you.

In a more specific sense, the intent is to explore the process of decision-making that people engage in when selecting a lifestyle for themselves. I have invited five people to share their experiences with us this afternoon—a married couple, a single person, a priest, and a religious. I've asked each of them to reflect on their lifestyle and on how they came to choose it. After each has shared his or her thoughts, we'll call them all back together for a panel discussion, at which time you'll be able to explore in greater depth any questions or concerns that their presentations prompt in you.

5. At this point, introduce the first speaker. No set order is required for this; decide the order based on your sense of how the various personalities are likely to blend and complement one another. Ask the retreatants to welcome each speaker, and encourage applause at the end of each presentation.

6. After the first two presentations, take a refreshment break of about 15 minutes. Then continue with the remaining speakers.

7. Follow the four presentations by gathering all the speakers together for an open-ended panel discussion. A number of variables make it difficult to predict the flow of this discussion. Naturally, the speakers you recruit will greatly influence the kind and degree of student feedback you can expect. However, at least as significant is the nature of your group, how extroverted its members are, and the degree of their maturity. Retreat leaders must be prepared to help stimulate conversation, particularly in the beginning as both retreatants and panel members warm to the situation. Try to keep the discussion focused on the issues involved in decision-making, such as dealing with doubts and anxiety about life choices, determining when one is ready to make a firm choice, and so on. Time will not allow extensive discussion of the particular characteristics of each lifestyle.

8. *Note well:* The plan for this retreat calls for an evening presentation by a marriage and family counselor on the characteristics of a successful marriage and the particular pitfalls of marriage in our society. If you intend to follow this plan, try to avoid a panel discussion that might "steal the thunder" of the later speaker. The nature of the two topics is distinct enough that this should not be a problem, but the open-ended nature of a panel discussion might lead to this kind of digression.

9. Bring the panel discussion to a close by 5:00. Thank the panelists and announce the time for dinner. Feel free to close the discussion if it runs its course earlier than 5:00. Allowing additional free time for the participants is not a problem. Consider inviting the panel members to linger after the discussion and join you for dinner. This would afford more opportunities for the retreatants to mingle with them in a relaxed manner.

5:00 Free time.

5:30 Dinner. The time frame for dinner is intended for a rather formal meal, with time for casual conversation. By "formal" I do not mean elegant. Rather, the meal itself can be quite simple—for example, spaghetti—yet the setting can convey special meaning. Many youth retreats include an *agape* meal, a term based on the Christian Testament word for love. See the SHARING III retreat, page 223, for a description of such a meal.

Consider the following special touches for this meal:
- candlelight
- colorful table coverings; perhaps a different arrangement of tables than has been used for the other meals
- appropriate background music
- an opening prayer ritual
- toasts made by the team leaders
- a special dessert

This kind of meal lends an air of special significance to the retreat; it becomes a symbol of your care and concern for the retreatants. You might even announce that your intent in preparing a special meal is to let the young people know how much you care for them.

6:30 Free time.

7:00 Guest speaker on marriage. The afternoon was devoted to a broad discussion of the various lifestyles available to the young people. The fact, however, is that the vast majority of them will eventually choose marriage. Therefore, that lifestyle deserves more discussion than do the others.

I suggest that, for this session, you invite a marriage and family counselor to speak to and discuss with the group the qualities of successful marriages. Marriage counseling centers have multiplied all over the country in recent decades. Many of these counselors make presentations to schools and church groups. You should have little difficulty finding a counselor, but you will want to choose one who has a positive track record in speaking to groups of young people. For suggestions, contact your diocesan religious education department or teachers of marriage and family life courses at the high schools or colleges in your area.

Ask the speaker to offer 45–60 minutes of information. This should be kept as practical as possible, including a great deal of anecdotal material gained from the counselor's experience with clients. Then schedule at least one hour of discussion time to follow the formal presentation. Young people have intense interest in this topic. If the speaker is dynamic and the student interest is high, you may need to extend the time beyond what is suggested here. Trust your intuitions on this.

9:00 Break.

9:15 Journal writing activity: "A Letter to Myself." See Student Handout C following this retreat outline. With the exception of a short time of personal reflection during the morning discussion activity, the young people have been asked to listen to and discuss a great deal of information. As the day draws to a close, give the retreatants some time for private reflection and a chance to sort out the meaning of the day for themselves as individuals. This activity is designed to facilitate this reflection.

1. When the young people have gathered after the break, briefly review the content of the day. Note the need for private time to reflect on what has been shared.

2. Distribute pencils and copies of Student Handout C, entitled "A Letter to Myself." Read the directions at the top of the handout. Emphasize that the retreatants will not be asked to share what they write, though they will be invited later to share their experiences of the activity.

3. Give the young people the freedom to go where they wish during this time. They will likely need some kind of hard surface on which to write. Clipboards might be purchased specifically for this purpose, but such an expense would likely not be warranted for a single retreat. If needed, consider making inexpensive boards by cutting up 4-by-8-foot sheets of hardboard. This material can be purchased at lumber yards and home improvement stores.

4. Announce the amount of time allowed for this activity, as well as the location for night prayer.

10:00 Evening prayer. The theme of this evening prayer service is "sharing the gift that is me." The following directions can be adapted as you wish.

1. You will need the following materials:
- a Bible
- a paschal or other large candle to represent Jesus
- small candles or tapers for each young person
- a box of sand in which the individual candles can be placed (An aluminum roasting pan filled with sand works well for this.)
- a small lamp or penlight by which to read if the lights in the room cannot be dimmed
- appropriate recorded music and a tape player

2. Have the room dimly lit as the young people gather, and play quiet, reflective music. Give each retreatant a small candle and invite them to join together in a tight circle on the floor. In the middle of the circle have the lighted candle representing Jesus, the Bible, and the box of sand.

3. Before formally beginning the prayer, offer the opportunity to share any insights gained from the private reflection and letter-writing activities. Consider these lead questions to spark their sharing:

- **How many of you found the exercise helpful?** (Ask for a show of hands.) **Could you identify what made the activity helpful to you?**
- **Describe what it felt like to spend that kind of focused time literally talking to yourself. Did that seem silly to you? Unnatural? Comfortable? Normal?**

- **The fact is, we all spend a great deal of time talking to ourselves. This kind of self-talk can dictate the moods we experience, our basic attitude toward life, even our relationships with other people. If we constantly say negative things to ourselves, we will act with negative attitudes. If, on the other hand, we say positive things to ourselves, we will feel and act more positively. How were you inclined to speak to yourself in your letters? Were you kind to yourself—gentle, affirming? Or did you tend to be critical, judgmental, and demanding? If your best friend sent you a letter like the one you just wrote, would you feel good or bad, happy or sad, angry or grateful?**
- **Some popular books on personal development suggest that it is important to try to be our own best friend. What do you think this means? Does that sound selfish? Why or why not?**

Note that this discussion is not essential to the prayer service. Your group may or may not respond comfortably. Posing questions such as these, however, will help the young people to reflect on the purpose of the activity. Do not press them to respond. If they are reluctant to discuss, move to the prayer itself.

4. Share the following thoughts:

One intent of this activity is to get in touch with ourselves as unique, individual persons on unique journeys. Though our uniqueness can at times make us feel lonely and misunderstood, it is also the foundation of our special worth as persons. As a unique person, we each have something to offer the world that no one else can give it. What a wonderful gift! Yet our uniqueness is only valuable if we share it, if we give it away; that is, our unique gifts will mean nothing to others if we hide them, if we keep them inside ourselves. God didn't create us to live in isolation from others. Listen to the way Jesus expressed this thought. (At this point, read Matthew 5:13–16.)

5. **Jesus calls us to be light to the world. If each of us beamed that unique light that is ours—small and insignificant as it may occasionally seem to us—we could light up the world. We want to symbolically celebrate that fact in prayer.**

6. At this point ask the retreatants to silently name their unique gifts, those attributes that they possess that make them special. Some of these characteristics may well have been identified in the letters that they just wrote. They are to try to identify one particular gift and to name that gift as specifically as they can—for example, a sense of humor, a good listener, a lover of music, sensitivity. You might play an appropriate song at this time. See the SHARING music guides for suggestions.

7. After the silent reflection, explain the following procedure: Each person, when he or she feels comfortable doing so, is to simply state the gift that he or she has identified. After doing so, he or she is to take the small candle, light it from the Christ candle, and then place it in the box of sand. As the retreatants begin to do this, the leader should turn off any lights other than the Christ candle. The effect will be to move from near total darkness to the considerable light of all the candles burning in the box of sand. Those candles then become a symbol of the entire group of unique persons united as one.

8. Close the service with a personal prayer of your own, emphasizing gratitude to God for the gifts of these young people. You may wish to conclude the service with another song.

9. Before breaking for recreation, ask for volunteers who are willing to meet this evening to help prepare tomorrow's closing liturgy. Directions for working with these volunteers are given later on page 162. Also remind everyone that morning prayer begins at 8:30 A.M.

10:30 Relaxation and recreation. Make decisions about the nature and the time limits of this recreation on the basis of your experience of the group to the point. A mature group will need less direction and monitoring than will one with young people who are either immature or shy. As noted earlier, I have often simply provided party games (e.g., Trivial Pursuit) and snacks and allowed the retreatants to choose their own form of relaxation. Some retreat centers also have Ping-Pong or pool tables and other forms of recreation.

One enjoyable—but messy!—activity is a pizza-making party. This works particularly well if your group is small, for example, fifteen participants or fewer. Young people love pizza and the project of making and eating their own pizza can be a wonderful community-building experience. Naturally, this requires the purchase of appropriate ingredients and access to your facility's kitchen, something that may not be allowed.

Though lights out time is adjustable, I would recommend it not be later than 1:00. Even as seniors, young people require sufficient sleep if they are to function effectively the next day.

Planning for the closing liturgy

See Student Handout D following this retreat outline.

The closing liturgy may, but need not, require extensive planning. The degree of planning required can be determined by the retreat leaders and, to a lesser extent, by those retreatants who volunteer to help plan it. That is, the retreat leaders can plan in advance the number of options and choices available to the volunteers. As a leader, you will make such decisions on the basis of your own liturgical background and preferences.

One resource offers helpful directions for those who wish to make liturgy planning a significant part of the retreat. In her manual *Youth Retreats: Creating Sacred Space for Young People* (Saint Mary's Press, 1986), Aileen Doyle includes a rather extensive appendix titled "Eucharistic Liturgy Preparation for Overnight and Weekend Retreats" (pp. 103–107). She thoroughly outlines a committee structure for organizing volunteers in charge of planning the liturgy, and then describes in detail the responsibilities of each committee. Take a good look at this material if you intend to do extensive planning for the liturgy in this retreat.

Minimally, the volunteers should select the readings and music for the liturgy and determine who will serve as lectors or song leaders. They can compose Prayers of the Faithful and choose readers for them. More ambitiously, they might make the offertory procession more meaningful by adding gifts that symbolize the group in special ways. Room arrangements and special decorations can also be planned. Again, Doyle's manual offers helpful advice on all these options. It also includes a liturgy planning sheet. This sheet is included in this manual. See Student Handout D, "Planning Sheet for Eucharistic Liturgy," found at the end of this retreat outline.

Sunday

8:00 Rising. Again, consider waking the young people with music. If you have it available, include "Desiderata" as one of the songs.

8:30 Morning prayer. The theme for this morning prayer is awareness of the gift of life. The intent is to increase our awareness of the great potential that exists for us as we awake each morning—the potential for growth, new learning, deepening relationships, and greater understanding of and participation in the mysteries of life.

1. Greet the young people and ask them to sit closely together on the floor.

2. Introduce the theme for the morning prayer as follows:

As we discussed yesterday morning, most of us awake either in a kind of fog or are so hurried and pressured that we start the day running and never slow down. As a result, life can become something that takes charge of us, and we spend much of our time reacting to it rather than directing it. Living life becomes a defensive effort of avoiding and hiding from life rather than a positive effort of finding ways to live it more fully. We can significantly change a negative approach to life by pausing each morning to briefly reflect on the great gift of life that is ours and by making a firm resolution to live our life consciously and fully. This morning's prayer is intended to help us do that today.

3. At this point, lead the young people through a series of relaxation and deep-breathing exercises, helping them to center themselves. By this time in the SHARING Program, this kind of preparation for prayer should be quite familiar to the group and rather easily accomplished. Once the retreatants have become relaxed and focused, ask them to locate the pulse on one of their wrists. Tell them that the pulse is a concrete and powerful reminder of a profound and mysterious reality—that we are, quite wonderfully, alive! To get in touch with this sense of aliveness, ask them to remain in a relaxed and centered posture, monitoring their pulse, while you play some quiet background music. (See the SHARING music guides for suggestions, noting especially the instrumental selections recommended in each.) As the music plays, the young people are to imagine the blood flowing throughout their body, pumped by the heart through miles of veins and capillaries—blood that nourishes each part of the incredible machine that is the human body. Tell them not to try to analyze the circulatory system; rather, they should allow themselves to simply get caught up in the wonder of it.

4. When the music has stopped, quietly reflect on the reality of God's presence in our life:

We cannot spend our days concentrating on the magical workings of our circulatory system. We necessarily take that wonderful facet of our bodies for granted, assuming that it will continue working while we get on with the other tasks of living. Occasionally calling to mind this reality can bring a new sense of richness to our life.

In a certain sense, our relationship with God is like our circulatory system. God's creative power and presence holds us in existence, ensuring that our body keeps working. We often take God's

presence for granted, much like we do the inner workings of our body. However, if we can occasionally and consciously call to mind the presence of God in our life, we can live much more fully.

5. Now share with the young people Luke 12:22–32 on trust in God's providence. Read slowly and prayerfully, asking the retreatants to savor each verse.

6. After the reading, pause for a moment of silent reflection. You might include another song at this point.

7. Invite the young people to offer intentions for the day, asking the group to respond to each one by saying together, "Lord, we place our life in your care."

8. Close the morning prayer by joining hands and together reciting the Our Father.

8:45 Breakfast.

9:15 Cleanup and packing. Depending on your facilities and the services it provides, cleanup and packing may take longer than the 30 minutes provided by this schedule. Adjust the time frame as required.

9:45 Closing presentation: "Signposts for the Journey of Life." The following is an outline for a keynote presentation that I was asked to present at a diocesan youth congress. The theme of the talk is that life is an ongoing journey in which each of us seeks to understand the meaning of life. In many ways, the search for meaning never ends, even for those who profess faith in God. For people with faith, the search often takes on even greater intensity and struggle as they attempt to search out the depths of divine mystery. The intent of the talk is to offer a series of signposts, or basic principles, that can help people to not only pursue their personal journey but to more fully enjoy the search that is a major part of that journey.

I provide illustrative anecdotes from my life for each of the points raised in this presentation. I encourage whoever presents this material to do likewise. Such personal stories commonly spell the difference between a mediocre talk with good content and a great talk with the power to move and change people.

1. Introduction: The Search for Meaning

a. I commonly open the talk by playing a popular song that centers on the search for meaning in life. Butch Ekstrom, author of the rock music guide in the SHARING director's manual, points out that this is a common theme of rock music. He suggests a category of song he calls "facing an unknown future." The songs he recommends for this category often capture the theme of this presentation. As I write this, the number one rock song in the country is "I Still Haven't Found What I'm Looking For" by the group, U2. This is a fine example of the kind of song I recommend using here.

b. I then do a brief commentary on the song as it relates to the theme of the talk. I stress that the search for meaning is shared by people of all ages; it is not an adolescent phenomenon. In many ways, the journey is an unending one. We are never fully satisfied in life, there is always a hunger for *more*—more joy, more intimacy, more fulfillment, more peace.

c. For some individuals, the unending nature of the search for meaning is a cause for despair. This sense of hopelessness comes from misunderstanding the journey itself. The joy of life is not in attaining some magical, idealistic answer "out there." Rather, the joy of life is the search itself. Fullness of life is not an end goal to be sought; rather, it is discovered and experienced in the process of searching.

2. *Five signposts for the journey of life:* Having introduced the theme for the talk, I next offer what I call signposts for the journey of life, basic principles, or guidelines, for pursuing the search for meaning in a way that brings richness to life. I have identified five such principles for this talk:

a. Embrace the questions of life, and reject the easy, pat answers that society offers for them.
   1) We have a tendency to seek easy answers to the questions of life, and society is always ready to respond to our desire for simple solutions. If we are lonely, we are offered casual sex and artificial intimacy. We are told that the accumulation of material things will provide us with a sense of security and personal value. If we are in pain of any kind, we are told an answer is available in pills, pot, or alcohol. Some even try to sell religion as an easy answer to all the problems of life.
   2) A popular bumper sticker once proclaimed, Jesus Is the Answer. That was quickly followed by another bumper sticker that stated, "But What Is the Question?" Both stickers missed the significant point. Jesus is not "the

answer." For those who listened to Jesus teach, few things were more exasperating than his practice of refusing to offer answers to questions that he saw as aimed in the wrong direction. When asked such a question, he would tell a story, one often ending with another question for the listener—a question aimed in the direction of his vision of life.
3) Jesus realized that asking the right question is fundamental to living a full life. The kind of questions we ask determine the nature and direction of our search. Some examples: Society's question is, How can I accumulate more material goods? Jesus' question is, How can I share what I have? Society's question is, How can I have power over people? Jesus' question is, How can I learn to better serve others? Society's question is, How can I become popular? Jesus' question is, How can I love others?
4) So the first major signpost for the journey of life is this: learn to ask and embrace the right questions, and be skeptical of simple answers to them.

b. The answers we seek are not to be found outside but rather within ourselves.
1) We live with the illusion that there is something or someone "out there" who has the ability to satisfy all our deepest desires. This is particularly true in our interpersonal relationships. We believe that there is a dream boy or dream girl who will make us happy. But there is no such person . . . anywhere, for anyone.
2) If we look to others to satisfy our deepest longing, what is likely to happen? While we drain such people in order to satisfy our own needs, who is tending to *their* needs? They quickly run dry and leave us while they seek satisfaction for their own needs, and the process starts over. What is required is that we take a different posture toward others. The question is not, Who can meet my needs? Rather the question is, What can I do to meet the needs of others? When we take that stance, friendships abound, and the people for whom we care consciously seek to care for us. Paradoxically, we gain all that we had hungered for by not trying to gain it at all!
3) At this point, I like to share the story of the poor man that is offered as an optional com-

ponent of the closing prayer service for session 7, pages 141–142 of this program. Consider it for use here if you did not use it then.

c. **We must recognize and embrace our uniqueness with both its promise and its pain.**
1) We have stressed throughout the SHARING Program that we have each been created unique in all the world by the God who loved us into existence. Our acceptance of that uniqueness is a critical step in the search for meaning in life. We must learn to embrace both the pleasing and the painful dimensions of our uniqueness.
2) One positive side of our uniqueness is the tremendous worth it gives us. If I am truly unique, then I have something to offer the world that no other human being can offer it. This gives my life great value and purpose.
3) However, if I am truly unique, then to a certain extent I will never find anyone—other than the One who created me—who will fully understand me. That means that loneliness is an inevitable experience for each of us. Society once again offers fast solutions to this sense of loneliness, but none of them can eliminate it. We must learn to embrace, even be grateful for, our periodic loneliness as a sure sign of the uniqueness that gives worth and value to our life.

d. **We must share the journey with others.**
1) There are many paradoxes in life, and one of them is this: one of the nice things about loneliness is that it is something we can share with others, and the sharing can help to alleviate some of the pain. Put another way, it is true that in one sense we all walk through this life alone, but, strange as it sounds, we can walk alone with others.
2) Sharing the journey of life with others requires two skills, both of which we have touched upon in this program. First, we must learn to be open with others in sharing our life experience—its ups and downs, its triumphs and tragedies. This takes courage, for we all fear rejection and ridicule. However, the alternative is to hide within a protective shell and to die of loneliness.
3) A second skill required in sharing the journey of life with others is the ability to listen to and affirm the stories that others share with us. This means listening with our minds and our hearts.

e. **We should make the journey one step at a time.**
1) We can get so bound up with the destination of our journey that we forget that all journeys are made one step at a time. We might dream

of a future, blissful marriage and ignore the chances to build relationships today. We can envision ourselves professionally successful, yet pass up the chances we have today to learn the skills we will later need.

2) Try to begin each day—perhaps in your own morning prayer—with an attitude of openness to what life will teach you this day. As our scriptural reading this morning said, the Lord is always present, even in the trials and tragedies of life—often, most tangibly in such times. Say yes to the mystery that is life.

3. I try to close the talk, as I open it, with a popular song. In this case, I select one that I feel is uplifting, positive, hopeful. Again, the SHARING rock music guide offers suggestions.

10:15 Break.

10:30 Group preparation for the liturgy. At this time, the volunteers who worked on the liturgy last evening prepare the group for active participation in it. This may include practicing songs, explaining symbolic gestures, and so on.

10:45 Private, personal preparation for the liturgy: "A Letter to God." Yesterday, the retreatants were asked to write letters to themselves. In preparation for the liturgy, ask them now to take pencil and paper, go off alone, and write a letter to God. They can address God any way they wish and then simply let their heart guide them, writing down whatever they wish. Tell them that they will be asked to have their letters read *anonymously* during the liturgy, so they should not sign their name.

11:15 Liturgy. During the offertory, ask them to place their letter to God on the altar. Explain that, during their private reflection, God may have spoken something to their heart that will also speak to the hearts of others. The celebrant might share those as part of his homily. Or he may prefer to use them as part of a post-Communion reflection. Before reading a letter, he should quickly scan it to make sure it contains no references or names that might reveal who wrote the letter.

12:00 Closing lunch. At the end of this meal, the leaders of the retreat can close with appropriate expressions of thanks to those who helped make it possible. The opportunity should also be given for the retreatants to share any final thoughts that they might have before leaving.* If you made memento cards of the reading "Desiderata," you may wish to distribute them at this time. (Note: You may wish to close with the liturgy and omit the closing lunch.)

---

*If you are providing the meditation program or other options following the retreat, make all relevant announcements about the programs at this time. If appropriate, you may wish to sign up interested students after the close of the meal for participation in a future program.

STUDENT HANDOUT A

What a Frightening Thought!

Directions

1. On your own and without discussing this with anyone, rank the human fears listed at the bottom of the page according to how you think most people commonly experience them. That is, in front of the fear that you believe is most commonly experienced by people, put the number 1. For the second most common fear, write number 2, and so on, until all the fears are ranked. You have 5 minutes to do this.

2. When all the participants in your group have individually ranked the items, you are to try to reach consensus or agreement **as a group** on how the fears should be ranked. Consensus implies that the rankings must be agreed upon, at least partially, by **all** the members of the group. Following are some suggestions for achieving group consensus:
   a. Approach the task on the basis of logic. Avoid simply defending your position for the sake of argument. Listen carefully to the reasons group members give for their ranking.
   b. At the same time, resist changing your opinion simply to reach agreement or to avoid conflict. Support only those rankings you can agree with, at least to some extent.
   c. Avoid techniques like majority voting, averaging, or trading off in order to reduce conflict. These are cop-outs to consensus-seeking.
   d. View differences of opinion as an asset rather than a hindrance in group decision-making.

3. When all the groups have completed the assignment, the retreat leader will share the results of a survey that indicate how the subjects of the survey actually ranked these fears.

Rank the fears listed below in the order in which you think survey respondents mentioned them most, from 1 (the most frequently mentioned fear) to 14 (the fear mentioned least often).

____ darkness

____ death

____ deep water

____ dogs

____ driving or riding in a car

____ elevators

____ escalators

____ financial problems

____ flying

____ heights

____ insects and bugs

____ loneliness

____ sickness

____ speaking before a group

Reproduction permission is granted if you wish to make copies for classroom use.
The photocopy master for this handout is found at the back of this manual.

Dyadic Encounter Guide

1. One of my favorite times of the year is . . .
2. A pleasant memory from my childhood is associated with . . .
3. (Quickly choose one of the following) The first time I
   - tried to swim, I . . .
   - was away from home overnight, I . . .
   - kissed someone from outside the family, I . . .
   - performed before a group, I . . .
   - went out on a "date," I . . .
4. A person whom I would like to visit is . . .
5. One of my favorite spots to spend some time is . . . If I could take you there right now, I . . .
6. I am eagerly looking forward to . . .
7. Look over the previous questions and pick one topic you would like to return to and share it with your partner . . .
8. What I remember most about my closest childhood friend is . . .

9. When I can find some time to be alone I like to . . .
10. I came to this retreat because . . . So far during this retreat I have felt . . .
11. Three things that I think I am really good at are . . .
12. One thing about me that I would like to change is . . .
13. Share with your partner a personal success that you have experienced and what it means to you.
14. A problem that I am dealing with right now is . . .
15. Pick a topic from the previous pages and ask your partner to tell you more about his or her response to it.
16. Now that we have reached the last page in this booklet, I feel . . .

Reproduction permission is granted if you wish to make copies for classroom use.
The photocopy master for this handout is found at the back of this manual.

STUDENT HANDOUT C

A Letter to Myself

Directions: The day has been a rich one, filled with information, questions, discussion, and challenges. At times such as these, collecting one's thoughts and reflecting on the personal meaning of all that has happened can be helpful. This exercise is intended to help you do that.

You are to find a place where you can be alone and quiet. Think for a few moments about the events of the day. What most impressed you? What disturbed you? What do you feel you have to spend more time thinking about? If you were now with your best friend, what would you want to tell him or her about the day?

After some reflection, write a letter below about the day to someone who may be your best friend—yourself! Start the letter as you would any other: "Dear (your name)." Then just let your thoughts unfold on the paper. You may be surprised to discover all the things you have never been able to tell anyone . . . even yourself.

Dear _____,

Reproduction permission is granted if you wish to make copies for classroom use.
The photocopy master for this handout is found at the back of this manual.

STUDENT HANDOUT D

Planning Sheet for Eucharistic Liturgy

Theme: _____ **Date:** _____

Decorations: _____

Musical accompaniment: _____

Leader of song: _____

Introduction: composed by _____ read by _____

Opening song: _____

First reading: _____ read by _____

Responsorial psalm: _____ antiphon _____

_____ said _____ sung _____

Second reading: _____ read by _____

Gospel acclamation: _____

_____ said _____ sung _____

Gospel: _____ read by _____

Prayer of the Faithful: composed by _____ read by _____

Offertory song: _____

Offertory gifts: _____

   presented by _____ explained by _____

Holy, Holy, Holy: said _____ sung _____ version (if sung) _____

Memorial acclamation: _____

_____ said _____ sung _____

Amen: said _____ sung _____ version (if sung) _____

Our Father: said _____ sung _____ version (if sung) _____

Lamb of God: said _____ sung _____ version (if sung) _____

Eucharistic ministers: _____

Communion song: _____

Communion meditation (if any): reading _____ read by _____

   song _____

Recessional song: _____

Reproduction permission is granted if you wish to make copies for classroom use.
The photocopy master for this handout is found at the back of this manual.

SHARING IV Designed Retreat

Retreat Planning Guide for SHARING IV

In session 2 of SHARING IV, I suggest that you form a retreat planning committee of volunteers to work with you in designing and conducting a retreat. Many variables in retreat planning are specific to each particular situation: the number of young people who actually volunteer to be part of the committee, the young people's past experiences with retreats, your own background in creating and directing retreat programs, the number of young people likely to attend a retreat program, available retreat facilities, and financial considerations. Consequently, a planning guide that gives specific directions in all of these variables is not possible. Yet there are a number of standard and predictable features of youth retreat planning that make a planning guide practical and effective. The standard features of retreat planning that can be described and given direction are the following:

a. identifying the tasks of the retreat planning committee

b. organizing the retreat planning committee

c. directing subcommittee work

With the directions for the facets of retreat planning offered in this guide you will be able to organize a process for creating and directing your own retreat.

Retreat Planning Committee

A. Tasks of the Retreat Planning Committee

Four major tasks must be accomplished whenever a retreat is planned and then conducted. These are identified below. Following each of the tasks is a brief description of the steps to be taken to accomplish the task. Detailed directions for each task are provided later in this planning guide.

1. The retreat program itself must be carefully planned. The planning involves the following steps:

a. Select an overall theme for the retreat.

b. Set major objectives related to the theme.

c. Design activities for achieving each objective.

d. Prepare a detailed schedule for the entire retreat.

e. Assess the financial implications of the retreat plan.

2. The leaders of the retreat must be recruited and trained. The recruiting involves the following steps:

a. Recruit at least one adult who is experienced in retreat work to help with the planning process and, if possible, to help lead the retreat itself.

b. Recruit an appropriate number of adult chaperones.

c. If needed or desired, identify, contact, and contract with outside speakers and other resource people.

d. Arrange for a priest if you should decide to include the Eucharist or sacramental Reconciliation.

e. Identify and train the young people who will serve as speakers and leaders during the retreat.

3. The facilities and the meals must be identified, planned, and prepared. This preparation involves the following steps:

a. Locate and contract for a facility for your retreat.

b. If necessary, prepare the site for the retreat.

c. Develop a menu and organize the preparation for all meals not provided with your facility.

d. Project the costs of the facilities and the meals and then add these to the costs associated with the program itself. Determine a participant fee, based on projected costs and the potential number of participants for the retreat.

4. The participants in the retreat must be recruited and then be properly prepared for their participation. This task involves the following steps:

a. Advertise and promote the retreat.

b. Decide if the retreat will be open to people outside your parish and, if so, contact and keep the leaders of those parishes informed.

c. Thoroughly inform participants of all information regarding the retreat: dates and times; clothing, toiletry, and bedding needs; transportation to and from the retreat site; rules and regulations regarding behavior.

d. Collect all the fees associated with the retreat.

B. Organizing the Retreat Planning Committee

The great number of variables involved in planning a particular retreat precludes the possibility of my suggesting a specific committee structure to suit your needs. However, based on the description of the committee tasks involved in the process, a workable approach is to form one subcommittee to be responsible for each of the four tasks. One major exception would be the elimination of the facility and meal subcommittee if you contract with a retreat center that provides all facilities and meals.

The number of members for each of the subcommittees will necessarily be dictated by the number of young people who volunteer. I do suggest that you try to recruit at least one adult to work with each subcommittee of young people. This will be particularly helpful for the program planning subcommittee, the one responsible for setting objectives and choosing or designing activities.

Clearly, the subcommittee planning the retreat program and the one recruiting and training leaders will have to work closely together. I separate these tasks primarily to control the amount of work expected of each subcommittee and to engage as many young people as possible in the planning process.

How often should the committees meet? The answer will be based on the number and level of experience of the volunteers, the requirements dictated by choice of facilities, and the length of time between the development of the committee and the date of the retreat itself. My recommendation would be for the committee as a whole to meet initially to decide the overall theme and the scope of the retreat. The subcommittees might then meet weekly, and the committee as a whole would continue to meet every two or three weeks, until the basic plans for the retreat are firmly in place. If the committee completes its work far in advance of the retreat, wonderful; this is far better than being overwhelmed with last-minute details and problems. The planning schedule you intend to follow should be explained to the young people in session 2 as you introduce the notion to them. The more informed they are before making any commitment, the more effective and satisfied they will be when the real work of planning begins.

What do you do if only a few young people volunteer for the committee? The basic principle is this: The fewer the number of volunteers, the more you will have to rely upon previously designed and published retreat models. Your decision about facilities and meals will also be dictated to some extent by the number of volunteers involved. The fewer the number of volunteers, the more you will need a retreat center that provides facilities and meals.

C. Directing Subcommittee Work

See Student Handout E following this retreat planning guide.

Sheer common sense may be the primary skill needed for carrying out the tasks of two of the subcommittees. The facilities and meals subcommittee will need to identify potential facilities and then contact them for available dates. A menu will have to be planned and all arrangements made for the purchase, preparation, serving, and cleanup of meals.

In a similar vein, the recruitment and promotion subcommittee will need to identify potential participants and then find creative ways to contact each of them. My one thought on this would be to keep the recruitment effort as personal as possible. Bulletin announcements, posters, and pulpit support from the pastor are so general in nature that individual young people are not attracted by them. Word-of-mouth and person-to-person promotion by the young people themselves is the most credible and effective approach to recruitment.

Ask the members of these two subcommittees with such clear-cut responsibilities to spend their first meeting brainstorming the jobs associated with their assigned task. Once these jobs have been identified, they should be listed in order of priority according to scheduling requirements. Then individual subcommittee members should be asked to assume responsibility for each one of the jobs on the list. As each task is accomplished, it can be scratched from the list. The subcommittee reports on its progress at regular meetings of the committee as a whole.

Regarding the tasks of the subcommittee responsible for recruiting and training leaders for the retreat, I refer you to the extensive material on this matter offered in the director's manual for the SHARING Program, Section 11, "Developing Leaders for SHARING" (pp. 123–136). Though designed for use with the program as a whole, the material explains principles of leader recruitment and training that can be applied directly to retreat leadership needs.

The subcommittee faced with the most daunting challenge in this planning process is the one responsible for setting the objectives for the retreat and then providing educational activities for each. Given such responsibilities, I will offer extensive directions for that subcommittee.

I suggest that members of this subcommittee begin their work by thoroughly studying and discussing Student Handout E entitled "A Model for Effective Lesson Planning." Based on the work of Richard Reichert, it is the most reasonable and practical approach I have seen in the development of effective learning experiences. The usefulness of this information may not be immediately apparent to the subcommittee members, but it will provide a helpful initial context for understanding their task and will later serve as an extremely helpful tool in developing the retreat activities.

In designing retreats, I have found two practices to be consistently helpful:

1. Prepare a rough schedule for the retreat. By "a rough schedule," I mean one that includes the following information:

a. Specify the starting and closing times of the retreat. Be as specific as possible, for example, from 7:30 P.M. on Friday until 3:30 P.M. on Sunday. (Check school and parish calendars to make sure that there will be no conflicts with other activities during the time of your retreat. I once inadvertently scheduled a retreat for homecoming weekend!)

b. Specify the times for morning rising and evening lights out. Some individuals may want to eliminate a formal lights out altogether, but experience has clearly shown the necessity for sufficient sleep during a retreat. Note that what is sufficient for seniors, however, will differ from that for ninth graders.

c. List all meal times.

d. List free time or organized recreation time.

e. Specify the times for all the set program elements. This will include, for example, the Eucharist or Reconciliation and morning and evening prayers.

By the time you have developed a rough schedule with this basic information, much of the fear of planning a retreat will begin to dissipate. You will discover that a full weekend retreat does not demand an overwhelming amount of time for the program proper since a great deal of the time is taken up with the necessities of sleeping, eating, praying, and relaxing. Also, this rough schedule reveals that you will be working with manageable blocks of time, for example, the time between lunch and dinner, rather than the whole weekend.

2. Set retreat objectives. The approach that I have found most helpful in setting objectives is to think of focuses that are organized in the following sequence:

a. Focus on the individual person and his or her needs, attitudes, and values. For a weekend retreat, I generally set aside Friday night for helping the retreatants get in touch with their own life and personal spirituality. Even though activities that engage them in interaction and conversation with one another will be used to break down barriers and to develop an initial sense of trust, the central focus is on the individual.

b. Focus on interpersonal or communal relationships. This might include anything from interpersonal communication to one's involvement in the Church. The basic idea is to build from reflection on the individual and his or her personal concerns and to broaden the discussion to include a person's relationships with others. On a weekend retreat, I might spend the better part of Saturday morning and afternoon on such objectives.

c. Focus on the participants' relationship with God. This focus is on faith and relationship with God. Having this focus follow the previous two almost guarantees its relevance to the personal and interpersonal lives of the young people. Also, the earlier concentration on matters of immediate and personal interest helps the retreatants warm up to one another and enhances later discussion of theological or spiritual topics. I usually save such topics for Saturday evening and Sunday morning. Incidentally, this sequential flow also leads logically to the celebration of the Eucharist or Reconciliation on Saturday evening or Sunday.

d. As the retreat nears its end, there should be an attempt to summarize the objectives and activities and relate them to one another. Often I will summarize by including a relatively formal presentation near the end of the retreat. This need not be lengthy (generally not more than 30 minutes) and should primarily tie up all the loose ends of the retreat.

e. Finally, I like to conclude a retreat with either a prayer service or a meal of celebration. The conclusion of a program should normally be festive, joyful, and affirming. A formal presentation will normally not convey these characteristics or attitudes. A meal would be most appropriate if the program is scheduled to end near a normal mealtime or if the retreatants are faced with a long trip home. A prayer service or Eucharist would be appropriate at other times.

f. If you are providing the meditation program or any other options following this retreat, make all the announcements about the programs at the conclusion of the retreat. If appropriate, you may wish to sign up interested students for participation in a future program.

This progressive flow of focuses—self, others, God, summation, and closing—provides a helpful framework for the program planning subcommittee. Its members can now plan a rough schedule for the entire program and can identify the objectives they wish to aim at during each of the blocks of time available after meals, recreation, and sleep have been taken into account. Once the objectives are set, the work will be to provide learning activities for each of the objectives.

Reichert's learning process provides practical guidance for the subcommittee. The subcommittee can now use the learning process to identify or develop learning activities for achieving each of the objectives that have been set. This is done by designing a learning activity according to each of the four steps, A through D, outlined at the bottom of the "Model for Effective Lesson Planning."

Step A in this lesson-planning process—identifying what we call the "starting point" of the learner—should actually come into play earlier in the planning, as the subcommittee sets the objectives for each focus. For example, on Friday evening we want to approach an objective focused on the individual. What personal issues will be of greatest concern, given the starting point of the people attending the retreat? Looking at the left-hand column at the bottom of the chart, what topics will be of high interest, given the retreatants' levels of development, their culture, their family background, and so on? The most reliable assessment of the starting point is one based on one's past personal experience with the potential learners, in this case the retreatants. Your experience with the group—assuming that you have conducted some or all of the seven 2-hour sessions before this retreat—will give you many insights into the starting point of your group.

After identifying a specific topic that is in touch with the starting point of your group, the subcommittee then plans activities related to step B. Given the topics selected, what "significant experiences" can be developed to work with each topic? That is, what can be done that will catch the attention of the retreatants and help them reflect on, evaluate, or in any other way consider the topic at hand? The chart lists a series of learning experiences to consider. For each of these experiences there are hundreds of possibilities, many of them contained in the "Helpful Resources" section below.

Once an experience for getting at a topic has been shared by the group—whether that experience is a film, a role-play, a guest speaker, or a game—the retreatants will have to be guided through step C in the learning process. That is, they will need a method of reflection on the significant experience. Each type of significant experience will lend itself to certain methods of reflection. In some cases, you will want to formally discuss the experience. Or, following a particularly powerful film or speaker, you may wish to have the retreatants go off to do some private journal writing. Perhaps prayer is called for.

Formally or concretely including step D of the process—assimilation—in the retreat itself may not be possible. This step involves the actual living out or application of that which has been learned, and it is a lifelong task that is largely the responsibility of the learner. On a retreat, however, you may want to occasionally address this issue from the point of view of looking forward to the future impact of the topic under consideration. For instance, a film might be presented, followed by a discussion of its meaning. You might conclude the discussion by asking, "How might we apply the lessons gained from this film to our life after we leave this retreat?"

This retreat program planning process may seem artificial or terribly complex, but practice with it will quickly demonstrate its value. To sum up, program planning for retreats requires that the subcommittee does the following:

1. Create a rough schedule for the retreat, identifying blocks of time that require learning experiences.
2. For each block of time in the schedule, set an objective that is consistent with both the retreat's theme and the focus of that part of the retreat.
3. For each objective, design a learning activity using the four steps of the lesson planning process:
- Select a topic that is in touch with the starting point of the retreatants.
- Provide a significant experience for the retreatants.
- Identify an appropriate approach to reflection on the experience.
- Suggest some practical means for assimilating new insights into living one's life.

D. Helpful Resources

A wide variety of published resources might prove helpful to the retreat planning committee, particularly for those committee members involved in setting objectives and providing learning experiences. I suggest the following:

1. If you have not used the SHARING I through III retreats, you can draw upon them, along with the SHARING IV designed retreat, in your preparation of this retreat.

2. Saint Mary's Press has published a very helpful manual titled *Youth Retreats: Creating Sacred Space for Young People* by Aileen A. Doyle (Saint Mary's Press, 1986). The manual includes a wide variety of retreat models, including three designed for a full weekend.

3. Group Books, one of the leading Protestant publishers of youth ministry resources, has published two valuable resources for those planning or guiding retreats:

- *The Group Retreat Book* by Arlo Reichter "and dozens of retreat designers" (Group Books, 1983). The book offers valuable information on everything from choosing a location to publicity, from planning meals to raising funds. In addition, it includes thirty-four retreat outlines. Order from Group Books, P.O. Box 481, Loveland, CO 80537.
- *More Group Retreats*, compiled by Cindy S. Hansen (Group Books, 1987). This book offers thirty retreat models on themes such as faith and commitment, self-image, loving others, and family.

4. The Center for Learning has created many fine resources for use with adolescents. The manual *Senior High Retreats* by Karen Jessie, William Griffin, Barry Katrichak, and Cheryl Rose is particularly helpful (Center for Learning, 1987). The manual includes ten planned retreats, three of which are full weekend models. Order from The Center for Learning, P.O. Box 910, Villa Maria, PA 16155.

5. A great number of other retreats—many of them intended for seniors—have been designed over the last two decades by diocesan offices and other groups all over the nation. Most of these have not been formally published, but manuals for them are available through the youth ministry or religious education offices of the dioceses in which they were developed. Most diocesan youth ministry personnel will be familiar with at least a few of these retreats and may even have the program manuals for some of them in their libraries. Check with your diocesan youth ministry or religious education offices for advice and guidance.

6. A number of other publications, though not offering actual retreat plans, provide numerous reflection activities, group exercises, and prayer experiences that would be invaluable resources with which you might construct your own retreat. Among the best are the following:

- A manual entitled *Ministering to Young Adults* by Carol Gura with Carl Koch, FSC (Saint Mary's Press, 1987). This manual includes thirty "practical programs for serious talk and spiritual development," all designed for use by or with young adults. Therefore, the manual would serve as a perfect complement or supplement to the SHARING IV Program.
- *The Jesus Difference* by Kieran Sawyer, SSND (Notre Dame, IN: Ave Maria Press, 1987). The book offers more than fifty "capsules" of youth ministry experiences that can be used like building blocks with which to construct retreat and other programs. Each capsule is a detailed explanation of how to conduct a specific youth activity—prayer service, scriptural study, presentation, values discussion, community building activity or game, and more.
- *The Risk of Faith and Other Youth Ministry Activities* by Kieran Sawyer, SSND (Notre Dame, IN: Ave Maria Press, 1988).

E. Conclusion

Having read this retreat planning guide, you might have a difficult time imagining yourself coping with such a seemingly complex task. Your eyes may glaze, your palms perspire, and your mind declare, "The redhead from Winona must be out of his mind to think I can do this!" I remember feeling that way myself about twenty years ago when I attempted my first retreat. If you react this way, remember that I developed all of the thoroughly designed retreats in SHARING just for you.

However, those leaders who have already conducted retreats and have experienced the joy and satisfaction that accompany them may now want to try their hand at creating a retreat to meet the unique situation of their young people. This planning guide has been developed for those leaders.

Whether you use a predesigned retreat or create your own, you will be providing your young people with a wonderful opportunity to experience, grow in, and celebrate the marvelous journey of faith.

STUDENT HANDOUT E

A Model for Effective Lesson Planning

Real learning—as distinct from the simple accumulation of knowledge—seems to take place in a consistent pattern:
  A. The potential learner's **starting point** is understood, respected, and taken into account in planning.
  B. **Significant experiences** are provided—information or experiences that allow the potential learner to question, reflect upon, evaluate, or become uncomfortable with his or her starting point.
  C. Opportunities are provided for **reflection,** for evaluating the import and effects of the new information; here the teacher can be properly defined as a "facilitator of reflection."
  D. The new information is assimilated into one's life. **Assimilation** is the responsibility of the learner; at this level the teacher becomes one who supports, encourages, challenges.

The following table shows the effects of this learning process on lesson plan development. For a particular topic or point of information to be effectively shared, that is, truly learned by the student, the effective teacher will do the following:

A.	B.	C.	D.

Attempt to understand and remain continually conscious of the student's **starting point** by . . .
 1. understanding basic patterns of psychological development
 2. studying the sociocultural environment(s)
 3. learning about family and immediate social influences (e.g., peer group, friends)
 4. ideally, meeting and developing a personal relationship with each student
	Determine the most **significant experiences** based on the topic, audience, available time, and so on. Possibilities include . . .
	 1. the current life experiences of the students
	 2. effective speakers
	 3. simulation games
	 4. group dynamics
	 5. field trips
	 6. prayer experiences
	 7. case studies
	 8. relevant reading
	 9. films, music, media
	 10. the teacher, who can be a significant experience in himself or herself
		Provide opportunities for **reflection** on information. Possibilities include . .
		 1. discussion:
		   a. teacher-student
		   b. student-student
		 2. questionnaires and reflectionnaires
		 3. prayer services
		 4. opportunities for private prayer
		 5. journal keeping
		 6. carefully designed quizzes and tests
		 7. interviews
		 8. essays, term papers, reports
			Facilitate **assimilation** to whatever degree possible by . . .
			 1. challenging students to accept responsibility
			 2. encouraging, supporting, affirming
			 3. following up on students' progress through
			   a. letters
			   b. phone calls
			   c. other personal contact
			 4. encouraging further study, providing book lists, and so on
			 5. being available if needed for support

Reproduction permission is granted if you wish to make copies for classroom use.
The photocopy master for this handout is found at the back of this manual.

Part 4
Learning to Meditate:
A Way to God

The Meditation Program: An Introduction

Program Goals

To introduce the young people to the skills of prayer and meditation; to help them identify and practice an approach to meditation that responds to their unique needs; to conclude the SHARING Program on a prayerful and positive note.

Program Objectives

That the young people develop an appreciation and desire for meditation; that they acquire the rudimentary skills required to pursue lifelong prayer and meditation; that they end their involvement in the SHARING Program with feelings of gratitude for the past and hope for the future.

Background Material

The background material for this monthlong meditation program provides information on the following points:

- rationale for the meditation program
- basic components
- an overview of the themes and exercises for each day of meditation
- the qualifications and responsibilities of the adult leader
- recruitment of young people for the program
- supplemental resources

Rationale

During workshops or in phone conversations I am often asked to describe and explain the SHARING Program. The listeners commonly seem satisfied, even highly impressed, as I summarize the curriculum content from SHARING I through most of SHARING IV. Then I close by saying, "And the SHARING Program then concludes with a thirty-day meditation program in which the participants contract to meditate privately once each day and to meet with fellow meditators once a week for a month." At this point, some members of the audience will glance in wonder at one another, or the caller on the end of the line will fall silent or mutter a somewhat tentative, "Oh, I see. . . ."

Why this kind of response? Why do some individuals find it so difficult to imagine young people enthusiastically participating in a program of prayer? Even more to the point, perhaps, why am I so convinced that young people not only want this kind of experience but will look back upon it as the highlight of the entire SHARING Program?

I believe that two stereotypes, or negative assumptions, prompt a skeptical response to a meditation program for young people. One of the stereotypes applies to young people, the other to prayer or meditation. First, young people are commonly characterized as "not interested in religion." I certainly hope that by this point in the SHARING Program such a false assumption has been eliminated. Although it may be true that many young people struggle to find meaning in their experience of institutional religion, the vast majority of older adolescents are very interested in their personal spirituality. They are profoundly interested in a faith relationship with God and in sharing that faith with others. Perhaps this is best reflected in the marvelous response of young people to retreats, to creative prayer services, and particularly to guided meditations as an approach to prayer. The entire SHARING Program is committed to nurturing within the young person the hunger for personal spiritual development.

The second stereotype affecting attitudes about a meditation program for young people is one regarding meditation itself. Many adult Catholics have been raised with a narrow understanding of prayer. This is not intended as a critical or judgmental statement; rather, this is simply a fact of history for many of us. It is only in recent years, for instance, that some of the prayer techniques of the oriental religions have found favor in the Church. Countless books on prayer, meditation, and spirituality now fill the shelves of Catholic bookstores. Many people are discovering that meditating can be satisfying and even downright fun.

As an aside here, readers familiar with the meditation program in the original SHARING 11/12 manual might also be a little skeptical about this revised meditation program. In the original manual published in 1979, I offered a very demanding thirty-day meditation program based on the Spiritual Exercises of Saint Ignatius. I had experienced the Exercises myself at about age twenty, and I was convinced that many young people were ready for a similar experience. In designing that program, however, I made a number of mistakes: (1) the program called for two meditation periods a day, too many given the schedules of young people; (2) it relied almost solely on the Ignatian method of meditation, failing to take into account the fact that individuals have differing prayer styles and needs; (3) the original program was too strictly limited to the Scriptures as a source of themes and focus of meditations; and (4) it was far too ambitious in terms of content, essentially attempting to review the entire plan of God in just thirty days. Over the years I have heard from a number of people who have used that program with wonderful results. Yet I am quite sure that far more people reviewed the program and were overwhelmed by it, and understandably so. I doubt that I have ever worked harder on a program that has served fewer people! For those familiar with that program, I encourage you to thoroughly review this one; you will find here something very different—and much better—than the original.

The primary focus of this meditation program is on the act of meditating rather than on specific content or themes. That is, the program is skill-centered, focusing on helping young people develop a personal approach to private meditation that meets their own spiritual needs. Participants learn to meditate by doing it, not by studying it. They regularly join with others to review their experience, to pray together, and to find peer support and affirmation as they work their way through the program. The information that follows will further clarify the rationale of the program.

Components

The basic format of the program asks the participants to meditate once each day for four weeks in periods of roughly 15 minutes each day. A booklet entitled "A Guide for Meditation" is given to each young person. This booklet is created by photocopying, collating, and stapling together the photocopy masters that are provided on pages 205–236. The guide for meditation thoroughly explains each daily meditation exercise and often asks the participants to do brief journal writing as part of their meditations. These booklets become the personal property of the participants. The participants' journal entries are often used as the focus of group discussions, but the participants are never asked to reveal anything that they wish to remain private.

In addition to the daily meditations, the program includes five weekly sessions of roughly two hours each. (The exact length of these sessions will depend on the number of participants and the personal desires of the group members.)

The first session is an orientation to the program in which the young people learn the details of the program, are introduced to a few basic meditation skills, and then formally sign a contract to participate. This formal contract is then returned to the participant at the end of the program, signed by the leader and the pastor as a certificate of participation and as a keepsake. The handout for photocopying the contract can be found on page 203. Daily meditations begin the day immediately following the orientation meeting.

The four remaining sessions of the program are "gatherings" at which the participants meet with their fellow meditators. The gatherings are held once each week during the program. I use the name "gathering" to try to counter the common impression that these are "meetings" or "classes" in the traditional sense. I want to clearly separate this experience from that of a conventional religious education program. More so than at any other level of the SHARING Program, the adult leaders and youth participants in this program are co-learners and, indeed, fellow meditators rather than students and teachers. Incidentally, you may wish to name these meetings something other than gatherings. Feel free to do so, but try to retain the idea that these are distinctly different than conventional classes.

The purposes of the gatherings are (1) to review the individual experiences of the participants and to offer assistance when needed or desired, (2) to allow the leader to introduce additional meditation techniques and other information to enhance the experience for the young people, and (3) to allow the participants to experience the benefits of group prayer and meditation. The gatherings follow a pattern that, once established, allows the gatherings to almost guide themselves. Each gathering includes the following elements:

- an opening period of silent meditation by the group
- a review of the personal experiences of the participants during their previous week of meditations
- some input by the leader, usually involving another meditation exercise
- a brief preview of the coming week using the short introductions to each week provided in the guide for meditation
- a closing prayer ritual that is repeated at each gathering

Note that even the participants' review of the previous week is made simple by the fact that, on the seventh day of meditation each week, the participants do a journal-writing activity that prepares them for the gatherings.

An Overview of Daily Themes and Exercises

The following is a summary of the daily meditations for the four weeks of the program. The title of each exercise is printed in boldface type and is followed by a brief statement identifying the meditation technique or purpose of the exercise. Remember that the focus of the program is on developing the skills of meditation rather than on specific themes or content.

Week 1

Major objectives: To introduce the participants to the basic components of effective meditation: proper place, time, posture, relaxation, and deep breathing.

1. **Creating Sacred Space:** select and prepare a space for meditation
2. **The Face of God in Nature:** find an item from nature that puts you in touch with God
3. **Practicing a Posture for Prayer:** choose a physical posture that is conducive to meditation
4. **The Sounds of Silence:** learn how to handle the distraction of noise
5. **Taking Time to Catch Your Breath:** learn the purpose and the practice of deep breathing
6. **Takin' It Easy:** practice a technique for relaxing the body
7. **Things Worth Sharing:** prepare for the first gathering

Week 2

Major objectives: To introduce body awareness exercises; to learn techniques for managing mental distractions; to learn to use a mantra; to begin journal writing.

1. **Coming to Your Senses:** become aware of and grateful for your body
2. **Picture in Your Mind:** learn to manage mental distractions
3. **Calling on the Name of the Lord:** learn and practice the Jesus Prayer
4. **Meditating with a Mantra:** practice with a mantra; expand use of journal writing
5. **This Is the Word of the Lord!:** use the Scriptures as a primary source for meditation
6. **Praying with the Scriptures:** further practice in praying the Scriptures
7. **Things Worth Sharing:** prepare for the second gathering

Week 3

Major objectives: To introduce and practice the technique of guided meditation; to use guided imagery to meditate on the Scriptures.

1. **Seeking a Place to Rest with God:** learn the basic techniques used in guided meditation
2. **The Saving Goodness of Love:** use a guided meditation to focus on a particular theme
3. **The Search for God:** experience a guided meditation on images of God

4. **Seeing Myself in a New Way:** perform a guided meditation on self-image
5. **Meeting Myself in the Scriptures:** learn to use guided imagery in meditating on the Scriptures
6. **Bringing the Scriptures to Life:** further practice meditating on the Scriptures with guided imagery
7. **Things Worth Sharing:** prepare for the third gathering

Week 4

Major objectives: To learn to use spiritual reading as a source for meditation; to help the participants experience gratitude for the past and hope for the future as they end their involvement in the SHARING Program.

1. **Embracing My History:** prayerfully reflect on and accept your past
2. **Living the Present Moment:** learn to live each moment of the day as God would have you live it
3. **Only Two Things Are Certain:** come to terms with the inevitability of future death and its implications for the present
4. **I Have My Mission:** learn to use spiritual reading for meditation; reflect on personal uniqueness and dignity
5. **Lead Me, Lord:** continue practice of spiritual reading in meditation; focus on trust in God as central to Christian spirituality
6. **For All That Has Been, For All That Will Be:** reflect on the significance of this program to you and look to the future with hope
7. **Things Worth Sharing:** prepare for the final gathering

Qualifications and Responsibilities of the Adult Leader

Some adults may look at the description of this meditation program and immediately feel unqualified to lead it. I hope that is not the case. The fact is that anyone who has successfully led the other components of SHARING IV—the two-hour sessions or the retreat—has already demonstrated his or her ability to lead this meditation program. Remember that the program almost leads itself because of the extensive guide for meditation provided for the participants and the nature of the gatherings. Reading the meditation guide and reviewing the plans for the gatherings should allay the fears of most volunteers.

However, one unique qualification is required of any adult wishing to lead this program—a sincere desire to pray with the young people. That is, the adult should make the same commitment to daily meditation as do the young people themselves. In fact, I would encourage the leader to sign the same contract that the young participants sign. This would affirm and reflect the ideal that the leader and the young people view themselves as co-learners in this program.

The responsibilities of the adult leader, other than the commitment to meditate regularly along with the young people, are not substantially different than those for other dimensions of the SHARING IV Program. Promoting the program, preparing facilities, convening and leading the gatherings—these and other routine responsibilities are also part of the meditation program.

Recruitment of Young People for the Meditation Program

The last of the SHARING IV two-hour sessions and the detailed directions for leading the weekend retreat both include reminders to the leaders of those components in the program to promote participation in this meditation program. These contacts with the young people provide the best opportunity for explaining the meditation program and boosting interest in it.

Whether promotion of the meditation part was included within other parts of SHARING IV, you will have the greatest likelihood of successful recruitment by personally contacting the young people who participated in the two-hour sessions or the retreat. By their previous participation they have already shown interest in religious programs, and you or other adult leaders have presumedly established a level of trust that will give credibility to the meditation program.

In promoting the meditation program, recognize that many young people carry the stereotypes about meditation alluded to earlier. Such negative assumptions are more a factor of our culture than they are a characteristic of a particular age-group. Therefore, expect some resistance to the meditation program among the young people. They will want to avoid looking like "holy rollers" among their peers. In your discussions with potential participants, tap into their past experience in order to sell the concept of meditation. Guided meditations and creative prayer services have been a regular feature of the entire SHARING Program. When talking to young people, remind them of those experiences and tell them that this meditation program will teach them how to experience such prayer on their own. This alone may be enough to catch their attention and generate enthusiasm.

Generally speaking, mass appeals for participation will have little effect in promoting a program that is as demanding as this one. Bulletin and pulpit announcements, posters in the church, and the like will have meager results. Yet curiously enough, I would not hesitate to use these methods for two reasons: (1) you may in fact motivate one or two people to investigate the meditation program, and (2) more importantly, you will be alerting the entire parish to the availability of the meditation program. This will presumedly enhance the reputation of the entire high school program in the eyes of parishioners and begin to build a higher level of awareness that can pay greater dividends in future years.

Ultimately, the most effective means of promoting the meditation program is to start small (you may not have a choice on that!), have a good experience with those who participate in the program initially, and then watch it build from there as younger participants in the parish program begin to look forward to this experience.

Building up the number of participants brings up the issue of group size for the meditation program. Most likely you will not be concerned, at least for a while, about having too many young people participate. That unfortunate fact may in the long run be beneficial in that a smaller group will place less pressure on the leader and allow for more individualized treatment for the participants. In any case, I recommend that the group size not exceed ten or so. A greater number than this will make it difficult to guide the discussions during the gatherings. If you have more participants than this, consider breaking into smaller groups for the gatherings. The orientation session could be attended by all, and the participants could meditate within a fairly common schedule, but you will need to increase the number of gathering times to accommodate additional small groups.

Can a group be too small? In the strict sense, no. One can even imagine this program serving as a basis for a kind of modified, individualized spiritual direction in which one leader works with one young person. Clearly the daily meditations are already intended for individual meditation. The nature and length of the gatherings would necessarily change from group discussion to more personal conversation between the leader and the young meditator, but the basic flow and methodologies of the gatherings would still prove helpful and largely workable. However, it would be an exceptional young person who would be comfortable in such a situation. My point here is that the program should not be eliminated if only three or four young people show interest.

Resources

The following published materials proved valuable to me in developing this meditation program. If you need or are interested in further study in this area, consider reading one or more of these resources. I am restricting the list primarily to those materials specifically developed for use with young people.

de Mello, Anthony. *Sadhana: A Way to God*. Saint Louis: Institute of Jesuit Resources, 1978. I can say without hesitation that I could not have developed this program without de Mello's *Sadhana*, though the book was not designed for use with adolescents. Given to me by a friend several years ago, this book has been an invaluable aid in my own prayer life. As the acknowledgments for this manual suggest, many of the techniques and exercises used in this meditation program are based in whole or in part on de Mello's work.

Kovats, Alexandra. *Prayer: A Discovery of Life*. Minneapolis: Winston Press, 1983. A helpful book intended for young adults and written from the perspective of creation-centered spirituality. Includes exercises and reflection activities useful for either individuals or groups.

Link, Mark. *You: Prayer for Beginners and Those Who Have Forgotten How*. Allen, TX: Argus Communications, 1976. A program for adolescents designed by an experienced high school teacher—one who has taught many young people how to pray.

———. *Breakaway: Twenty-eight Steps to a More Reflective Life*. Allen, TX: Argus Communications, 1980. A follow-up to his book *You*, this program includes audiocassette tapes and a booklet for journal writing.

Meegan, Mary. *Climbing the Mountain: A Journey in Prayer*. Allen, TX: Argus Communications, 1984. Developed as a course to be used in high schools, this book is based on the author's many years of experience in teaching her students how to pray.

Vetter, Bernadette. *My Journey, My Prayer*. Rev. ed. Villa Maria, PA: Center for Learning, 1985. Heavily centered on journal writing, the program includes a marvelous collection of short readings by spiritual giants throughout the Church's history.

In addition to these published resources, the growing interest in videotape as an educational tool has resulted in the development of a number of video programs on prayer and spirituality. Of particular interest is Anthony de Mello's *A Way to God for Today*. Allen, TX: Tabor Publishing, 1984. The program includes reflections and meditation exercises on the major Christian themes of silence, peace, joy, life, freedom, and love. My meditation program does not suggest or demand the use of this video program primarily because of the expense involved. However, you may find that your diocesan media center owns the series, or your parish may decide to invest in it. This would be a wonderful aid in preparing leaders for this meditation program and would offer an attractive follow-up to it if some young people want to continue their meditations and gatherings. In addition, contact Argus Communications for a list of their other video materials.

Directing the Meditation Program

Orientation Meeting

Purposes

- To provide the participants with complete information about the nature, the components, and the procedures for the meditation program
- To define prayer and identify the forms and elements of prayer
- To help the participants make initial personal decisions about the elements of meditation, particularly regarding preferred place, time, and posture as they begin to meditate
- To have the young people formally contract to participate in the program

Materials Needed

- A personal copy of "A Guide for Meditation" for each participant (See pages 205–236.)
- A chalkboard, newsprint, or poster paper prepared as directed for a presentation on prayer
- Firm, straight-backed chairs (one for each participant) for use in practicing one of the prayer postures
- Copies of the contract for the program and pens for formally signing them
- A Bible, candles, and other desired elements for the closing prayer service for this orientation

Special Notes

Note these three points as you prepare for this orientation to the meditation program:

1. The design of this orientation session presumes that the young people attending it already understand the meditation program enough so that they come to this session with the firm intent of completing the entire monthlong program. This understanding is possible because the leaders of SHARING IV were asked to explain and promote the meditation program among the young people at the end of both the seven 2-hour sessions and the weekend retreat. If that was done, only highly interested young people should be attending this orientation.

If you find that some of the young people attending this orientation session are not at all familiar with the meditation program's basic design and demands, your focus during this meeting will have to shift. You may even consider offering a separate introductory session intended only to explain the basics of the program. You would then have to schedule another orientation session like this one for the individuals who seriously want to pursue the program. A second option would be to offer a simple overview of the program and then take a break, allowing the individuals who decide not to participate to leave before continuing on with the remainder of the meeting. If such options are not available, some young people may feel pressured into contracting for this program even though they have little idea what they are committing themselves to. That situation could cause significant difficulties later on. If the program is to be successful, it requires an informed and free decision by the participants to join the program.

2. Mention was made earlier that determining an exact length of time for the gatherings is difficult. As you will see, one of the major focuses of the gatherings is on individual participants sharing their experience of meditation and dialoguing about it with others in the group. The focus on sharing and dialoguing implies two variables that will significantly affect the time needed for a gathering: the number of participants in the group and their willingness or ability to share and dialogue. Therefore, the sharing and prayer sections of the gathering are the only elements in the entire SHARING Program for which I resist identifying a specific schedule or time frame.

This orientation session may last up to two hours; many things have to be accomplished. I suggest that the gatherings last no longer than two hours. You may find with experience that you can finish in 90 minutes or less. With younger adolescents, such unpredictability might be a concern, but the fact that the participants in this program are older allows you more freedom in this regard. Most participants will be able to drive, so rides to and from the gatherings will not be a problem. Stating a maximum time limit for the gatherings can eliminate possible problems for those few individuals who may have to arrange rides.

3. A final point related to schedules: As a leader of this program, you may occasionally experience a tension between maintaining the rigidity of a controlled and organized educational program and allowing for a more relaxed, spontaneous, comfortable conversation among friends. Young people who begin to feel close to you and to one another may want to hang around for hours. If this happens, it may be a high compliment and perhaps enjoyable. However, if the program loses its central focus of meditation and prayer and becomes more of a social gathering, its effectiveness will be diminished. Far better to be very clear on your purposes during the gatherings, move things along at a steady pace, and end by or before your agreed upon time limit. You can always meet on other occasions for parties.

Procedure

A. Welcome, introductions, and opening prayer (10–15 minutes)

1. The way that you handle the preliminaries for this meeting will be determined in part by your current familiarity with the young people who attend as well as the degree of understanding about the program that they already have. As noted above, this orientation presumes that they already are quite familiar with the nature of the program and will probably be coming to this session with openness and enthusiasm. If that is the case, the welcome, introductions, and opening prayer can be quite relaxed and spontaneous. Handle this as you would if you were inviting friends to your home for a meal. Make sure each person is introduced to the others and allow for some small talk. When you wish to formally begin, call the participants together, and ask them to join with you for a short opening prayer.

2. If you believe a formal introduction is required, gather the young people together. Spend a few minutes introducing yourself and sharing your own hopes and expectations about the program. Then ask each young person to briefly introduce himself or herself, perhaps stating their school (if they come from different schools) and what attracted them to this program. After these initial introductions, offer a brief spontaneous prayer of your own.

B. Background information on the meditation program (15 minutes)

1. Create a brief presentation on the nature and components of the program based on the information provided on pages 180–182. Include explanations of the following elements:

a. the primary focus on learning the skills of meditation

b. daily private meditation exercises of 15 minutes each, all fully explained in "A Guide for Meditation"

c. weekly meetings of the group, called "gatherings" to distinguish them from "classes"

d. a formal contract agreeing to be part of the program that will be signed by the participants at the end of this orientation session

2. Follow this brief overview with specific information about each part of the program. Distribute copies of "A Guide for Meditation." Leaf through the guide with the young people, pointing out how clearly each exercise is presented. Note as well the role of journal writing in the program, but mention the brevity of each journal-writing activity to avoid threatening them with a lot of writing. Emphasize the private, personal nature of the journal writing; they will never be asked to share anything they do not want to share freely.

3. Next, give a more detailed explanation of the four gatherings and their purposes. Stress that the gatherings are times to share experiences and to support one another. Though you as leader will occasionally be offering information about meditation techniques, and so on, the gatherings are not intended to be classes or learning situations in the strict sense. The primary purpose is to gather as believing friends to pray together and share experiences of God. Once again, emphasize that there will be no pressure during these meetings to reveal anything they wish to keep private.

4. At this point ask if there are any questions, and respond to them as clearly and specifically as possible. To repeat: It is important that all participants thoroughly understand what they are getting involved in before they contract to join the program.

C. Presentation on prayer (15–20 minutes)

Note: Time is dependent on the number of anecdotes offered for each point.

1. After completing the introductory explanation of the program and its components, point out that it is important to have a general understanding of prayer and, more particularly, of meditation as the program begins. Tell them that this will be the only time in the entire program that you will be "talking at them" like a teacher, but that this is necessary in order to cover a lot of information as quickly as possible.

2. Prepare in advance, on a chalkboard or on paper, the following outline of the information to be presented at this time. With this outline extensive notes are unnecessary. The outline will also help the young people see the information unfold.

a. **Prayer is "communication in a relationship of love."** (Prepare the diagram indicated below "Prayer as Communication.")

b. **Forms of prayer include:**
   - conversation
   - meditation
   - contemplation

c. **Elements involved in meditation include:**
   - an appropriate place
   - an appropriate time of day for the individual
   - the proper posture
   - the ability to center through relaxation and deep breathing
   - an awareness of and openness to God

3. Reveal the outline to the young people, and begin a relaxed commentary on the points listed. I offer here an example of how I would do this. As always, however, you are encouraged to personalize the discussion and make it your own. Illustrate several of the points with anecdotes from your own experience.

Defining prayer

With a subject as broad and varied as prayer, we could find all kinds of definitions. As children we may have been told that prayer is the act of lifting our heart and mind to God or, more simply, talking to God. One of the problems with such definitions is that they seem one-sided; they make it sound as if we're doing all the work, all the talking. What is God doing in this?

Prayer can be defined as communication in a relationship of love. If you take that definition apart a bit, it reveals all kinds of insights about the nature of prayer:

- *Communication* implies a unity between persons, a give-and-take kind of sharing.

- The use of the word *relationship* extends the notion of communication. In prayer we do more than mouth words and hope for some mysterious sign from on high. A relationship with God implies the existence of a God who is reachable, who is in touch with us.

- When it is stated that the relationship involved is one of love, the sense of what's happening in prayer becomes clearer. Real prayer must be founded on the firm conviction that our God cares enough about us to want to communicate with us. It is the nature of all love to do this. If you love someone, you need to become one with that person, to share, to express yourself. If God loves us as we profess, then that love demands similar expression. If we don't believe that there is a God who loves us, of course, then the whole idea of prayer becomes foolish. Why bother? God certainly doesn't need our nice words, and if God doesn't care about us, all the talk in the world isn't going to change that. If we do believe that God loves us, on the other hand, it would be foolish not to pray, not to open ourselves to the power and joy of a love that is infinite.

Prayer as communication

In prayer we experience our deepest selves in touch with the deepest dimensions of life. Consider the following illustration:

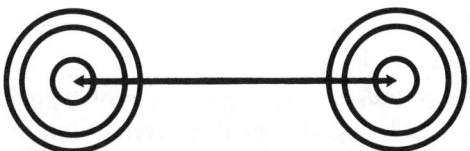

The two sets of concentric circles represent two individuals. The outer circle represents our contact with the physical world, with the ground we walk on, the trees we bump into, the strangers we pass without a word. The next circle represents the level of personal relationships in our life—the level on which we move beyond just physical contact and begin to develop communication and friendship with others outside ourselves and, in a sense, with the world. When we look at the stars in awe, for example, we are operating more on the second level than on the first. Finally, the interior circle represents our contact with the dimension of life that is most interior and mysterious. This is the deepest level of our existence, the point at which we are most fully in touch with what it truly means to be human. It is at this interior level that ultimately we will find and experience God in the most personal and intimate way.

Significantly, it is also at the interior or innermost level that we will be most personally and intimately in touch with other people, demonstrated by the line connecting the center circles. We can relate to others as objects, in which case we are in a sense rubbing outer circles with each other with no communication. We can move beyond treating people as objects to a meeting of minds, to the development of a degree of communication, in which case we would be relating on the second level. However, it is in the experience of love that we can relate on the level of our center, our deepest self. It is also on this level of love that we become one with God. This explains why, in the experience of many, we are never closer to other persons than when we are together in touch with God. This is why communal prayer—praying with other people—can be so exhilarating, so uplifting, and why communal prayer is such a central part of this program.

Many contemporary writers in spirituality use the term *centering* for that action or activity of getting in touch with our deepest self. Basically that is what is being referred to here: the process or experience of being in touch with our own center and those of others. During this program we will be practicing techniques that can help us do that.

Forms of prayer

There are almost as many different forms of prayer as there are definitions of it. For our purposes, the many forms of private prayer—as distinct from communal prayer like the Mass or other experiences of group prayer—can be summarized under three categories:

- *conversation,* which means simply speaking to God and, essential to all conversation, listening creatively to God's response
- *meditation,* which is a more structured attempt to get in touch with and communicate with God, to center our heart and thoughts on the Mystery that is God and to reflect more deliberately on what God is trying to reveal to us about both ourselves and about the mysteries of life
- *contemplation,* what some writers call "resting in God," the experience of not needing words, not consciously analyzing or reflecting on the reality of God but simply yet profoundly *being with God*

Comparing these forms of prayer to levels of communication experienced in our other relationships can be helpful. Think for a moment of your relationship with your best friend or with any person you love deeply. Most of the time, communication between the two of you is spontaneous, and relaxed, involving a lot of chitchat and banter. You enjoy being together and sharing your lives. This is similar to the level of conversational prayer with God. This form of prayer can take place anywhere at any time.

At times, however, you and your friend experience a kind of intense dialogue and sharing. He or she calls you and says, "We've really got to get together!" and you know immediately you're in for a long conversation. The two of you find a quiet place to get together without interruption. You watch each other intently, exchanging all kinds of signals with your eyes and body language. You share and listen deeply, and such encounters affirm and deepen the love you have for each other.

Finally, there is another delightful kind of communication shared by friends who deeply love each other. At times they can share an experience—watching a sunset, sitting together on a porch during a summer evening, listening to music—and they say nothing. In fact, it almost feels like words would break the magic of the moment. The friends are with each other, but so totally with each other that they feel as one. In other words, to recall our illustration, they are meeting each other at their center, and no words are necessary. Perhaps no other form of communication between friends is more wonderful, energizing, and moving.

These are also the ways we encounter God—in conversation, meditation, and contemplation. In this program we are going to concentrate heavily on meditation, a focused and formal attempt to get in touch with our God. Contemplation is within the reach of all Christians, not just the saints, but it cannot be programmed or scheduled anymore than those moments of intimacy with our friends can be forced. It is quite possible, however, that many of you will experience moments of true contemplation during this program.

Elements involved in meditation

What elements are involved in the experience of meditation, and how do we learn to meditate? At this point, we will only identify and define the elements involved in meditation. Then we'll take a short break, after which we will explore a few of these elements at greater depth in preparation for your first week of meditation. Basically, five elements are involved in meditation:

- *An appropriate place:* When you and your friend really need to talk, you don't go to a rock concert or a movie theater. You need privacy, an environment that helps you to relax and focus on each other. The same need exists in meditation. During the first week of this program you will spend some time creating what we will call a sacred space in which you can practice your meditation.

- *An appropriate time of day for the individual:* Everyone has his or her own *biological clock,* a kind of built-in system that makes some people, for example, morning people and others night owls. If you don't really wake up until the school day is over, it wouldn't make sense to try to meditate the first thing in the morning. Again, this week you will begin to gain a sense of the best time of day for you to meditate.

- *The proper posture:* Through the centuries, masters of meditation have discovered a variety of physical postures that are conducive to meditation. We'll identify and experience a few of these postures after our break, and you will try to settle on one posture to use for this coming week.

- *The ability to center through relaxation and deep breathing:* Relaxation and deep breathing are two basic meditation techniques that will help you get in touch with your center in preparation for communication with God. You'll be practicing various centering approaches throughout this program.

- *An awareness of and openness to God:* In many ways, awareness of the presence of God is both a goal and by-product of all the other elements of meditation. This awareness also includes the ability to listen to God, to comprehend what God is revealing to you in prayer. This will be the focus of one of our later gatherings.

Invite any immediate questions if you wish at this point, particularly if you sense that some of the young people are confused by any of this information. If no questions or comments arise, break for simple refreshments. If you prefer, take just a stretch break at this point, and offer refreshments at the close of the orientation when some relaxation time might be appreciated.

D. **Break** (10 minutes)

E. **Experiencing the elements of prayer**
(30 minutes)

1. At this point, you are to lead the young people through some focused reflection and discussion on three of the basic elements of prayer—place, time, and posture. The goal is to provide them with the kind of general information that will make their first week with the program an enjoyable experience. You will be introducing them to options for each of the three elements, which they are then to consider on their own or, if necessary, discuss with the group. They are then to make some initial decisions about how they as individuals will deal with these elements as they begin their meditations.

2. Explain the purpose of this part of the orientation. Provide the young people with the pens that will later be used for signing the contracts. Ask them to turn to the back cover of their guide for meditation and fill in their name and phone number. Then explain that they may want to make a few notes to themselves in their booklet on page 62, labeled "Notes for Orientation" as they begin to make some decisions about their own meditation style. Once again, the boldface type below indicates how I would present this information. Feel free to adjust this to suit your personal style.

3. *Information on and decisions about a place for prayer:* **Certainly there are all kinds of options available with regard to the place for prayer. In fact, the possibilities are unlimited in the sense that one can pray in virtually any place, from a mountaintop to a dungeon. However, it stands to reason that some places are more conducive to prayer than others. Among the more popular are the following:**

a. **A private bedroom removed from the rest of the house in which one can find some degree of privacy.**

b. **Perhaps another room of the house that is available for decorating in a way conducive to prayer, for example, with low lighting and candles.**

c. **Nature settings have always been popular with people committed to prayer. With the obvious limitations of weather, it is remarkably helpful to be in touch with a peaceful scene from nature: the isolation and peace of the forest; the exhilaration of hills from which one can see great distances; the relaxing sounds of water brushing the shores of a creek and slapping against the**

Directing the Meditation Program 189

rocks. Nearly all geographical areas have some place, even a public park, that at certain times offers an appropriate environment for meditation.

d. Other options, perhaps not as obvious as one might imagine, are chapels and churches, whose entire purpose for existence is to offer an environment for prayer. We tend to think of churches as reserved for public, communal worship rather than for private prayer. Yet few places are more conducive to private prayer than a beautiful church in the evening, lights out and quiet, a candle or two flickering, and the distant, muffled sounds of the street all but blocked out.

At this point, ask the young people to take a moment to reflect on all the places for prayer that they have reasonably available to them, that is, places they can expect to have easy access to on a daily basis. For example, they should normally not choose their parish church unless they live in the neighborhood of the church and can get there quickly and easily. Keep in mind that most tape recorders, which will be used in the guided meditations, are battery-powered and portable. If the young people wish, they can list all of these options for a place to meditate in their guide. After a minute or so, ask them to make an initial decision about where they will begin to meditate. As an aside here, make the following comment:

In the directions for the daily meditations in your guide, the presumption will always be that you are meditating in a special space in your house, one that you have prepared just for this purpose. In fact, your first meditation period is devoted to creating such a space. However, on occasion you may decide to meditate somewhere else, and you should feel comfortable doing so.

4. *Selecting a time for prayer.* Though the Scriptures tell us to "pray always," some times of the day seem more conducive to prayer than others. It's a little hard to get into prayer during lunch in the school cafeteria, and it's rather dangerous to attempt meditation while driving! Two times that have traditionally been preferred for prayer are early morning, perhaps before other members of the family awake, or late at night, just before bedtime. Yet there are some individuals for whom both of these times would prove unworkable: the kind of person who takes hours to wake up, for instance, or the one who passes out as soon as he or she gets near a bed. For such people, maybe a time at midday is required, perhaps stopping briefly at church on their way home from school. Others might find that the time immediately after supper is appropriate, for example, just before studying, when they can be alone without feeling uncomfortable about it. When do you think your best time of day for prayer might be?

Again, provide a minute or two for reflection, and then ask the young people to jot down the time of day that they initially feel will be best for their meditation periods. Tell them that, during their first week of meditation, the guide for meditation will ask them to practice with alternate times of the day for meditation. If they are already convinced about a particular time that is best for them, they can feel free to stick with that throughout the week.

5. Choosing a posture for prayer: For this part of the discussion of the elements of prayer, I suggest that you actively engage the young people in experiencing each posture described here. You will be able to practice each posture only for a minute or two, but this should be enough time for them to come to an initial decision on which posture they prefer. This approach is based on the assumption that you will have a small group to work with, for example, ten or less. If you have a large group, you may want to create a more involved activity in which smaller groups are assigned one of the postures, allowed to practice it for 5 minutes, and then asked to share with the large group their reactions to it. This would necessarily involve more time and require a slight change in the schedule for this orientation.

Tell the young people that experts in meditation have identified at least five basic physical postures or positions that are conducive to meditation. As you describe each, ask them to practice it for a minute. Note that they may keep their eyes open but directed straight ahead, opened only slightly, or closed completely. They will have to experiment to find which way works best for them. The five postures are the following:

a. Kneeling with the back straight and the hands folded in front of the body, the hands resting on something—perhaps a chair or couch—to give support and aid balance.

b. Kneeling, again, but this time allowing the body to relax with the buttocks resting on the heels of the feet. The back remains straight, and the hands are allowed to rest on the thighs, often with the palms turned upward in a gesture of openness to God.

c. Seated in a firm, straight-backed chair, the upper body erect, the feet together and firmly on the floor, the hands gently resting on the lap, with the palms facing upward. (Note: You will need to provide appropriate chairs for this posture, e.g., kitchen or dining room chairs. Also, mention that some people prefer to sit on the edge of the chair rather than with the back against the back of the chair.)

d. Reclining on the floor, either on the back or the belly, but in such a way that one feels relaxed yet attentive. The body should be straight, the legs not crossed, and the hands in a relaxed but prayerful position. (Note that, for obvious reasons, this posture is the most predisposed to inducing sleep.)

e. The famous lotus position, seated on the floor, the legs folded close to the body, the back straight —perhaps held so against a wall—the hands resting on the knees with upraised palms. Note that most people can only do a modified version of this posture, as we do not normally have the flexibility to assume the traditional version of this posture.

After the young people have experienced all five postures, ask them to briefly note all five in their guide. They should then rank order these postures in terms of their apparent effectiveness for them, admitting that they will need practice before making a final decision. The participants should then choose the posture they want to start with this week.

6. Close this experience of the elements of prayer by noting that the other two elements identified—centering techniques and listening to God—will be experienced and discussed throughout the program. As usual, allow for any questions the young people may want to ask.

F. Contracting and closing prayer (20 minutes)

See Student Handout F on page 203.

1. As you now bring the orientation meeting to a close, distribute copies of the formal contract for the meditation program. (The participants should still have their pens from the previous exercise.) See page 203 for the photocopy master. I suggest that you have these copied on high quality, parchment-like paper in order to increase the sense of importance attached to the program. Most photocopy businesses have such paper. The contracts are to be signed by the participants and returned to you. At the end of the meditation program, both you and the pastor will sign the contracts, which are then returned to the participants during the closing prayer service.

2. To guide this prayer service, you may wish to sit on the floor behind a table, such as a coffee table, with the young people gathered about you on the floor. Have a candle or two and a Bible on the table.

3. Begin the prayer service with a short spontaneous prayer of your own, calling the presence of God to mind and asking the Spirit to be with the group, both during this time of commitment to the program as well as throughout the course of the next month of prayer and meditation.

4. Have the following places marked in your Bible for easy reference, and be prepared to select the readings *in this order*: Mark 1:35; Matthew 7:7–11; John 11:41–42; and Matthew 26:36–39. Tell the young people that, as in all others areas of the Christian life, Jesus is our model for prayer. Ask them to listen as you slowly read the passages, which reflect the primary role prayer played in Jesus' life.

5. Note that, if we hope to learn to pray with the same conviction of God's love as Jesus did, we must make a firm commitment to work at it. Like any skill, meditation takes real effort and practice. If this program is to be effective, we must all make a firm commitment to God, to one another, and even to ourselves to do what is necessary to make it so. That is the purpose of the contract.

6. At this point, read through the contract out loud, asking the young people to read along. When you are done, invite them to spend a moment in silent prayer, asking God to help them live out the commitment that they are about to make. When they feel ready, the participants should sign their contract. After all the participants have signed their contract, invite them to slowly come forward to present them to you by laying them on the table. You may wish to shake each person's hand at this time as another sign of the commitment you are making to one another. You may also decide to play music during this time, allowing people to reflect for a few minutes after they have presented their contract. See the SHARING music guides for suggestions. (*Special note:* Do not forget to sign a contract yourself!)

7. Close the service by asking all the young people to share the prayer that Jesus taught us, the Our Father. You may wish to join hands for the prayer.

G. Final announcements (5 minutes)

Make certain that everyone knows exactly what is to be done as they begin meditating the next day.

Tell the young people that all they need to do is read the directions for the first meditation and follow them. Also, remind them of the first gathering to be held in a week. As noted earlier, you may wish to offer refreshments at this time.

Gatherings: General Information

In the background information for the meditation program provided earlier, the general format of the gatherings was briefly described. Each gathering includes the following elements:

- An opening period of silent meditation by the group
- A review of the personal experiences of the participants during their previous week of meditations
- Some input by the leader, usually involving another meditation exercise
- A brief preview of the coming week
- A closing prayer ritual that is repeated each week.

Because these elements are to be repeated during each gathering, I will describe them in detail here. In the explanations of procedure for each gathering that follow, then, I will simply remind you to repeat what is described here.

A. Opening period of silent meditation

One of the major purposes of the gatherings is to allow the participants to pray together. The conventional image of group prayer is that of people reciting prayers together or, perhaps, sharing in spontaneous prayer. These approaches to prayer will be part of the gatherings, but the opening prayer for each session will no doubt be something unique for the participants.

I encourage you to begin each session with a period of silent group meditation. This will perhaps initially seem a little odd or uncomfortable for both the leader and the participants, but I am convinced that with experience the group will quickly warm to the idea. When teaching meditation to groups of people, Anthony de Mello suggests a minimum of 30 minutes of such meditation. Consider what he says about group meditation:

> If you make these [meditation] exercises in a group you will also notice the group benefits that they will bring. The highest of these benefits is an increase of love among the members of the group. Many attempts are being made today, and very laudable ones, to bring about a greater union of hearts among members of religious communities and families through dialogue, group sharing and group encounter. There is an additional way of achieving this result: through group contemplation, when all of the members of the group sit together for at least half an hour each day, preferably in a circle (I do not know why this helps, but it does) in total silence. It is important that the silence be not just external—no physical movements in the room, no fidgeting, no verbalization of prayer—but internal too, namely, that the group members strive to create a silence of words and thoughts within themselves. . . .
>
> Silence, when it is deep, can unite. Words can sometimes be used to impede communication! One retreat master who conducts retreats very similar to Zen retreats at which the participants spend hours together in total silence and in emptying the mind of all thought content, told me that he always gets his retreatants to practise their contemplation together in a hall. The reason: it helped enormously to bring all these people—as many as eighty of them, generally total strangers to one another—together and give them a deep sense of union with one another. (From *Sadhana: A Way to God* [Saint Louis: Institute of Jesuit Resources, 1978], pp. 53–54)

If the intent of this program is to provide participants with the basic skills of meditation and to encourage them to make meditation a regular feature of their life, then we want also to expose them to the joys and benefits of group meditation. The approach I recommend in this program is modified and minimalist compared to that suggested by de Mello. You may discover, however, that the young people will request more than what I propose, and you should feel free to accommodate them.

I recommend the following approach to group meditation:

1. At the beginning of the first gathering, introduce the concept of silent group meditation to the young people, perhaps referring to or even quoting some of de Mello's thoughts. Tell them that the pattern for this group meditation will be as follows:

a. for gathering one, 5 minutes of silent meditation, with quiet background music to help alleviate tension

b. for gathering two, up to 10 minutes with background music

c. in gathering three, 5 minutes without background music

d. in gathering four, 10 minutes without music

2. Gather the participants in a circle. For group meditation, it is advisable that all the participants assume the same prayer posture as a sign of their unity. Allow the group to share opinions on which posture to assume, and try to achieve a consensus on this rather than simply resorting to a majority vote. You may want to use a different posture at each gathering.

3. For the first gathering, the leader will have to provide some instructions. The need for these instructions should virtually disappear by the final gathering. The group begins with some centering activities. Then I recommend an exercise adapted from de Mello that he titles "God in My Breath." I offer here the way in which I would direct this during the first gathering. Remember, however, that the goal is to keep reducing the number of oral instructions as you experience this in successive gatherings. As always, the series of periods (. . .) indicates a pause in the instructions.

> **As we gather this evening, let's all assume a common prayer posture as a sign of our unity. . . . Now close your eyes, and take a moment to relax your body. Identify any part of your body that seems particularly tense. Tighten the muscles in that part of your body, become conscious of the tension there, and then allow the muscles to relax. . . .**
>
> **Now become aware of your breathing. . . . Spend a minute or two steadying the rate of your breathing and deepening it. . . .**
>
> **Now imagine that the air that you are breathing in is charged with the power and the presence of God. . . . Think of the air as an immense ocean that surrounds you . . . an ocean heavily colored with God's presence and God's being. . . . While you draw the air into your lungs, you are drawing God in as well. . . .**
>
> **As you exhale, imagine that you are breathing out all your distractions, your concerns, your fears, your negative feelings. . . . Imagine that you see your whole body becoming radiant and alive through this process of breathing in God's life-giving Spirit and breathing out all those things that keep you from being one with God. . . . Rest in the peace of God's loving presence.**

(Adapted from de Mello, p. 32)

4. As noted, I suggest that you provide some quiet background music for the first two gatherings to aid the young people in this exercise. Silence, particularly among strangers, can be discomforting. As the young people grow comfortable with one another, the discomfort will become less a problem. Choose music unfamiliar to the participants so that it will not provoke distracting memories or feelings. Use instrumental music only, and play it softly. For suggestions, see the guide for religious music in the SHARING director's manual, especially that identified in Margaret Cassidy's essay as "Instrumental Music for Meditation." Because you will be joining the group in the prayer circle, you will either need to have your tape player near you or have someone else who is not a participant of the group take care of the music for you. For the first week, select a musical piece roughly 5 minutes in length. For the second week, increase the length to 10 minutes.

5. When the period of meditation is completed, gently invite the participants to thank God in their hearts for this time of prayer. Then ask them to leave their prayer posture and prepare for the next part of the gathering.

6. For the first two gatherings, you may want to briefly process the experience of group meditation with the participants. Ask the young people to freely share how they felt during the meditation or how they now feel after it. Invite suggestions from them on how you might change the experience next time. By the third gathering, however, allow the experience to speak for itself, that is, do not feel compelled to analyze it rationally. The primary purpose of meditation, after all, is to experience a level of life that goes beyond words.

B. Reviewing the experience of the past week

The seventh day of each week of meditations includes a journal-writing activity to help the participants review their experiences of the week and to prepare for the gathering. These activities, entitled "Things Worth Sharing," are to be the focus of this part of the gatherings. The individual statements or questions that make up each of these journal-writing activities are commonly phrased to ensure that they can be used for open dialogue with the group. For example, a statement might read, "One thing that I would like to share with the group about this week is . . ." Nevertheless, remind the participants that their privacy is always viewed as sacred; they are to share only what they feel comfortable sharing.

You may decide to review the "Things Worth Sharing" material step-by-step, inviting group members to respond to each successive point. Or, as you grow to know the group, you may know that some points are far more interesting and important than others. Feel free to use this material in the way it best fits the character of the group. Always remember that the program is only a tool to facilitate individual and group meditation. God and what God reveals must be the ultimate "program," the ultimate concern. Trust the Spirit working through you and the others to lead the group.

C. Leader options

This part of the gatherings is necessarily somewhat unpredictable and, to a certain extent, optional. That is, if God is to be truly in charge of the gatherings, you will have to trust the prompts of the Spirit. You may find, for example, that the group reflection on "Things Worth Sharing" stimulates so much discussion that no time is left for this additional information or exercise. In such cases, trust your intuitions and drop this material. As a kind of guideline, keep this principle in mind: The primary focus of the gatherings is to be on prayer—the opening silent meditation and the closing prayer ritual. The secondary purpose is to allow the participants to discuss their past experiences through the "Things Worth Sharing" activities. The third purpose is to provide additional information and meditation experiences *when time permits*.

This section of the gatherings commonly offers a meditation exercise that either builds upon the meditations of the previous week or helps to introduce what is coming in the next week. In one case—the third gathering—the leader is asked to provide information and to lead discussion on the question of how God responds to prayer.

D. Preview of the coming week

Each week of meditations in "A Guide for Meditation" is introduced by a one-page essay. Simply refer the participants to that information at this point in the gatherings and, if you wish, read through it with them. Also, in preparation for each gathering read through the coming week's meditations on your own, and offer any additional information that you feel might be helpful for the participants, given your understanding of their needs. For example, you may discover during a discussion that some people have had difficulty doing guided meditations when listening to their own voice on the tape player. You may, in light of that, provide alternatives when you see that another guided meditation is scheduled for the coming week. This is another way to personalize the program for your group.

E. Closing prayer ritual

In his program *Breakaway: Twenty-eight Steps to a More Reflective Life* (Allen, TX: Argus Communications, 1980), Mark Link describes an approach to shared prayer that he developed for use with groups of young people that he was teaching to pray.

The group prayer follows Link's format:

1. All the participants take a comfortable posture, close their eyes, and relax completely.

2. The leader recalls Jesus' promise: "Where two or three come together in my name, I am there with them." This is followed by a minute or so of silence.

3. After the silence, the leader invites each person to share a short prayer aloud with the group. Concretely, this is the way the participants share their prayers:

a. Moving from left to right, each person gives thanks for a recent blessing. For example, "Dear God, you know how hard it is for me to be honest in a class that I'm having difficulty with. It's very hard! But with your help, I managed it this past week. Thank you for this, Lord."

b. Again, moving from left to right, each person asks pardon for a recent failure. For example, "Jesus, you taught us how to love by word and by example. Forgive me for not showing love this week to someone who deserves it the most, my mother."

c. Finally, moving again from left to right, each person asks God's help for something. For example, "Holy Spirit, giver of light, I want to do what is right, but I'm not always sure what that is. Help me to know how to act toward my father who is under great stress and who is drinking rather heavily" (adapted from Link, p. 20).

4. I suggest one caution and one addition to Link's approach:

a. The caution is that I would provide the option, at least initially, for a person to pray privately during each of these cycles of prayer if he or she is uncomfortable sharing the prayer publicly. My basic guiding principle is always that a person's freedom must never be threatened. Paradoxically, once that principle is firmly established and the participants relax, they tend to become more open with their thoughts and prayers.

b. The addition is to consider finding or purchasing an attractive crucifix or other religious artifact that can be passed from one person to the next as the prayer cycle is repeated. On one level, this will serve as a helpful, nonverbal sign that an individual is done with his or her prayer, something particularly helpful if one chooses not to pray aloud. On another level, religious symbols have a particular power of their own to prompt prayer.

Using a religious artifact offers a third possibility that you might consider. Try to find a crucifix or other artifact of a size that makes it functional for group use (that is, four or five inches) but that is also available in a smaller version. Then, at the closing gathering, present each of the participants with one of the smaller artifacts as a permanent memento of this experience. If possible, choose an artifact—again like a crucifix or a religious medal—that might be worn on a cord around the neck or as a piece of jewelry. This may well be treasured by the young people for years to come.

5. To finish the closing prayer, have the young people hold hands and recite the Our Father.

These basic components make up the major portion of all the gatherings. Remember that the length of the gatherings will necessarily vary from group to group but should not be allowed to run more than two hours.

Gathering 1

Purposes

- To establish procedures that will be followed for all the gatherings
- To help the participants become comfortable with the group dimension of the meditation program
- To reflect on the experiences of the first week of meditations
- If time allows, to lead an exercise intended to teach the importance in meditation of awakening and sharpening all of our senses

Materials Needed

- Suitable chairs for all the participants if you expect that they will be needed for the opening period of silent meditation
- An orange, a dish, and a napkin for each participant for the sense experience

Procedure

A. Welcome and silent meditation (10 minutes)

1. Greet all the participants as they arrive, and make an effort to address each one by name. Help make them comfortable until all the young people are present.

2. When all the participants have arrived, use the information provided earlier (page 192) to explain the nature and purpose of the silent meditation period that will open each gathering. Explain that the first session will call for just 5 minutes of meditation with music, and that this procedure will be changing from one gathering to the next. Then lead the silent meditation as described in the general information for the gatherings on pages 192–193.

B. Review of the first week's meditations (time flexible)

1. Briefly explain that, following the opening prayer of each gathering, the group will review the previous week's experience of meditation. To do this you will use the "Things Worth Sharing" material from day 7 of each week. Ask the participants to turn to that material in their guide.

Some individuals may have left their guide at home. If so, be very firm on how important this guide is for the success of the gatherings, and encourage them all to bring their guide each week. If several have forgotten their guide, you may have to refresh their memory on the "Things Worth Sharing" material for the first week by reading from your own guide. Do not expect those who did bring guides to share them with those who did not, as this would compromise the privacy of the guides that is guaranteed during the orientation meeting.

2. Review each point of "Things Worth Sharing" in order, inviting the people to respond to each. Being in a group, the members may initially and quite naturally be reluctant to share. Be ready for some silence until someone volunteers a response. Given the nonthreatening nature of the points raised for the first gathering, feel free to call upon specific people to respond, always allowing them to pass if they wish. On points for which there is prompt or enthusiastic discussion, allow the sharing to continue until you feel that its value has waned. If little interest surfaces for some points, move on quickly. The major purpose of this part of the gatherings is to allow the participants to share and discuss *if they need or desire it*. During some gatherings the need to share may be quite strong; during others, this sharing may take relatively little time.

C. Optional exercise on experiencing the senses (20–30 minutes)

1. This is a very enjoyable exercise on the need to sharpen all of our senses as an aid to meditation. Remind the young people that several of the exercises of the first week touched upon this point in limited ways: the search for a symbol of God may have put them in touch with their sense of sight and touch; the exercise handling the distraction of noise involved the sense of hearing; deep breathing and relaxation exercises are both intended, at least in part, to relax the body in order to become *more*, rather than less, attuned to the world about us.

Mention also that, in the coming week, the young people will be completing a meditation exercise that more explicitly addresses the need for alertness to our sensory experience, primarily to the sense of touch that covers virtually our entire body. The point is this: In the richest sense of the term, *meditation* can be, and in fact must be, a very sensual experience.

2. To further explore the marvelous world of the senses, you are going to ask the participants during this gathering to perform a routine act but to *do it as a prayerful exercise*. After noting this, pass to each person an orange, a dish, and a napkin. (Note: Be selective in your choice of oranges, which will vary in size and quality, depending on the season and the part of the country in which you live. Test several varieties if you can, selecting one that is particularly rich in color, texture, juiciness, and taste. Experiment by peeling and eating one before the gathering, making sure that it can be peeled and broken into sections with relative ease.)

3. Tell the young people that they are to spend the next 15 minutes or so eating the oranges, quietly and with prayerful attentiveness. They are to do this alone if possible, or at least in a part of the room where they can experience some solitude. When they find such a place, they are to follow these instructions:

a. **Take a moment to become centered. You need not assume your prayer posture unless you wish to do so, but try to remain centered and alert throughout the activity.**

b. **For a minute or two, carefully explore the orange without peeling it. Feel its texture in your hands, smell its skin, study its contours, even try to taste the skin without breaking it.**

c. **Then very slowly and with a meditative attitude begin to peel the orange. Break the skin while the orange is close to the face, so that the rush of its aromas and the fine spray of the skin's juice can be experienced. Carefully explore the inside of the skin and then the fruit itself.**

d. **Next, separate the sections of the orange, and slowly begin to eat each one. Hold a section in the mouth for a moment without biting it; roll it around your mouth with your tongue. Then very consciously bite down, feeling the gush of juices explode in your mouth. Continue this routine until the orange is completely consumed.**

e. **Finally, while you are doing this exercise, reflect upon the God who created that orange, who designed it and gave it life, who loves the hand of every worker who has been responsible for its care. Thank that God as your different senses experience the simple but glorious product of God's love that is the common orange.**

4. After all the participants have completed the exercise, call them back together to share their reactions and insights. Expect and allow some humorous exchanges as they begin to share their thoughts, but then move to more serious reflection on the exercise:

What did the exercise teach you? In what sense can something as simple as eating an orange be called a religious experience? What insights into God can be gained from this kind of sensory experience? How might we train ourselves to achieve greater sensory awareness in our daily life? What attitudes would direct our life if we could become more conscious of the world about us?

D. Preview of the coming week (5 minutes)

1. Ask the participants to open their guide to the introduction to week 2 on page 15. Either read through or summarize that information.

2. Particularly note the addition of journal writing as a component of the program. Emphasize the two points raised in the introduction about journal writing: (1) this is not a test of writing skills or grammar, so the young people can relax and enjoy it; (2) no one will ever see what they write in their guide unless they choose to share it.

3. Ask if there are questions about any dimension of the program to this point or about what they are to do next week.

E. Closing prayer ritual (time flexible)

1. Begin by explaining the format of the closing prayer ritual as described in the general information

about the gatherings (pp. 194–195). Acknowledge that some may naturally feel a little uncomfortable with the ritual the first one or two times, but note also that such discomfort will quickly pass, especially if they truly enter into the experience of prayer. Then lead the service as described.

2. Remind the young people of the time, date, and place of the next gathering. Share any concluding thoughts you may have, based on this experience of the first gathering.

Gathering 2

Purposes

- To review the experience of the meditations from the second week
- To offer a basic introduction to the technique of guided meditation
- To preview the meditations of week 3
- To continue providing support for the participants through group sharing and prayer

Procedure

A. Welcome and silent meditation (15 minutes)

1. For this gathering, increase the length of silent meditation to 10 minutes, but once again provide reflective music to help ease any tension or embarrassment.

2. As noted in the general information provided for the gatherings, feel free to discuss the experience of the silent group meditation if you feel that would be valuable for the participants. However, do not feel compelled to do so.

B. Review of the second week's meditation (time flexible)

1. Review the results of the young people's journal writing for day 7 of week 2. Be alert to any patterns that emerge for the most satisfying and most difficult experiences that they had with the meditation. If any patterns are evident, try to identify their causes and what they might imply regarding the needs of the participants.

2. Be sure to discuss the last two points raised in the "Things Worth Sharing" of the second week: (1) "The thing I would most like our leader or our group to do for me at this point is . . ." and (2) "If God were trying to say one thing to my fellow meditators at this time, I think God would want to say . . ." These points move the discussion beyond the concrete matters of individual meditations to the broader issues of personal need and deeper spirituality. Do not attempt to force discussion on these points if the young people are reluctant. However, if sharing is enthusiastic or intense, allow it to continue for as long as it remains profitable.

C. Optional exercise on the fundamentals of guided meditation (20–30 minutes)

1. In the coming week, the young people will practice the technique of guided meditation. Those students who have participated in other dimensions of the SHARING Program likely have had some experience with this approach to prayer. Even those individuals, however, probably have not fully comprehended the basic dynamics of this technique or its potential power to deepen and expand their personal spirituality and prayer life. One hope during this week of the program is that they not only enjoy their experience of this approach but also grow to more fully understand it. Such understanding will enable them to effectively use guided meditations on their own in the future.

2. Ask the young people to find a comfortable place in the room in which they can assume their preferred posture. When all have done so, ask them to spend a minute or two to center themselves. When all are centered, share the following instructions in your own words:

Try to remember a specific incident or event in your life from more than five years ago that you recall as being a time of real joy and happiness for you. Try to identify in your mind exactly where you were and what you were doing at that time that made you so happy. . . . Once you have called that event or incident to mind, try to bring back to your mind everything you can about that event. Who was involved? What did they look like at that time. What did you look like? Exactly what happened that made you so happy? Try to get in touch with the entire experience. . . . (Allow a couple minutes of reflection at this point.)

3. Now interrupt the exercise to make the following comment:

Stay in your posture and remain focused if you can, but I want you now to spend a moment consciously analyzing what has been going on in your mind. Consider these questions: Did you simply

remember what was going on in your life at that time, or did you actually begin to *relive the experience?* Did you see the event happening again as if it were recorded on film? If so, that is your memory at work. This isn't necessarily wrong, but memory alone will not allow you to truly gain the benefits of guided meditation. To make the most of this approach to prayer, we must learn to *imagine* an event, whether a real or a fictional one, with such intensity and clarity that we actually *feel* the event happening for us. Let's try the same exercise again, but this time we will try to imagine, not just remember.

4. Ask the young people to spend another minute or so becoming centered if your comments have distracted them. Then ask them again to recall the event that they identified earlier. This time, however, they are to not only remember it but truly relive it. To help them do so, offer the following reflective questions, and provide plenty of time during the indicated pauses for them to respond to each question in their mind:

See the scene of the event as clearly and precisely as you can. What is the setting? Look closely at all the surroundings. If it is outdoors, what are the things you see? . . . What colors are part of the scene? . . . Are there aromas in the air, sounds you hear? . . . If the event takes place indoors, what are the colors of the walls, and what pictures or other objects are hanging on them? . . . Are there any distinguishing sounds or aromas that you associate with that place? . . .

Now, what about the people involved, if any? Don't simply identify who they are. See what they are wearing. Hear their voices. Do any aromas come to mind when you think of them—things like perfume or pipe tobacco? Truly be in their presence once again. . . .

Finally, try to relive the feelings that you experienced then. See the expression on your face change as the feelings do. Pause for a moment and truly enjoy the feeling. . . . Now open your eyes and return to the group.

5. Help the young people reflect on and discuss the differences between their first and second experiences of this activity. Ask for specific examples:

Was anyone able to actually recapture the sensations of the past experiences? For example, could you recall the aromas and sounds associated with the event? Were you more able to do that the second time than the first time? What does that teach us?

The point you must emphasize here is that each of us has the capacity to recreate past events in our imaginations or to imagine future or fictional events with such clarity that we actually feel part of what is going on. However, this capacity generally only comes into play if we consciously work at it and if we allow ourselves enough time to make it happen for us. Effort and time are two requirements that will be necessary if the participants are to fully appreciate and enjoy the meditations for the coming week.

D. Preview of the coming week (5 minutes)

1. To some degree, you have already previewed the week in your discussion of guided meditations. Now simply read or summarize the introduction to week 3 on page 31 of the guide.

2. *Note well:* The introduction to week three in "A Guide for Meditation" mentions the need to prepare recordings of the scripts for each of the guided meditations. Check to be sure that everyone has access to a tape player for this purpose. As the leader, you have the option of recording and duplicating the scripts for the young people. This may be a particular interest of yours or of one of your friends and a service that you wish to provide. Weigh the merits of this service, however, against the possible benefits gained by the participants if they record their own scripts. One consideration: If the participants are poor readers or not highly motivated, they may do a poor job of making the recordings, and that will negatively affect their meditations. In such cases, you might make the recordings for them. If, on the other hand, they are highly motivated and good readers, let them experience making their own recordings.

E. Closing prayer ritual (time flexible)

1. Repeat the prayer ritual, adjusting it as you think is necessary based on your experience with the ritual last week.

2. Remind participants of the time, date, and place of the next gathering.

Gathering 3

Purposes

- To review the experience of the meditations from the third week
- To offer information on the ways in which God responds to our prayer

- To preview the meditations for the fourth week
- To continue providing support for the participants through group sharing and prayer

Materials Needed
- A chalkboard or paper with notes for the presentation on God's response to prayer
- Pens or pencils

Procedure

A. Welcome and silent meditation (10 minutes)

The silent meditation for this week is to be attempted for 5 minutes without the benefit of background music. Use your discretion on this, however. If your past experience leads you to believe that the young people will not handle this well, trust your intuitions. You might also consider a change in prayer posture for this period of meditation as a way to further broaden the experience of the group.

B. Optional input by the leader on God's response to prayer (20–30 minutes, including discussion)

1. Does God respond to our prayer? No question or issue involved in our entire course on prayer and meditation is more pivotal than this one. If God does not respond to prayer in a way that is intelligible, for what purpose do we pray? For our own gratification? We would hardly be gratified by the thought of struggling in prayer without a conviction that someone out there cares. Do we pray for God's sake? The thought of God in some way needing our prayer would appear to contradict the very concept of God. On the other hand, as pointed out earlier in this course, if God truly loves us and communicates with us in prayer—that is, not only listens but responds—then prayer becomes not only reasonable but something greatly desired. In this presentation, you will explore with the young people the issue of God's response to prayer.

2. Begin by noting that for this gathering, rather than doing an exercise, you want to discuss a major issue involved in the experience of prayer and meditation. Then introduce the question of God's response to prayer by paraphrasing the comments above.

3. Lead a brief discussion of the young people's past experience with and present understanding of the way God responds to their prayer or to specific prayers.

Have you ever felt strongly convinced that God was in fact listening to you when you prayed? (Explore examples if the participants are willing to offer any.) **What convinced you that God was truly responding to you?**

On the other hand, have any of you seriously questioned God's response? Why? When you raised such questions to parents or teachers, what answers did you receive from them? Did those answers satisfy you? Why or why not?

4. At this point, read the following quote taken from John Powell's book *He Touched Me* (Niles, IL: Argus Communications, 1974). Before reading, mention that one of the techniques of meditation that we will be practicing in the coming week is that of *spiritual reading*, in which we use selections from books or other reading material as a source of meditation. This selection from Powell is one example of such writing, so ask the young people to listen *prayerfully*. Note that before Powell has been talking about how he believes God speaks to us through our faculties of the mind, will, emotions, imagination, and memory. Powell then says:

> **Of course I feel sure that God can and does reach us in [many] ways. I think of the whole Bible as simply a written record of such religious experience, of God invading human history and human lives, of God speaking to men [and women]. I also believe that this God is available and anxious to speak to you and me. Yes, just as anxious as [God] was to speak to Abraham, Isaac and Jacob, Isaiah and Jeremiah. I believe that [God] has spoken to others before me, that [the Lord's] inspirations have resulted in many beautiful lives and deeds for God and [humanity]. . . . But would [God] come to me? This was harder for me to grasp until I stopped asking the wrong question and began to ask the meaningful question. I had been asking: Who am I, O my God, that you would come to me in tenderness and intimacy? How could I ever be so important to you? What do I have to offer? I was trapped in my old preoccupation with myself. The real question is, of course, who are you, my God? Who are you that you would come to me and speak to me, that you would fill my poor finite mind with your thoughts and perspectives, that you would enable me to see this world through your eyes, that you would put your strength and desires in my frail will, that you would pour your divine grace into this vessel of clay? Who are you that you graciously accept the loaves and fishes of my life to feed the hungry throughout the world? Who are you? Show me your face,**

fold me and my life into your loving arms, let me feel your fire and the soothing touch of your hand on the face of my thirsting soul. (Pp. 71–74)

5. After the reading, reveal to the young people the chalkboard or paper on which you have prepared the following notes:

God responds to my prayer by touching my
- mind
- will
- emotions
- imagination
- memories

How do I know that this is God and not my own wishful thinking? I can use three tests:
- the time test
- the reality test
- the charity test

Then comment on the notes along the following lines:

After writing the material that I have shared with you, Powell goes on to explain how he feels God touches our human faculties:

- Prayer can open my *mind* and widen my vision, so that God's response to my prayer is a clearer perception of reality.
- God empowers me in prayer to live according to what I know in my heart is truth; God touches my *will* and strengthens it.
- God calms my *emotions* in prayer and brings tranquillity to what was a confused mind.
- God fills my *imagination,* helping me to arrive at new solutions to problems that confront me.
- Finally, God speaks to me in my *memories,* using them to help me learn from past mistakes and to encourage me by recalling those times when the Lord's touch was real and evident.

It is a fair question to ask, "How do I know this is God's response and not my own wishful thinking?" One answer, never quite satisfying, is faith—I believe it even if I can't explain it. Another logical possibility is that if a God who loves us *does* exist, that God must be trying to get in touch with us, to communicate with us, on a level at which we can understand. There is another way, however, to judge whether God in fact has touched us or influenced us in our prayer. Jesus said, "You will be able to tell them [false prophets] by their fruits" (Matthew 7:16). He was not referring to prayer at the time, but the connection is a valid one to make. The only way to judge whether we are in touch with God is to look at the results of our actions, attitudes, and prayer. Powell suggests three tests for identifying when one is touched by God:

- *The time test:* One touched by God will never be quite the same again. The effects last. Although emotional kicks come and go, God's touch endures.

- *The reality test:* Jesus was a man in and for the world. He took on the world as it was, not as he wanted it to be. One touched by God becomes even more immersed in the real world, sees it in a new way, perhaps, but does not live in a vacuum. One touched by God does not live in an ivory tower oblivious to the suffering and misery of his or her brothers and sisters, nor does he or she fall into despair. Prayer creates within one a sense of realistic optimism.

- *The charity test:* "God is love, and whoever remains in love remains in God and God in him" (1 John 4:16). The final and most evident test of the Christian life is the degree to which we reach out in love to others. God has touched us if, because of that contact, we are more gentle, patient, understanding, joy-filled, kind, and tender.

If our interpretation of God's response in our prayers meets the criteria of these three tests we can be reasonably sure that what we are hearing is God's voice.

There will be times when God's voice is not heard at all, times when we are certain God is not there, is silent, is unavailable to us. The same is true for all of our relationships. We don't live on a constant high; we never feel completely at one with those we love. However, if we hang in there, the touch of God will return, and there will be times when God will not only seem present but will appear to be shouting at us!

6. At this point, ask for reactions to the above ideas. Do the ideas make sense? Offer the opportunity for the young people to illustrate from personal experience any of the points raised here. Finally, mention that some participants might find it helpful to copy the notes of this presentation somewhere in their guide for future reference.

D. Preview of the coming week (5 minutes)

1. Read or summarize the material in the introduction to week 4 on page 47 of the guide.

2. Note that, in a slight change from the previous two, this week's meditations not only introduce new techniques for meditating but also focus on specific themes related to the meditators' lives right now. During the first three meditations, the young people will meditate on their past, present, and future through the use of journal-writing activities and a guided meditation. In the next three meditations, then, they will meditate on the Christian virtues of faith and hope as they prepare to leave this program and their high school years and move into the future. For these reasons, the young people will likely find the meditations for this week particularly meaningful and important. Encourage them to enter into the week with a heightened sense of prayerfulness and openness to what God might reveal to them.

E. Closing prayer ritual (time flexible)

1. Adjust your use of the ritual as dictated by past experience.

2. Announce the day, time, and location of the final gathering.

Note: A special party or celebration would certainly be appropriate as you close this meditation program. You may wish to involve the young people in planning this. If so, you will need to start this planning at the end of gathering 3. However, if you feel that having the young people plan a closing party would detract from the final week of meditation and the final gathering, you might have adult volunteers do the planning.

Gathering 4

Purposes

- To review the experience of the meditations from the fourth week
- To bring the meditation program to a satisfying and prayerful close
- As an option, to conclude the program with a party or other appropriate expression of gratitude and hope

Materials Needed

- The contracts for the program, signed by the program leader and the pastor
- The crucifixes or other mementos that are to be presented to the participants during the closing prayer
- Supplies for a closing party (optional)

Procedure

A. Welcome and silent meditation (15 minutes)

1. Welcome the young people by noting that this is the final gathering for this program, one that may bring many mixed feelings—gratitude, joy, perhaps a little sadness. More than during any other gathering, the young people may feel a need for one another and may require both a willingness to share personally and to support one another. Begin with a period of silent meditation. Ask the participants to strive for true unity of hearts and minds during the meditation.

2. Ask the young people to meditate silently and without background music for 10 minutes. Adjust these plans as you believe necessary.

B. Review of the fourth week's meditations (time flexible)

1. The meditations for the fourth week of the program are particularly personal and potentially quite moving. This includes both the daily meditations as well as the journal-writing activity for the "Things Worth Sharing." Therefore, you will want to prepare with particular sensitivity for this review of the meditations. How will you lead discussions on the individual points raised in the "Things Worth Sharing" section of day 7? Are there some points that you feel you should simply allude to but avoid discussing publicly? Given your understanding of the participants, how involved are they likely to become in this review, and what impact will that have on your planning for the rest of this session?

2. You may feel that points 1 through 3 of the "Things Worth Sharing" of week 4 are too personal to share openly. However, be sure to reflect with the group on their responses to points 4 and 5: "The most helpful thing I have learned from this entire meditation program is . . ." and "During this program, our group has shared many special moments. I realize that we will never be together again in quite this way. As the program comes to an end, I would like to tell the others that . . ." Naturally, you will want to handle these points with sensitivity.

3. Note that I did not include point 6 from "Things Worth Sharing" among the points to be discussed during the review. Consider adjusting your closing prayer ritual to include this point,

which reads, "During our final prayer as a group, I will want to say this to God . . ."

C. Optional exercise: "I'd like to teach the world . . ." (15 minutes)

1. You may well believe that the schedule for this session does not allow or require this activity. Feel free to eliminate it. However, this is a simple exercise that is one more way to tap into some of the ideas and feelings that are the focus of this final gathering.

2. Ask the young people to assume their prayer posture and to spend a couple minutes becoming centered.

3. Share the following instructions:

I want you to now imagine that you have been given a very special gift from God. God has called you to the top of the highest mountain in the world. Imagine yourself there for a moment, just you and God, looking together at the world spread out before you. . . . Now God gives you this gift: God tells you that you have one minute to speak to the world, with the guarantee that all five billion people will hear and understand you. All language barriers have been abolished for this minute. The people of the world are awaiting your message. What do you say to them? . . .

At this point you may want to play some reflective music. When a few minutes have elapsed or the music has ended, ask the participants to thank God for this time that they have shared, and then invite them to rejoin the group.

4. Invite the young people to now share what they would say to the world. As always, this is strictly an invitation, with no pressure to respond. Comment appropriately to each response, or offer the chance for others to do so. Close the exercise with the following ideas:

We commonly refer to Jesus as "the Word of God," the perfect expression of God to the world. It is also true that each of us is a word of God spoken in time—not of the same importance of Jesus, perhaps, but nevertheless tremendously valuable in the eyes of God. You may have experienced great difficulty in finding a way to express to the world what you felt in your heart as you stood on that mountaintop with your God. What you were struggling to do was, in a sense, to find words to express that unique "word of God" that is you. That is your challenge and your mission and your source of joy now and for the rest of your life—to live your life in such a way that the voice of God speaks to the world through you.

D. Closing prayer ritual (time flexible)

1. As noted above, you may want to somewhat alter your closing prayer for this gathering. One possibility is the addition of the participants' responses to point 6 of the "Things Worth Sharing" material for the last week. Reflect on how you might best incorporate that material here.

2. Remember the suggestion, made earlier, to make the presentation of the signed contracts a part of this closing prayer ritual.

3. Remember as well the suggestion regarding mementos, *made in the general information section for the gatherings.* If you have planned to offer each participant a crucifix or other keepsake at the conclusion of the program, it would be appropriate to do so during this closing ritual. I suggest that you present the mementos to the young people at the same time you return to them the signed contracts for the program.

4. You may also wish to include a scriptural reading in your closing prayer. I especially recommend Ephesians 3:14–21 and Philippians 1:3–11. Check different translations to see which best expresses your thoughts and feelings.

E. Optional party or other celebration

STUDENT HANDOUT F

Meditation Program Contract

A Contract with My God, with My Fellow Meditators, and with Myself

As I begin my participation in this meditation program, I commit myself to freely and sincerely do the following:

I commit myself to meditate once a day for the duration of the program. I recognize this as a top priority in my life for the coming month and will do everything possible to fulfill this commitment. If, in the case of unavoidable circumstances, I am unable to complete a period of meditation, I will attempt to make up for it during the following day.

I commit myself to attend all four gatherings during the program. I know that I attend these not only for my own benefit but also for the good of my fellow meditators. I recognize that a failure to attend a gathering results in a weakening of the group as a whole. If an emergency demands that I miss a gathering, I will contact the leader of the program immediately.

I commit myself to share my thoughts, insights, and questions with the group during the gatherings. The strength of the group depends on the willingness of the individual meditators to share what they have gained in prayer. I also recognize, however, that at no time will my personal privacy be threatened or abused. What I choose to offer will be freely given.

I commit myself to be open to the Spirit of Jesus, praying that the Spirit will open my mind and heart to the message of God and give me the courage and insight to act upon God's Word in my daily life.

I hereby pledge my earnest intent to do these things by the grace of God and with the support and encouragement of my fellow meditators in this program.

Date _____ Signature _____

We, the undersigned, confirm that _____
has faithfully completed the program *Learning to Meditate: A Way to God.*

_____   _____
Program leader   Pastor

_____
Date

Reproduction permission is granted if you wish to make copies for classroom use.
The photocopy master for this handout is found at the back of this manual.

Directing the Meditation Program   203

A Guide for Meditation: Instructions and Photocopy Masters

Each person involved in the meditation program will require a copy of the meditation guide. The necessary photocopy masters for making the guide follow these instructions. Creating the guide is not difficult if you carefully follow the directions provided here. Do each of the following steps in order:

1. Begin by photocopying the following pages *exactly as they are presented here*, that is, making sure that *the pages that are printed back-to-back here are photocopied back-to-back as well*. If you are making a copy just to review the program, you need only photocopy each page once. However, if you are quite certain that you will be using this program, make as many copies as you will likely need, rather than having to repeat the process later.

Note: You may wish to make the guide more attractive by using colored paper for the text and, perhaps, a heavier paper for the cover.

2. After all the pages have been photocopied front and back, the pages are to be collated as follows: The first page to place before you is the cover of the guide. This should be placed so that the inside of the front cover faces you to the left. Next, when looking at the lower left-hand corner of the pages, the first interior page you should place before you should be numbered 4. Then, on top of that page, place the one for which the lower left-hand corner shows the number 6. Repeat this process with the remaining page numbers appearing in the lower left-hand corner in the following order: 8, 10, 12, 14, 16, 18, 20, 22, 24, 26, 28, 30, and 32.

3. All the pages should now be collated properly. Next, align all of the pages and fold them over to form the booklet. Hint: If you fold the pages in groups of four or five, rather than all together, you can form a finer crease in the middle of the pages that will result in a neater looking guide.

4. To join the pages together, use a conventional, desk-size stapler, one that can be opened up to a tacking position. Turn the collated and creased pages of the guide over so that you are looking at the cover, and place the pages against some thin carpeting or carpet-like material. A good choice would be kitchen carpeting or firm indoor-outdoor carpeting. This will allow the staples to pierce the pages without being bent over. Then, holding the stapler in its open position, staple the pages together along the crease at both ends and in the middle of the crease.

5. Finally, turn the stapled pages over. You will see the unbent staples coming through the crease of the pages. Take a letter opener or other hard object and bend each staple over. The guide is now assembled. Close the booklet and firmly press down along the crease.

A GUIDE FOR MEDITATION

Your name

Telephone number

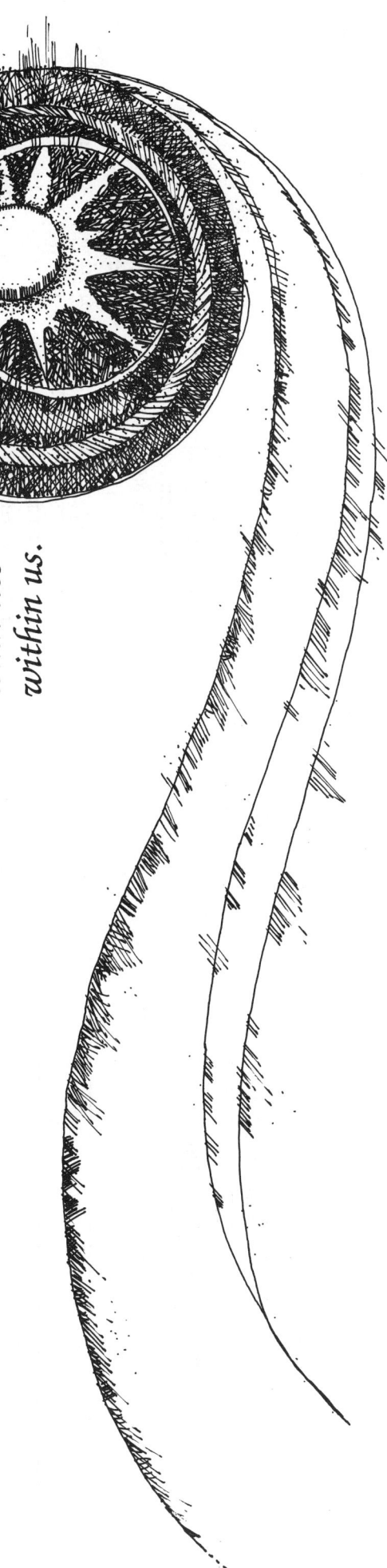

What lies behind us and what lies before us are small compared to what lies within us.

How to Use This Guide

This guide provides all the information that you will need to complete the daily exercises that make up the private, individual part of this meditation program. The meditation program, and therefore this guide, is divided into four weeks. Each of the four weeks begins with a brief introduction that identifies the meditation techniques that you will be practicing during that week. These introductions are then followed by detailed instructions on what you are to do each day of the week.

The format of each day's instructions is as follows:

- The week and the day on which the exercise is to be done is identified in the upper left-hand corner of the page.
- Following the title of the exercise, there is a statement of purpose, which clearly identifies what you hope to accomplish during that particular meditation.
- The statement of purpose is followed by a detailed explanation of the exercise for that day. The exercise is commonly explained in a step-by-step fashion, guiding you from beginning to end.
- From the second through the fourth weeks of the program, you will frequently be asked to complete the daily exercises by doing brief journal-writing activities in which you respond to specific questions or directions.
- Finally, each day concludes with a suggestion on how you might prepare for the next day's meditation. You are encouraged to prepare for each exercise by at least reading the directions for it the evening before you actually complete it. On occasion, more specific preparation might be asked of you. Doing such preparation thoughtfully can help make each meditation all the more enjoyable for you.

This guide for meditation is yours, and it need never be shared with anyone. Take care of it. Be honest in what you write here, and be sure to save this guide when the program is completed. You may grow to treasure it and the memory of this program for years to come.

This meditation guide is part of the SHARING IV "Learning to Meditate" program. Permission to reproduce it is granted only to purchasers of SHARING IV.

**Saint Mary's Press
Christian Brothers Publications
Winona, Minnesota**

Notes for Orientation

Review of Basic Meditation Techniques

During the first week of this program, you will be introduced to several basic techniques for effective meditation. Once these techniques have been introduced and practiced, your knowledge of them will be presumed. These basics will not continually be redefined. Yet experience has shown that, when people experience difficulties with meditation, it is often because they have failed to remember these simple but important factors in meditation. Therefore, these factors are listed here for your convenience. This can serve as a kind of troubleshooting guide for you. If you experience difficulties in your meditation, refer to this list for possible solutions.

1. **Select a sacred space.** *Where* you choose to meditate can greatly influence *how* you meditate. In your first meditation exercise, you will be asked to select a place in your house or apartment that is conducive to meditation. However, only experience will teach you whether your first choice is the best one for you. If, after some experience, you find that you are having difficulties with your meditation, they may be caused by distractions around you that you can control or eliminate by moving or in some way changing your space for prayer.

2. **Seek the sounds of silence.** We live in a culture that is so saturated with sound that many people, young and old alike, are uncomfortable with silence. Yet it is in silence that one can most readily and powerfully encounter God. Particularly during the first two weeks of the program, try to free yourself as much as possible from distracting sounds—radio, television, records, and tapes. You may find this almost impossible, so thoroughly is our culture dominated by noise of various kinds. If you find that you must have some sounds around you ("I can't stand the silence anymore!"), at least try to select sounds that are relaxing and that help you center on God.

3. **An upright back straightens out a lot of problems.** Longtime meditators have discovered that, for undetermined

reasons, keeping the back straight is essential to effective meditation. Whatever posture you choose for meditation—whether sitting upright in a chair, cross-legged on the floor, even stretched out on your back—make sure that you keep your back and spine straight. Don't allow yourself to slump. Also, if you prefer to sit in a chair, choose one that is hard and straight-backed. Some individuals even prefer to sit on the edge of the seat. Keep both feet flat on the floor, and rest your hands comfortably in your lap, perhaps with palms turned upward as a sign of openness to God.

4. **The nighttime isn't necessarily the right time.** Everyone's biological clock is unique. Practice meditating at different times of the day until you find the time that works best for you.

5. **Relax the body and the mind and heart will follow.** In this program, you will learn exercises to help you relax. One basic technique is to identify a part of the body that is tense, consciously tighten the muscles in that area, and then consciously allow those muscles to relax. Doing this just twice can normally relax those muscles. Anytime you feel particularly tense during meditation, feel free to repeat this exercise.

6. **Catch your breath and it will free you.** As you will learn, breathing properly is perhaps the most basic yet most important factor in meditation. You can base an entire period of meditation just on your breathing. In fact, some styles of meditation center their entire approach on breathing alone. One mystic suggested that "God is the breath within the breath." The breathing pattern of most of us is too rapid and shallow. Anytime you find yourself struggling with meditation, check your breathing. Slow down the pace, breathe deeply, and relax.

4. The most helpful thing I have learned from this entire meditation program is . . .

_____
_____
_____
_____

5. During this program, our group has shared many special moments. I realize that we will never be together again in quite this way. As the program comes to an end, I would like to tell the others that . . .

_____
_____
_____
_____

6. During our final prayer as a group, I will want to say this to God:

_____
_____

Introduction to Week 1

During the first week of this meditation program, you will learn and practice a few basic techniques that will help you to meditate. These techniques are so basic, in fact, that you will use them over and over again throughout this program and, I hope, throughout your lifetime.

In our culture, we tend to think of meditation as primarily an activity of the head. That is, we view it as a thinking activity, something we accomplish with our mind alone. Certainly meditation, like many forms of communication, includes some brain power. In reality, though, meditation is an activity that involves the entire person, not just the mind.

Consider this: If you have a toothache, will it affect your ability to do homework? If you have an argument with a close friend, will it affect your performance in an athletic activity? Certainly. We cannot divide who we are into neat little packages. We are whole people.

The techniques that you will learn this week are based on the fact that, in meditation, the whole person is involved. By practicing certain exercises with our body, we can prepare ourselves for the deep, internal dialogue with God that is meditation.

Week 4, Day 7

Things Worth Sharing

■ **Purpose**
To prepare for the last gathering

■ **Exercise**
Respond in writing to each of the following points as indicated. Be prepared to share this information with your fellow meditators.

1. The first three meditations for this week focused on my past, present, and future. If I had to find one word or short phrase to express how I now feel about these periods in my life it would be (write one word or phrase to describe each):

■ about my past: _____

■ about my present: _____

■ about my future: _____

2. Through the meditation on my own funeral, I realized that . . .

_____
_____
_____

3. During my imaginary funeral, I heard people talking about me. When I think of the things I would most want people to say about me, I would feel best if they would say . . .

Week 1, Day 1

Creating Sacred Space

- **Purpose**
 To identify and prepare a place in your home that will provide the atmosphere required for your daily meditations

- **Exercise**
 Your task this day is to identify some place in your house or apartment that will provide you with privacy when you need it, and then to arrange and decorate that sacred space in a way that promotes a prayerful attitude. Naturally, each person will have to deal with the possibilities or limitations afforded by his or her own situation. Keep the following suggestions in mind as you create your sacred space:

- If you have a private bedroom, consider preparing one corner of the room for your daily meditations.

- If you must share your prayer space with other family members, keep the furnishings and decorations as simple as possible. You may only need a simple prayer rug or mat or a straight-back chair and a small candle in an otherwise bare corner. These items can then be put in place or removed in a matter of seconds each day.

- Many individuals find that a Christian religious symbol or image is helpful in their meditation. The most popular of these is likely the crucifix. Other possibilities would be a portrait of Jesus, an open Bible, or a religious statue.

- Be cautious in preparing a prayer space in front of or near a window. A view of a peaceful nature setting, for example, may help your meditating. A view of a busy street, on the other hand, will likely be distracting.

- **To Prepare for Tomorrow**
 Read the directions for tomorrow's meditation. Try to think of an item from nature that might symbolize for you the presence of God.

After you have completed your use of the mantra, write a letter to God expressing your thoughts and feelings as you near the end of this program.

- **Journal Writing**

_____

_____

_____

_____

_____

_____

_____

_____

_____

_____

- **To Prepare for Tomorrow**
 Reflect on tomorrow's review questions in preparation for the final gathering.

Week 1, Day 2

The Face of God in Nature

■ **Purpose**

To discover and reflect upon an item from nature that calls to mind the presence of God

■ **Exercise**

Today look for an item in nature that reminds you of the presence of God. Then add it to your sacred space to help you to get in touch with the presence of God each day. The very act of looking for such an item can be prayerful in itself, and reverently reflecting upon and then placing the item in your prayer space will help make that space more special to you. Here are a few suggestions to help you:

- Some things in nature seem particularly rich in symbolic power and meaning: rocks or stones, seashells, flowers or plants, leaves or bark from trees, sand as a symbol of the desert experiences of the Jews and of Jesus.
- If you select living things (e.g., a flower), the symbol will gradually die and will have to be replaced. This natural cycle of life and death can in itself provoke prayer.
- When you have found a symbol that speaks to you of God, spend a few minutes in your prayer space reflecting upon the symbol. Do not so much analyze it as a scientist might, but look upon it with reverence as it reveals to you the creative presence of God.
- After these moments of prayerful reflection on the item you have chosen, say a prayer of thanks to God for the wondrous gifts to be found in the created universe.

■ **To Prepare for Tomorrow**

Before going to bed tonight, read the directions for tomorrow's meditation. Prepare to awaken a little earlier than usual tomorrow morning and to meditate before breakfast. During the remainder of the week, you will be experimenting with other prayer times.

Week 4, Day 6

For All That Has Been and All That Will Be

■ **Purposes**

To reflect on the personal meaning of this meditation program; to look forward with hope to the future

■ **Exercise**

This meditation program concludes with the most simple prayer form you have used, the mantra, and with journal writing. You are offered two different mantras from which to choose. The first option is the statement by Jesus on the cross referred to in the last meditation: "Father, into your hands I commit my spirit." Praying these words as a mantra can help to make the trustful attitude of Jesus the very foundation of our own spirituality.

The second mantra suggested is a statement made by Dag Hammarskjöld, former secretary general of the United Nations who died in an air crash in Northern Rhodesia in 1961 while on a peace mission. He had kept a journal of his own spiritual life, which was published after his death under the title *Markings*. One sentence summed up his perspective on life, one that might serve well as a signpost for our journeys: "For all that has been—Thanks! To all that shall be—Yes!" What a wonderful attitude toward life!

Before entering your prayer space, decide on the mantra you wish to use. You may want to consider alternating the suggested two mantras in your meditation. An option is to say one for as long as it seems to speak to you, and then say the other. You may also wish to synchronize the mantra's phrases with your breathing, saying the first half while inhaling, the second half while exhaling. Finally, remember that you can pause as you wish during your meditation, allowing yourself to rest peacefully in the presence of God; use the mantra whenever you feel that your attention is drifting.

Practicing a Posture for Prayer

Week 1, Day 3

■ **Purpose**
To practice a physical posture that for you promotes prayer and meditation

■ **Exercise**
In your first meeting for this program, you were introduced to several postures for prayer, including sitting upright in a straight-backed chair and sitting on the floor in a modified version of the familiar lotus position. You were asked to decide which position you wished to use for your first meditations. Your only task this morning is to assume that position for just 5 minutes. A few suggestions:

■ Check the time as you enter your prayer space, but do not look at a watch or clock while you meditate.

■ As soon as you have prepared your sacred space, quickly assume your chosen prayer posture.

■ Be careful to keep your back erect while meditating.

■ You may find that tightly closing the eyes is a disruption to prayer; the closed eyelids can act like movie screens filled with distracting images. It may be helpful to keep your eyes not tightly closed but slightly open. Rest your eyes on a spot or object (perhaps the nature item you found yesterday) about three feet away from you.

■ Avoid shifting about or moving during this 5-minute experiment. If you experience the urge or desire to move or to scratch an itch, simply note that urge or desire in your mind for later reflection. When you believe that 5 minutes have elapsed, stop the exercise. Check the clock to determine how much time has actually passed.

■ **To Prepare for Tomorrow**
Select a midday time (e.g., after school or just before the evening meal) for tomorrow's meditation. Read the directions for that meditation.

Nor do I really know myself,
and the fact that I think I am following your will
does not mean that I am actually doing so.
But I believe that the desire to please you
does in fact please you.
And I hope that I have that desire
in all that I am doing.

I hope that I will never do anything
apart from that desire.
And I know that if I do this,
you will lead me by the right road
though I may know nothing about it.

Therefore will I trust you always
though I may seem to be lost
and in the shadow of death.
I will not fear, for you are ever with me,
and you will never leave me
to face my perils alone.

(Thomas Merton)

■ **Journal Writing**
Write whatever comes to your heart in response to your prayer.

_____

_____

_____

_____

_____

■ **To Prepare for Tomorrow**
No preparation is required.

Week 4, Day 5

Lead Me, Lord

■ **Purposes**

To practice another approach to spiritual reading; to reflect on personal trust in God as the central characteristic of Christian spirituality

■ **Exercise**

Some writers in the area of Christian spirituality have suggested that the very core of Christian faith can be summed up with the few words uttered by Jesus as he neared his death on the cross: "Father, into your hands I commit my spirit" (Luke 23:46). This act of incredible trust in God expresses perhaps more clearly than any other words of Jesus what his vision and mission were all about.

Each of us will inevitably face the same kinds of times that prompted Jesus to speak these words. At such times it is gratifying and affirming to know that Jesus himself faced similar moments—in fact, moments of far greater desperation—but he never lost touch with the God who ultimately saves.

One of the most influential writers on Christian spirituality in modern times is Thomas Merton. Merton seems to have the ability to capture the fears and yearnings, concerns and dreams of contemporary people and the words to place them in God's hands as Jesus did. Below you will find one of Merton's prayers that does this. After becoming centered in your prayer space, meditate on this prayer as a spiritual reading. You may use the Benedictine method while doing so. Or just slowly read the prayer in its entirety, and then speak to God about what the reading means to you. You may find it helpful to actually speak out loud to God, or in a whisper if you wish not to be heard.

My Lord God, I have no idea where I am going.
I do not see the road ahead of me.
I cannot know for certain where it will end.

Week 1, Day 4

The Sounds of Silence

■ **Purpose**

To learn to accept sounds and noise as a backdrop for prayer rather than as distractions or impediments to it

■ **Exercise**

If we are to meditate effectively, we must learn to deal with the common distraction of sounds or noise. This exercise can help those who are distracted by household noises or street sounds during prayer.

- Prepare your sacred space and assume your prayer posture.
- Take a moment to close your eyes, quiet yourself, steady your breathing, relax your body, and place yourself in the presence of God. Plug your ears with your thumbs, and then place the palms of your hands over your closed eyes. The only sound you will likely hear is that of your own breathing. Listen to the sound of your breathing.
- After taking ten full breaths in this position, gently remove your hands from your face and rest them on your lap. Keep your eyes closed. Now listen to all the sounds that surround you—within your room, throughout your house, outdoors—every sound. Identify each sound in terms of its source and its distance from you—the stair creaking upstairs, the clock ticking in the next room, the sound of a passing truck—every sound.
- Finally, recognize that all sounds—both in their origins and in your ability to hear them with your ears—are reflections of the creative and sustaining power of God. Thank God for the sounds and your gift of hearing. Allow yourself to rest peacefully in the midst of the sounds.

■ **To Prepare for Tomorrow**

Select a time in the evening, perhaps just before sleep, for tomorrow's meditation. Read the directions for it.

Taking Time to Catch Your Breath

Week 1, Day 5

- **Purpose**
To make real the important role of deep breathing during meditation

- **Exercise**
Meditators have learned that control of one's breathing can be an immense aid to relaxation, concentration, and the ability to open one's mind and heart to God during prayer. Some center their entire method of meditation on the act of slowly inhaling and exhaling. This exercise is intended to introduce what is commonly called deep breathing and some of its benefits.

As you prepare to meditate, sit upright and quiet yourself. Become conscious of your breathing. Don't try to control or analyze the process of breathing. Simply become conscious of the act of breathing.

Now gently attempt to control the pace of your breathing as follows: Slowly inhale through your nostrils, filling not only your lungs but also your stomach with air. Then slowly and gently exhale through your mouth. Again, inhale deeply and slowly exhale. Do this ten times.

As you continue to breathe deeply, imagine that each time you inhale you are filling yourself more and more with God's peace. Imagine as well that each time you exhale, you are literally breathing away your cares, concerns, tensions, fears, and preoccupations. Continue this exercise for 5 minutes or until you feel that you have exhausted its value for you. When you are done, thank the God who is for you and all people the Breath of Life.

- **To Prepare for Tomorrow**
Based on the experience of the previous days of meditation, choose the time of day that you now feel is best suited for your daily meditations. Then read the directions for tomorrow's meditation.

- In your prayer space, assume your posture and spend a few moments becoming centered.

- Begin by slowly reading the words of Newman. Pause whenever a word, a phrase, or a sentence catches your attention. Then repeat those words prayerfully, allowing them to take root in the fertile soil of your heart.

- When you feel so moved, speak to God about what is in your heart. If you wish, you may then resume reading and repeat the process. You need not do any journal writing for today.

God has created me to do Him some definite service.
He has committed some work to me which He has not committed to another.
I have my mission.
I may never know it in this life.
But I shall be told it in the next.
I am a link in a chain,
a bond of connection between persons.
He has not created me for nothing.
I shall do good. I shall do His work.
Therefore, I will trust Him.
Whatever, wherever I am,
I cannot be thrown away.
If I am in sickness, my sickness may serve Him.
In perplexity, my perplexity may serve Him.
If I am in sorrow, my sorrow may serve Him.
He does nothing in vain.
He knows what He is about.
He may take away my friends.
He may throw me among strangers.
He may make me feel desolate, make my spirits sink, hide my future from me—
still, He knows what He is about.

(John Cardinal Newman)

- **To Prepare for Tomorrow**
No preparation is required.

Week 1, Day 6

Takin' It Easy

■ **Purpose**

To learn a relaxation technique to assist meditation

■ **Exercise**

This week you have been experimenting with a number of basic techniques that can help prepare you for meditation: creating a sacred space, selecting a proper posture, and breathing deeply. Today you will practice a technique for relaxing your body in preparation for meditation.

- In this exercise you are to try to relax your body by alternately tightening and then relaxing one part of your body at a time. To begin, in your prayer space assume your chosen posture and spend 2 or 3 minutes in deep breathing. Then concentrate on your feet. Feel your feet inside your shoes or socks or against the floor. Consciously tighten the muscles in your feet and hold them tight for 5 seconds. Then very consciously allow the feet to relax. Tighten them again for 5 seconds, then relax. Now move to your calf muscles and repeat the process: Become conscious of your calf muscles, tighten them, relax, tighten them once again, and then relax.
- Repeat this process until you are totally relaxed.
- Here is a helpful sequence for this exercise: relax first the feet, then the lower legs, upper legs, neck and head, shoulders and upper back, hands, arms, buttocks, stomach, and chest. However, don't become too concerned about the order in which you do this. Do what feels natural to you. Feel free to return to one part of the body a second time if you begin to feel tension there. When you are thoroughly relaxed, just rest for a moment in the peace of God.

■ **To Prepare for Tomorrow**

Read the directions for tomorrow's meditation, and begin to reflect on the questions asked in the journal activity.

Week 4, Day 4

I Have My Mission

■ **Purposes**

To learn to use spiritual reading in meditation; to reflect on the truth that my unique life has purpose and meaning

■ **Exercise**

As we move toward the conclusion of this program, we want to introduce one more helpful method of meditation. This is an approach commonly attributed to the great Saint Benedict of Nursia, "the father of Western monasticism" and the founder of the Benedictine religious order. Benedict popularized an approach to prayer that is centered on what is commonly referred to as *spiritual reading*.

We have already experienced a modified version of this approach to prayer. Three steps typify this method:

1. Begin by selecting a short reading that has the power to make you aware of the loving presence of God. The reading may be taken from a book of poetry, a book of prayers, a biography of a saint or other holy person, or other source. Certainly, the greatest source of spiritual reading is the Bible, and within it, some books in particular—among them the Psalms and the Gospels. Read until a particular word, phrase, or sentence catches your attention.

2. Next, spend time simply repeating the word, phrase, or sentence that has captured your attention, allowing the words to sink deeply into your heart. The intent is not to analyze or study the words; rather, the words are used like a mantra, which is repeated over and over, allowing the words to speak to the heart.

3. Finally, speak to God of the meaning that the words have for your life at the present time.

This simple, three-part method—read, meditate, speak to God—is a wonderful way to pray. In today's meditation, we will practice the method on a beautiful reading by John Cardinal Newman. In your meditation, do these three things:

Things Worth Sharing

Week 1, Day 7

■ **Purposes**

To review your meditation experience this week in preparation for the next gathering; as an option, to practice once again the basic techniques learned this week

■ **Exercise**

Your primary task today is to prepare for the next gathering with your fellow meditators by responding in writing to the questions asked below. This will take you about 15 minutes. If you are short of time today, there is no need to do the optional exercise suggested here.

As an option, practice putting together all the techniques for meditation that you learned this week into a single prayer routine. For example: reverently enter and prepare your sacred space for prayer; take your preferred posture; do 2 minutes of deep breathing exercises; spend a few minutes relaxing your body; listen to, accept, and praise God for the sounds you hear; rest in God's loving presence. Please respond to the following items as directed:

1. I feel that the sacred space I have chosen and prepared is (check one response): just what I need and want ____; adequate, but needs some change ____; very poor, and I must create another ____.

2. Briefly describe why you responded to number 1 as you did, noting especially things you discovered in preparing your sacred space that might help your fellow meditators.

Look again at the faces of your friends who have come to attend your funeral.... Imagine all the good things they will be saying about you when they return home from your funeral.... What do you feel now?....

Is there something you would like to say to each of your friends before they go home?... Do you have some final farewell to share in response to all that they are thinking and feeling about you?... Say it now, even though they cannot hear you, and reflect on what speaking those words means to you.

The funeral rites have ended. In your imagination, picture yourself standing above the grave in which your body lies, watching your friends leave the cemetery. What are your feelings now?... Look back on your life and your experiences from that unique perspective.... Was it all worthwhile?....

Now become aware of yourself right now as you meditate, and realize that you are still alive. You still have time remaining in your life.... Think of your friends, those you had imagined attending your funeral. Do you see them in a different light than before?... Think of yourself now.... Do you feel differently about yourself and about your future as a result of this exercise?... Thank God for the gift of your life....

■ **Journal Writing**

At this point, write whatever words come to your heart and your mind in response to this exercise.

■ **To Prepare for Tomorrow**

No preparation is required.

Week 4, Day 3

Only Two Things Are Certain

■ **Purpose**

To meditate on the certainty of my death and the implications of that reality for my present life

■ **Exercise**

It is often said, not entirely in jest, that only two things in life are certain—death and taxes! Most of us would rather ignore both of these realities than prepare for them. But accepting, even embracing with joy, the reality of death can add immeasurably to the pleasure that we gain from living.

In this exercise, you will experience a guided meditation on your funeral as you imagine the funeral might be. A script is provided here for the meditation, and you are encouraged to record it before starting the exercise. Enter your prayer space, spend a few moments becoming centered, and then turn on your tape player to be led through the meditation. When you are done, complete the journal writing-activity as directed.

Imagine your body lying in a coffin in a church, prepared for the funeral rites.... Take a good look at your body, especially at the expression on your face.... How old are you?... Are you surprised by the way you look?...

Now look at all the people who have come to your funeral.... Go slowly from one pew to another, looking at the faces of those people.... Stop before each person and become aware of what he or she is thinking and feeling at this moment....

Now listen to the sermon that is being preached by the priest. Who is he?... Do you know him?... What is he saying about you?... Can you accept all the good things he is saying about you?... If you cannot, can you identify why you resist what he is saying?... Which of the good things he is saying about you can you accept?... How do you feel as you listen to him speak?...

---

3. Below are listed four basic elements involved in the practice of meditation—posture, time of day when meditating, deep breathing, and relaxation. For each element, briefly describe your experience and note anything you discovered regarding it that might help other meditators. Be prepared to share your ideas during the gathering.

Regarding my prayer posture: _____
_____

Regarding my preferred time for prayer: _____
_____

Regarding deep breathing: _____
_____

Regarding the relaxation of my body: _____
_____

4. My feeling about the meditation program so far is
_____
_____

"The secret of living without frustration and worry… is to avoid becoming personally involved in your own life…."

Ziggy © 1974, Universal Press Syndicate. Reprinted with permission. All rights reserved.

■ Journal Writing
Complete the following schedule of your day:

7:00 A.M. _____
8:00 _____
9:00 _____
10:00 _____
11:00 _____
12:00 _____
1:00 P.M. _____
2:00 _____
3:00 _____
4:00 _____
5:00 _____
6:00 _____
7:00 _____
8:00 _____
9:00 _____
10:00 _____
11:00 _____
12:00 _____

■ To Prepare for Tomorrow
Record the script for the guided meditation used in tomorrow's meditation.

Introduction to Week 2

You have been introduced to a variety of basic aids to meditation: creating a sacred space for prayer, deep breathing, relaxing the body, and so on. You will be reminded throughout this program to make these basic techniques regular features of your meditation. If you find yourself having difficulty with your meditating, you may be forgetting some of the basics. At such times, review the basic meditation techniques on pages 3-4 of this guide.

This week, you will learn additional techniques to help in your meditation. You will learn to become more aware of and in touch with yourself—your body, your mind, your relationship with God. You will learn techniques for dealing with mental distractions during prayer. You will practice a special kind of prayer called a mantra. You will also meditate on a beautiful reading from the Scriptures. All of these exercises will prepare you for more effective meditating in the coming weeks.

You will also be asked this week to begin using journal writing as another particularly helpful tool for prayer and meditation. Journal writing is a way to focus consciously on your life and experiences by struggling to find words to capture or express the richness of life. It is a powerful means of reflection, even for those who have never considered themselves good writers. For each meditation during the remainder of the program, you will be asked to write brief responses to exercises or to specific questions. Write your thoughts honestly and openly, without worrying about spelling, grammar, or word choice. *No one will ever see what you write here.* A journal is not a diary. A diary normally records what is going on outside of one's self—events, relationships, and so on. Journal writing is the recording of a journey *inside* one's self—into one's hopes, dreams, beliefs, fears. Such a journey is one of the most important any of us can take. For it is inside ourselves that we ultimately encounter our God.

Week 4, Day 2

Living in the Present Moment

■ **Purpose**

To learn to embrace my present life and to discover God during each moment of my day

■ **Exercise**

Many people get so caught up in regretting the past and fearing the future that they fail to live the present moment. Yet in reality the present moment is all that we truly own. The past can be appreciated and learned from, but it cannot be changed. We can and should try to prepare for the future, but we will inevitably be surprised by it. Furthermore, we must admit, an earthly future may not even exist for us; we may die tomorrow. Recognizing the certainty of death need not be morbid or depressing, as we shall learn in tomorrow's meditation. In this meditation, we learn to embrace and fully live the present moment.

In this exercise, you are asked to do four things:

- Enter your prayer space and become centered.
- You will find below a schedule for a day beginning at 7:00 a.m. and ending at midnight. Imagine that this is a schedule for you for tomorrow. For each hour of the day on the schedule, note what you can reasonably expect to be doing during that time. Be as specific as possible.
- After completing your schedule, imagine the day unfolding before your eyes as if it were captured on film. Try to see yourself in your mind's eye, living the day that lies before you.
- Finally, replay the imaginary film of your day, but this time see yourself living the day *as you believe God would want you to live it*. See yourself reacting to people, eating your meals, and doing your work with Christian attitudes and behavior.

Week 2, Day 1

Coming to Your Senses

■ **Purpose**

To become aware of and grateful for your body as a means of contact and communication with all creation—with nature, with other people—as well as with the One who creates, God

■ **Exercise**

During the first week of this meditation program, we learned some techniques and exercises for preparing our body for meditation—posture, deep breathing, and relaxation. We also considered our sense of hearing and the fact that it can pose a problem during meditation when it detects potentially distracting sounds. Such exercises point to an important reality in prayer and meditation: We must learn to control our body if we hope to free our mind and heart to communicate with God.

The notion of controlling the body during meditation may lead some individuals to incorrectly view the body as a kind of necessary evil, a problem, a stumbling block in our relationship with God. At times during Christian history, people of goodwill have taken this false notion to an extreme, viewing the body as evil and seeing its natural needs and desires as threats to our relationship with God. Such a negative view of the body can cause great problems for us, limiting our ability to accept ourselves or to relate openly to others, and even restricting us from experiencing God as gracious and caring.

Controlling the body does not require condemning it. On the contrary, your body is a marvelous gift from God to be treasured, regardless of how our society might evaluate how you look. Your body allows you to take in and be refreshed by all creation—its sights, sounds, tastes, aromas, textures. Your body enables you to gently cradle an infant, hold the hand of a loved one, embrace a friend in pain. An awareness of your body can also put you in touch with the God who created you.

sense of gratitude, *even for the painful and sad memories*. Embracing the painful moments of our life allows us to heal the hurts of the past and to learn to trust difficult times. Failure to do this can lead to bitterness and repression of feelings or lack of hope, all of which can cripple us emotionally and spiritually.

■ **Journal Writing**

For each period of your life given below, identify in writing both your happiest and saddest memories.

From birth to age 5

Happiest memory: _____

Saddest memory: _____

From ages 5-10

Happiest memory: _____

Saddest memory: _____

From ages 10-15

Happiest memory: _____

Saddest memory: _____

From ages 15-present

Happiest memory: _____

Saddest memory: _____

■ **To Prepare for Tomorrow**

Read the directions for tomorrow's meditation. You may wish to begin working on the daily schedule called for in that meditation.

Week 4, Day 1

Embracing My History

■ Purpose

To meditate on and accept my past as a necessary step to fully living the present and anticipating the future with hope.

■ Exercise

If we hope to live rich and fulfilling lives, we must learn to embrace our past history, with all its joys and pains, all its delights and heartaches. This exercise is an attempt to help you do that. Because your periods of meditation are kept relatively short during this program, this is a simplified approach to an exercise that can become much more complex and extended. After doing this exercise, you may experience a need to spend more meditation time with the issues of the past that this exercise presents to you. You might consider continuing this meditation after the program has concluded.

This meditation exercise asks you to do three things:

- Enter your prayer space and take a few minutes to become centered. Ask the Lord to open your eyes and your heart to your past.

- You will find below a series of questions regarding specific periods of your life. Reflect upon each stage of your life and identify in writing both the happiest and saddest memories you can recall from each period. Be as specific as you can, but don't worry if you have difficulty identifying a particular incident for each period. You may only be able to recall general impressions of a given time or remember recurring experiences like moving or going to the lake in the summertime.

- After doing the written part of the exercise, slowly review each incident that you have recalled. Try to get in touch with the feelings generated by each one. Let yourself feel both the sadness and the joy of those memories. Then pray in your heart *in response to each of those events*, "My God, for that part of my life, I thank you." Feel free to change the way you phrase this prayer, but retain the

- For this meditation, enter your prayer space, assume your prayer posture, and close your eyes. Allow yourself to relax and become centered. Then, beginning with your head and moving down, become conscious of every part of your body. Don't *think* about your body; try to simply *feel* it, all parts of it, every sensation you can. Feel the touch of your hair against your forehead or ears or neck. Become aware of the touch of your clothes on your shoulder. Focus for a moment on the touch of your back against the chair . . . the shirt or blouse on your arms . . . your hands touching one another or resting on your lap . . . your buttocks and thighs touching the chair or floor . . . your feet within your shoes or against the floor.

- Repeat the exercise: head . . . shoulders . . . arms . . . right hand . . . left hand . . . thighs . . . feet. Repeat it again if time allows.

■ Journal Writing

When done with the above exercise, complete this statement: When I reflect on my body, I honestly feel . . .

_____

_____

_____

_____

_____

■ To Prepare for Tomorrow

Try to remain conscious of your body throughout this day—its marvelous workings and the joys it allows you to experience. Be thankful to God for this gift. Before going to bed tonight, read tomorrow's meditation.

Picture in Your Mind

Week 2, Day 2

- **Purpose**
  To learn techniques for dealing with distractions during meditation

- **Exercise**
  One of the most frustrating problems encountered in meditation is that of mental distractions. The meditator tries to focus on God, or perhaps tries to clear her or his mind of all images, yet feels besieged by every thought imaginable. Schoolwork, the big game, the next date, whether the car will be available when needed, a favorite television show, the next meal—countless thoughts seem to carry on a relentless battle for attention. Here are some suggestions for dealing with such distractions:

- First, acknowledge that the problem of mental distractions has been experienced by every person who has seriously attempted prayer or meditation, including the Church's greatest saints. You are in good company, so relax! View your experience with distractions as a kind of curious game, an intriguing way to better know yourself. Becoming conscious of those things that distract you can give you some interesting insights into yourself.

- Second, distractions are usually a minor nuisance. It is when you allow yourself to get too frustrated by them that they become a major distraction to prayer.

- Finally, at times you may experience a mental distraction that carries with it a strong emotional dimension. Some passing thoughts may trigger feelings of fear, sorrow, guilt, or loneliness, and others trigger positive feelings like joy or peace. You can make such emotionally-laden thoughts the focus of some further reflection, journal writing, or prayer. Try to determine why the thought sparked the emotion it did. This can be an avenue for significant growth in self-understanding.

Introduction to Week 4

This fourth and final week of the meditation program will include the following elements:

1. You will use the technique of journal writing in a different way than you have before in this program. In previous weeks, journal writing has normally been used to help you respond to an exercise. This week you will be doing two journal-writing activities that are themselves the focus of meditation.
2. You will learn one more technique for meditation, the use of what is known as *spiritual reading*.
3. You will experience another guided meditation and practice one more form of mantra.
4. Finally, all of the meditations during the week will focus on themes appropriate to your life right now. You are moving not only out of this program but also out of high school, and you are moving more deeply into a new stage in your life, that of young adulthood. You have a lot of things to think and pray about. This week will help you do that.

The conclusion of almost any program, event, or special occasion brings with it a variety of feelings. One often feels happy, even proud, that a task has been successfully accomplished. Yet feelings of sadness or loss are also common as we realize that it is time to end what we are doing and to move into the future. All of those feelings and more may be part of what you are experiencing as this program comes to an end. Prayer, especially when experienced with others, possesses tremendous power to influence our life. When we meditate with others, a kind of bonding and deep closeness often occurs, a sense of unity with others that is seldom experienced in our life. Be grateful for what you have shared in this program, and use your experience here to move into your future with optimism, joy, and peace. In the words to be used in the final meditation of this program—words you may choose to say over and over again, "For all that has been, thanks. For all that will be, yes!"

For today's meditation, assume your prayer posture and allow yourself a few minutes for deep breathing, relaxation, and centering. Once centered, peacefully allow all thoughts to pass through your mind as follows:

- Consciously name each thought as it enters your mind. For example, say to yourself, "Now I'm thinking about my homework." Or "Here comes a thought about Jack."
- Try to imagine the thought as "passing by" in your mind. Simply acknowledge the thought; say to yourself, "That's interesting," and then let it go. Don't dwell on or analyze these thoughts. Treat each one like a bird that arrives, lights for a brief moment, and then flies away. Stay observant and peaceful. Do this for 5 minutes or until you tire of the exercise.

■ **Journal Writing**
After meditating, respond in writing as indicated:

1. List as many of the distracting thoughts as you can remember, using the names you gave them as you experienced them during your meditation.

_____

_____

2. React to this statement: "As soon as I tell myself I'm thinking of something, I stop thinking of it."

_____

_____

■ **To Prepare for Tomorrow**
Read the directions for tomorrow's meditation.

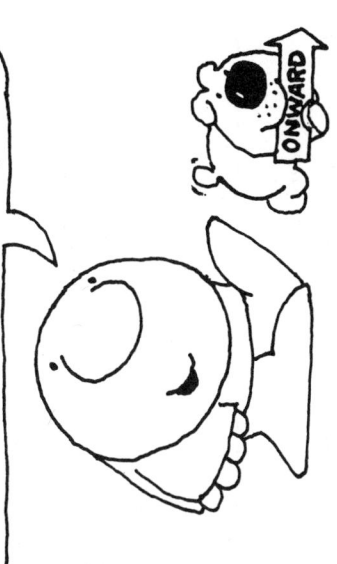

Ziggy © 1976, Universal Press Syndicate. Reprinted with permission. All rights reserved.

Week 2, Day 3

Calling on the Name of the Lord

- **Purpose**

  To learn the use of a mantra in prayer

- **Exercise**

Hindu masters of meditation have a saying regarding distractions during prayer: "One thorn is removed by another." By this they mean that the meditator, rather than being constantly distracted by random thoughts, can consciously choose one helpful thought upon which to focus. She or he then calls that thought or image back to mind whenever a distraction appears. In a sense, the helpful thought so fills the mind that no room remains for distractions.

This basic principle can be applied in many ways to prayer and meditation. The most popular application is the use of a word, phrase, or sound that one repeats over and over during meditation. This is called a *mantra*. The meditator can choose or create a mantra that works for him or her. Or a spiritual guide might suggest or even assign a mantra based on his or her knowledge of the meditator's needs. Today you will practice the most popular Christian mantra, called the Jesus Prayer. In succeeding days you will learn other mantra techniques.

The Jesus Prayer is practiced in various ways in different traditions. In some cases, only the name "Jesus" is slowly pronounced over and over. Another version is reciting the name with the rhythm of one's breathing, saying the first syllable of the name while inhaling and the second syllable while exhaling.

One approach to this prayer is known as "the Jesus Prayer formula." The formula is "Lord Jesus Christ, have mercy on me." Again, this can be combined with the pace of one's breathing, saying the first half of the formula while inhaling and the second half while exhaling.

Another variation of the Jesus Prayer suggests that the meditator choose a phrase that best reflects his or her own

4. Looking back at that experience, one thing that could have made it better for me would have been if I had . . .

_____

_____

5. I think that the thing I most need at this point to improve my experience with meditation is . . .

_____

_____

6. Of all the insights that I gained during my meditation this week, the one that I believe would be most helpful to my fellow meditators is . . .

_____

_____

7. If God were trying to say one thing to my fellow meditators at this time, I think God would want to say . . .

_____

_____

_____

_____

relationship with Jesus or one that best expresses a current personal need. Examples include, "Jesus, my Brother, heal my loneliness," or "Jesus, my Lord, give me peace." In all cases, however, the name Jesus is included, and the mantra is kept short.

A helpful aid in saying the Jesus Prayer is to imagine that you are in the physical presence of Jesus. Picture him in your mind as you most like to imagine him. Look into his eyes, and imagine him looking into yours. If you have a favorite portrait of Jesus, feel free to place the picture in your prayer space as an aid for this meditation.

- Before meditating, choose the approach to the Jesus prayer that most appeals to you, using one of the examples given or one of your own design.
- Prayerfully enter your prayer space, take your preferred posture, and spend a moment relaxing your body. Imagine Jesus present. Then begin deep breathing, this time using the Jesus Prayer of your choice while inhaling and exhaling. Practice for 5 minutes.

■ **Journal Writing**
Note here the Jesus Prayer formula that you used today and evaluate your experience with it.

_____

_____

_____

■ **To Prepare for Tomorrow**
Select another version of the Jesus Prayer for tomorrow's meditation. Change the words that you will use for your mantra. If you wish, consider other changes that you would like to experiment with in your prayer space, posture, or the image of Jesus you call to mind in your prayer.

Week 3, Day 7

Things Worth Sharing

■ **Purpose**
To prepare for the next gathering

■ **Exercise**
Review your experience with the meditation program this week by looking over the exercises and your journal writing for each of the last six days. Then respond in writing to each of the following points as indicated. Be prepared to share this information with your fellow meditators.

1. I had the most satisfying experience with meditation this week when . . .

_____

2. I think the main reason that meditation was so satisfying was that . . .

_____

3. The most difficult time I had meditating this week was when . . .

_____

Meditating with a Mantra

Week 2, Day 4

■ **Purposes**

To further practice the use of a mantra in meditation; to deepen the experience of journal writing as an aid to prayer.

■ **Exercise**

Yesterday you experimented with one approach to the Jesus Prayer, the most popular Christian mantra. It was then suggested that, in preparation for today's meditation, you consider changing your approach to the Jesus Prayer—experimenting with a new word or phrase, altering your posture during the prayer, or perhaps in some way changing the image of Jesus that you call to mind as you begin to meditate.

■ Before you enter your prayer space, make your final decisions regarding these matters. Then practice the new approach to the Jesus Prayer for at least 5 minutes.

■ When you have completed your use of the Jesus Prayer, write whatever comes to your mind and heart in the space provided below. If you wish, consider it a letter to Jesus that is prompted by your meditation. Or you may feel moved to write directly to yourself. Maybe you will feel like writing a poem. Let the words flow on the paper spontaneously, without concern for spelling, grammar, or even content. You need not fill the entire space provided.

■ **Journal Writing**

_____
_____
_____
_____

■ The Miracle of the Loaves in Mark 6:30-44
■ Jesus in the Garden of Gethsemane in Mark 14: 32-42
■ The Call of the First Disciples in Luke 5:1-11
■ Jesus and the Sinful Woman in Luke 7:36-50
■ The Story of Zacchaeus in Luke 19:1-10

■ **Journal Writing**

Indicate below the passage you selected. Then summarize the dialogue you had during your meditation with either Jesus or another gospel character.

_____
_____
_____
_____
_____
_____

■ **To Prepare for Tomorrow**

Reflect on the questions asked in tomorrow's preparation for your next gathering.

Week 3, Day 6

Bringing the Scriptures to Life

■ **Purpose**

To practice using your imagination to recreate Bible stories for use in guided meditation

■ **Exercise**

Yesterday you were provided with a script with which to meditate on a particular story from the Gospels—that of the blind man cured by Jesus. Today you are asked to develop your own imaginary retelling of a gospel story for use in your meditation.

- Below are listed a series of gospel passages. You are asked to briefly review the passages and select one that appeals to you. Use yesterday's prepared script on the cure of the blind man as a model for your imagined retelling of the passage. Place yourself at the scene. Try to get in touch with the event on every level of your senses: touch, smell, hearing, taste, sight. See yourself at the event, either as an involved witness or as one of the characters in the story. Be sure to include in some way a dialogue involving yourself—either with Jesus or with another character.

- You may find it helpful to prepare in advance a script for your meditation. You can write or record the script and then use it to guide you during prayer.

- Enter your prayer place, assume your preferred posture, and spend a few moments becoming centered. Then prayerfully read your selected passage. After doing so, replay the story as vividly as you can, either mentally or by using a written script or taped recording. When you are done, complete the journal-writing section as indicated.

Suggested gospel passages
- Cure of the Paralytic in Matthew 9:1–8
- The Danger of Riches in Matthew 19:16–26

■ **To Prepare for Tomorrow**

Read the directions for tomorrow's meditation. Be prepared to begin the exercise as soon as you enter your prayer space.

Week 2, Day 5

This Is the Word of the Lord!

- **Purpose**
  To learn to use the Scriptures as a source for meditation

- **Exercise**
  In this exercise, you will practice combining the use of the mantra with a prayerful reading of the Scriptures. Below is a familiar passage from the Sermon on the Mount. Have this passage available as you enter your prayer space. (You may want to have your Bible opened to this passage; reading directly from the Scriptures can enhance the sense of prayer.)

- Take your prayer posture, relax, and center yourself with a minute or two of deep breathing. Then slowly read the scriptural passage. Consider saying the words out loud, perhaps in a whisper. When you are done with the reading, scan the passage and look for a word or phrase that strikes a chord within you, that seems to speak directly to your heart. Reflect on the words; what do they mean to you today? Each time your mind seems to drift away from prayer, slowly repeat the word or phrase, using it as a mantra. Let the words find a fertile place in your heart, where they can take root and become part of you.

- After a few minutes of meditation, record any feelings or thoughts you have in the space provided for journal writing.

That is why I am telling you not to worry about your life and what you are to eat, nor about your body and what you are to wear. Surely life is more than food, and the body more than clothing! Look at the birds in the sky. They do not sow or reap or gather into barns; yet your heavenly Father feeds them. Are you not worth much more than they are? Can any of you, however much you worry, add one single cubit to your span of life? And why worry about clothing? Think of the flowers growing in the fields; they never have to work or spin; yet I assure you that not even Solomon in all his does his voice sound like? . . . You realize now that the man is blind. . . . What does he look like? . . . How is he dressed? . . . See and listen to the response of the people in the scene—the people around you in the crowd; those near the blind man who are apparently embarrassed by his behavior. And you—how do you feel? . . .

Finally the blind man catches Jesus' attention. Jesus stops and turns toward the man. You work your way through the crowd to get closer to Jesus, anxious to see how he will handle the situation. The crowd noise lessens as people wait in anticipation. . . . Then Jesus looks at those who have been trying to silence the blind man and demands that they bring the man to him. What do those people feel like? . . . How does the blind man feel as he realizes that the crowd has grown silent? Does he feel that they are all watching him? . . . As the man is brought forward, he stumbles against you. What does he say to you? . . . Do you say anything to the blind man? . . . How do you feel? . . .

The blind man now stands before Jesus. Jesus asks him, "What do you want me to do for you?" "Sir," the blind man replied, "let me see again." How does Jesus look upon the man? . . . Jesus then says, "Receive your sight. Your faith has saved you." And the man's eyes slowly open. He can see! How does he respond? . . . How does the crowd react? . . . Look at Jesus' face. What does he look like? . . . How do you feel, and how do you respond to what you have seen? . . . Jesus unexpectedly turns toward you. He looks into your eyes and says, "What do you want me to do for you? What things are blinding you? How might I heal you? What do you say to Jesus? . . .

- **Journal Writing**
  On page 62 of your guide for meditation, record the dialogue between you and Jesus as the two of you talk of the things in your life that require healing.

- **To Prepare for Tomorrow**
  Read the directions for tomorrow's meditation and decide how you will prepare for it.

Week 3, Day 5

Meeting Myself in the Scriptures

■ **Purpose**

To learn to use your imagination in praying the Scriptures

■ **Exercise**

Saint Ignatius, the founder of the Jesuits, developed a method of prayer that consists of selecting a scene from the life of Jesus and reliving it as if it were occurring right now. The meditator imagines him or herself actively participating in the event, at times assuming the role of one of the primary characters involved or, perhaps, as simply an observer on the scene. Often one is asked to imagine a dialogue with Jesus taking place within the context of the story. The meditator actually feels as if he or she is a part of all that is happening.

Enter your prayer space and spend a few minutes becoming centered. Then read from your Bible the brief story about the cure of the blind man on the road to Jericho recorded in Luke 18:35-43. "Replay" the passage using the script provided below. This script can be recorded in advance if you wish, though you may not feel that recording it is necessary. Prayerfully reflect on the passage as follows:

Imagine yourself walking amid the crowd that is following Jesus on the road to the town of Jericho. How many people are present? . . . Feel and smell the dust of the road in the air as the crowd moves along. . . . What sounds do you hear? How do you feel as a member of the crowd? . . . Excited? . . . Anxious? . . . Tired? . . . Are you talking with others in the crowd or sticking by yourself as you watch Jesus? . . .

Suddenly, there is commotion by the side of the road. Someone is screaming, "Jesus, Son of David, have pity on me." Jesus apparently can't hear the man calling, and others around the man are trying to shut him up. But he calls out more loudly, "Jesus, Son of David, have pity on me." What

---

royal robes was clothed like one of these. Now if that is how God clothes the wild flowers growing in the field which are there today and thrown into the furnace tomorrow, will he not much more look after you, you who have so little faith? So do not worry; do not say, "What are we to eat? What are we to drink? What are we to wear?" . . . Your heavenly Father knows you need [these things]. Set your hearts on his kingdom first, and on God's saving justice, and all these other things will be given you as well. So do not worry about tomorrow: tomorrow will take care of itself. (Matthew 6:25-34)

■ **Journal Writing**

_____

_____

_____

_____

■ **To Prepare for Tomorrow**

For tomorrow's meditation, you are again asked to meditate on a passage from the Scriptures. In this case, however, you are to use a passage of your own choosing. Before going to sleep this evening, slowly leaf through one of the Gospels. (Many individuals find John's Gospel to be a particularly rich source for this exercise). When you come to a gospel story or scene that appeals to you or catches your attention, simply place a bookmark at that page in your Bible in preparation for tomorrow. You need not read or reflect on the passage until then.

Praying with the Scriptures

Week 2, Day 6

■ **Purpose**
To practice using the Scriptures as a basis for meditation

■ **Exercise**
Today you are to again use the Scriptures as a source of meditation, this time meditating on a passage of your own choosing. If you found the approach used yesterday helpful—that is, repeating a particular word or phrase from the passage whenever you felt distracted—feel free to use it again. Or consider using the following approach:

■ Before entering your prayer space, select a passage from one of the Gospels that for any reason catches your attention. The particular passage you select is not critical to the exercise; your goal is to learn to meditate on any part of the Bible.

■ Enter your prayer space and spend a few minutes becoming centered.

■ Slowly and prayerfully begin to read the passage. If you have enough privacy to read aloud without embarrassment, feel free to do so. This can aid concentration.

■ In this case, pause for prayer and reflection any time you are struck by a verse, a phrase, an idea, a statement by a character in the scene—anything that strikes a chord in you. Speak to God about the meaning of the passage in your own life. When you feel ready, begin reading again, stopping for prayer and reflection whenever a verse catches your attention. Continue this for at least 5 minutes.

■ **Journal Writing**
Write whatever comes from your heart in response to your meditation today.

Jesus must now leave. You return to yourself, and you look once more at your statue. Has it changed at all? . . . Have you changed at all, that is, do you feel differently than you did before? . . .

Now say good-bye to your statue . . . leave the room . . . and open your eyes.

■ **Journal Writing**
Imagine that you are Jesus writing a letter *to you*, expressing what you feel would be his thoughts about you at this time.

_____

_____

_____

_____

_____

_____

_____

■ **To Prepare for Tomorrow**
Read the directions for tomorrow's meditation and decide how you wish to prepare for it.

Week 3, Day 4

Seeing Myself in a New Way

■ **Purpose**

To meditate on your self-image and personal relationship with Jesus

■ **Exercise**

Assume your prayer posture and spend a few minutes centering yourself. Then turn on your tape player and follow these directions as you recorded them earlier:

Imagine that a sculptor has been hired to make a statue of you. You have just heard that the statue is ready, and you are invited to see it before it is shown to the public. You go to the sculptor's studio. She gives you the key to a room where your statue is on display and tells you that you can examine it privately. The sculptor then leaves.

You unlock the door to the room. The room is dark, with just enough light to allow you to see the statue, covered with a cloth, in the middle of the room. You slowly walk up to the statue, and you remove the cloth....

You step away from the statue to get a good view of it. What is your first impression of it?... Are you happy with it?... Disappointed?... Notice all the details: its size... what it's made of... what color it is.... Walk around it and look at it from different directions and angles. ... Touch the statue. Is it rough or smooth?... Cold or warm?...

Say something to your statue.... What does it reply? ... What do you then say?...

Now imagine that you have become your statue.... What does it feel like to be your statue?...

Imagine that, while you are your statue, Jesus walks into the room.... How does he look at you?... What do you feel like when he looks at you?... What does he say to you?... How do you reply?...

■ **To Prepare for Tomorrow**

Your primary task tomorrow is to prepare for the next gathering by responding in writing to the questions asked of you. However, if you wish to do another meditation in addition to the writing, consider this possibility: Review the first two weeks of this meditation guide, and repeat any of the exercises that you have particularly enjoyed or found helpful. Virtually any exercise in this meditation program can be repeated countless times with new and deeper results.

Week 2, Day 7

Things Worth Sharing

- **Purpose**
  To prepare for the next gathering

- **Exercise**
  Respond in writing to each of the following points as indicated. Be prepared to share this information with your fellow meditators.

  1. I had the most satisfying experience with meditation this week when . . .

  _____
  _____
  _____
  _____

  2. I think that the main reason this meditation was so satisfying was that . . .

  _____
  _____
  _____
  _____

  3. The most difficult time I had meditating this week was when . . .

  _____
  _____
  _____

where to go to search for God. . . . Where in the city do you decide to go? Don't go where you think you *ought* to go. Rather, go where your heart truly leads you. . . .

What happens when you arrive at this place? What do you find there? . . . Do you find God? . . . In what way? . . . What does God say to you if anything? . . . How do you respond? . . . Are you disappointed? . . . Relieved? . . . Confused? . . . Joyful? . . . What do you do then? . . . Do you want to go somewhere else or stay where you are? . . .

Now imagine that you are leaving that place, that you return to the edge of the city, and that you climb up to the top of the hill that you were on before. There you again meet the holy man, and he asks you to tell him what you learned about God. What do you tell him? . . .

Now say a brief prayer in your heart to God, and then open your eyes . . .

- **Journal Writing**
  Describe below the God that you encountered in your meditation today. Consider the following reflection questions:
  - Where in the city did you seek the presence of God?
  - What did God look like?
  - Could you hear God's voice?
  - Did you like the way God looked and sounded?
  - What did you tell the hermit that you learned about God?

- **To Prepare for Tomorrow**
  Record the script for tomorrow's meditation.

4. Looking back at this experience, one thing that could make it better for me would be if I . . .

___

5. If there is one thing I need a lot more practice with in meditation, it is . . .

___

6. The thing I would most like our leader or our group to do for me at this point is . . .

___

7. If God were trying to say one thing to my fellow meditators at this time, I think God would want to say . . .

___

Week 3, Day 3

The Search for God

■ Purpose
To gain insights into your images of God

■ Exercise

Today and tomorrow you will experience two guided meditations that you may have previously experienced in this high school religion program. They are so popular with young people that many students have asked to do them over and over again. Providing the scripts for these meditations here will allow you to use them anytime you wish.

Each evening, record the script for the next day, adding the centering instructions and pausing wherever the series of periods (. . .) indicates. Feel free to change the wording anytime you wish to better suit your own tastes or speaking style.

Imagine that you are sitting on a hilltop overlooking a large city. It is dusk, and the sun is slowly setting over the city. As it does so, the lights of the city begin to burn, and slowly the city begins to look like a sea of lights. You are all alone, gazing at the marvelous sight. . . . After a while you hear the footsteps of someone behind you, but you are not afraid. You know that they are the footsteps of a holy man who lives on the mountain, a hermit. He comes up to you and stands by your side. He looks gently at you and says just one sentence to you: "If you go down into the city tonight, you will find God." He then turns and walks away. No explanation, no time to ask any questions.

You know that the holy man is trustworthy and that he knows what he is talking about. What do you feel like doing? Do you want to act on what he said and go into the city, or do you want to stay where you are? . . .

Whatever you might want to do, imagine now that you are going down into the city in search of God. Soon you find yourself on the outskirts of the city. Now you must decide ahead of you.... Butterflies float among the flowers.... One stops near you.... You barely breathe so that it won't wing away.... Now you inhale the fragrances carried on the wind.... You breathe in and out deeply several times....

Slowly, you continue to walk toward the woods.... A man sits on a log in the shade.... With a slight wave of his hand he invites you to share the log with him.... When you are close, he says "Peace be with you."... Your eyes are opened and you know that it is Jesus.... You look deeply into his eyes.... Jesus reaches out and takes your hand in his and says, "I love you with an everlasting love."... Softly he says, "Now, my friend, tell me of the people you love. Share with me stories of those you love and who love you." You see before you the faces of several people who you love.... Now you tell Jesus about the loved ones who reside deeply in your heart.... He listens carefully. [Longer pause here.] When you are finished, Jesus stands to go, saying, "Your sins are forgiven because you have loved much." He embraces you.... Then you watch as he walks slowly into the forest.... When he has disappeared, you gaze at the scene around you once more.... When you are ready, return from the scene and open your eyes.

■ Journal Writing

Ziggy © 1976, Universal Press Syndicate. Reprinted with permission. All rights reserved.

■ To Prepare for Tomorrow
Record the script for tomorrow's meditation.

Introduction to Week 3

During the third week of our meditation program, we are going to practice an approach to prayer and meditation that many people have found not only helpful but also enjoyable. It is a type of prayer that uses the power of the imagination and is usually referred to as *guided meditation*.

The imagination is one of the most marvelous human faculties. It enables us to experience worlds that we may never actually visit; well-written stories can make us feel as if we are crawling through caves with prehistoric people or walking on the moon with astronauts. Keeping in mind that God is always more than we can imagine, we can use our power of imagination to expand our ability to pray.

If you have experienced guided meditations before, you know that hearing someone lead you through these experiences is often more helpful than reading them. One way to accomplish this in private prayer is to use tape recordings of the instructions. Your group leader may provide the recordings for you. If not, learn to do this for yourself. The evening before one of the guided meditations, record the instructions on your tape player. Then place the player conveniently in your prayer space for use the next morning. When recording the instructions, imagine how they might best sound when played. Speak with a slow, peaceful pacing and tone. Leave plenty of pauses to allow you to reflect. You might even want to add musical background. In this way you will learn techniques that will enable you to create your own guided meditations.

A final thought: Most people find their own recorded voice distracting. This feeling usually passes with experience. Or you may want to ask a friend whose voice you enjoy to make the recordings with you. In this way, you will be teaching your friend to pray while he or she helps you out!

Week 3, Day 2

The Saving Goodness of Love

■ **Purpose**
To use guided meditation to focus on a particular theme

■ **Exercise**
Guided meditations can be designed to help the meditator focus on a theme of his or her own choosing. In today's meditation the theme is love as we have experienced it in our personal relationships. By slightly changing the instructions, however, you can focus this meditation on any theme that you wish to explore in prayer—your relationship with God, your future, a particular fear you are struggling with.

Following is a script for this meditation. This should be recorded, and the tape player should then be placed conveniently in your prayer space so that it is ready to go when you need it. In the script, a series of periods (. .) indicates a pause; at these points you should allow enough silence to permit your imagination to create the scene suggested by the script. Then move on to the next part of the instructions. The script opens with directions for centering. Feel free to replace these with others if you have developed a centering technique that works well for you. When you have completed the meditation, jot down whatever thoughts come to your mind in the journal-writing space provided.

Assume your prayer posture. . . Relax. . . Let all tension leave your body. . . Breathe deeply in and out. . . Feel the tension leave your feet. . . your legs. . . Relax your stomach and chest. . . Now let all the tension escape from your arms . . . and from your neck. . . Let your jaw and face relax. . . Slow down. . . Breathe in and out slowly. . . .

Now imagine taking a long walk. . . See and feel yourself slowly walking through a clearing in a woods. . . . Tall grass and wildflowers wave in the soft breeze. . . The sun caresses your face. . . You stop to take in the scene. . . Birds flit among the wildflowers and fly into the pine trees

Seeking a Place to Rest with God

Week 3, Day 1

- **Purpose**
  To practice the use of the imagination in guided meditation

- **Exercise**
  Today you are going to practice the technique of a guided meditation. Though recorded directions are not required here, you might experiment by taping the instructions for this exercise.

  A great help to meditation is to find a place that lends itself to prayer. That is why you began the program by creating a sacred space for your daily meditations. However, even if you have been enjoying that space, it is necessarily limited. Most of us have favorite environments in other places that can lead us to prayer—a quiet church in the evening, a lakeshore at sunset, a mountain peak, a campsite on a starlit night, the seashore at daybreak with the waves slowly lapping at the sand. Such settings have a special power to place us in the presence of God. Perhaps that is why Jesus, who certainly knew well the art of praying, often climbed a hill or went to the desert to pray. Our imagination has the power to carry us to these places in our mind and heart. We can place ourselves in our favorite places, no matter how drab our real environment.

  In this exercise, you are to choose one of your favorite environments and then imagine yourself there with God. Here are some suggestions on how to achieve this:

  - Before entering your prayer space, identify the environment you find most conducive to prayer. Choose a location that you have actually experienced. It makes the imagining more realistic. Do not choose a mountaintop if in fact you have never climbed a mountain.

  - Enter your prayer space, and take a few minutes to center yourself with relaxation exercises and deep breathing.

  - When you are centered, begin to imagine yourself in the place that you have chosen. Use as many of your senses as you can to make the place real to you: try to see all the details of the place with your mind's eye; try to hear all the sounds, including those that might not immediately be identified—the breeze in the trees or the chirp of crickets; feel the air touching your skin; you may even be able to taste the environment, as one tastes the salty air by the sea. Totally immerse yourself in that place.

  - When you have fully imagined yourself in your special place, start to talk to God from your heart. You may find it helpful to imagine the man Jesus present. Some of the saints found it distracting to try to imagine Jesus physically, and they preferred to simply sense his presence. Or you may want to speak to God or to the Spirit. Do what feels most natural and comfortable to you.

  - When you have shared your thoughts with God, try to imagine God responding to you. This communication need not take the form of words. You may simply rest in God's presence. Imagine that everything in your environment is speaking to you of God. Let yourself be touched by the very life of God.

- **Journal Writing**
  Write below whatever comes to your mind or heart in response to this experience.

  _____

  _____

  _____

- **To Prepare for Tomorrow**
  Prepare a recording of the directions for tomorrow's guided meditation.

Acknowledgments (continued)

The scriptural excerpts are from *The New Jerusalem Bible*, copyright © 1985 by Darton, Longman & Todd, Ltd., and Doubleday, a division of Bantam, Doubleday, Dell Publishing Group, Inc. Reprinted by permission of the publisher.

The ten tasks listed on pages 57–58 and in Student Handout 1–B are adapted from *Moving Into Adulthood: Themes and Variations in Self-Directed Development for Effective Living*, by Gerard Egan and Michael A. Cowan (Monterey, CA: Brooks/Cole Publishing Company, 1980), page 32. Copyright © 1980 by Wadsworth, Inc.

The excerpt on page 58 is from *The Seasons of a Man's Life*, by Daniel J. Levinson et al. (New York: Alfred A. Knopf, 1978), page 102.

The poem "This Is Who I Am" on Student Handout 1–C is adapted from *Why Am I Afraid to Tell You Who I Am?* by John Powell, SJ (Allen, TX: Argus Communications, 1969), pages 8 and 9 and guide excerpt. Copyright © 1969 by Tabor Publishing, a division of DLM, Inc. Used with permission.

The prayer "You Have Great Plans for Me" on Student Handout 1–C is adapted from a prayer card by the Vocation Center (Saint Paul, MN: Archdiocese of Saint Paul–Minneapolis). Used with permission.

The activities "Lifeline" and "Rest in Peace" on pages 70–71 and on Student Handout 2–A are adapted from *Meeting Yourself Halfway*, by Sidney B. Simon (Niles, IL: Argus Communications, 1974), pages 1–4 and guide excerpt. Copyright © 1974 by Tabor Publishing, a division of DLM, Inc. Used with permission.

The excerpts after the Beatitudes on Student Handout 2–C are quoted in *The Beatitudes: Lenten Prayer Guide*, by Jacqueline Bergan and S. Marie Schwan (Crookston, MN: Center for Christian Renewal, n.d.). Used with permission.

The excerpt on page 82 is from *The Annotated Alice: Alice's Adventures in Wonderland and Through the Looking Glass*, by Lewis Carroll, with an introduction and notes by Martin Gardner (New York: Clarkson N. Potter, 1960).

The story on page 99 is from *Putting Forgiveness into Practice*, by Doris Donnelly (Allen, TX: Argus Communications, 1982), page 50. Copyright © 1982 by Tabor Publishing, a division of DLM, Inc. Used with permission.

The excerpt on page 104 is from *Will the Real Me Please Stand Up?* by John Powell and Loretta Brady (Allen, TX: Argus Communications, 1985), page 18. Copyright © 1985 by John Powell, SJ. Used with permission.

The poem "Celebrate You" on page 124 is adapted from *Celebrate the Temporary*, by Clyde H. Reid (New York: Harper & Row Publishers, Inc., 1972). Copyright © 1972 by Clyde H. Reid. Reprinted by permission of Harper & Row Publishers, Inc.

The self-test on Student Handout 6–B and the chart on Student Handout 6–C are adapted from "Counseling Youth on Sex, Love and Infatuation," an audiotape of a lecture by Dr. Ray E. Short presented at the Religious Education Congress, Archdiocese of Los Angeles, Anaheim, CA, 1983.

The quotation on pages 138 and 142 and page 58 of the meditation guide is from *Markings*, by Dag Hammarskjöld, translated by W. H. Auden and Leif Sjöberg (New York: Alfred A. Knopf, Inc., 1976), page 89.

The folktale on pages 141–142 is from *Storytelling: The Enchantment of Theology*, by Belden C. Lane. Saint Louis: Bethany Press, 1981. Sound cassette.

The exercise on page 151 and Student Handout A on page 166 are reprinted from J. William Pfeiffer and John E. Jones, eds., *A Handbook of Structured Experiences for Human Relations Training*, vol. 7 (San Diego, CA: University Associates, Inc., 1979). Used with permission.

The poem on pages 155–156 is "Desiderata," by Max Ehrmann. Copyright © 1927 by Max Ehrmann. All rights reserved. Copyright renewed 1954 by Bertha K. Ehrmann. Reprinted by permission. Robert L. Bell, Melrose, MA 02176.

Student Handout D on page 169 entitled "Planning Sheet for Eucharistic Liturgy" is reprinted from *Youth Retreats: Creating Sacred Space for Young People*, by Aileen A. Doyle (Winona, MN: Saint Mary's Press, 1986).

Student Handout E on page 176 entitled "A Model for Effective Lesson Planning" is adapted from *A Learning Process for Religious Education*, by Richard Reichert (Dayton, OH: Pflaum Publishing, 1975).

The excerpts on pages 192 and 193 and the exercises on pages 9, 10, 16, 19, 36–37, 38–39, and 52–53 of the meditation guide are adapted from *Sadhana: A Way to God*, by Anthony de Mello, SJ (Anand, India: Gujarat Sahitya Prakash), pages 53, 54, 43, 11–12, 21, 79–82, and 90–91, respectively. Copyright © 1978 by Anthony de Mello, SJ. Used with permission of the Institute of Jesuit Sources and Gujarat Sahitya Prakash.

The exercise on pages 34–35 of the meditation guide entitled "The Saving Goodness of Love" is reprinted from the teaching manual for *Creating a Christian Lifestyle*, by Carl Koch, FSC (Winona, MN: Saint Mary's Press, 1988).

The closing prayer ritual on page 194 is adapted from *Breakaway: Twenty-eight Steps to a More Reflective Life*, by Mark Link (Allen, TX: Argus Communications, 1980), page 20. Copyright © 1980 by Tabor Publishing, a division of DLM, Inc. Used with permission.

The excerpt on pages 199–200 and the three tests on page 200 are adapted from *He Touched Me*, by John Powell (Niles, IL: Argus Communications, 1974), pages 71–74. Copyright © 1974 by John Powell. Used with permission.

The prayers on pages 55 and 56–57 of the meditation guide by Cardinal John Newman and Thomas Merton, respectively, are quoted in *My Journey, My Prayer*, by Sr. Bernadette Vetter (Villa Maria, PA: The Center for Learning, 1985).

The Ziggy cartoons on pages 14, 30, and 46 of the meditation guide are by Tom Wilson. (Kansas City, MO: Universal Press Syndicate, 1974). Copyright © 1974 by Universal Press Syndicate. Used with permission.

The photographs on pages 51, 80, 91, 102, 114, and 133 are by James L. Shaffer.

The photograph on page 66 is by Vivienne della Grotta.

Photocopy Masters for Student Handouts

List of Student Handouts

Session 1
1-A Discussion Booklet for the Film *Solo*   61
1-B Ten Tasks for Young Adults   63
1-C Keepsake Prayers   64

Session 2
2-A Rest in Peace   75
2-B The Dream of a Lifetime   76
2-C Prayer Service: The Dream of Jesus   78

Session 3
3-A Guidelines for Creating Your Story   89
3-B A Step-by-Step Decision-making Guide   90

Session 4
4-A Reflecting on My Relationships   101

Session 5
5-A Imagining Myself as a Communicator   110
5-B Assignments for Role-playing   112

Session 6
6-A Small-Group Discussion Assignments for *A Question of Intimacy*   126
6-B Love or Infatuation? A Confidential Self-test   128
6-C Is It Love or Infatuation?   130

SHARING IV Designed Retreat
A What a Frightening Thought!   166
B Dyadic Encounter Guide   167
C A Letter to Myself   168
D Planning Sheet for Eucharistic Liturgy   169

Retreat Planning Guide for SHARING IV
E A Model for Effective Lesson Planning   176

Directing the Meditation Program
F Meditation Program Contract   203

A Guide for Meditation: Photocopy Masters   205

STUDENT HANDOUT 1-A

Discussion Booklet for the Film *Solo*

1

It seems to me that growing as a person is a lot like climbing a mountain because . . .

2

Sometimes mountain climbing can be fun and exciting, while at other times it can be scary, risky, thrilling, peaceful, prayerful, painful. Comparing my life to the process of climbing a mountain, I would describe my present stage in life as . . .

3

At times, individual experiences in life can be viewed as mountains in themselves—difficult challenges we must face and, it is hoped, endure, conquer, or grow through. In the last five years, one of the most difficult mountains I had to climb was when . . .

4

At this point, tell your partner as much as you feel comfortable sharing about the mountain climbing experience you just identified. Possible points to consider include, Who were the significant people involved? What exactly happened? How did you first react to the situation? What made it such a challenge?

5

The name of the film is *Solo,* referring to the fact that the climber in the film accomplishes his task all alone. In what sense must each of us face the major challenges of life alone? Is that good or bad?

6

How would you interpret the significance of the mountain climber finding, protecting, and later releasing the small toad? What might that symbolize about life?

7

If our lives are to be exciting and fulfilling— even just plain fun—it seems that we have to be willing to take some risks. Either that, or we spend all our time on the ground in fear and boredom and never climb the mountains in life.
At this point in my life, the greatest risks I probably have to take are . . .

8

If I were asked to sum up the main message of the film, I think it is that . . .

STUDENT HANDOUT 1-B

Ten Tasks for Young Adults

The following developmental tasks have been identified by researchers as the primary challenges facing young adults who are striving for maturity and fulfillment as persons. The tasks are stated here as personal decisions or commitments in order to affirm the fact that success in each area is indeed attainable.

1. Becoming Competent: As a young adult, I will acquire a belief in my ability to "get things done," a sense that I can handle all the other tasks that I will face in the next few years.

2. Achieving Autonomy: I am a person who chooses to be in relationships with others, but I do not depend on the approval of other people to sustain me. I freely choose interdependency; I reject total dependency upon others.

3. Developing and Implementing Values: I will personally choose a set of values that will give guidance and meaning to my life.

4. Forming a Personal Identity: I will strive to rid myself of the masks that I wear. People who encounter me will meet the **real** me, not an artificial role that I assume.

5. Integrating Sexuality into Life: I will develop values regarding sexuality and sexual expression that reflect my total value system and that support my goal of living with moral and personal integrity.

6. Making Friends and Developing Intimacy: I will strive to develop the friendship skills that allow me to be trustful, open, forgiving, and nurturing in my relationships with others.

7. Loving and Making a Commitment to Another Person: Should my life bring me to the point of choosing a permanent relationship with another person, I will have developed the maturity and personal integrity necessary to make it a lifelong relationship of caring, interdependency, and true intimacy.

8. Making Initial Job and Career Choices: In the years ahead, I will test and slowly refine my career choice. My life's work will reflect my values and contribute to my sense of personal integrity.

9. Becoming an Active Community Member and Citizen: Knowing that my primary concern in the next few years is the development of my personal and interpersonal skills, I resist the notion that I am responsible only to myself. I am a member of a community, and I will seek ways to share my gifts and skills with others.

10. Learning How to Use Leisure Time: I will learn to use my leisure time as an invitation to **re-creation**—that is, for "re-creating" myself—rather than allowing my free time to be a wasted opportunity to grow.

STUDENT HANDOUT 1-C

Keepsake Prayers

This Is Who I Am

My person is *not* a little hard core inside of me, a fully-formed statue that is real and authentic, permanent and fixed. If I am anything as a person, it is what I . . .
think
judge
feel
value
honor
esteem
love
hate
fear
desire
hope for
believe in
and am committed to.
These are the things that define my person, and they are constantly in process, in the process of change. In other words, if you knew me yesterday, please do not think that it is the same person you are meeting today. I have experienced more of life, I have encountered new depths in those I love, I have suffered and prayed, and I am different.

Approach me, then, with a sense of wonder, study my face and hands and voice for the signs of change—for it is certain that I have changed.

Adapted from John Powell, SJ

This Is Who I Am

My person is *not* a little hard core inside of me, a fully-formed statue that is real and authentic, permanent and fixed. If I am anything as a person, it is what I . . .
think
judge
feel
value
honor
esteem
love
hate
fear
desire
hope for
believe in
and am committed to.
These are the things that define my person, and they are constantly in process, in the process of change. In other words, if you knew me yesterday, please do not think that it is the same person you are meeting today. I have experienced more of life, I have encountered new depths in those I love, I have suffered and prayed, and I am different.

Approach me, then, with a sense of wonder, study my face and hands and voice for the signs of change—for it is certain that I have changed.

Adapted from John Powell, SJ

This Is Who I Am

My person is *not* a little hard core inside of me, a fully-formed statue that is real and authentic, permanent and fixed. If I am anything as a person, it is what I . . .
think
judge
feel
value
honor
esteem
love
hate
fear
desire
hope for
believe in
and am committed to.
These are the things that define my person, and they are constantly in process, in the process of change. In other words, if you knew me yesterday, please do not think that it is the same person you are meeting today. I have experienced more of life, I have encountered new depths in those I love, I have suffered and prayed, and I am different.

Approach me, then, with a sense of wonder, study my face and hands and voice for the signs of change—for it is certain that I have changed.

Adapted from John Powell, SJ

This Is Who I Am

My person is *not* a little hard core inside of me, a fully-formed statue that is real and authentic, permanent and fixed. If I am anything as a person, it is what I . . .
think
judge
feel
value
honor
esteem
love
hate
fear
desire
hope for
believe in
and am committed to.
These are the things that define my person, and they are constantly in process, in the process of change. In other words, if you knew me yesterday, please do not think that it is the same person you are meeting today. I have experienced more of life, I have encountered new depths in those I love, I have suffered and prayed, and I am different.

Approach me, then, with a sense of wonder, study my face and hands and voice for the signs of change—for it is certain that I have changed.

Adapted from John Powell, SJ

You Have Great Plans for Me

Lord, I know you love me
    and have great plans for me.
But sometimes I am overwhelmed
    by the thought of my future.
It's scary, Lord!
Show me how to walk forward one day at a time.
May I take heart while I search openly,
    learn about all the choices I face,
    listen to others for advice,
    and pay attention
    to my own feelings.
By doing these things may I hear your call
    to a lifestyle and a career
    that will let me love
    as only I can,
    and let me serve others
    with the special gifts
    that you have given me.
Lord, thank you for the hope you have in me.
Amen.

                Adapted from the Vocation Center
           Archdiocese of Saint Paul–Minneapolis

Rest in Peace

RIP

Here lies _____
who died this day, _____.
The deceased is survived by _____.
At the time of death, the deceased was best known for _____.
He or she will be remembered by _____
for _____.
The deceased always hoped that he or she _____.
As it turned out, _____.
Those wishing to honor the memory of the deceased, should _____.
On his or her deathbed, the final words of the deceased were _____.

REST IN PEACE

RIP

Here lies _____
who died this day, _____.
The deceased is survived by _____.
At the time of death, the deceased was best known for _____.
He or she will be remembered by _____
for _____.
The deceased always hoped that he or she _____.
As it turned out, _____.
Those wishing to honor the memory of the deceased, should _____.
On his or her deathbed, the final words of the deceased were _____.

REST IN PEACE

STUDENT HANDOUT 2-B

The Dream of a Lifetime

Note to the leader: The following are statements of eighteen possible life goals. Make one copy of the handout for each student in your group. Then divide them into individual slips of paper by cutting along the dotted lines. Bind the individual slips together with clips or rubber bands in separate packets, each containing all eighteen life goals. Give each student a full packet. Note the large slip of paper at the end titled "I Have a Dream." Distribute that slip to the young people only **after** they have completed their work with the life goals, as described in the directions for this activity given in the session plan.

A COMFORTABLE LIFE, a prosperous life

AN EXCITING LIFE, a stimulating, active life

A SENSE OF ACCOMPLISHMENT, lasting contribution

A WORLD AT PEACE, free of war and conflict

A WORLD OF BEAUTY, beauty of nature and the arts

EQUALITY, equal opportunity for all

FAMILY SECURITY, taking care of loved ones

FREEDOM, independence, free choice

HAPPINESS, contentedness

INNER HARMONY, freedom from inner conflict

MATURE LOVE, sexual and spiritual intimacy

NATIONAL SECURITY, protection from attack

PLEASURE, an enjoyable, leisurely life

SALVATION, saved, eternal life

SELF-RESPECT, self-esteem

SOCIAL RECOGNITION, respect, admiration

TRUE FRIENDSHIP, close companionship

WISDOM, a mature understanding of life

I Have a Dream

Now take your highest rated life goals—using at least the top four of them—and below write a statement of your dream, modeled somewhat on the form of Martin Luther King, Jr's, famous statement of his own vision.

I _____ have a dream, that one day

_____.

I have a dream, that _____

_____.

I have a dream, that _____

_____.

I have a dream, that _____

_____

_____.

STUDENT HANDOUT 2-C

Prayer Service: The Dream of Jesus

Reader 1: A reading from the Gospel of Mark:

One of the scribes . . . put a further question to him, "Which is the first of all the commandments?" Jesus replied, "This is the first: Listen, Israel, the Lord our God is the one, only Lord, and you must love the Lord your God with all your heart, with all your soul, with all your mind and with all your strength. The second is this: You must love your neighbour as yourself. There is no commandment greater than these." The scribe said to him, "Well spoken, Master; what you have said is true, that he is one and there is no other. To love him with all your heart, with all your understanding and strength, and to love your neighbour as yourself, this is far more important than any burnt offering or sacrifice." Jesus, seeing how wisely he had spoken, said, "You are not far from the kingdom of God." (Mark 12:28–34)

Leader: Let us now respond to Jesus' call to help build up the kingdom of God through love of God and neighbor by prayerfully reading and reflecting on the Beatitudes, Jesus' wonderful description of the hearts of those people who will be called "blessed."

Reader 2: Blessed are the poor in spirit, for theirs is the kingdom of God.

The spirit of poverty consists . . . in seeing the universe and everything in it (ourselves included) as held in existence from moment to moment by nothing save God's continuing will to hold it there and . . . in setting our hearts upon God and loving Him above all things. (John Wu)

Reader 3: Blessed are the meek, the gentle, for they shall have the earth for their heritage.

A first step to inner gentleness is thus to gratefully love myself as a unique gift and to admit and accept my weakness. Gentleness with self is possible only when I recognize and "own" all the vulnerability of the treasure I am. I must be able to look at myself with a forgiving eye. (Adrian van Kaam)

Reader 4: Blessed are those who mourn, for they shall be comforted.

When things go well it is possible to live for years on the surface of things; but when sorrow comes a person is driven to the deep things of life, and, if one accepts it aright, a new strength and beauty enter into one's soul. (William Barclay)

Reader 5: Blessed are those who hunger and thirst for justice, for they shall be filled.

Maybe our children, our husband, our wife are not hungry, are not naked, are not homeless. But are you sure there is no one there who feels unwanted, unloved? Let us look straight into our own families. For love begins at home. We don't have to think of numbers. We can love one person at a time, serve one person at a time. (Mother Teresa)

Reader 6: Blessed are the merciful, for they shall receive mercy.

Be kind and merciful. Let no one ever come to you without coming away better and happier. Be the living expression of God's kindness: kindness in your face, kindness in your eyes, kindness in your smile, kindness in your warm greeting. . . . To the children, to the poor, to all who suffer and are lonely, give always a happy smile; give them not only your care, but also your heart. (Mother Teresa)

Reader 7: Blessed are those who are persecuted for the cause of right; theirs is the kingdom of heaven.

It is not likely that death awaits us because of our loyalty to the Christian faith. But . . . mockery awaits the person who practices Christian love and forgiveness. . . . Christ still needs his witnesses; he needs those who are prepared, not so much to die for him as to live for him. (William Barclay)

Reader 8: Blessed are the single-hearted, for they shall see God.

Persons [who are pure in heart] have no weapon in their hands, no defensive wall around their heart. They open their arms to embrace, knowing that one may be crucified when his or her arms are open, but unable to approach others in any other manner. (Anthony Padovano)

Reader 9: Blessed are the peacemakers, for they shall be called the children of God.

We all long for heaven where God is, but we have it in our power to be in heaven with him at this very moment. But being happy with him now means: loving as he loves, helping as he helps, giving as he gives, serving as he serves. . . . (Mother Teresa)

Leader: Lord, we pray that the Spirit of Jesus will find a home in our hearts, so that we may be witnesses of God's love to all who meet us. We ask this in the name of Jesus, whom we believe to be alive and with each of us at this moment and always.

All: Amen.

STUDENT HANDOUT 3-A

Guidelines for Creating Your Story

You are to create a story or situation in which a decision needs to be made, centered on the topic for discussion chosen by the group. Your story should include as many details as you can provide in the time allowed (about 15 minutes). You can be creative, even humorous if you wish, perhaps presenting your story in the form of a summary of a soap opera script or a letter to "Dear Abby." Or you can make your story serious, perhaps retelling a true situation with which you are familiar. You should answer the following questions to some degree in your story:

- Who are the people involved? Be specific, giving the characters' names.
- Precisely what is the character's dilemma or problem? Remember, this should reflect the topic chosen by the group.
- Close your story with a direct question that sums up the situation and clearly presents all the issues at hand. This question will be the focus of the decision-making process that the group will explore later.

Notes on your story:

_____
_____
_____
_____
_____
_____
_____
_____
_____
_____
_____
_____
_____
_____
_____

STUDENT HANDOUT 3-B

A Step-by-Step Decision-making Process

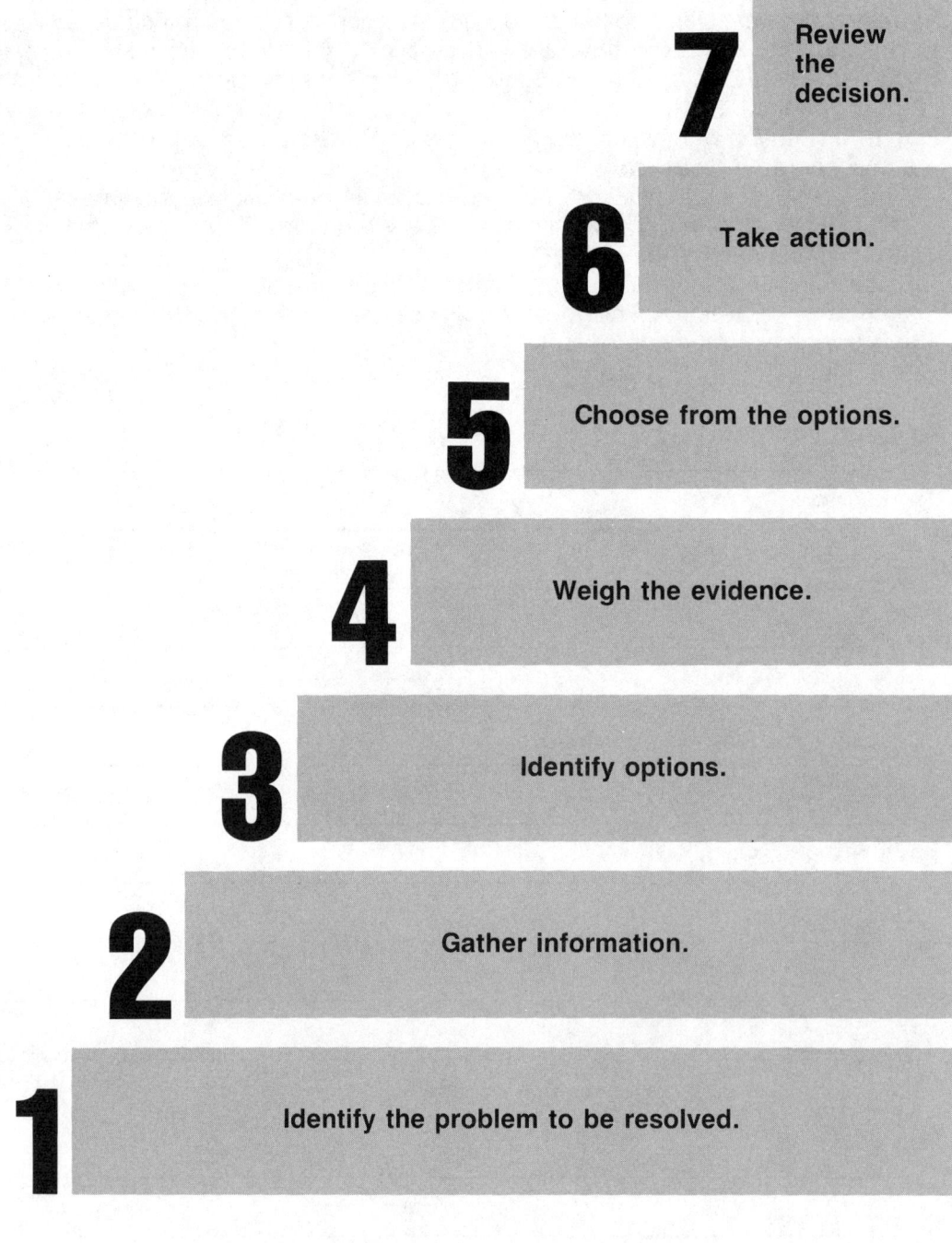

STUDENT HANDOUT 4-A

Reflecting on My Relationships

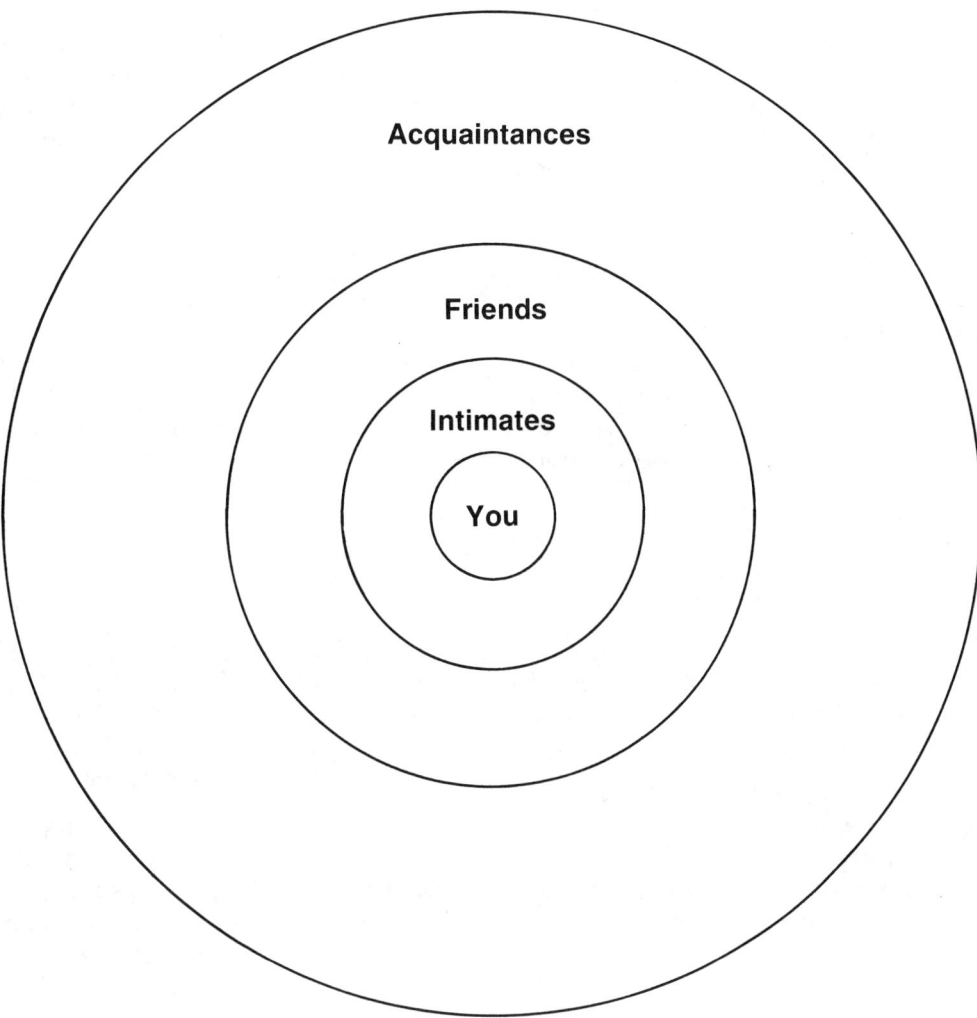

On the lines below, list characteristics, actions, attitudes — whatever comes to your mind — regarding each type of personal relationship identified in the circles above.

Acquaintances	Friends	Intimates
_____	_____	_____
_____	_____	_____
_____	_____	_____
_____	_____	_____
_____	_____	_____
_____	_____	_____

STUDENT HANDOUT 5-A

Imagining Myself as a Communicator

Directions: Find a place where you can be alone and left undisturbed. Assume a comfortable position that you can maintain for a reasonable length of time. Spend a few minutes relaxing your body and focusing your attention by using the breathing exercises practiced in group sessions. Then slowly and deliberately read each of the following affirmations. After reading each one, pause briefly and try to imagine yourself possessing the quality or characteristic reflected in the statement. Do this on a regular basis (twice a week or more) until the attitudes imagined become part of you and the way you act.

- I am fully committed to the hard work of communicating with others. I will work at it even when the results are frustrating or difficult to see.

- I believe that I am a gift to be offered to others and that all people I meet are gifts offered to me.

- I am determined to be completely honest with myself. I try to stay in touch with my thoughts and feelings, their origins, and their expression. If I am to be honest with others, I must first be honest with myself.

- I am fully responsible for all my actions and reactions. I blame no one and no thing for how I behave or for what I feel.

- I try always to speak the truth that is within me. I also respect the truth that is within others. I do not impose what I believe upon others, nor do I try to interpret the beliefs of others to suit my needs or desires.

- In communicating with others, I share my feelings as well as my thoughts. I do so with gentleness and sensitivity, not out of a desire to satisfy my own emotional needs or to manipulate others.

- I am willing to be open and honest with my thoughts and feelings even when rejection or ridicule by others is possible. To grow, I must be open to some pain in life.

- I am deeply grateful for all who love and care for me, and I let them know of my gratitude.

- When others approach me, I try to focus on their thoughts, feelings, and needs rather than on my own. I try always to be truly present and available to those I meet.

- I accept others just the way they are, without judging who they are or demanding that they become what I would like them to be.

- I avoid judging the intentions and motives of others. I recognize that people are complicated, and I resist the arrogant attitude that people are exactly what I believe them to be.

- When others attempt to share themselves with me, I try to see and feel the world through their eyes and heart. I try to understand their experience of life, not interpret their life in terms of my own experiences.

- I try to fully understand what others are sharing with me. When I am not sure if I understand, I always ask them to explain or clarify what they mean so that I do not falsely judge them.

- When others ask for my advice, I offer suggestions and honest opinions but never orders or directions. Only they can decide what is right for them.

- In a culture that fills our time with electronic sights and sounds and endless ways to waste time, I am committed to spending quality time with friends and loved ones.

- I recognize that many thoughts and feelings are better expressed with a touch of the hand or a hug than with words. I do not invade the privacy of others but touch them with tenderness and sensitivity.

- As one who is fully human, I make mistakes and hurt those I love. When I do so, I quickly apologize and ask their forgiveness.

- When I sense a problem in my communication with someone, I quickly seek the source of the problem and try to correct it. I do not allow small problems to grow into big ones through my neglect or denial.

- When a communication problem arises that is beyond my power to solve, I seek the advice and help of those who can provide it.

- In all my efforts at communication—in all my attempts to share my own thoughts and feelings and in my struggles to be attentive and accepting of those of others—my motive and guide is love.

- Finally, as one who believes in the presence of a loving God within all loving relationships, I regularly pray for God's guidance as I try to communicate with others.

STUDENT HANDOUT 5-B

Assignments for Role-playing

You have a good friend whose father has recently died unexpectedly. The friend has been out of school for several days and has just returned to school. You see this friend in the hall after school. What do you say or do?

In preparing this role-play, one person should be a narrator who explains the above scene to the rest of the group. The others in your small group are then to role-play two scenes:
1. an improper or poor way to respond in this situation
2. a proper or positive way to respond in this situation

You have just 15 minutes to prepare your role-play.

Your brother or sister has just had a big fight with your parents. He or she had made some plans for next Saturday but has just found out from your parents that they had already made commitments for the family without remembering to tell the kids. Your sibling has yelled at your folks and stomped up the stairs and into your bedroom, where he or she begins to grumble about how unfair the whole situation is. What do you do or say?

In preparing this role-play, one person should be a narrator who explains the above scene to the rest of the group. The others in your small group are then to role-play two scenes:
1. an improper or poor way to respond in this situation
2. a proper or positive way to respond in this situation

You have just 15 minutes to prepare your role-play.

One of your grandparents is dying of cancer. The illness has been lengthy, requiring many visits by family members, and your relatives have been taking turns visiting the grandparent in the hospital. When you are taking your turn, you find that your grandparent is particularly depressed and begins to talk of regrets about life and fears of death. What do you say or do?

In preparing this role-play, one person should be a narrator who explains the above scene to the rest of the group. The others in your small group are then to role-play two scenes:
1. an improper or poor way to respond in this situation
2. a proper or positive way to respond in this situation

You have just 15 minutes to prepare your role-play.

You are at a birthday party, and everyone is having a good time. However, one of your friends seems to be down and getting more depressed by the minute. Just when the birthday cake is being presented and everyone starts to sing the birthday song, your friend mumbles something and, near tears, runs out of the room. The party seems to come to a halt, and everyone feels very uncomfortable. You leave to find your friend and find him or her sitting on the steps. What do you say or do?

In preparing this role-play, one person should be a narrator who explains the above scene to the rest of the group. The others in your small group are then to role-play two scenes:
1. an improper or poor way to respond in this situation
2. a proper or positive way to respond in this situation

You have just 15 minutes to prepare your role-play.

You are at a dance, and you have told your parents that you will be home by midnight. At 11:30 P.M., one of your friends shows up and he or she obviously has been drinking heavily. The friend wants to talk to you about "something very serious." You spend over an hour with your friend, who manages to spill some liquor on you while you talk. You finally arrive home after 1:00 A.M., smelling of liquor, your angry parents waiting for you. What do you say or do?

In preparing this role-play, one person should be a narrator who explains the above scene to the rest of the group. The others in your small group are then to role-play two scenes:
1. an improper or poor way to respond in this situation
2. a proper or positive way to respond in this situation
You have just 15 minutes to prepare your role-play.

You have been going steady with the same person for nearly two years. Recently, you have been feeling less and less enthusiastic about the relationship and have been trying to find some way to break up without hurting the person. Just as you are ready to bring up the subject, the person suggests that the two of you get married. Obviously, she or he has had no inkling of what you have been feeling. What do you say or do?

In preparing this role-play, one person should be a narrator who explains the above scene to the rest of the group. The others in your small group are then to role-play two scenes:
1. an improper or poor way to respond in this situation
2. a proper or positive way to respond in this situation
You have just 15 minutes to prepare your role-play.

STUDENT HANDOUT 6-A

Small-Group Discussion Assignments for
A Question of Intimacy

---

1. The film suggests several words or phrases that are related to the meaning of intimacy:

    security, closeness, fear, sense of belonging and being loved, knowing something special about oneself, ultimate trust, overall acceptance of another, vulnerability to rejection

    Your assignment is this: Using these or other words of your own choosing, develop a one-sentence definition of intimacy. You may write it on the back of this paper.

---

2. Keith Miller, the narrator of the film, says at one point, "Unfortunately, intimacy and pain come through the same doorway, so that if we block the pain, we block the intimacy." Identify three kinds or examples of pain associated with intimacy to which he might have been referring. Jot your answers on the back of this paper.

---

3. Below are listed all of the fears associated with intimacy that are identified by members of the group in the film. Rank these fears in terms of which are most prevalent or strong **for people your age.** Do so by putting number 1 in front of the most common fear for your age-group, number 2 in front of the second most common, and so on, for each fear. Be prepared to explain your top choices.

    ____ fear of not being known or recognized
    ____ fear of being awkward in expressing affection
    ____ fear based on one's upbringing, in which one has been told to "save intimacy for marriage"
    ____ fear of being rejected when one reveals his or her real self
    ____ fear that, after risking intimacy, the relationship won't last
    ____ fear based on past failures
    ____ fear of revealing something about oneself that will be used against you later
    ____ fear of losing control of the relationship

---

4. The narrator of the film suggests that there are basically two kinds of people:

    a. "skunks" find ways to keep people at a distance
    b. "turtles" withdraw into a shell to hide from people

    He goes on to say, "Unfortunately, skunks and turtles almost always marry each other!"
    From your experience, do you believe that "opposites attract one another" in human relationships? If so, why do you think this happens? Do you agree with the narrator when he claims this is "unfortunate"? Why or why not?

---

5. Using the image of a chicken in an egg, Miller summarizes two schools of thought about helping people to "come out of their shells" to reveal their true selves:
   a. We can use a hammer to break open their shells.
   b. We can surround them with a warm, caring environment and let them break out of their own shells.

   Give examples of how this imagery relates to human relationships. Why does Miller suggest that the second approach has the better chance of leading to intimacy?

6. Miller suggests that ultimately there is only one way for two people to initiate an intimate relationship: Someone has to take the risk to make it happen. Give three reasons of your own that such a risk seems worth taking:

   a. _____

   b. _____

   c. _____

7. One woman in the film suggests that a major problem in establishing intimate relationships with the opposite sex is having one's intentions misunderstood. A person might want to be a caring friend but can be misunderstood as wanting a romantic, sexual relationship. Is this a common concern of young adults? How might one overcome this problem without withdrawing or hiding from people?

8. Miller states twice that we need a sense of personal security before we can reach out to others in intimate relationships. He says we can find such security in two ways: We can look within ourselves and count on our own resources. Or we can look outside ourselves—to psychotherapy, support groups, religious faith, and so on. Do you agree with him that faith in God can provide the security one needs to seek intimacy? Why or why not?

STUDENT HANDOUT 6-B

Love or Infatuation?
A Confidential Self-test

Directions: In preparation for a discussion on determining whether one is in a true love relationship or merely infatuated with another person, you are asked to complete this confidential self-test. **No one will see what you write, and you will not be asked to share with anyone anything you write on this paper that you do not wish to share.** This is only intended to spark your interest in and focus your attention on this complex issue.

Look at the three columns of boxes below. In the first column is a series of questions regarding romantic relationships. You are to do the following:
- In the second column across from each question, jot down a few words that summarize the characteristic response to the question when people are infatuated with one another;
- In the third column, briefly summarize a likely response to the question when a person is truly in love.

Later in the session, answers to these questions will be provided that are based on social scientists' research on love and marriage. You will be able to check your opinions and intuitions against "the facts" as the research has determined them.

Regarding the questions below	. . . when one is infatuated?	. . . when one is truly in love?
What is the major attraction between the persons . . .		
How many different things attract them to each other . . .		
How did the relationship begin . . .		
How will the relationship end, if at all . . .		
How consistent are their levels of interest in each other . . .		

Regarding the questions below	. . . when one is infatuated?	. . . when one is truly in love?
How does one react to the other's faults and weaknesses . . .		
How does their relationship with each other affect their relationships with others . . .		
How do they react to distance of time or space away from each other . . .		
How frequent and severe are their arguments or quarrels . . .		
How do one's friends respond to the other person and to the relationship . . .		
How does the relationship affect their personalities as individuals . . .		
How does each refer to the other in casual speech . . .		
What is a person's attitude toward his or her own needs . . .		
In what ways, if at all, is jealousy of the other expressed in the relationship . . .		

STUDENT HANDOUT 6-C

Is It Love or Infatuation?

The following chart summarizes the results of research done by social scientists on the phenomena of love and infatuation. In the left-hand column are key questions, the answers to which can serve as clues as to whether one is involved in a relationship based on infatuation or on love. The middle and right-hand columns indicate responses reflective of relationships of infatuation or love, respectively.

    Clearly, romantic personal relationships are so complex in reality that they cannot be easily evaluated and judged. However, one sociologist—Dr. Ray Short, the originator of this material—suggests that before deciding to marry, a couple should be able to answer positively to at least eleven of the fourteen responses in the right-hand column. Or, on the negative side, if a couple agrees with five or more of the responses listed in the middle column, they are likely involved in a relationship of infatuation and should avoid or delay a decision to get married.

Regarding the questions below	**. . . when one is infatuated?**	**. . . when one is truly in love?**
What is the major attraction between the persons . . .	The major attraction is physical appearance.	The major attraction is the total personality.
How many different things attract them to each other . . .	Only a few things attract one to the other.	One finds many things attractive in the other.
How did the relationship begin . . .	The relationship began very fast; "love at first sight."	The relationship grew more slowly, steadily.
How will the relationship end, if at all . . .	The relationship will end as it began—fast.	The relationship will stand the test of time.
How consistent are their levels of interest in each other . . .	The interest will come and go, and will be uneven and unreliable.	Interest will have fewer peaks and valleys, and will be more consistent.

Regarding the following question . . .	. . . when one is infatuated?	. . . when one is truly in love?
How does one react to the other's faults and weaknesses . . .	The other's faults are never seen; the person is idealized.	The faults and weaknesses are recognized but accepted.
How does their relationship with each other affect their relationships with others . . .	The universe narrows to this relationship; all others are excluded.	All other relationships are enhanced and enriched.
How do they react to distance of time or space away from each other . . .	Distance and time apart kills the relationship.	The two may actually grow closer when separated; they can overcome it.
How frequent and severe are their arguments or quarrels . . .	Arguments become more frequent and increase in intensity.	Arguments lessen as they find better ways to resolve conflict.
How do one's friends respond to the other person and to the relationship . . .	One's friends tend not to like the other; they have differing interests.	Friends support and affirm the relationship; they share interests.
How does the relationship affect their personalities as individuals . . .	Persons become disorganized, forgetful, spacey.	Persons become more organized, structured, together.
How does each refer to the other in casual speech . . .	Tends to speak as "he and I" or "she and I."	Begins to refer to selves as "we" or "us."
What is a person's attitude toward his or her own needs . . .	Emphasis will be on satisfying one's own needs.	Emphasis will be on the needs of the other.

Regarding the following question...	...when one is infatuated?	...when one is truly in love?
In what ways, if at all, is jealousy of the other expressed in the relationship...	One tends to speak of being "insanely" jealous.	Little or no jealousy exists; one desires to share loved one with others.

Regarding the following question . . .	. . . when one is infatuated?	. . . when one is truly in love?
How does one react to the other's faults and weaknesses . . .	The other's faults are never seen; the person is idealized.	The faults and weaknesses are recognized but accepted.
How does their relationship with each other affect their relationships with others . . .	The universe narrows to this relationship; all others are excluded.	All other relationships are enhanced and enriched.
How do they react to distance of time or space away from each other . . .	Distance and time apart kills the relationship.	The two may actually grow closer when separated; they can overcome it.
How frequent and severe are their arguments or quarrels . . .	Arguments become more frequent and increase in intensity.	Arguments lessen as they find better ways to resolve conflict.
How do one's friends respond to the other person and to the relationship . . .	One's friends tend not to like the other; they have differing interests.	Friends support and affirm the relationship; they share interests.
How does the relationship affect their personalities as individuals . . .	Persons become disorganized, forgetful, spacey.	Persons become more organized, structured, together.
How does each refer to the other in casual speech . . .	Tends to speak as "he and I" or "she and I."	Begins to refer to selves as "we" or "us."
What is a person's attitude toward his or her own needs . . .	Emphasis will be on satisfying one's own needs.	Emphasis will be on the needs of the other.

Regarding the following question . . .	. . . when one is infatuated?	. . . when one is truly in love?
In what ways, if at all, is jealousy of the other expressed in the relationship . . .	One tends to speak of being "insanely" jealous.	Little or no jealousy exists; one desires to share loved one with others.

STUDENT HANDOUT A

What a Frightening Thought!

Directions

1. On your own and without discussing this with anyone, rank the human fears listed at the bottom of the page according to how you think most people commonly experience them. That is, in front of the fear that you believe is most commonly experienced by people, put the number 1. For the second most common fear, write number 2, and so on, until all the fears are ranked. You have 5 minutes to do this.

2. When all the participants in your group have individually ranked the items, you are to try to reach consensus or agreement **as a group** on how the fears should be ranked. Consensus implies that the rankings must be agreed upon, at least partially, by **all** the members of the group. Following are some suggestions for achieving group consensus:
   a. Approach the task on the basis of logic. Avoid simply defending your position for the sake of argument. Listen carefully to the reasons group members give for their ranking.
   b. At the same time, resist changing your opinion simply to reach agreement or to avoid conflict. Support only those rankings you can agree with, at least to some extent.
   c. Avoid techniques like majority voting, averaging, or trading off in order to reduce conflict. These are cop-outs to consensus-seeking.
   d. View differences of opinion as an asset rather than a hindrance in group decision-making.

3. When all the groups have completed the assignment, the retreat leader will share the results of a survey that indicate how the subjects of the survey actually ranked these fears.

Rank the fears listed below in the order in which you think survey respondents mentioned them most, from 1 (the most frequently mentioned fear) to 14 (the fear mentioned least often).

____ darkness

____ death

____ deep water

____ dogs

____ driving or riding in a car

____ elevators

____ escalators

____ financial problems

____ flying

____ heights

____ insects and bugs

____ loneliness

____ sickness

____ speaking before a group

STUDENT HANDOUT B

Dyadic Encounter Guide

1. One of my favorite times of the year is . . .

2. A pleasant memory from my childhood is associated with . . .

3. (Quickly choose one of the following) The first time I
   - tried to swim, I . . .
   - was away from home overnight, I . . .
   - kissed someone from outside the family, I . . .
   - performed before a group, I . . .
   - went out on a "date," I . . .

4. A person whom I would like to visit is . . .

5. One of my favorite spots to spend some time is . . . If I could take you there right now, I . . .

6. I am eagerly looking forward to . . .

7. Look over the previous questions and pick one topic you would like to return to and share it with your partner . . .

8. What I remember most about my closest childhood friend is . . .

9. When I can find some time to be alone I like to . . .

10. I came to this retreat because . . .
    So far during this retreat I have felt . . .

11. Three things that I think I am really good at are . . .

12. One thing about me that I would like to change is . . .

13. Share with your partner a personal success that you have experienced and what it means to you.

14. A problem that I am dealing with right now is . . .

15. Pick a topic from the previous pages and ask your partner to tell you more about his or her response to it.

16. Now that we have reached the last page in this booklet, I feel . . .

STUDENT HANDOUT C

A Letter to Myself

Directions: The day has been a rich one, filled with information, questions, discussion, and challenges. At times such as these, collecting one's thoughts and reflecting on the personal meaning of all that has happened can be helpful. This exercise is intended to help you do that.

You are to find a place where you can be alone and quiet. Think for a few moments about the events of the day. What most impressed you? What disturbed you? What do you feel you have to spend more time thinking about? If you were now with your best friend, what would you want to tell him or her about the day?

After some reflection, write a letter below about the day to someone who may be your best friend—yourself! Start the letter as you would any other: "Dear (your name)." Then just let your thoughts unfold on the paper. You may be surprised to discover all the things you have never been able to tell anyone . . . even yourself.

Dear _____ ,

STUDENT HANDOUT D

Planning Sheet for Eucharistic Liturgy

Theme: _____ **Date:** _____

Decorations: _____

Musical accompaniment: _____

Leader of song: _____

Introduction: composed by _____ read by _____

Opening song: _____

First reading: _____ read by _____

Responsorial psalm: _____ antiphon _____

_____ said _____ sung _____

Second reading: _____ read by _____

Gospel acclamation: _____

_____ said _____ sung _____

Gospel: _____ read by _____

Prayer of the Faithful: composed by _____ read by _____

Offertory song: _____

Offertory gifts: _____

    presented by _____ explained by _____

Holy, Holy, Holy: said _____ sung _____ version (if sung) _____

Memorial acclamation: _____

_____ said _____ sung _____

Amen: said _____ sung _____ version (if sung) _____

Our Father: said _____ sung _____ version (if sung) _____

Lamb of God: said _____ sung _____ version (if sung) _____

Eucharistic ministers: _____

Communion song: _____

Communion meditation (if any): reading _____ read by _____

    song _____

Recessional song: _____

STUDENT HANDOUT E

A Model for Effective Lesson Planning

Real learning—as distinct from the simple accumulation of knowledge—seems to take place in a consistent pattern:
- **A.** The potential learner's **starting point** is understood, respected, and taken into account in planning.
- **B.** **Significant experiences** are provided—information or experiences that allow the potential learner to question, reflect upon, evaluate, or become uncomfortable with his or her starting point.
- **C.** Opportunities are provided for **reflection,** for evaluating the import and effects of the new information; here the teacher can be properly defined as a "facilitator of reflection."
- **D.** The new information is assimilated into one's life. **Assimilation** is the responsibility of the learner; at this level the teacher becomes one who supports, encourages, challenges.

The following table shows the effects of this learning process on lesson plan development. For a particular topic or point of information to be effectively shared, that is, truly learned by the student, the effective teacher will do the following:

A.	B.	C.	D.

Attempt to understand and remain continually conscious of the student's **starting point** by . . .
1. understanding basic patterns of psychological development
2. studying the sociocultural environment(s)
3. learning about family and immediate social influences (e.g., peer group, friends)
4. ideally, meeting and developing a personal relationship with each student
	Determine the most **significant experiences** based on the topic, audience, available time, and so on. Possibilities include . . .
	1. the current life experiences of the students
	2. effective speakers
	3. simulation games
	4. group dynamics
	5. field trips
	6. prayer experiences
	7. case studies
	8. relevant reading
	9. films, music, media
	10. the teacher, who can be a significant experience in himself or herself
		Provide opportunities for **reflection** on information. Possibilities include . .
		1. discussion:
		  a. teacher-student
		  b. student-student
		2. questionnaires and reflectionnaires
		3. prayer services
		4. opportunities for private prayer
		5. journal keeping
		6. carefully designed quizzes and tests
		7. interviews
		8. essays, term papers, reports
			Facilitate **assimilation** to whatever degree possible by . . .
			1. challenging students to accept responsibility
			2. encouraging, supporting, affirming
			3. following up on students' progress through
			  a. letters
			  b. phone calls
			  c. other personal contact
			4. encouraging further study, providing book lists, and so on
			5. being available if needed for support

STUDENT HANDOUT F

Meditation Program Contract

_____

 **A Contract with My God, with My Fellow Meditators, and with Myself**

As I begin my participation in this meditation program, I commit myself to freely and sincerely do the following:

I commit myself to meditate once a day for the duration of the program. I recognize this as a top priority in my life for the coming month and will do everything possible to fulfill this commitment. If, in the case of unavoidable circumstances, I am unable to complete a period of meditation, I will attempt to make up for it during the following day.

I commit myself to attend all four gatherings during the program. I know that I attend these not only for my own benefit but also for the good of my fellow meditators. I recognize that a failure to attend a gathering results in a weakening of the group as a whole. If an emergency demands that I miss a gathering, I will contact the leader of the program immediately.

I commit myself to share my thoughts, insights, and questions with the group during the gatherings. The strength of the group depends on the willingness of the individual meditators to share what they have gained in prayer. I also recognize, however, that at no time will my personal privacy be threatened or abused. What I choose to offer will be freely given.

I commit myself to be open to the Spirit of Jesus, praying that the Spirit will open my mind and heart to the message of God and give me the courage and insight to act upon God's Word in my daily life.

I hereby pledge my earnest intent to do these things by the grace of God and with the support and encouragement of my fellow meditators in this program.

Date _____ Signature _____

We, the undersigned, confirm that _____
has faithfully completed the program *Learning to Meditate: A Way to God.*

_____   _____
Program leader   Pastor

_____
Date

ORDER FORM (Please type or print)

Name _____

Parish or School _____

Address _____

City, State, Zip _____

Phone _____

Please send me the following:

____ **SHARING I,** spiral bound, 8½" × 11", $18.95

____ **SHARING II,** spiral bound, 8½" × 11", $18.95

____ **SHARING III,** spiral bound, 8½" × 11", $18.95

____ **SHARING IV,** spiral bound, 8½" × 11", $18.95

____ **Director's Manual,** loose-leaf binder,
8½" × 11", two cassettes, $54.00

For fast service call our toll-free number, 1-800-533-8095, or send to:

Saint Mary's Press
Terrace Heights
Winona, MN 55987